CARTOON NETWORK 2-IN-1

BEN 10: ALIEN FORCE
THE SECRET SATURDAYS

Sean Ryan Elisabeth V. Gehrlein Joan Hilty *Editors-Original Series*
Rex Ogle *Assist. Editor-Original Series*
Bob Harras *Group Editor-Collected Editions*
Sean Mackiewicz *Editor*
Robbin Brosterman *Design Director-Books*

DC COMICS
Diane Nelson *President*
Dan DiDio and Jim Lee *Co-Publishers*
Geoff Johns *Chief Creative Officer*
Patrick Caldon *EVP-Finance and Administration*
John Rood *EVP-Sales, Marketing and Business Development*
Amy Genkins *SVP-Business and Legal Affairs*
Steve Rotterdam *SVP-Sales and Marketing*
John Cunningham *VP-Marketing*
Terri Cunningham *VP-Managing Editor*
Alison Gill *VP-Manufacturing*
David Hyde *VP-Publicity*
Sue Pohja *VP-Book Trade Sales*
Alysse Soll *VP-Advertising and Custom Publishing*
Bob Wayne *VP-Sales*
Mark Chiarello *Art Director*

CARTOON NETWORK 2-IN-1: BEN 10: ALIEN FORCE /
THE SECRET SATURDAYS
Published by DC Comics. Cover and compilation Copyright © 2010
DC Comics. All Rights Reserved.

Originally published in single magazine form in CARTOON NETWORK
ACTION PACK 26-42. Copyright © 2008, 2009 Cartoon Network.
All Rights Reserved. The stories, characters and incidents featured
in this publication are entirely fictional. DC Comics does not read
or accept unsolicited submissions of ideas, stories or artwork.
CARTOON NETWORK, the logo, BEN 10: ALIEN FORCE, THE SECRET
SATURDAYS and all related characters and elements are trademarks
of and © 2010 Cartoon Network.

DC Comics, 1700 Broadway, New York, NY 10019
A Warner Bros. Entertainment Company
Printed by Quad/Graphics, Dubuque, IA, USA. 10/13/10. First Printing.
ISBN: 978-1-4012-2878-1

SUSTAINABLE
FORESTRY
INITIATIVE
Certified Chain of Custody
Promoting Sustainable
Forest Management
Fiber used in this product line meets the
sourcing requirements of the SFI program.
www.sfiprogram.org PWC-SFICOC-260

BEN 10 **created by** Man of Action

THE SECRET SATURDAYS **created by** Jay Stephens

Matt Wayne
Charlotte Fullerton
Amy Wolfram
Jason Hall
Jake Black
Writers

Rob Haynes
Mike Cavallaro & Mike DeCarlo
Min S. Ku
Artists

Rob Haynes
Heroic Age
Hi-Fi
Colorists

Randy Gentile
Travis Lanham
Sal Cipriano
Letterers

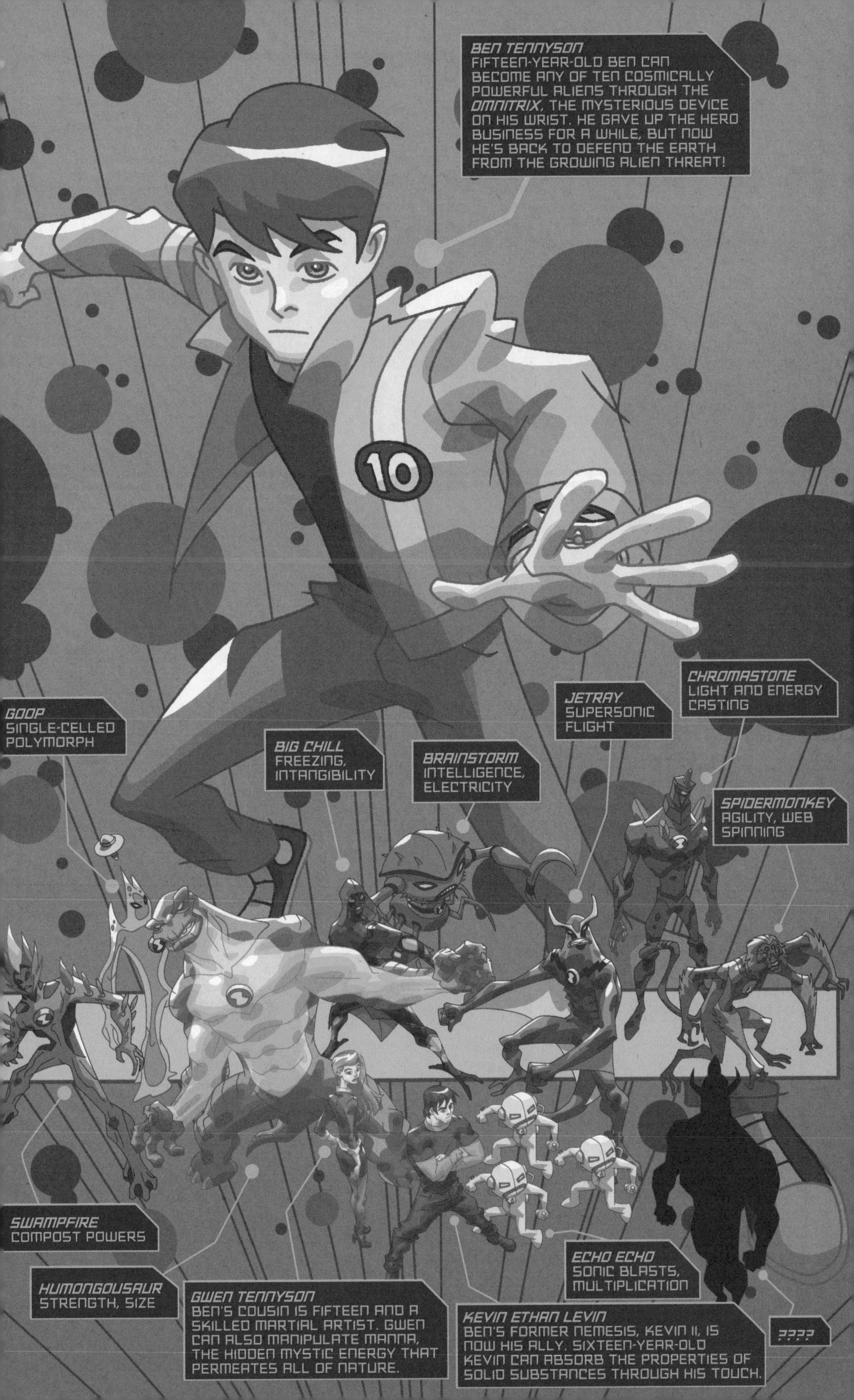
BEN TENNYSON
FIFTEEN-YEAR-OLD BEN CAN BECOME ANY OF TEN COSMICALLY POWERFUL ALIENS THROUGH THE OMNITRIX, THE MYSTERIOUS DEVICE ON HIS WRIST. HE GAVE UP THE HERO BUSINESS FOR A WHILE, BUT NOW HE'S BACK TO DEFEND THE EARTH FROM THE GROWING ALIEN THREAT!
10
GOOP
SINGLE-CELLED POLYMORPH
BIG CHILL
FREEZING, INTANGIBILITY
BRAINSTORM
INTELLIGENCE, ELECTRICITY
JETRAY
SUPERSONIC FLIGHT
CHROMASTONE
LIGHT AND ENERGY CASTING
SPIDERMONKEY
AGILITY, WEB SPINNING
SWAMPFIRE
COMPOST POWERS
HUMONGOUSAUR
STRENGTH, SIZE
GWEN TENNYSON
BEN'S COUSIN IS FIFTEEN AND A SKILLED MARTIAL ARTIST. GWEN CAN ALSO MANIPULATE MANNA, THE HIDDEN MYSTIC ENERGY THAT PERMEATES ALL OF NATURE.
ECHO ECHO
SONIC BLASTS, MULTIPLICATION
KEVIN ETHAN LEVIN
BEN'S FORMER NEMESIS, KEVIN 11, IS NOW HIS ALLY. SIXTEEN-YEAR-OLD KEVIN CAN ABSORB THE PROPERTIES OF SOLID SUBSTANCES THROUGH HIS TOUCH.
????

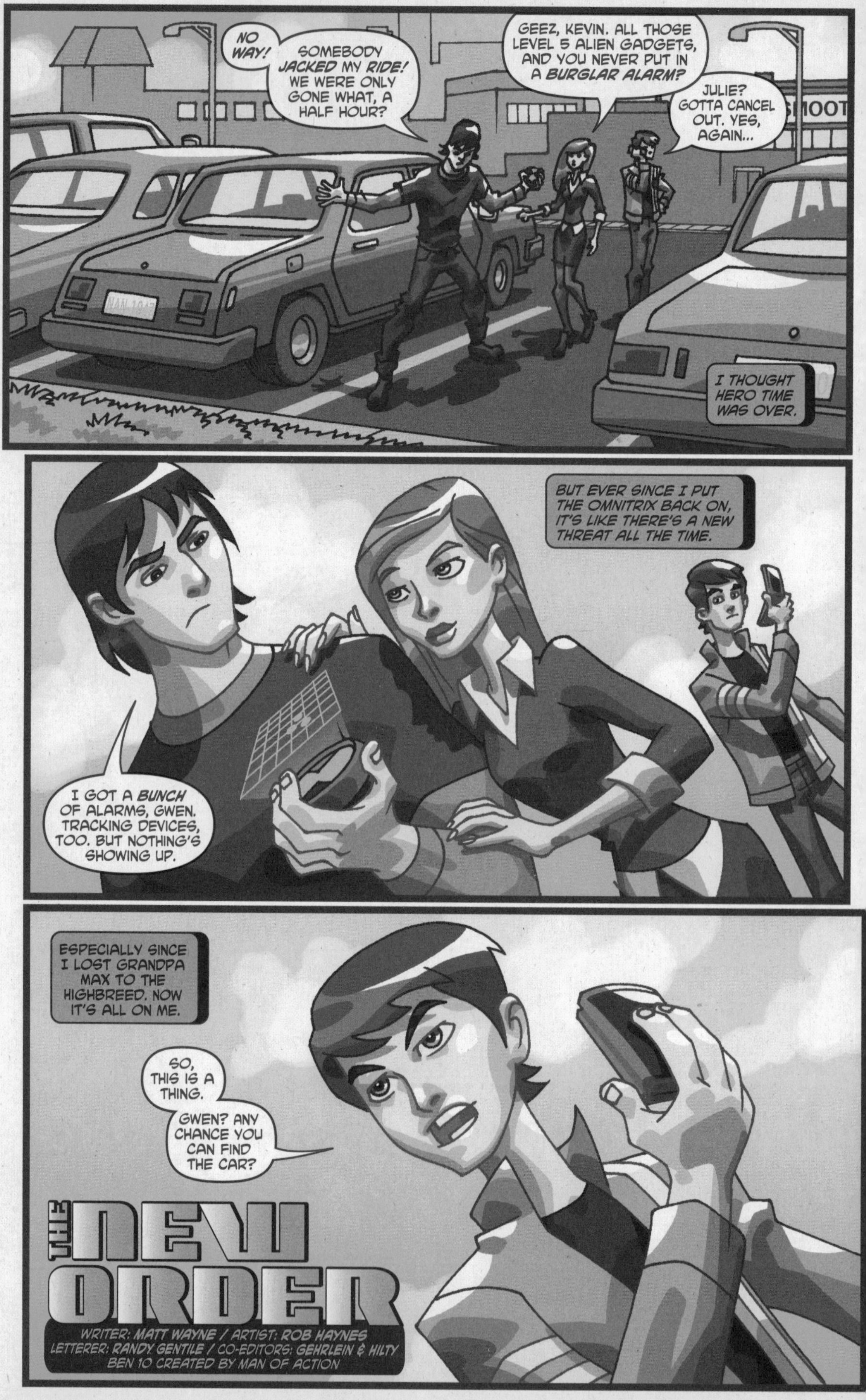
NO WAY!
SOMEBODY JACKED MY RIDE! WE WERE ONLY GONE WHAT, A HALF HOUR?
GEEZ, KEVIN. ALL THOSE LEVEL 5 ALIEN GADGETS, AND YOU NEVER PUT IN A BURGLAR ALARM?
JULIE? GOTTA CANCEL OUT. YES, AGAIN...
I THOUGHT HERO TIME WAS OVER.
BUT EVER SINCE I PUT THE OMNITRIX BACK ON, IT'S LIKE THERE'S A NEW THREAT ALL THE TIME.
I GOT A BUNCH OF ALARMS, GWEN. TRACKING DEVICES, TOO. BUT NOTHING'S SHOWING UP.
ESPECIALLY SINCE I LOST GRANDPA MAX TO THE HIGHBREED. NOW IT'S ALL ON ME.
SO, THIS IS A THING.
GWEN? ANY CHANCE YOU CAN FIND THE CAR?
THE NEW ORDER
WRITER: MATT WAYNE / ARTIST: ROB HAYNES
LETTERER: RANDY GENTILE / CO-EDITORS: GEHRLEIN & HILTY
BEN 10 CREATED BY MAN OF ACTION

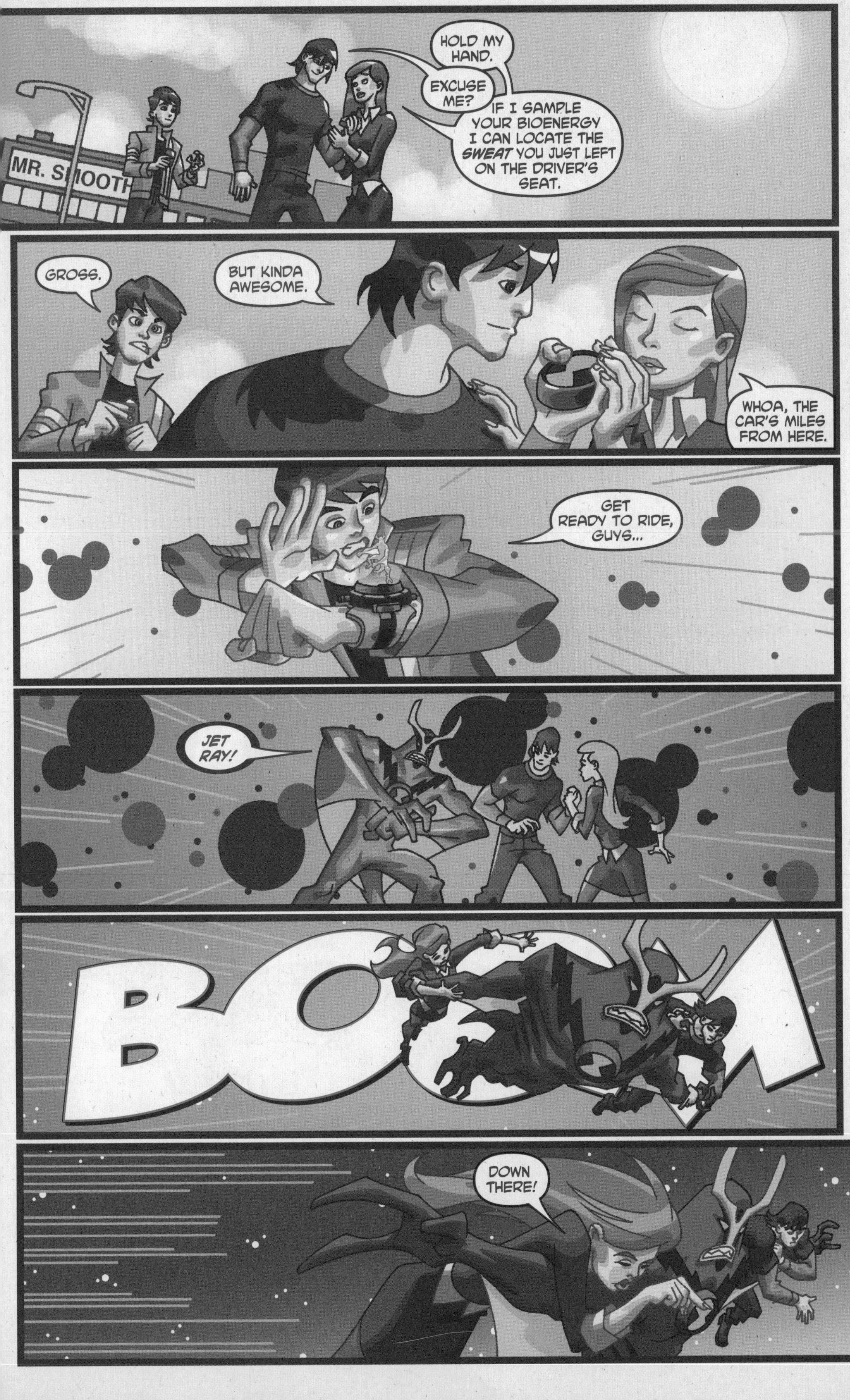

MR. SMOOTH
HOLD MY HAND.
EXCUSE ME?
IF I SAMPLE YOUR BIOENERGY I CAN LOCATE THE SWEAT YOU JUST LEFT ON THE DRIVER'S SEAT.
GROSS.
BUT KINDA AWESOME.
WHOA, THE CAR'S MILES FROM HERE.
GET READY TO RIDE, GUYS...
JET RAY!
BOOM
DOWN THERE!

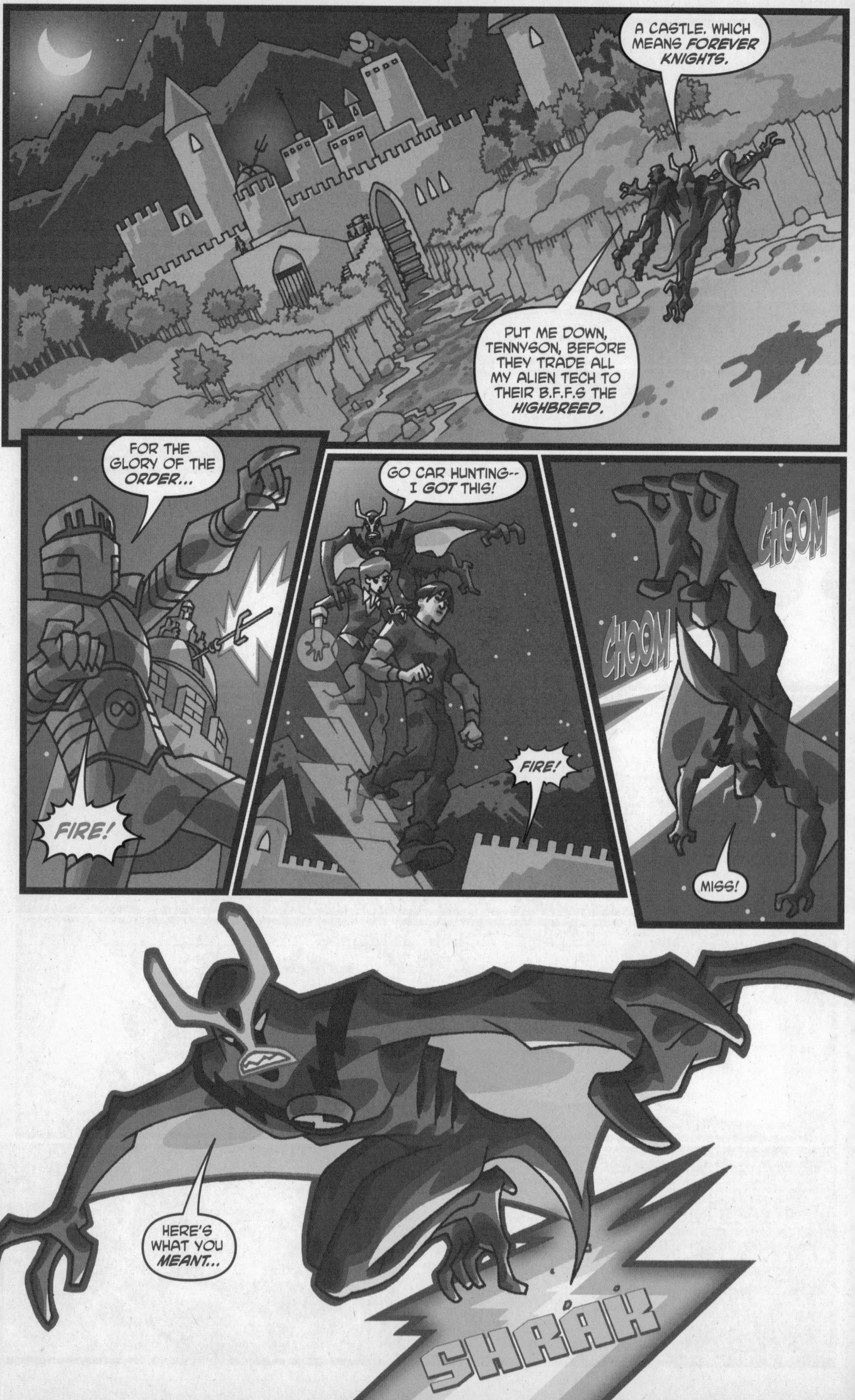
A CASTLE. WHICH MEANS *FOREVER KNIGHTS.*
PUT ME DOWN, TENNYSON, BEFORE THEY TRADE ALL MY ALIEN TECH TO THEIR B.F.F.S THE *HIGHBREED.*
FOR THE GLORY OF THE *ORDER...*
FIRE!
GO CAR HUNTING-- I *GOT* THIS!
FIRE!
CHOOM
CHOOM
MISS!
HERE'S WHAT YOU *MEANT...*
SHRAK

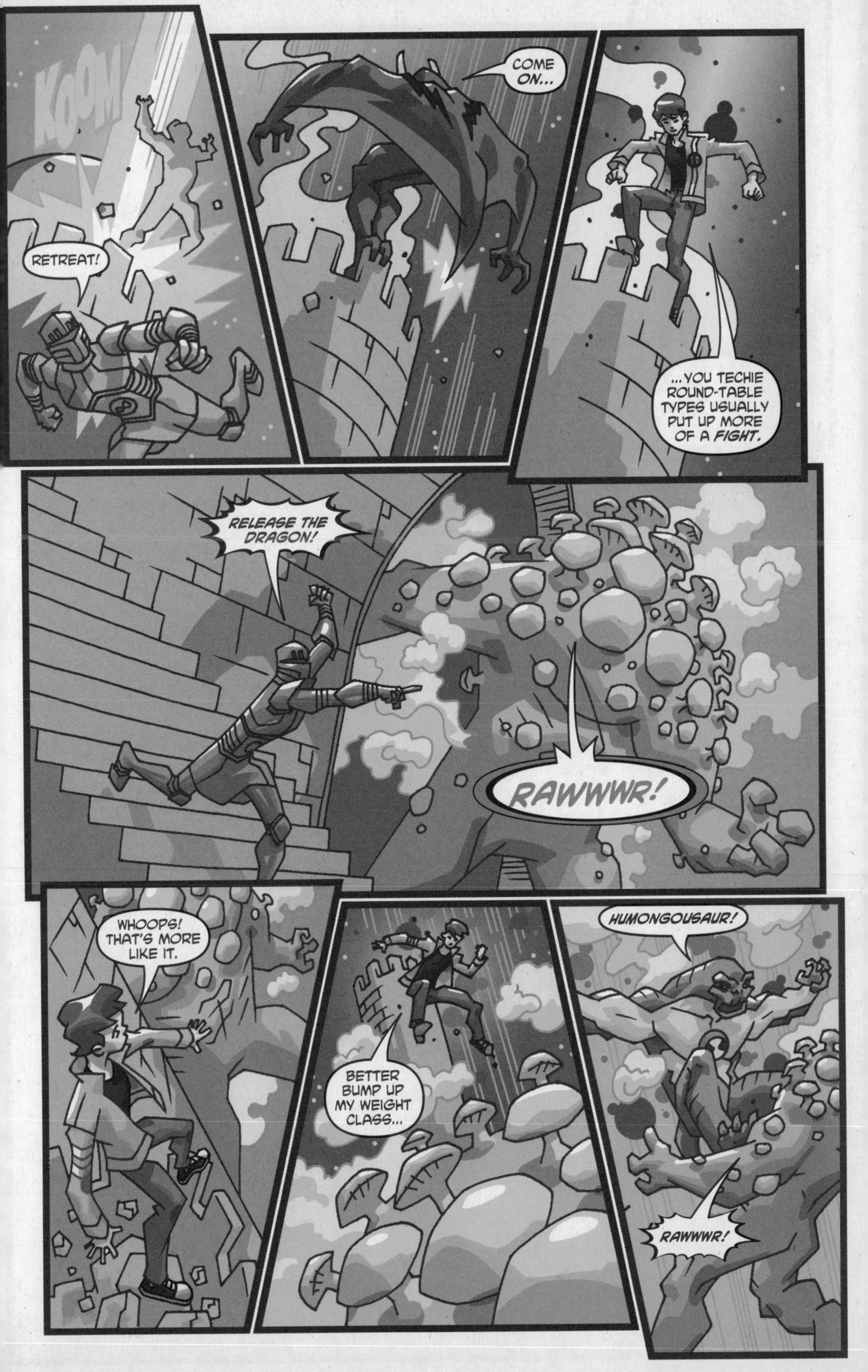
KOOM
RETREAT!
COME ON...
...YOU TECHIE ROUND-TABLE TYPES USUALLY PUT UP MORE OF A *FIGHT*.
RELEASE THE DRAGON!
RAWWWR!
WHOOPS! THAT'S MORE LIKE IT.
BETTER BUMP UP MY WEIGHT CLASS...
HUMONGOUSAUR!
RAWWWR!

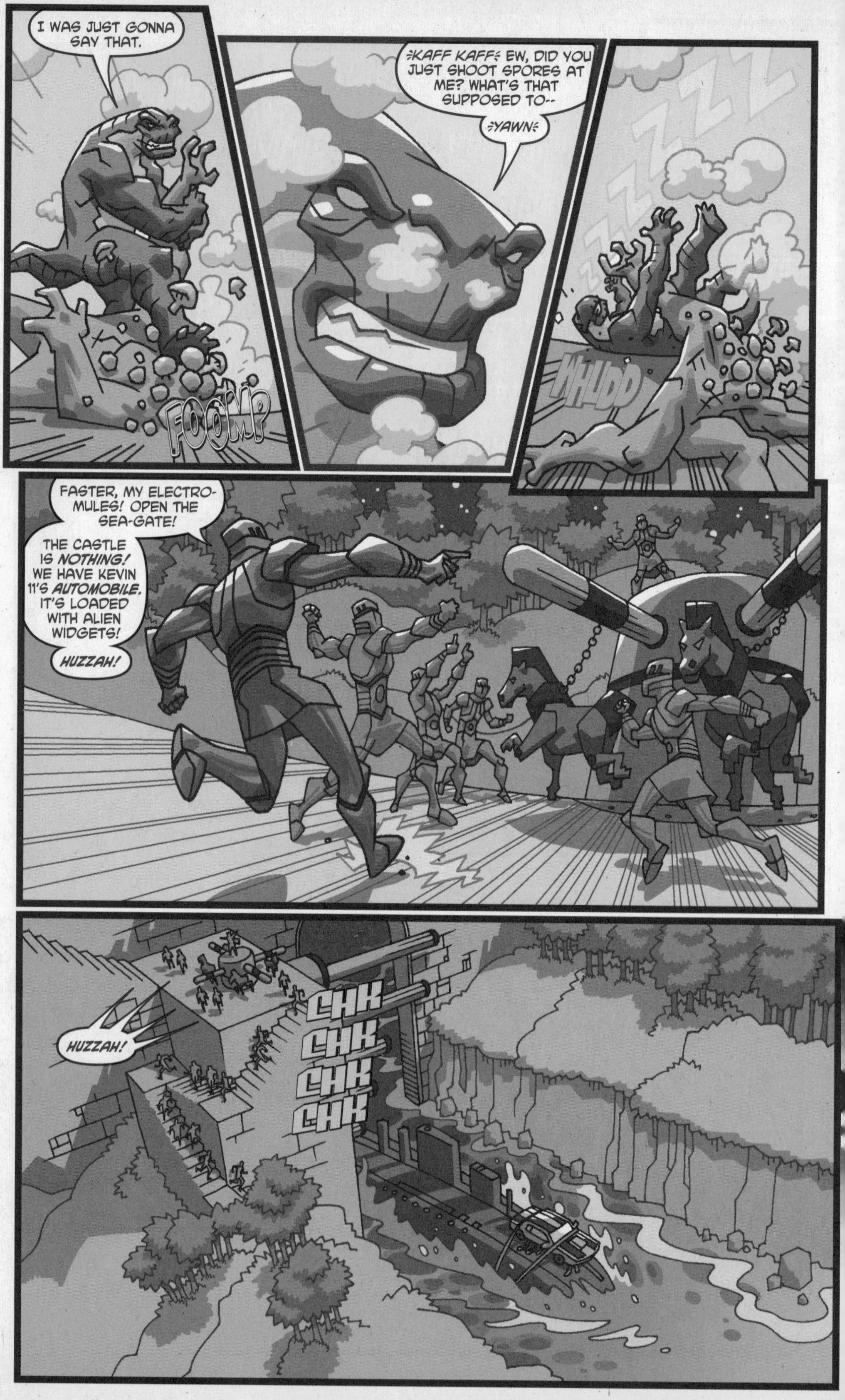
I WAS JUST GONNA SAY THAT.
FOOMP
≈KAFF KAFF≈ EW, DID YOU JUST SHOOT SPORES AT ME? WHAT'S THAT SUPPOSED TO--
≈YAWN≈
ZZZZZ
WHUDD
FASTER, MY ELECTRO-MULES! OPEN THE SEA-GATE!
THE CASTLE IS NOTHING! WE HAVE KEVIN 11'S AUTOMOBILE. IT'S LOADED WITH ALIEN WIDGETS!
HUZZAH!
HUZZAH!
CHK
CHK
CHK
CHK

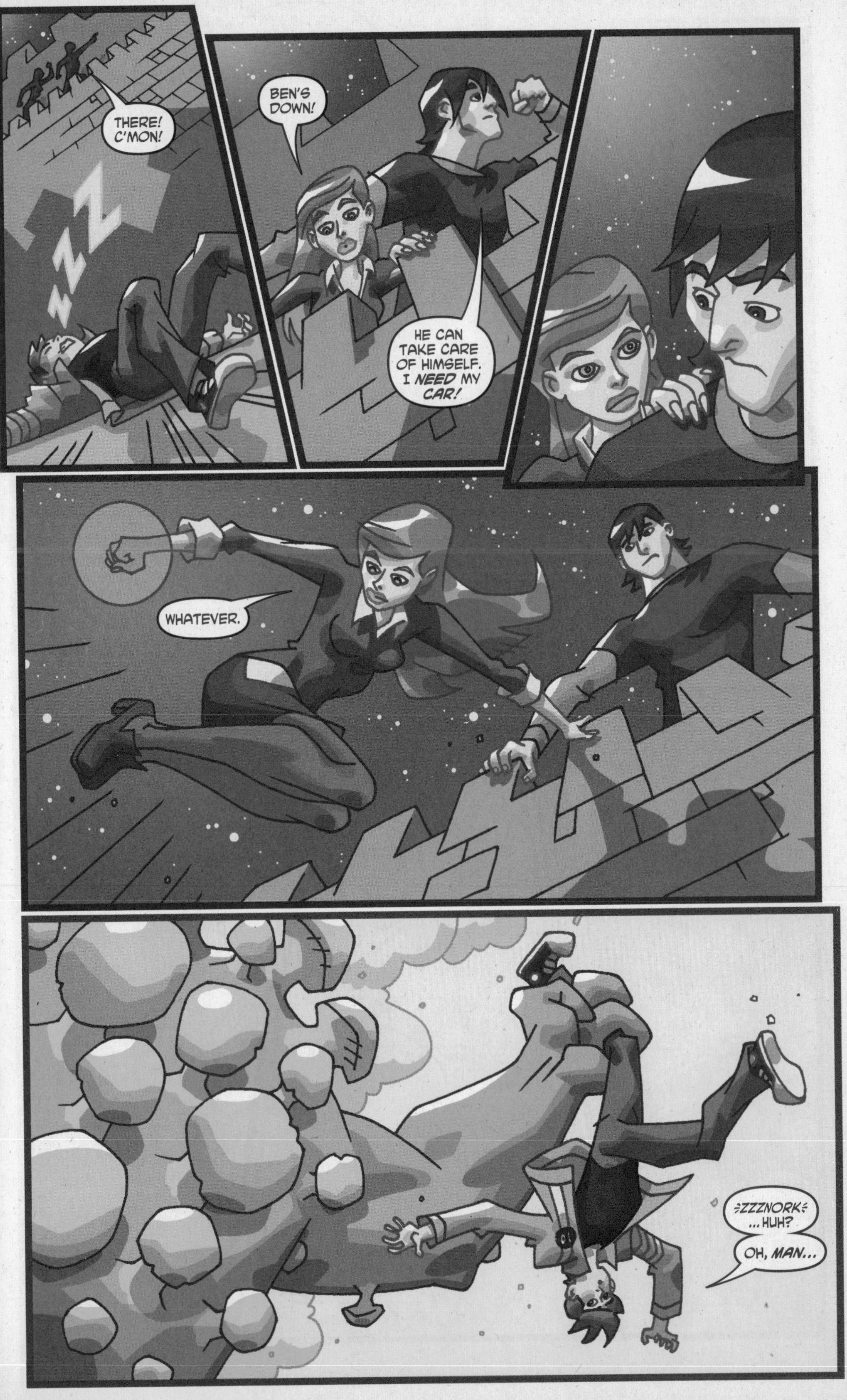

THERE! C'MON!
ZZZ
BEN'S DOWN!
HE CAN TAKE CARE OF HIMSELF. I *NEED* MY *CAR!*
WHATEVER.
≈ZZZNORK≈ ...HUH?
OH, *MAN*...

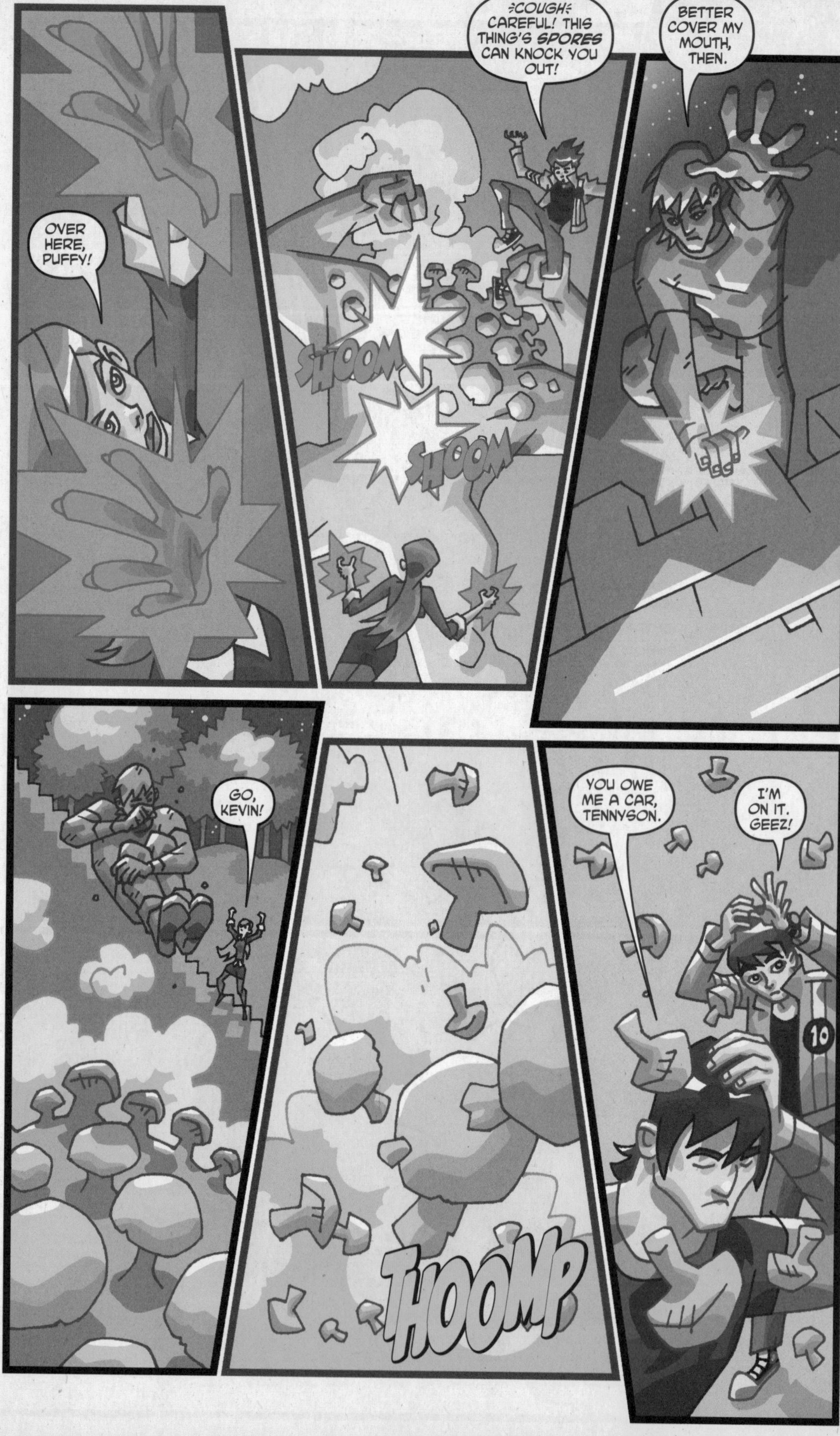
OVER HERE, PUFFY!
COUGH CAREFUL! THIS THING'S SPORES CAN KNOCK YOU OUT!
SHOOM
SHOOM
BETTER COVER MY MOUTH, THEN.
GO, KEVIN!
THOOMP
YOU OWE ME A CAR, TENNYSON.
I'M ON IT. GEEZ!

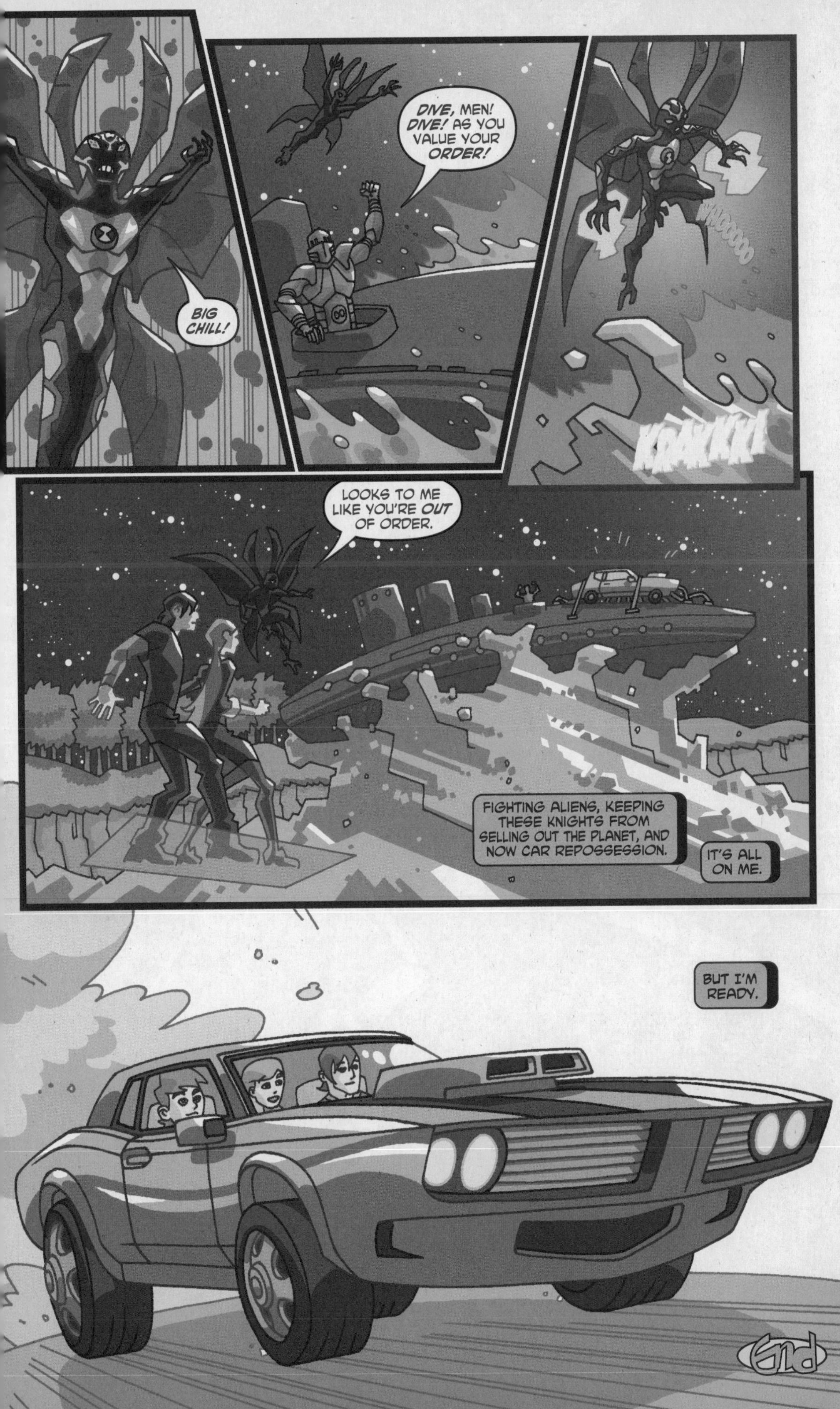
BIG CHILL!
DIVE, MEN! DIVE! AS YOU VALUE YOUR ORDER!
WHOOOOO
KRAKKK!
LOOKS TO ME LIKE YOU'RE OUT OF ORDER.
FIGHTING ALIENS, KEEPING THESE KNIGHTS FROM SELLING OUT THE PLANET, AND NOW CAR REPOSSESSION.
IT'S ALL ON ME.
BUT I'M READY.
End

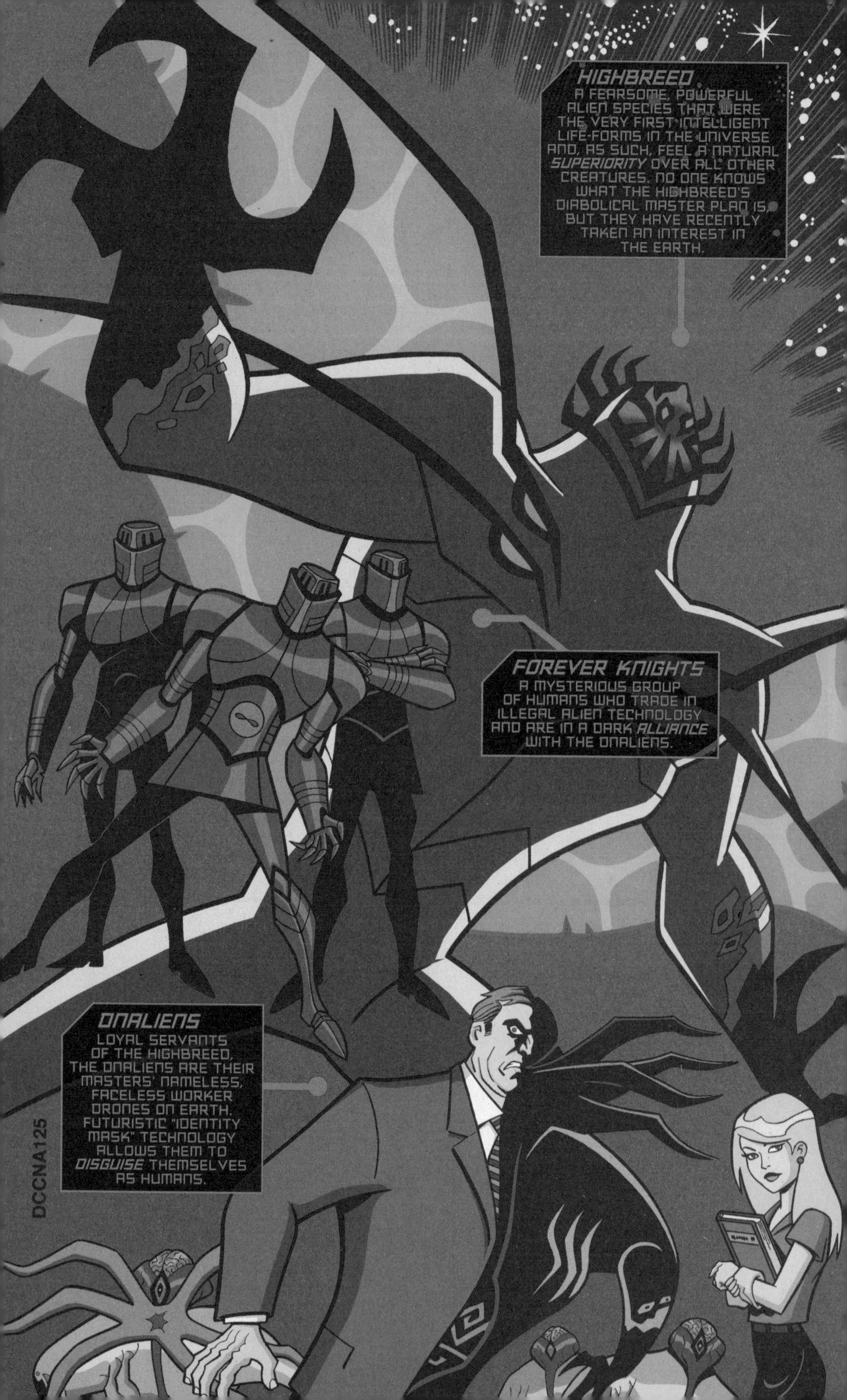
HIGHBREED
A FEARSOME, POWERFUL ALIEN SPECIES THAT WERE THE VERY FIRST INTELLIGENT LIFE-FORMS IN THE UNIVERSE AND, AS SUCH, FEEL A NATURAL *SUPERIORITY* OVER ALL OTHER CREATURES. NO ONE KNOWS WHAT THE HIGHBREED'S DIABOLICAL MASTER PLAN IS, BUT THEY HAVE RECENTLY TAKEN AN INTEREST IN THE EARTH.
FOREVER KNIGHTS
A MYSTERIOUS GROUP OF HUMANS WHO TRADE IN ILLEGAL ALIEN TECHNOLOGY AND ARE IN A DARK *ALLIANCE* WITH THE DNALIENS.
DNALIENS
LOYAL SERVANTS OF THE HIGHBREED, THE DNALIENS ARE THEIR MASTERS' NAMELESS, FACELESS WORKER DRONES ON EARTH. FUTURISTIC "IDENTITY MASK" TECHNOLOGY ALLOWS THEM TO *DISGUISE* THEMSELVES AS HUMANS.
DCCNA125

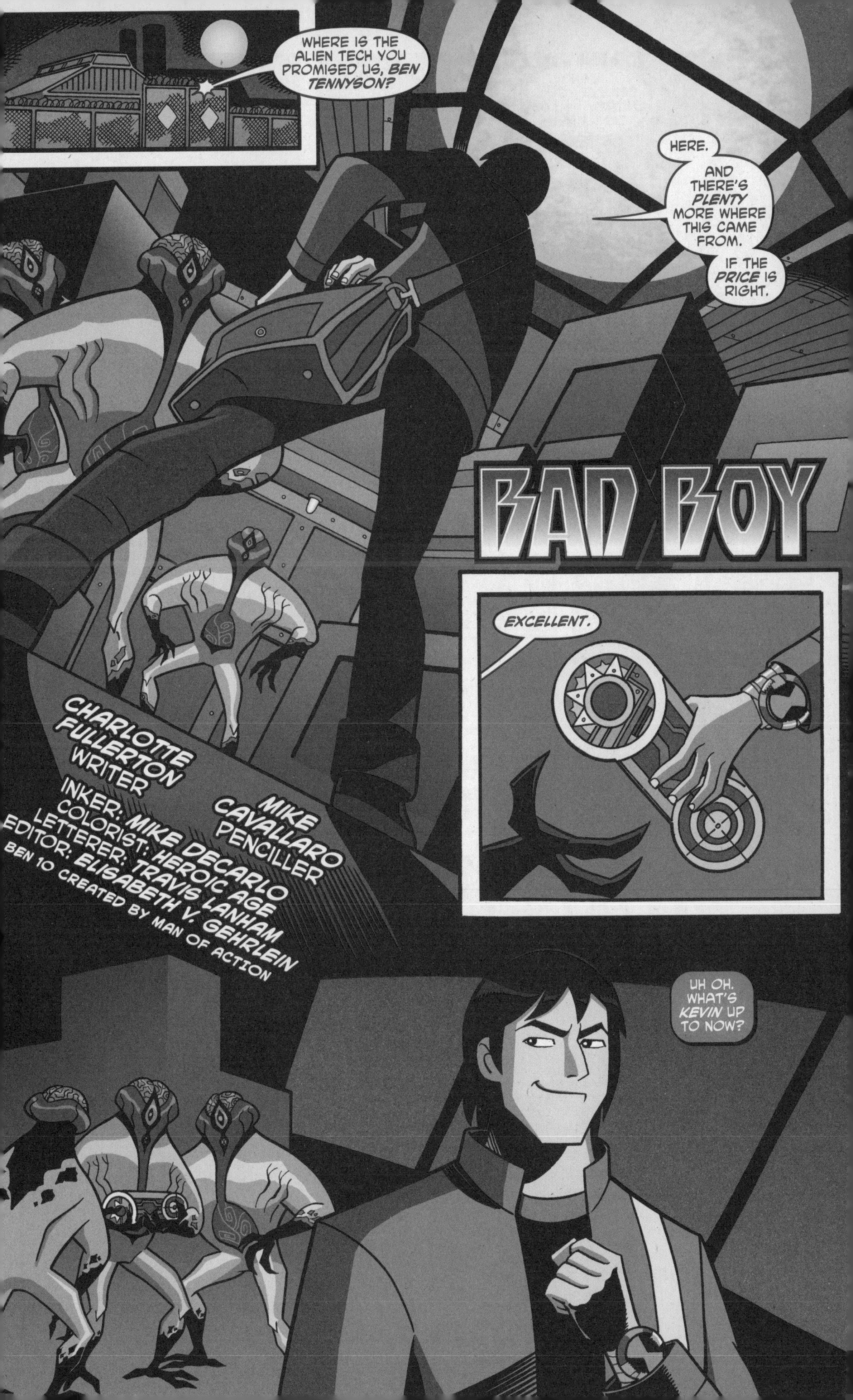
WHERE IS THE ALIEN TECH YOU PROMISED US, BEN TENNYSON?
HERE.
AND THERE'S PLENTY MORE WHERE THIS CAME FROM.
IF THE PRICE IS RIGHT.
BAD BOY
EXCELLENT.
CHARLOTTE FULLERTON WRITER
MIKE CAVALLARO PENCILLER
INKER: MIKE DECARLO
COLORIST: HEROIC AGE
LETTERER: TRAVIS LANHAM
EDITOR: ELISABETH V. GEHRLEIN
BEN 10 CREATED BY MAN OF ACTION
UH OH. WHAT'S KEVIN UP TO NOW?

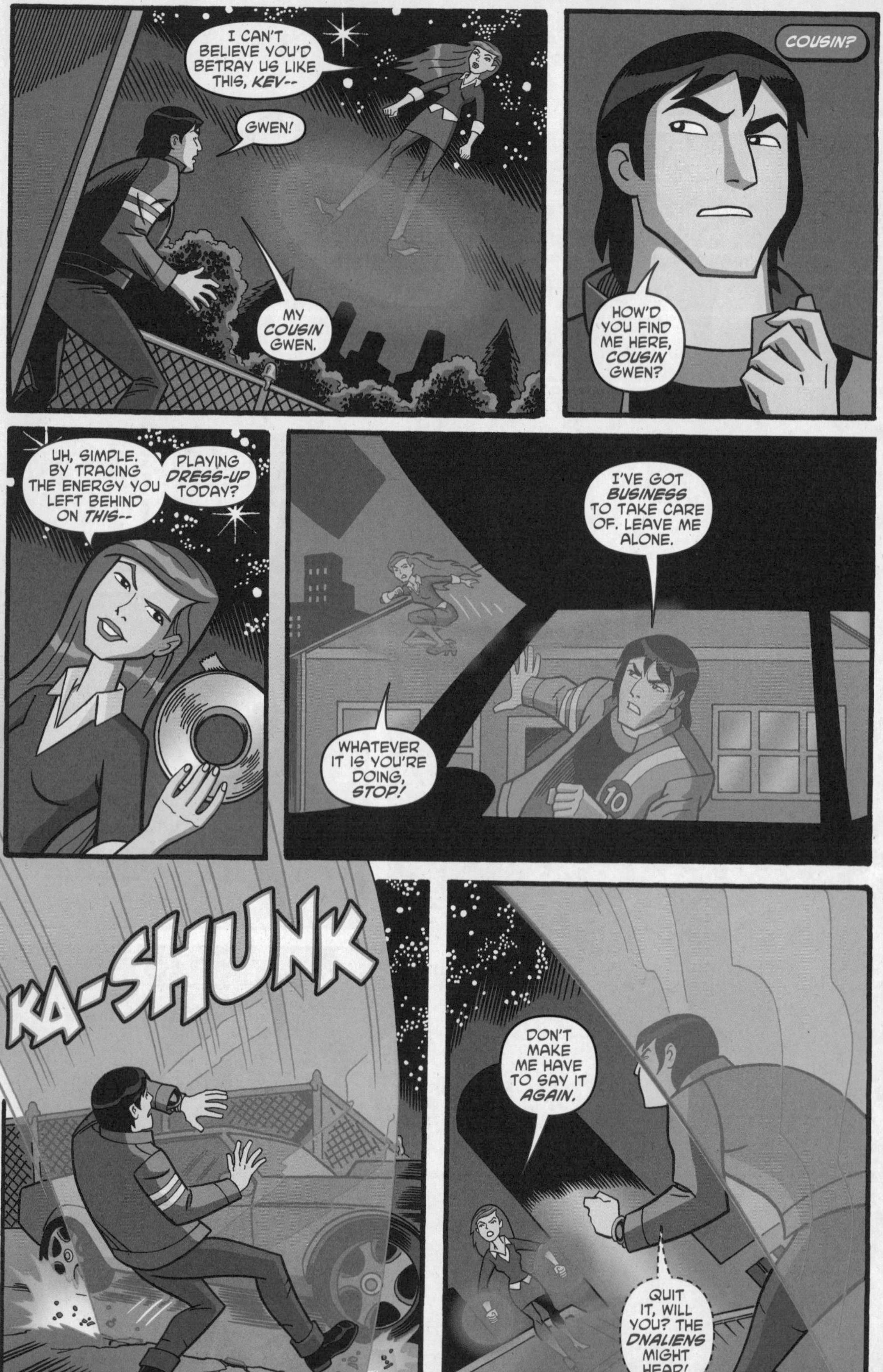
I CAN'T BELIEVE YOU'D BETRAY US LIKE THIS, KEV--
GWEN!
MY COUSIN GWEN.
COUSIN?
HOW'D YOU FIND ME HERE, COUSIN GWEN?
UH, SIMPLE. BY TRACING THE ENERGY YOU LEFT BEHIND ON THIS--
PLAYING DRESS-UP TODAY?
I'VE GOT BUSINESS TO TAKE CARE OF. LEAVE ME ALONE.
WHATEVER IT IS YOU'RE DOING, STOP!
10
KA-SHUNK
DON'T MAKE ME HAVE TO SAY IT AGAIN.
QUIT IT, WILL YOU? THE DNALIENS MIGHT HEAR!

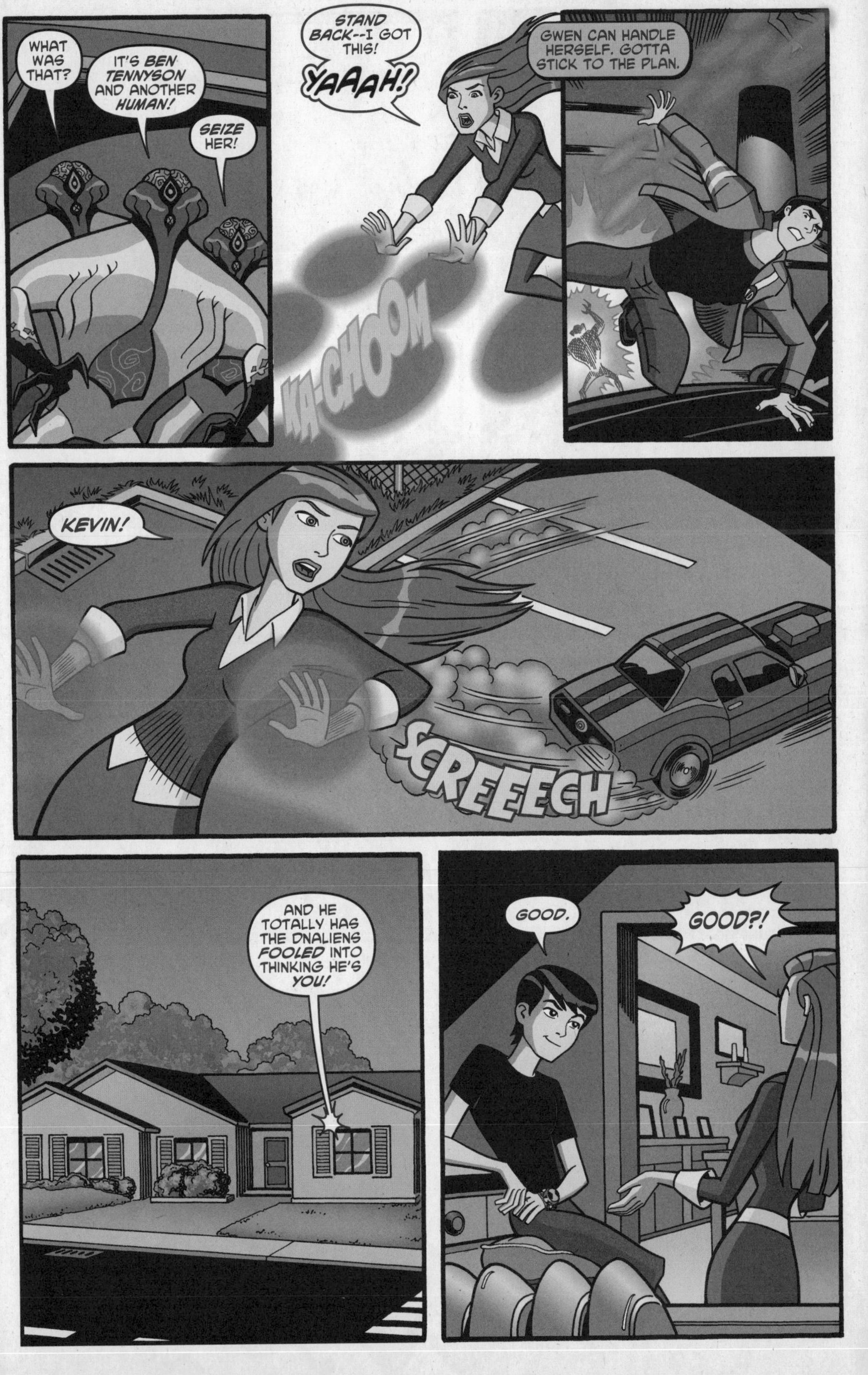

WHAT WAS THAT?
IT'S BEN TENNYSON AND ANOTHER HUMAN!
SEIZE HER!
STAND BACK--I GOT THIS!
YAAAH!
KA-CHOOM
GWEN CAN HANDLE HERSELF. GOTTA STICK TO THE PLAN.
KEVIN!
SCREEECH
AND HE TOTALLY HAS THE DNALIENS FOOLED INTO THINKING HE'S YOU!
GOOD.
GOOD?!

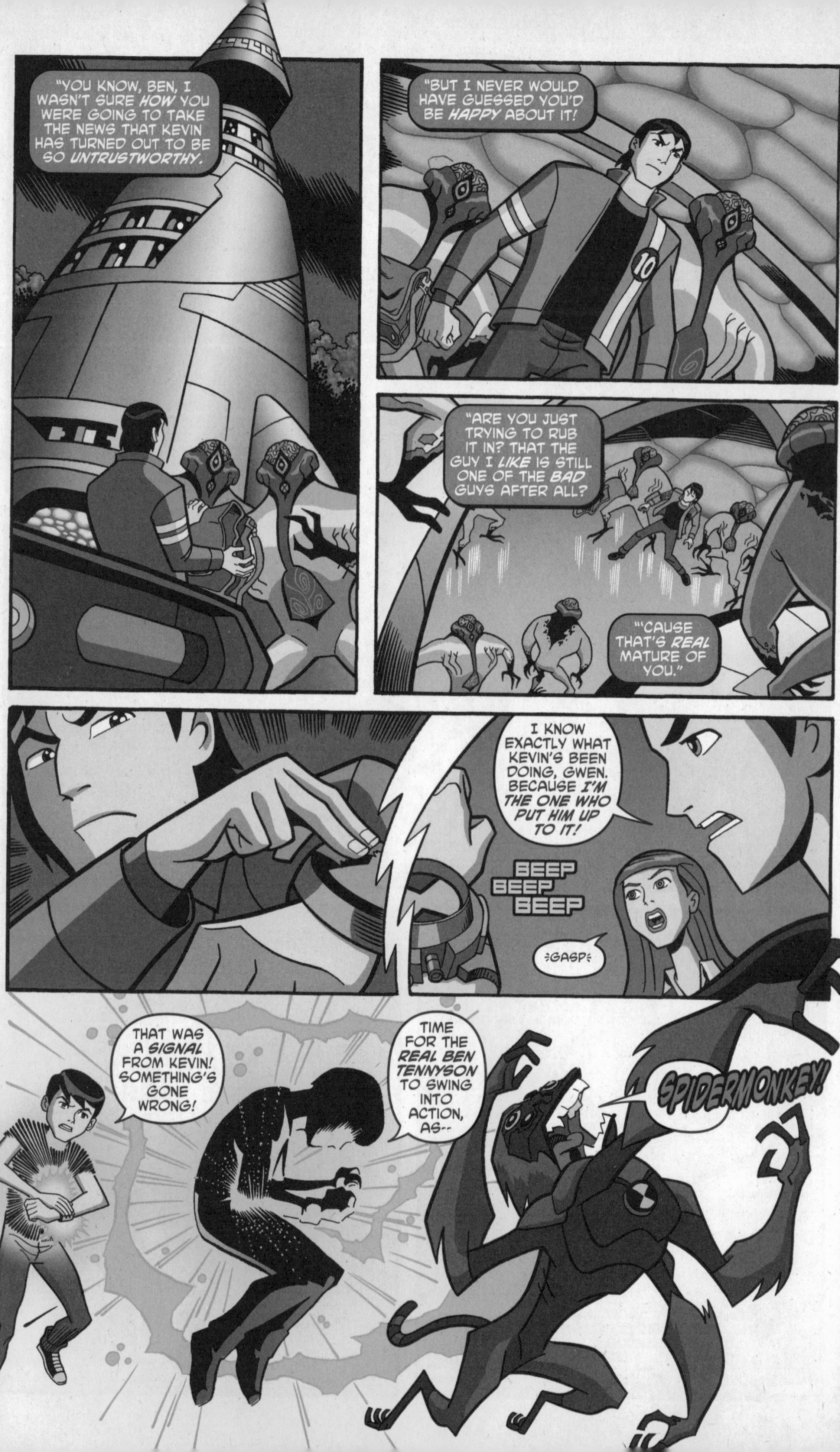
"YOU KNOW, BEN, I WASN'T SURE HOW YOU WERE GOING TO TAKE THE NEWS THAT KEVIN HAS TURNED OUT TO BE SO UNTRUSTWORTHY.
"BUT I NEVER WOULD HAVE GUESSED YOU'D BE HAPPY ABOUT IT!
"ARE YOU JUST TRYING TO RUB IT IN? THAT THE GUY I LIKE IS STILL ONE OF THE BAD GUYS AFTER ALL?
"'CAUSE THAT'S REAL MATURE OF YOU."
I KNOW EXACTLY WHAT KEVIN'S BEEN DOING, GWEN. BECAUSE I'M THE ONE WHO PUT HIM UP TO IT!
BEEP BEEP BEEP
GASP
THAT WAS A SIGNAL FROM KEVIN! SOMETHING'S GONE WRONG!
TIME FOR THE REAL BEN TENNYSON TO SWING INTO ACTION, AS--
SPIDERMONKEY!

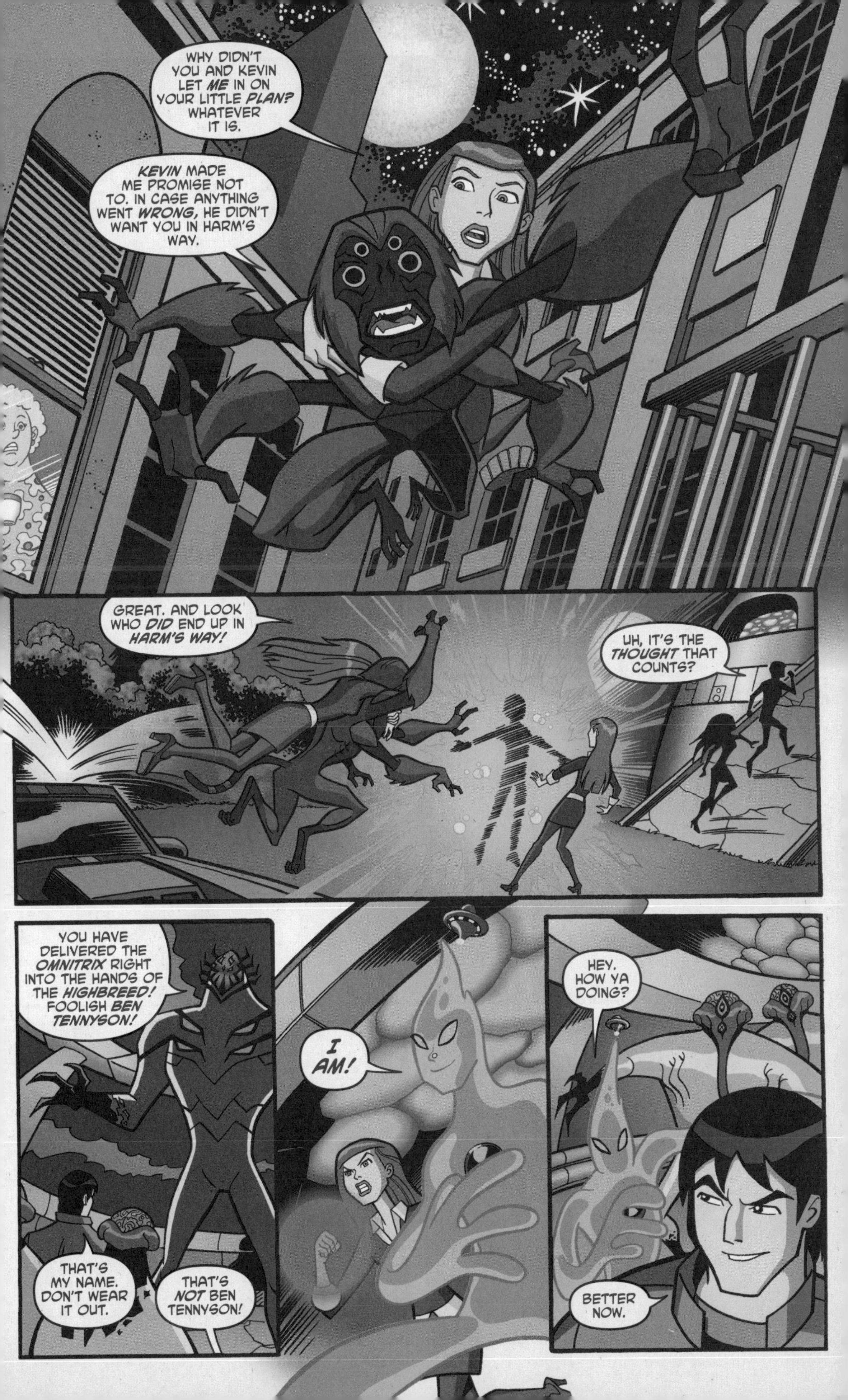

WHY DIDN'T YOU AND KEVIN LET *ME* IN ON YOUR LITTLE *PLAN?* WHATEVER IT IS.
KEVIN MADE ME PROMISE NOT TO. IN CASE ANYTHING WENT *WRONG,* HE DIDN'T WANT YOU IN HARM'S WAY.
GREAT. AND LOOK WHO *DID* END UP IN *HARM'S WAY!*
UH, IT'S THE *THOUGHT* THAT COUNTS?
YOU HAVE DELIVERED THE *OMNITRIX* RIGHT INTO THE HANDS OF THE *HIGHBREED!* FOOLISH *BEN TENNYSON!*
THAT'S MY NAME. DON'T WEAR IT OUT.
THAT'S *NOT* BEN TENNYSON!
I AM!
HEY. HOW YA DOING?
BETTER NOW.

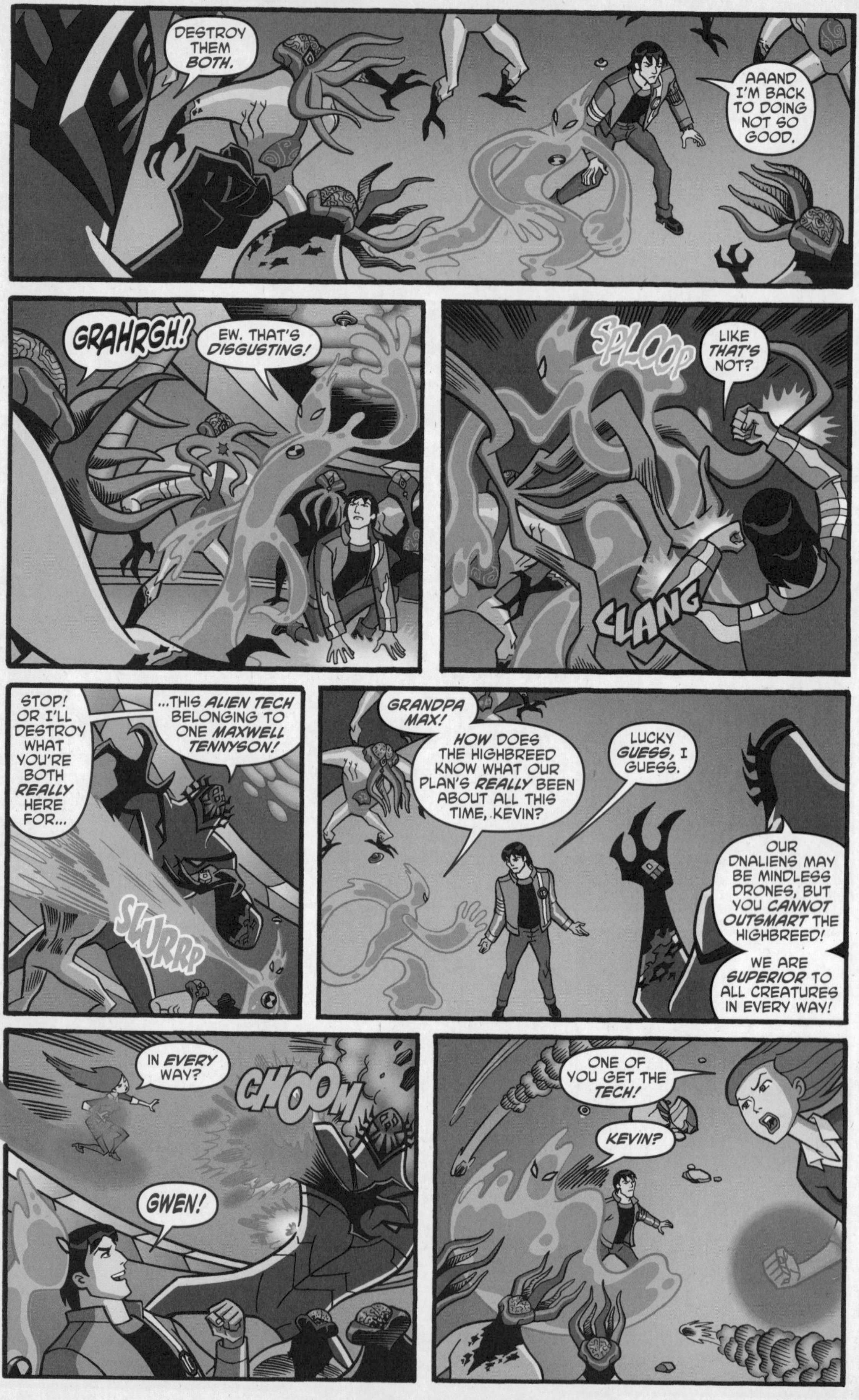
DESTROY THEM BOTH.
AAAND I'M BACK TO DOING NOT SO GOOD.
GRAHRGH!
EW. THAT'S DISGUSTING!
SPLOOP
LIKE THAT'S NOT?
CLANG
STOP! OR I'LL DESTROY WHAT YOU'RE BOTH REALLY HERE FOR...
...THIS ALIEN TECH BELONGING TO ONE MAXWELL TENNYSON!
SLURRP
GRANDPA MAX!
HOW DOES THE HIGHBREED KNOW WHAT OUR PLAN'S REALLY BEEN ABOUT ALL THIS TIME, KEVIN?
LUCKY GUESS, I GUESS.
OUR DNALIENS MAY BE MINDLESS DRONES, BUT YOU CANNOT OUTSMART THE HIGHBREED!
WE ARE SUPERIOR TO ALL CREATURES IN EVERY WAY!
IN EVERY WAY?
CHOOM
GWEN!
ONE OF YOU GET THE TECH!
KEVIN?

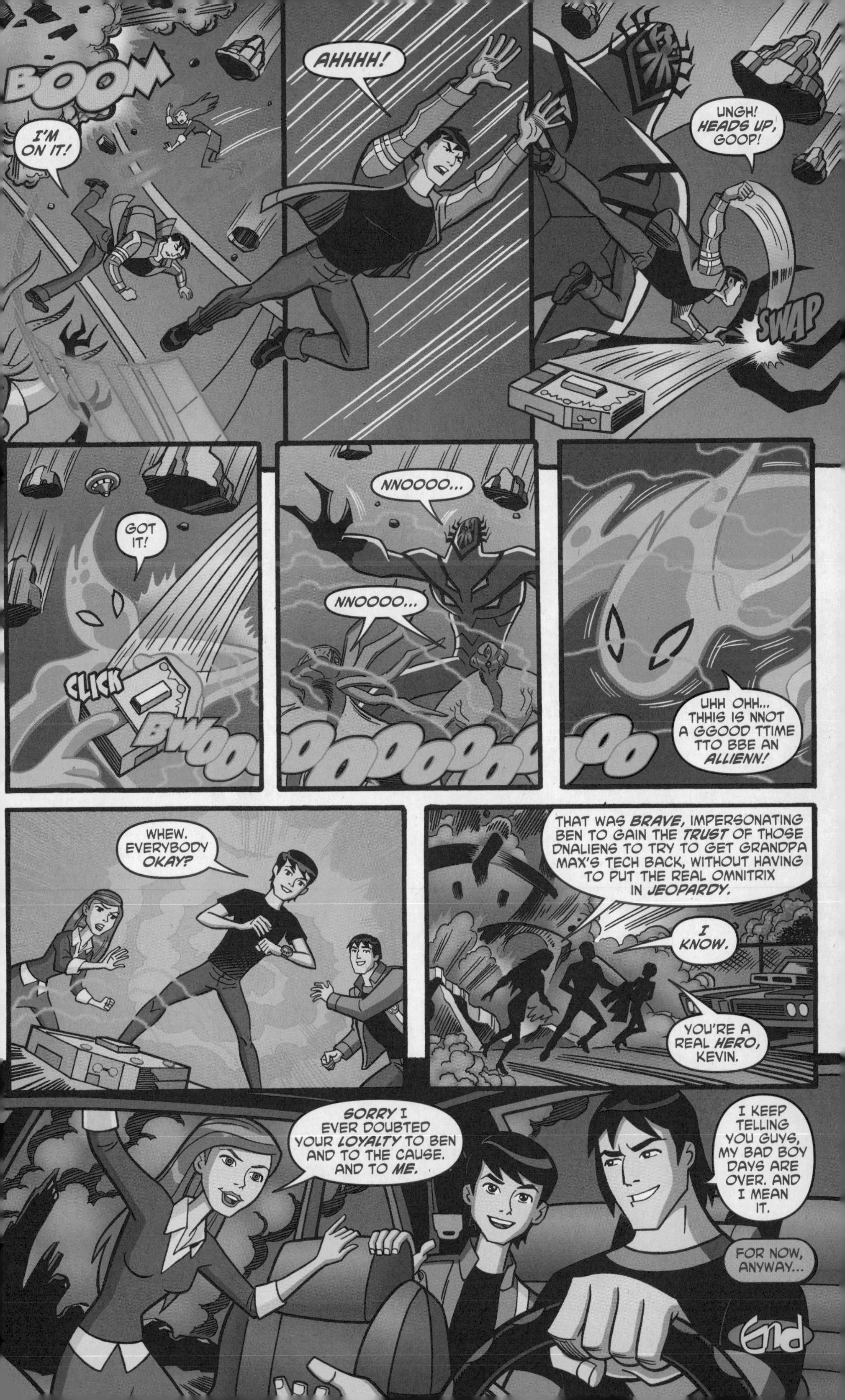
BOOM
I'M ON IT!
AHHHH!
UNGH! HEADS UP, GOOP!
SWAP
GOT IT!
CLICK
NNOOOO...
NNOOOO...
BWOOOOOOOOOOOOOO
UHH OHH... THHIS IS NNOT A GGOOD TTIME TTO BBE AN ALLIENN!
WHEW. EVERYBODY OKAY?
THAT WAS BRAVE, IMPERSONATING BEN TO GAIN THE TRUST OF THOSE DNALIENS TO TRY TO GET GRANDPA MAX'S TECH BACK, WITHOUT HAVING TO PUT THE REAL OMNITRIX IN JEOPARDY.
I KNOW.
YOU'RE A REAL HERO, KEVIN.
SORRY I EVER DOUBTED YOUR LOYALTY TO BEN AND TO THE CAUSE. AND TO ME.
I KEEP TELLING YOU GUYS, MY BAD BOY DAYS ARE OVER. AND I MEAN IT.
FOR NOW, ANYWAY...
End

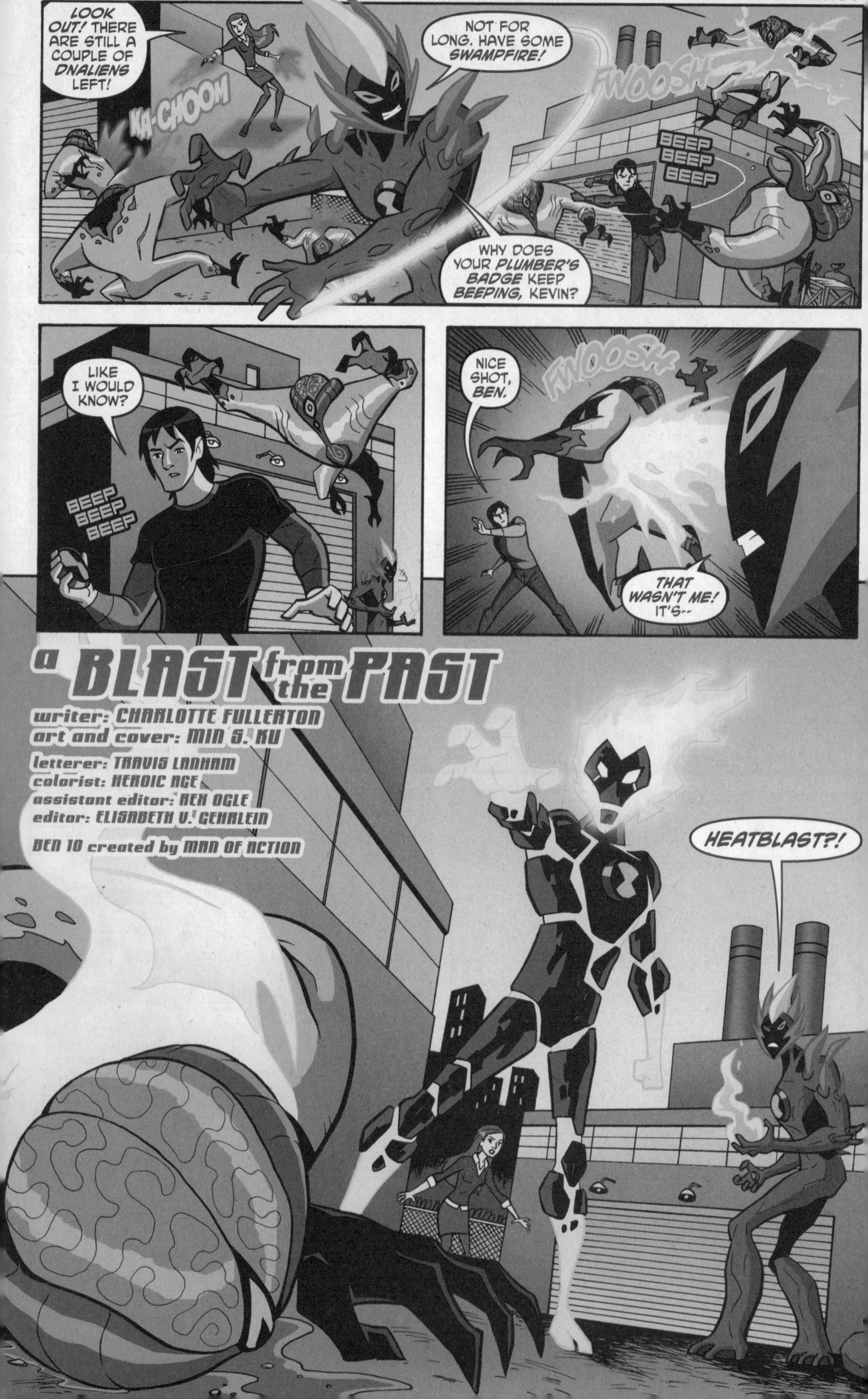
LOOK OUT! THERE ARE STILL A COUPLE OF DNALIENS LEFT!
KA-CHOOM
NOT FOR LONG. HAVE SOME SWAMPFIRE!
FWOOSH
BEEP BEEP BEEP
WHY DOES YOUR PLUMBER'S BADGE KEEP BEEPING, KEVIN?
LIKE I WOULD KNOW?
BEEP BEEP BEEP
NICE SHOT, BEN.
FWOOSH
THAT WASN'T ME! IT'S--
a BLAST from the PAST
writer: CHARLOTTE FULLERTON
art and cover: MIN S. KU
letterer: TRAVIS LANHAM
colorist: HEROIC AGE
assistant editor: REX OGLE
editor: ELISABETH V. GEHRLEIN
BEN 10 created by MAN OF ACTION
HEATBLAST?!

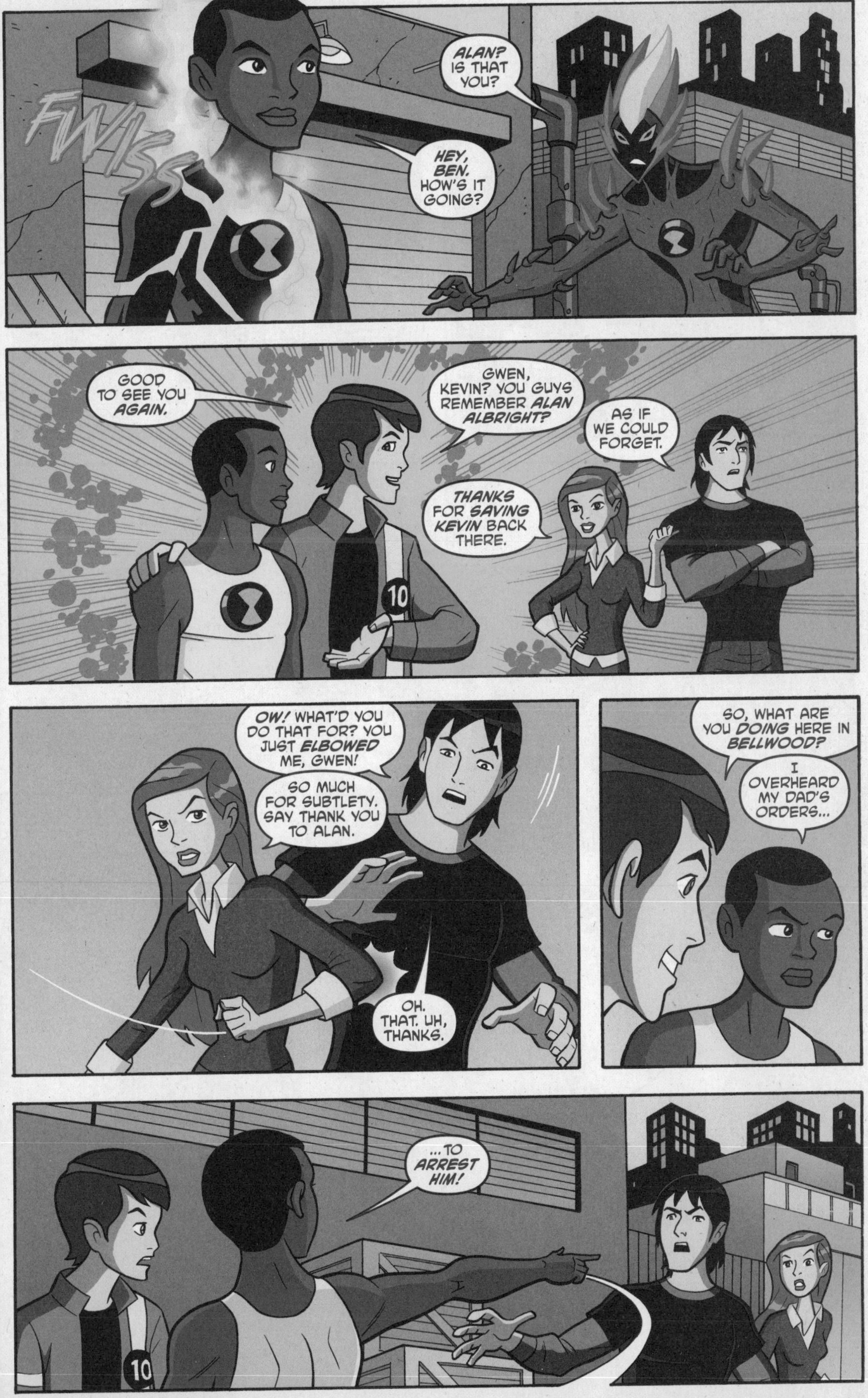
FWISS
ALAN? IS THAT YOU?
HEY, BEN. HOW'S IT GOING?
GOOD TO SEE YOU AGAIN.
GWEN, KEVIN? YOU GUYS REMEMBER ALAN ALBRIGHT?
AS IF WE COULD FORGET.
THANKS FOR SAVING KEVIN BACK THERE.
OW! WHAT'D YOU DO THAT FOR? YOU JUST ELBOWED ME, GWEN!
SO MUCH FOR SUBTLETY. SAY THANK YOU TO ALAN.
OH. THAT. UH, THANKS.
SO, WHAT ARE YOU DOING HERE IN BELLWOOD?
I OVERHEARD MY DAD'S ORDERS...
...TO ARREST HIM!

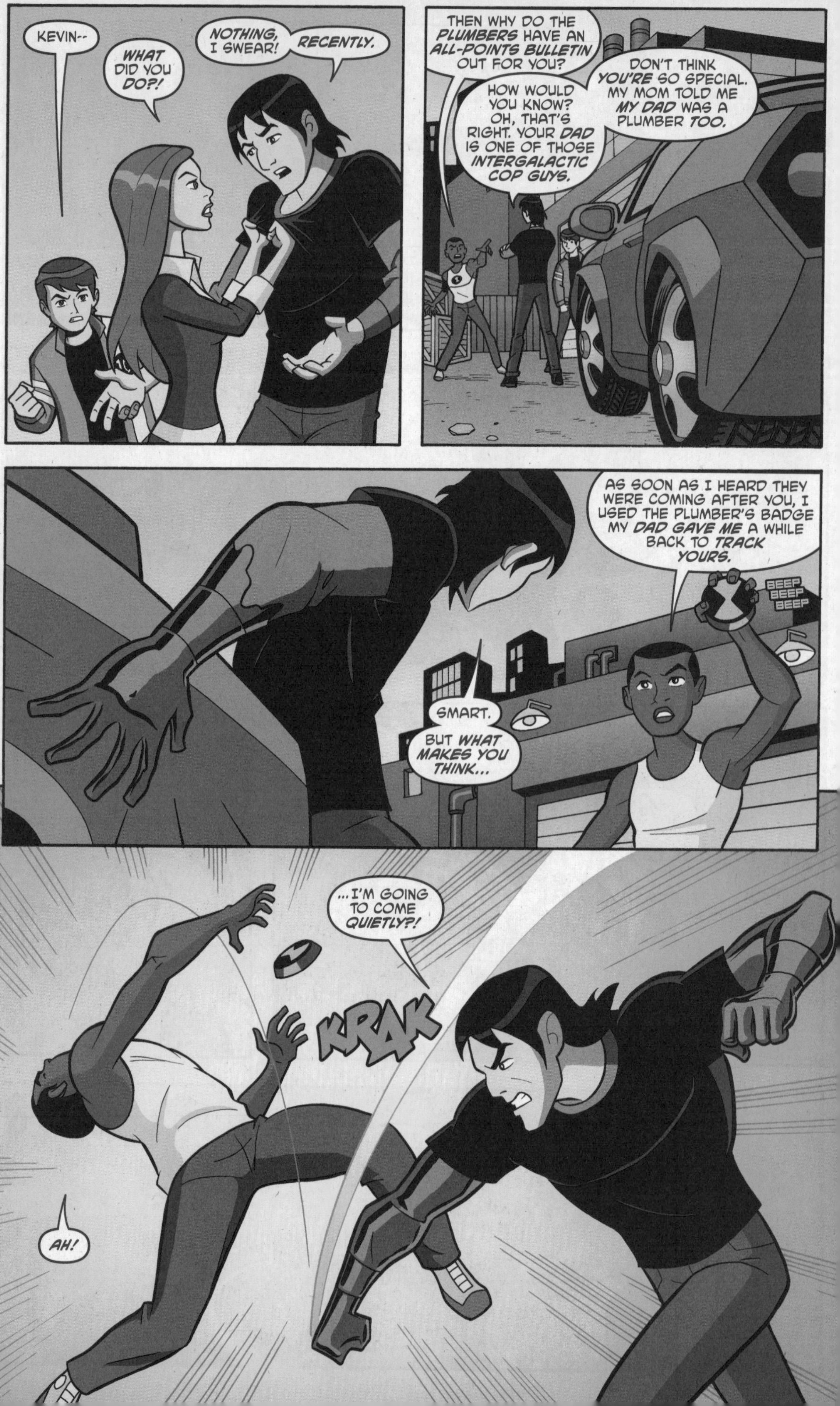
KEVIN--
WHAT DID YOU DO?!
NOTHING, I SWEAR!
RECENTLY.
THEN WHY DO THE PLUMBERS HAVE AN ALL-POINTS BULLETIN OUT FOR YOU?
HOW WOULD YOU KNOW? OH, THAT'S RIGHT. YOUR DAD IS ONE OF THOSE INTERGALACTIC COP GUYS.
DON'T THINK YOU'RE SO SPECIAL. MY MOM TOLD ME MY DAD WAS A PLUMBER TOO.
AS SOON AS I HEARD THEY WERE COMING AFTER YOU, I USED THE PLUMBER'S BADGE MY DAD GAVE ME A WHILE BACK TO TRACK YOURS.
BEEP BEEP BEEP
SMART.
BUT WHAT MAKES YOU THINK...
...I'M GOING TO COME QUIETLY?!
KRAK
AH!

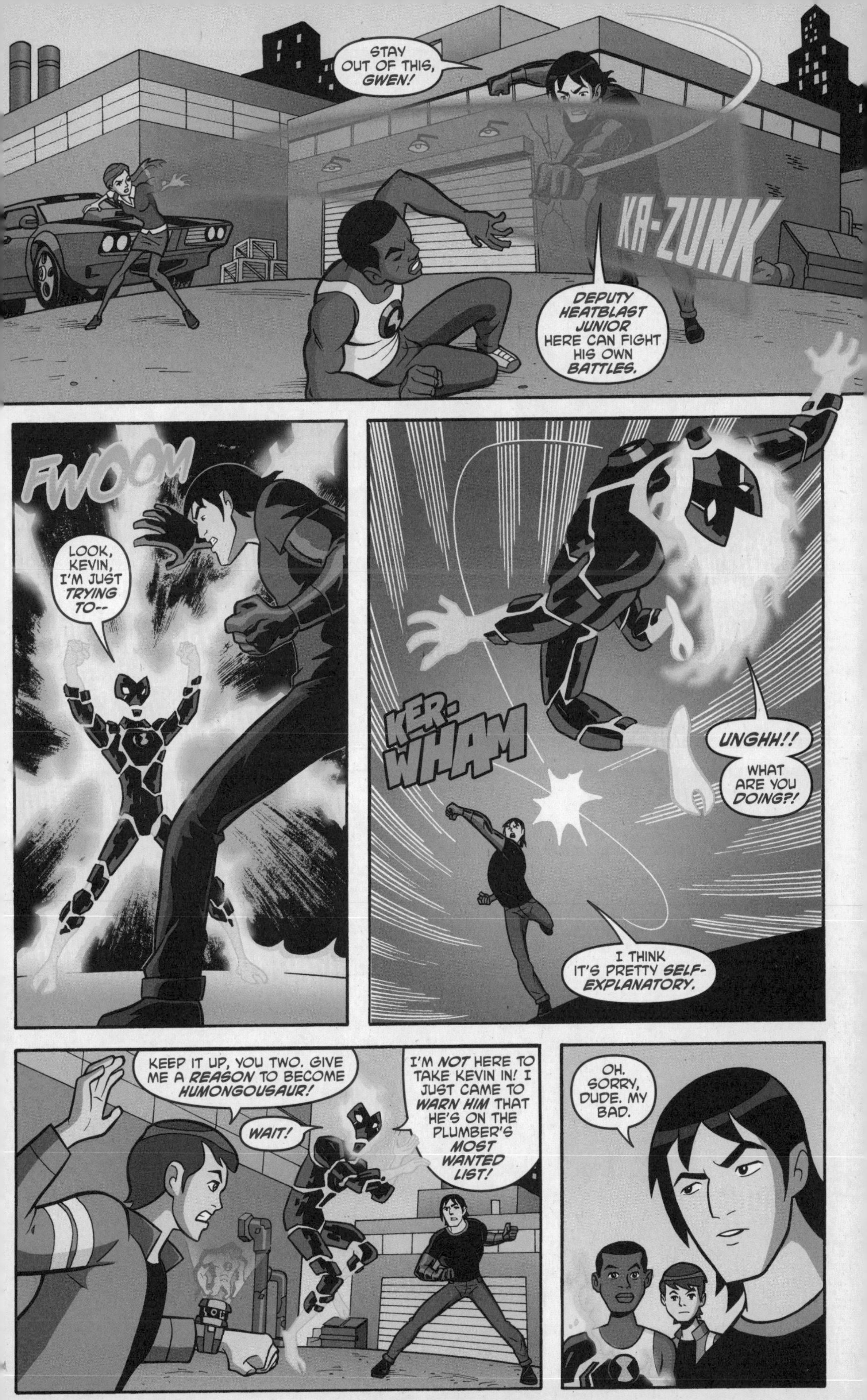
STAY OUT OF THIS, GWEN!
KA-ZUNK
DEPUTY HEATBLAST JUNIOR HERE CAN FIGHT HIS OWN BATTLES.
FWOOM
LOOK, KEVIN, I'M JUST TRYING TO--
KER-WHAM
UNGHH!!
WHAT ARE YOU DOING?!
I THINK IT'S PRETTY SELF-EXPLANATORY.
KEEP IT UP, YOU TWO. GIVE ME A REASON TO BECOME HUMONGOUSAUR!
WAIT!
I'M NOT HERE TO TAKE KEVIN IN! I JUST CAME TO WARN HIM THAT HE'S ON THE PLUMBER'S MOST WANTED LIST!
OH. SORRY, DUDE. MY BAD.

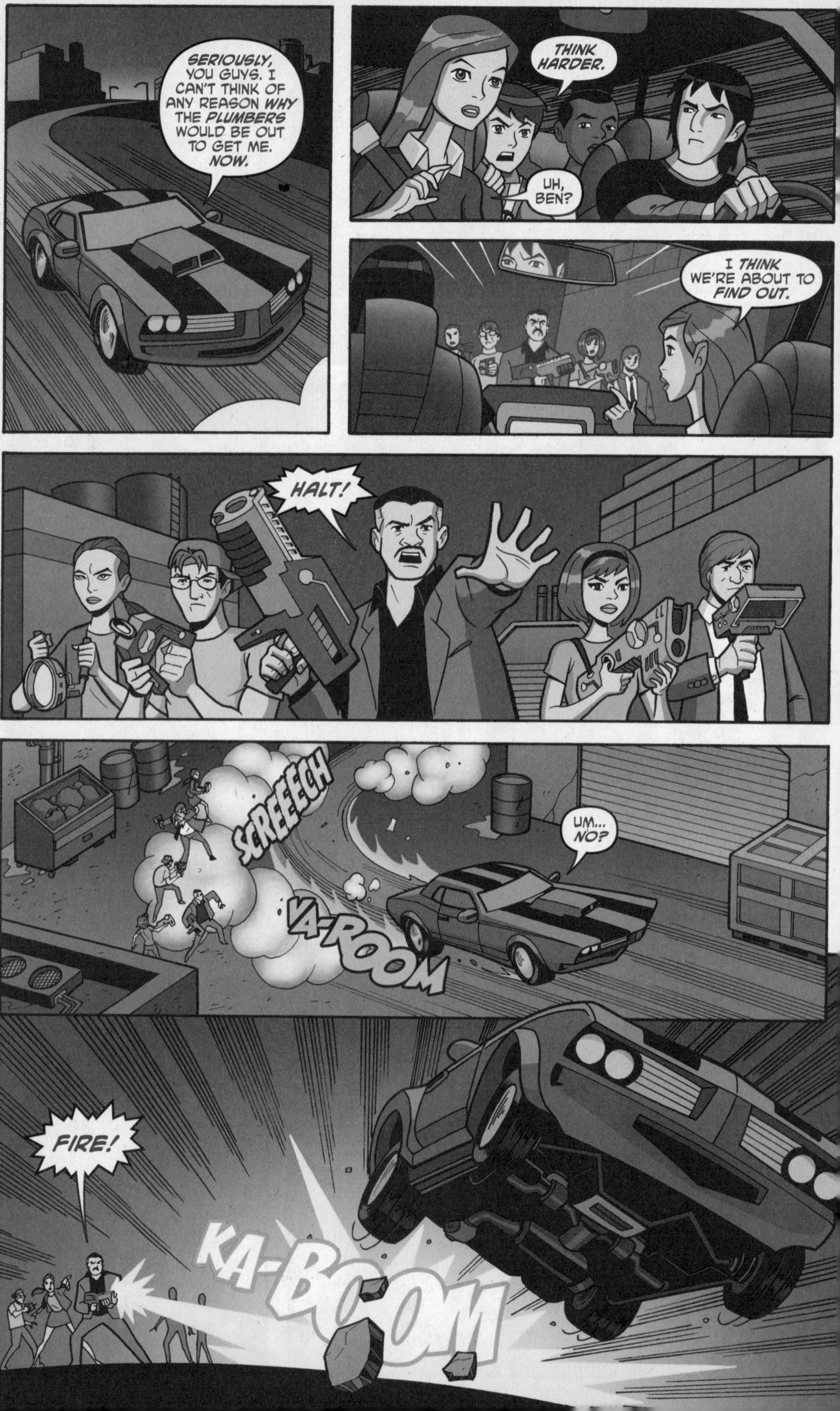
SERIOUSLY, YOU GUYS. I CAN'T THINK OF ANY REASON WHY THE PLUMBERS WOULD BE OUT TO GET ME. NOW.
THINK HARDER.
UH, BEN?
I THINK WE'RE ABOUT TO FIND OUT.
HALT!
SCREEECH
UM... NO?
VA-ROOM
FIRE!
KA-BOOM

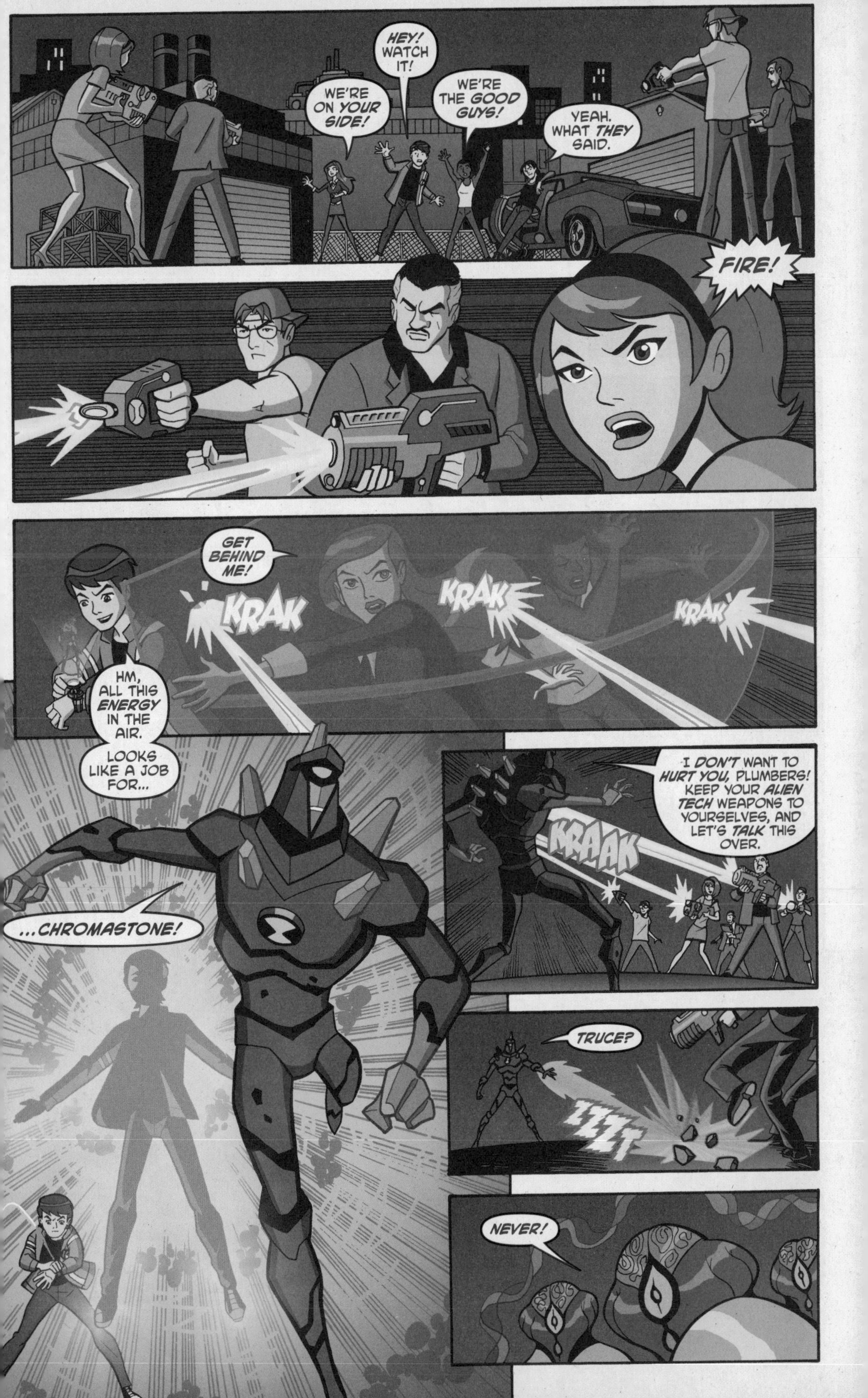
WE'RE ON YOUR SIDE!
HEY! WATCH IT!
WE'RE THE GOOD GUYS!
YEAH. WHAT THEY SAID.
FIRE!
GET BEHIND ME!
KRAK
KRAK
KRAK
HM, ALL THIS ENERGY IN THE AIR.
LOOKS LIKE A JOB FOR...
...CHROMASTONE!
I DON'T WANT TO HURT YOU, PLUMBERS! KEEP YOUR ALIEN TECH WEAPONS TO YOURSELVES, AND LET'S TALK THIS OVER.
KRAAK
TRUCE?
ZZZT
NEVER!

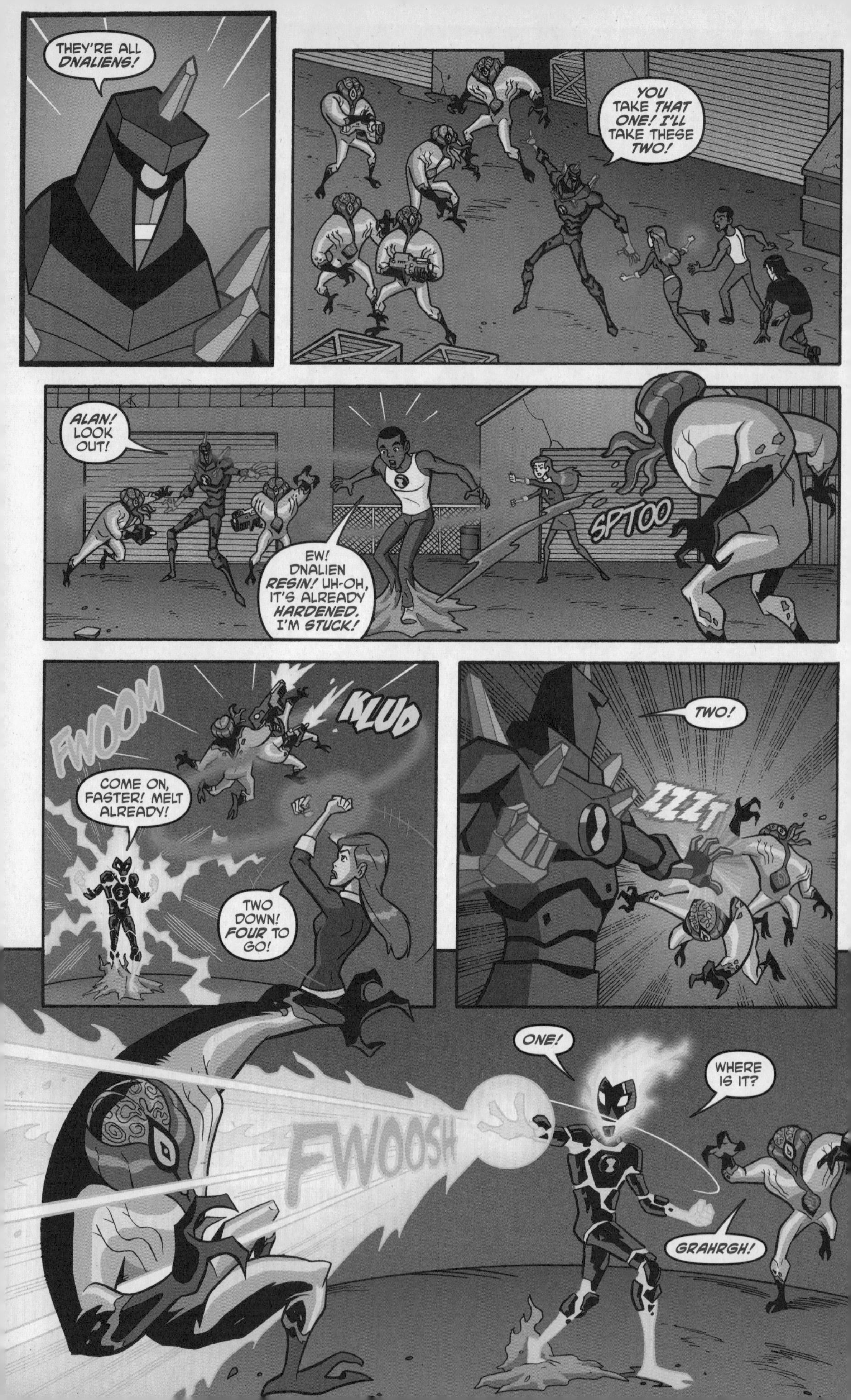
THEY'RE ALL DNALIENS!
YOU TAKE THAT ONE! I'LL TAKE THESE TWO!
ALAN! LOOK OUT!
EW! DNALIEN RESIN! UH-OH, IT'S ALREADY HARDENED. I'M STUCK!
SPTOO
FWOOM
KLUD
COME ON, FASTER! MELT ALREADY!
TWO DOWN! FOUR TO GO!
TWO!
ZZZT
ONE!
WHERE IS IT?
FWOOSH
GRAHRGH!

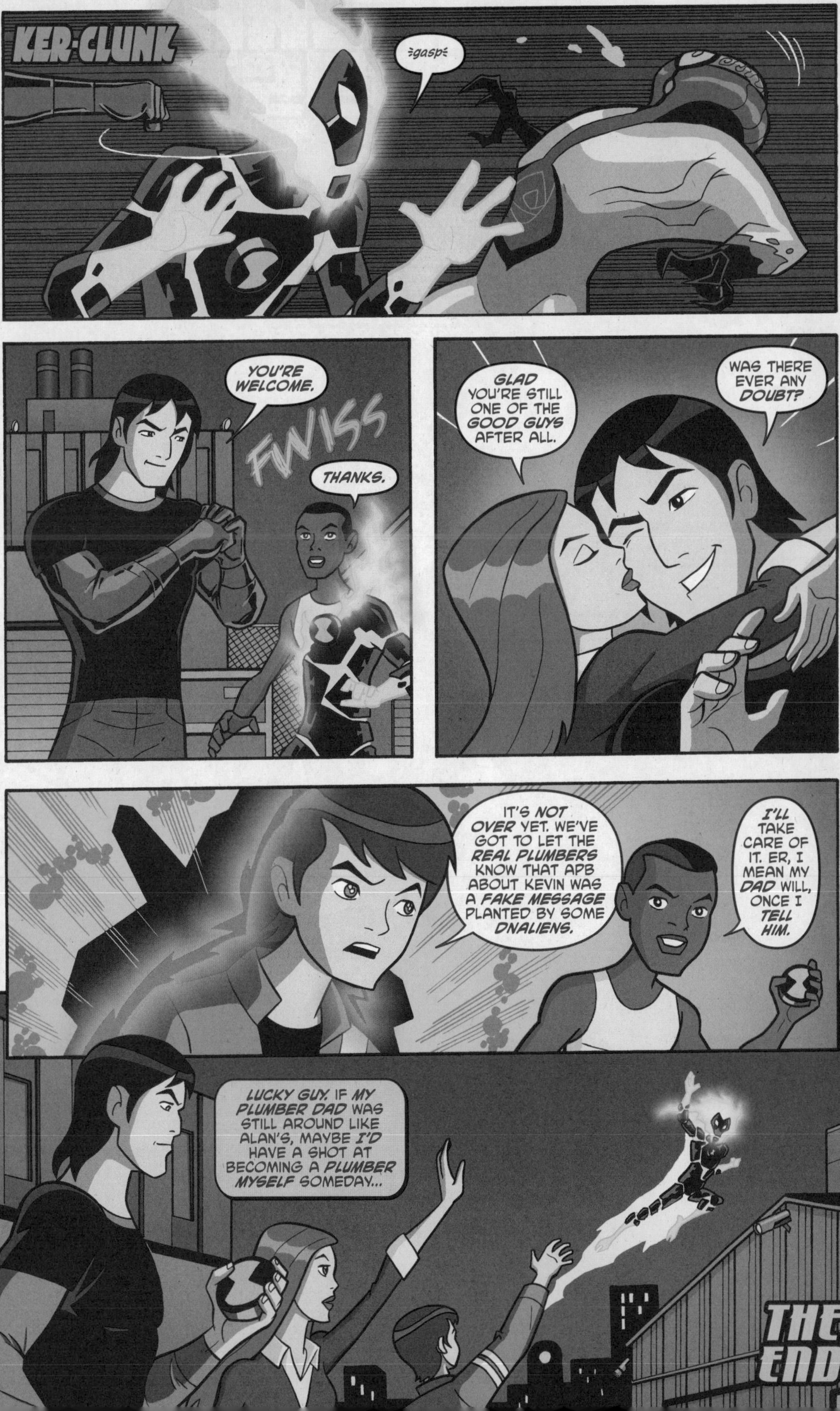
KER-CLUNK
gasp
YOU'RE WELCOME.
FWISS
THANKS.
GLAD YOU'RE STILL ONE OF THE GOOD GUYS AFTER ALL.
WAS THERE EVER ANY DOUBT?
IT'S NOT OVER YET. WE'VE GOT TO LET THE REAL PLUMBERS KNOW THAT APB ABOUT KEVIN WAS A FAKE MESSAGE PLANTED BY SOME DNALIENS.
I'LL TAKE CARE OF IT. ER, I MEAN MY DAD WILL, ONCE I TELL HIM.
LUCKY GUY. IF MY PLUMBER DAD WAS STILL AROUND LIKE ALAN'S, MAYBE I'D HAVE A SHOT AT BECOMING A PLUMBER MYSELF SOMEDAY...
THE END

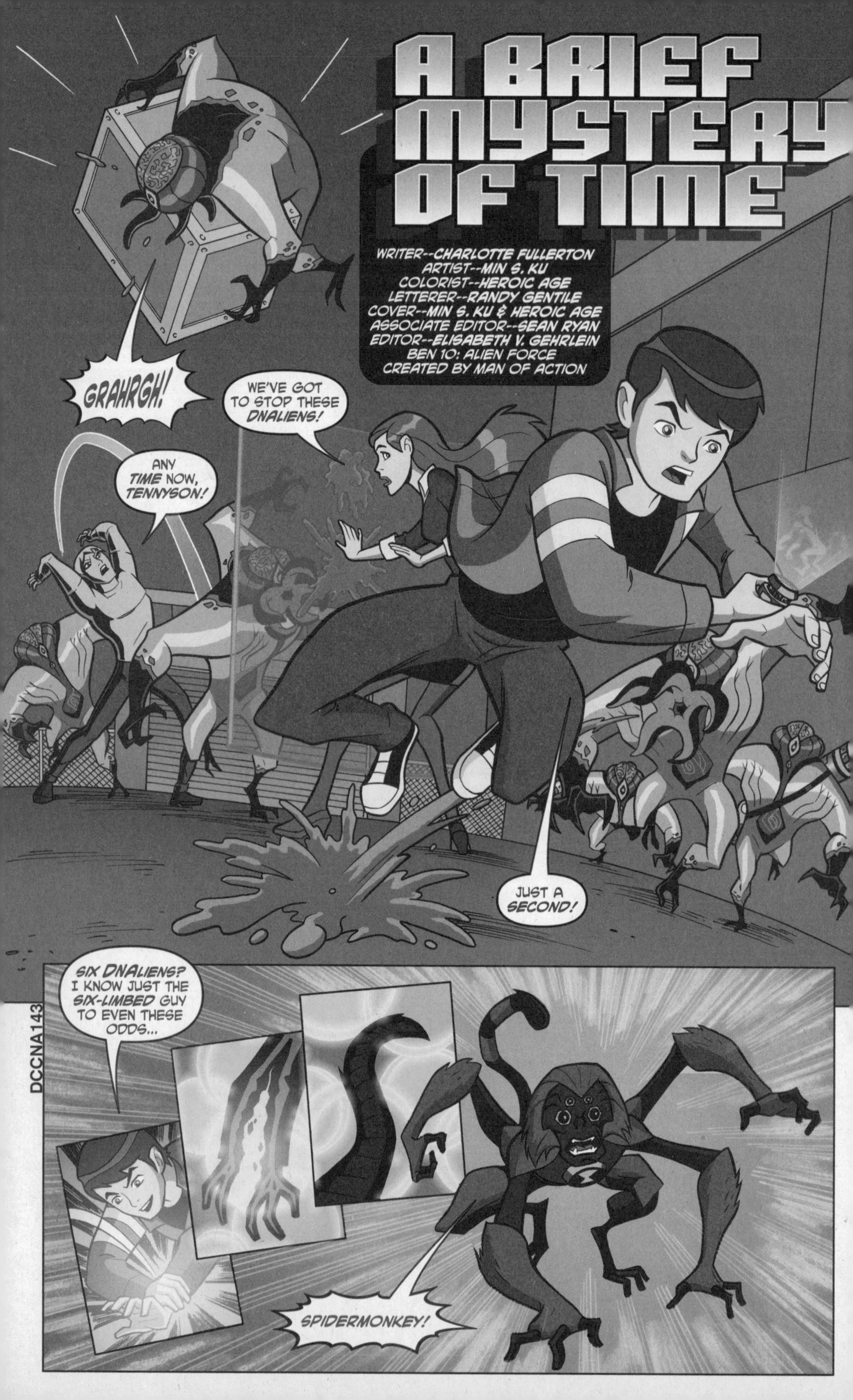
A BRIEF MYSTERY OF TIME
WRITER--CHARLOTTE FULLERTON
ARTIST--MIN S. KU
COLORIST--HEROIC AGE
LETTERER--RANDY GENTILE
COVER--MIN S. KU & HEROIC AGE
ASSOCIATE EDITOR--SEAN RYAN
EDITOR--ELISABETH V. GEHRLEIN
BEN 10: ALIEN FORCE
CREATED BY MAN OF ACTION
GRAHRGH!
WE'VE GOT TO STOP THESE DNALIENS!
ANY TIME NOW, TENNYSON!
JUST A SECOND!
SIX DNALIENS? I KNOW JUST THE SIX-LIMBED GUY TO EVEN THESE ODDS...
SPIDERMONKEY!

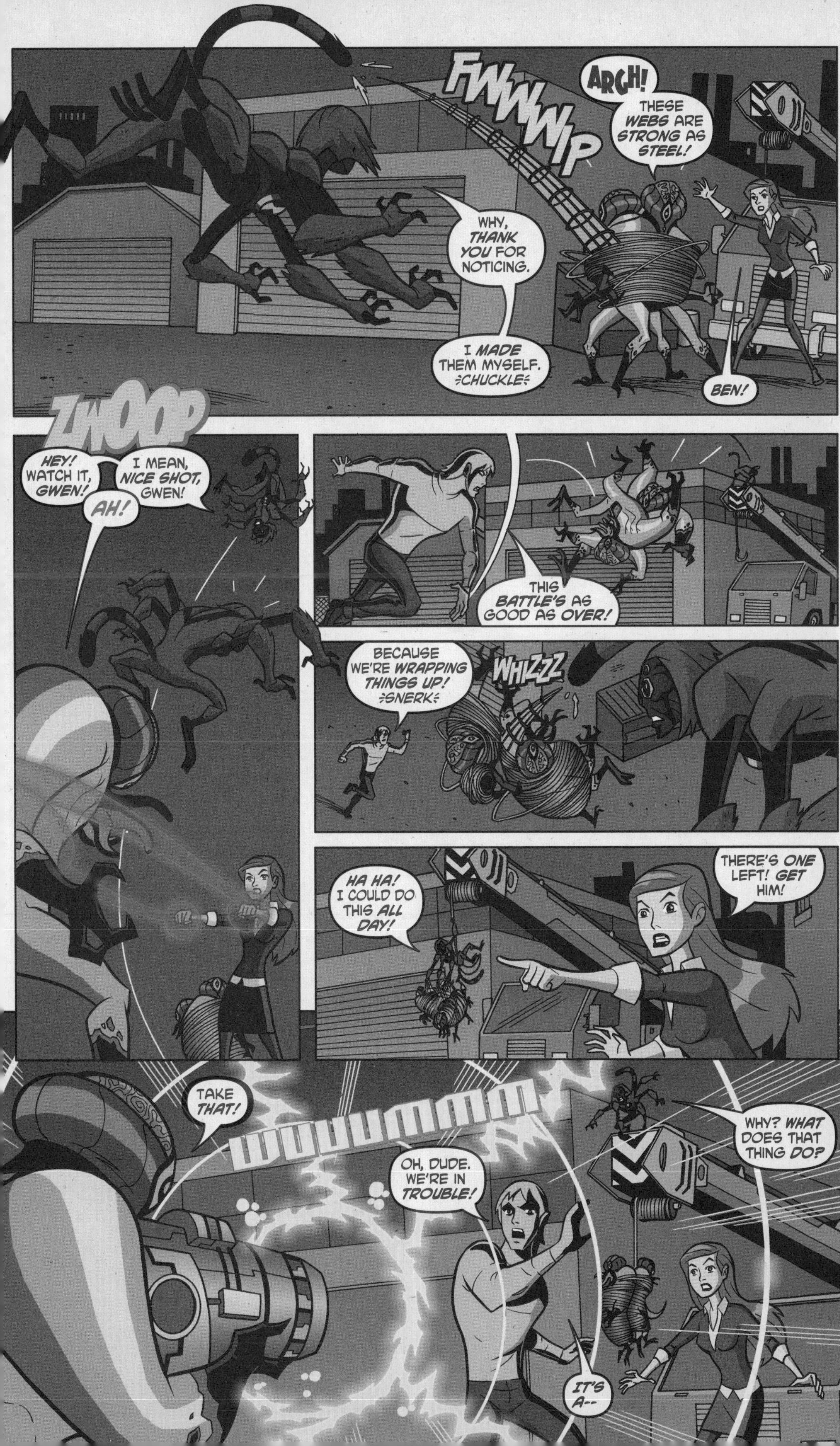
FWWWIP
ARGH!
THESE WEBS ARE STRONG AS STEEL!
WHY, THANK YOU FOR NOTICING.
I MADE THEM MYSELF. ≈CHUCKLE≈
BEN!
ZWOOP
HEY! WATCH IT, GWEN!
AH!
I MEAN, NICE SHOT, GWEN!
THIS BATTLE'S AS GOOD AS OVER!
BECAUSE WE'RE WRAPPING THINGS UP! ≈SNERK≈
WHIZZZ
HA HA! I COULD DO THIS ALL DAY!
THERE'S ONE LEFT! GET HIM!
TAKE THAT!
WUUUMMM
OH, DUDE. WE'RE IN TROUBLE!
WHY? WHAT DOES THAT THING DO?
IT'S A--

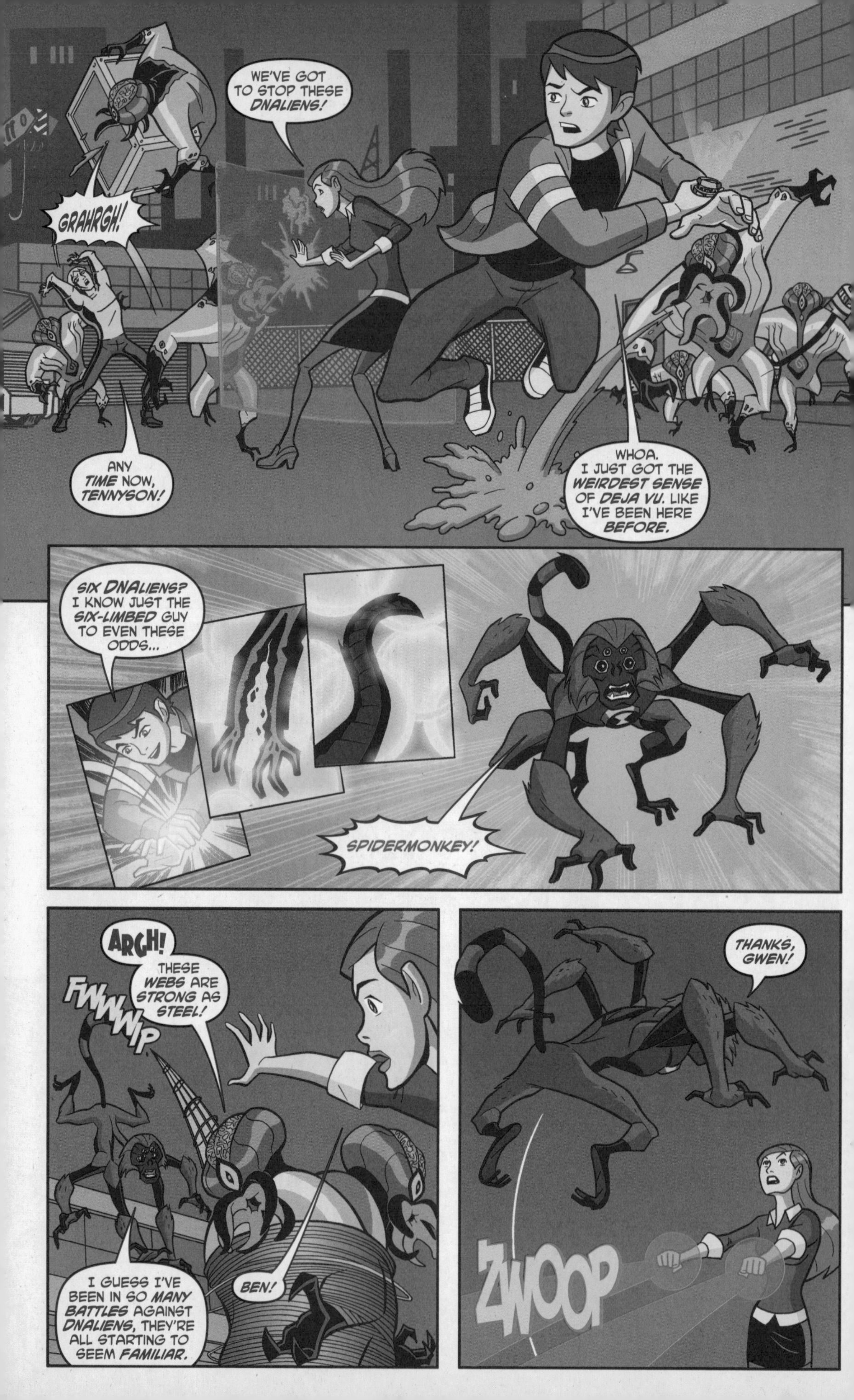
WE'VE GOT TO STOP THESE DNALIENS!
GRAHRGH!
ANY TIME NOW, TENNYSON!
WHOA. I JUST GOT THE WEIRDEST SENSE OF DEJA VU. LIKE I'VE BEEN HERE BEFORE.
SIX DNALIENS? I KNOW JUST THE SIX-LIMBED GUY TO EVEN THESE ODDS...
SPIDERMONKEY!
ARGH!
THESE WEBS ARE STRONG AS STEEL!
FWWWWIP
I GUESS I'VE BEEN IN SO MANY BATTLES AGAINST DNALIENS, THEY'RE ALL STARTING TO SEEM FAMILIAR.
BEN!
THANKS, GWEN!
ZWOOP

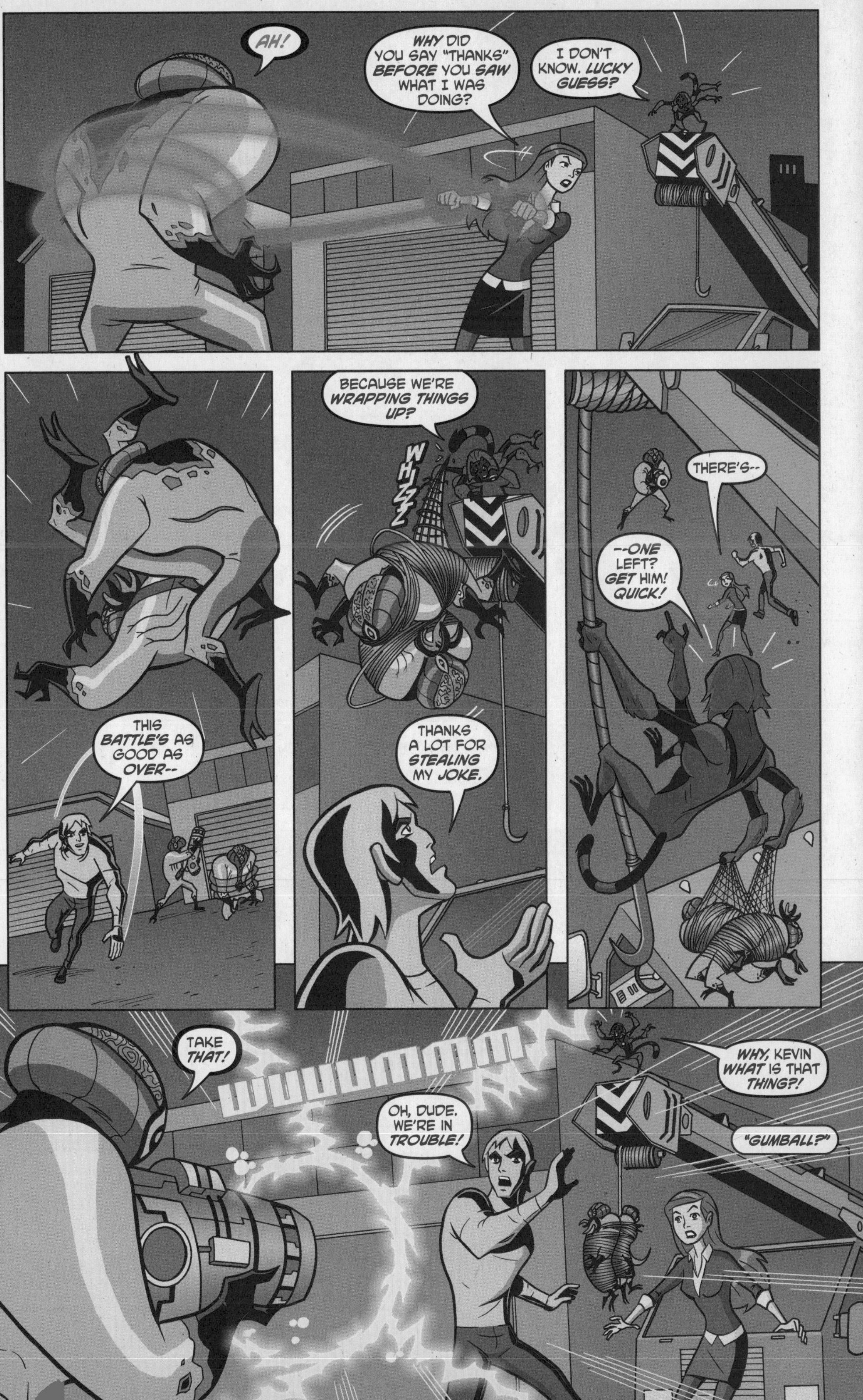
AH!
WHY DID YOU SAY "THANKS" BEFORE YOU SAW WHAT I WAS DOING?
I DON'T KNOW. LUCKY GUESS?
THIS BATTLE'S AS GOOD AS OVER--
BECAUSE WE'RE WRAPPING THINGS UP?
WHIZZZ
THANKS A LOT FOR STEALING MY JOKE.
THERE'S--
--ONE LEFT? GET HIM! QUICK!
TAKE THAT!
WUUUMMM
OH, DUDE. WE'RE IN TROUBLE!
WHY, KEVIN WHAT IS THAT THING?!
"GUMBALL?"

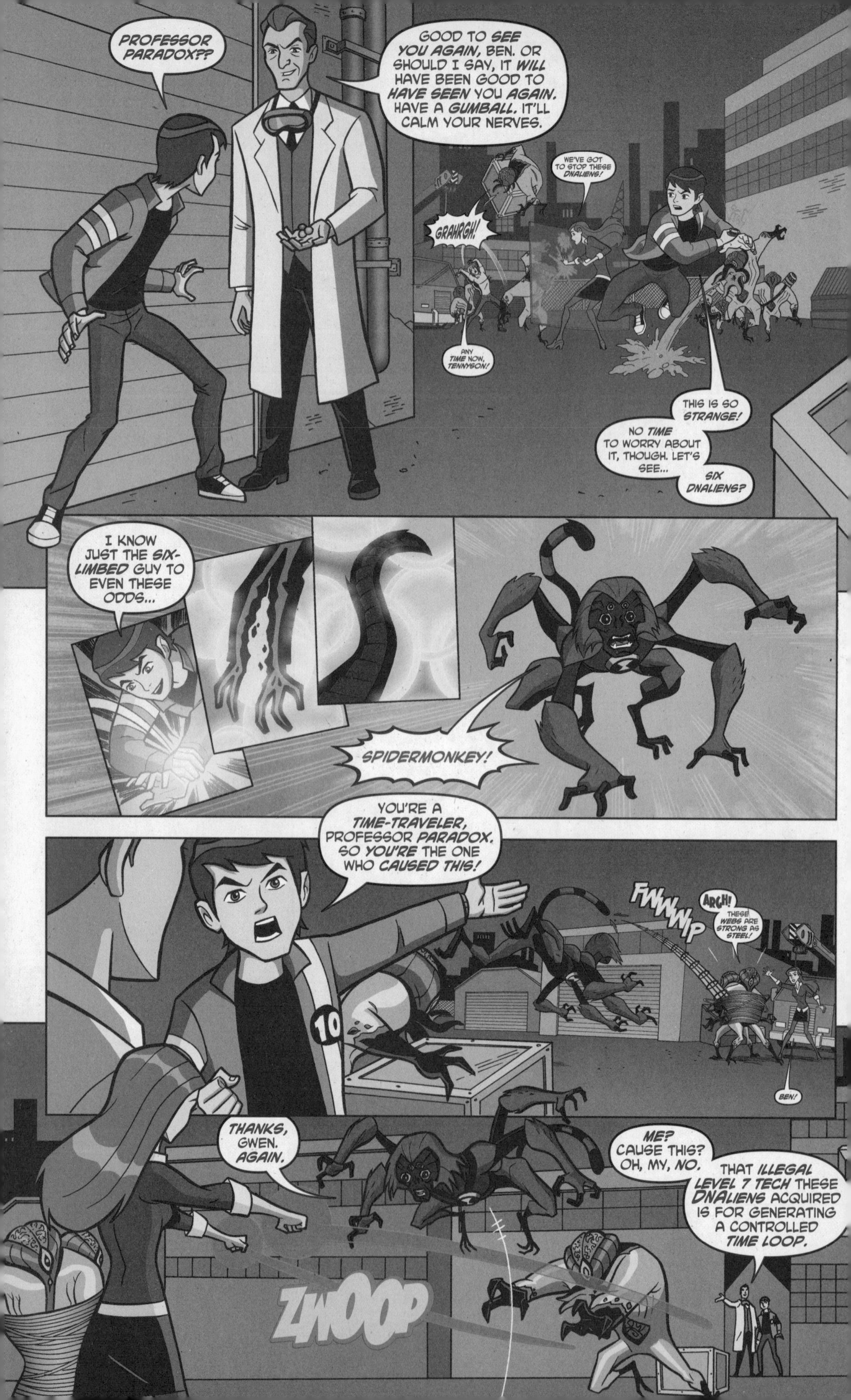
PROFESSOR PARADOX??
GOOD TO SEE YOU AGAIN, BEN. OR SHOULD I SAY, IT WILL HAVE BEEN GOOD TO HAVE SEEN YOU AGAIN. HAVE A GUMBALL. IT'LL CALM YOUR NERVES.
WE'VE GOT TO STOP THESE DNALIENS!
GRAHRGH!
ANY TIME NOW, TENNYSON!
THIS IS SO STRANGE!
NO TIME TO WORRY ABOUT IT, THOUGH. LET'S SEE...
SIX DNALIENS?
I KNOW JUST THE SIX-LIMBED GUY TO EVEN THESE ODDS...
SPIDERMONKEY!
YOU'RE A TIME-TRAVELER, PROFESSOR PARADOX. SO YOU'RE THE ONE WHO CAUSED THIS!
FWNWIP
ARGH!
THESE WEBS ARE STRONG AS STEEL!
BEN!
THANKS, GWEN. AGAIN.
ME? CAUSE THIS? OH, MY, NO.
THAT ILLEGAL LEVEL 7 TECH THESE DNALIENS ACQUIRED IS FOR GENERATING A CONTROLLED TIME LOOP.
ZWOOP

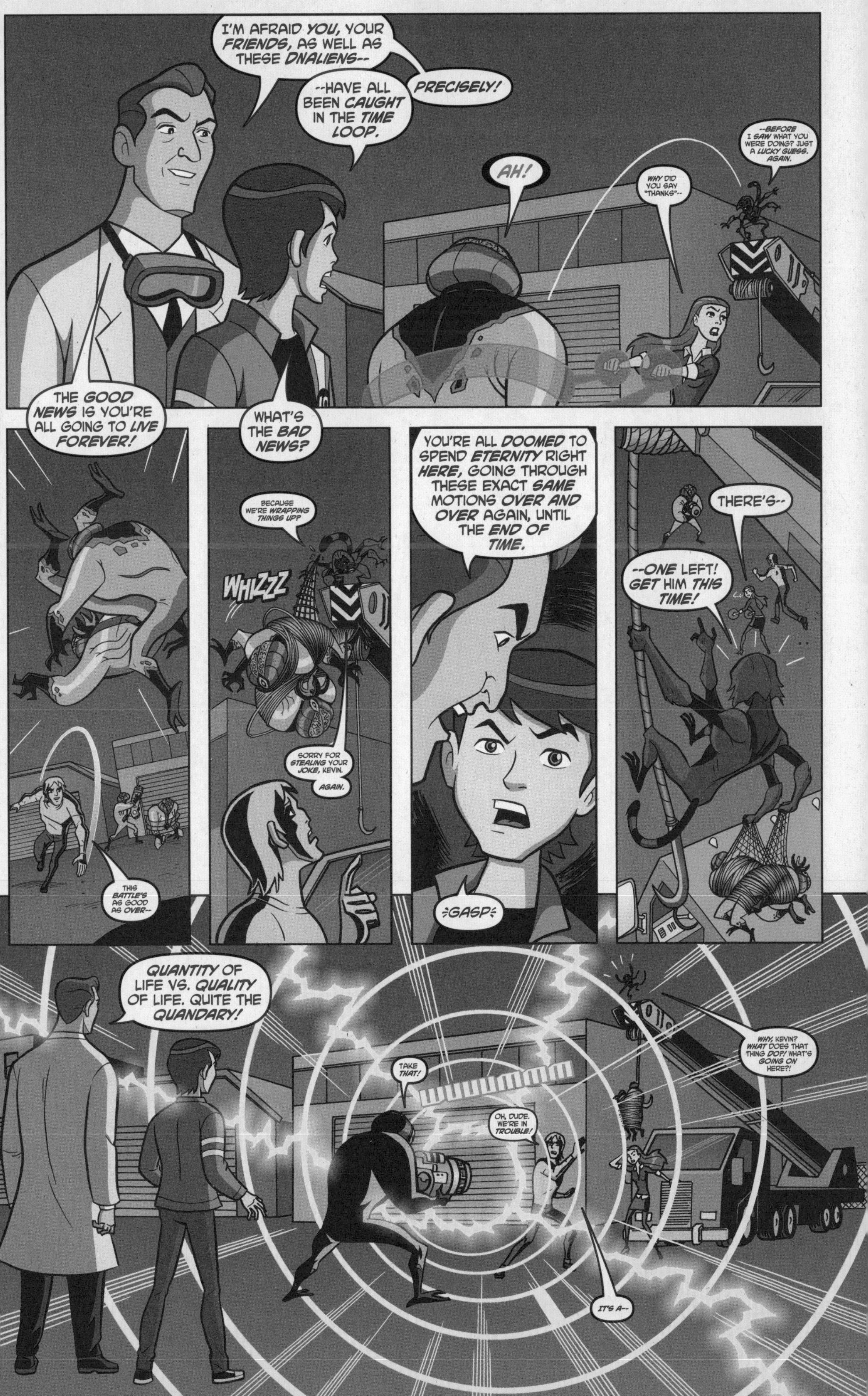
I'M AFRAID YOU, YOUR FRIENDS, AS WELL AS THESE DNALIENS--
--HAVE ALL BEEN CAUGHT IN THE TIME LOOP.
PRECISELY!
AH!
WHY DID YOU SAY "THANKS"--
--BEFORE I SAW WHAT YOU WERE DOING? JUST A LUCKY GUESS. AGAIN.
THE GOOD NEWS IS YOU'RE ALL GOING TO LIVE FOREVER!
THIS BATTLE'S AS GOOD AS OVER--
WHAT'S THE BAD NEWS?
BECAUSE WE'RE WRAPPING THINGS UP?
WHIZZZ
SORRY FOR STEALING YOUR JOKE, KEVIN.
AGAIN.
YOU'RE ALL DOOMED TO SPEND ETERNITY RIGHT HERE, GOING THROUGH THESE EXACT SAME MOTIONS OVER AND OVER AGAIN, UNTIL THE END OF TIME.
GASP
THERE'S--
--ONE LEFT! GET HIM THIS TIME!
QUANTITY OF LIFE VS. QUALITY OF LIFE. QUITE THE QUANDARY!
TAKE THAT!
WUUUMMM
OH, DUDE. WE'RE IN TROUBLE!
WHY, KEVIN? WHAT DOES THAT THING DO?! WHAT'S GOING ON HERE?!
IT'S A--

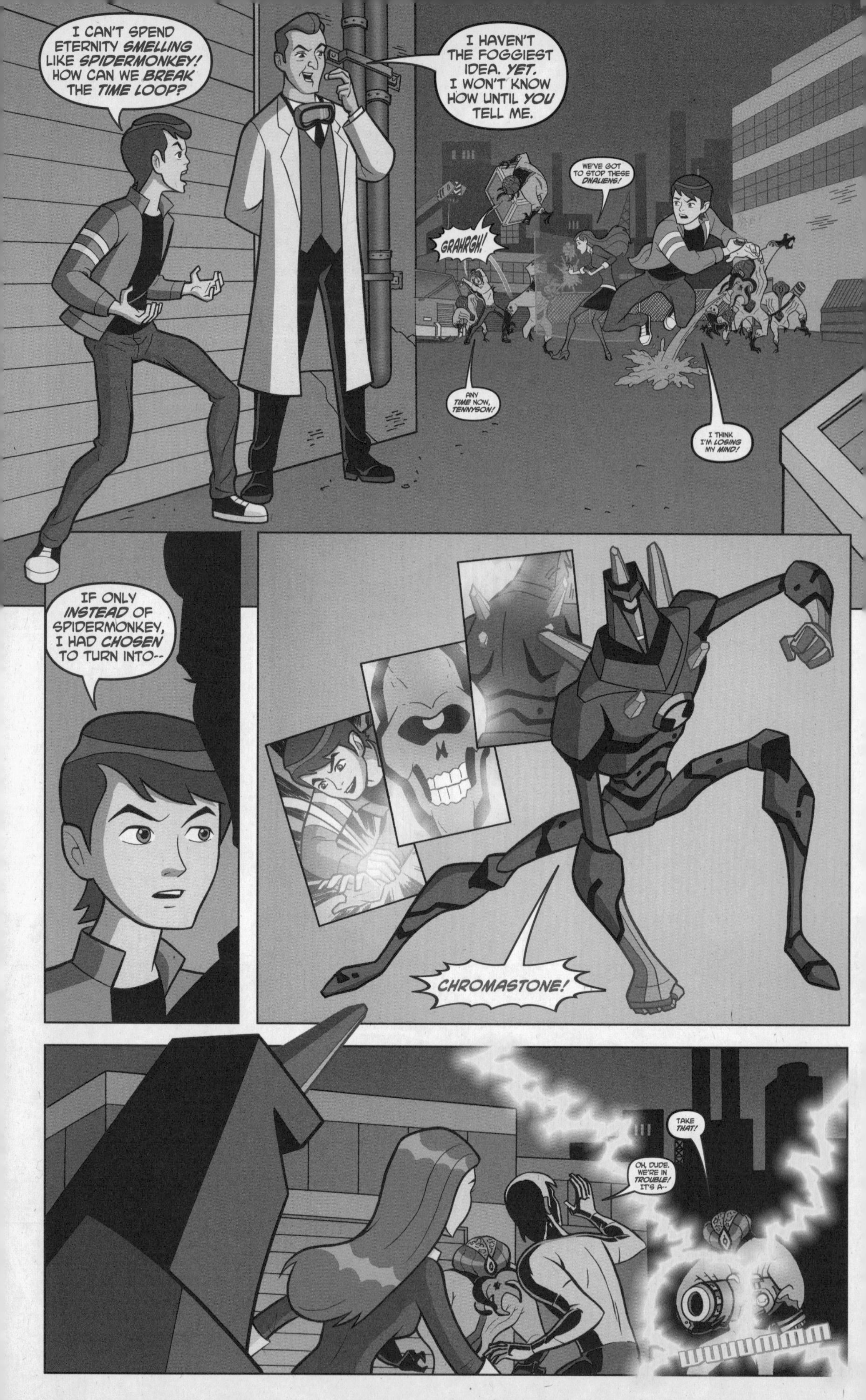
I CAN'T SPEND ETERNITY SMELLING LIKE SPIDERMONKEY! HOW CAN WE BREAK THE TIME LOOP?
I HAVEN'T THE FOGGIEST IDEA. YET. I WON'T KNOW HOW UNTIL YOU TELL ME.
GRAHRGH!
WE'VE GOT TO STOP THESE DNALIENS!
ANY TIME NOW, TENNYSON!
I THINK I'M LOSING MY MIND!
IF ONLY INSTEAD OF SPIDERMONKEY, I HAD CHOSEN TO TURN INTO--
CHROMASTONE!
TAKE THAT!
OH, DUDE. WE'RE IN TROUBLE! IT'S A--

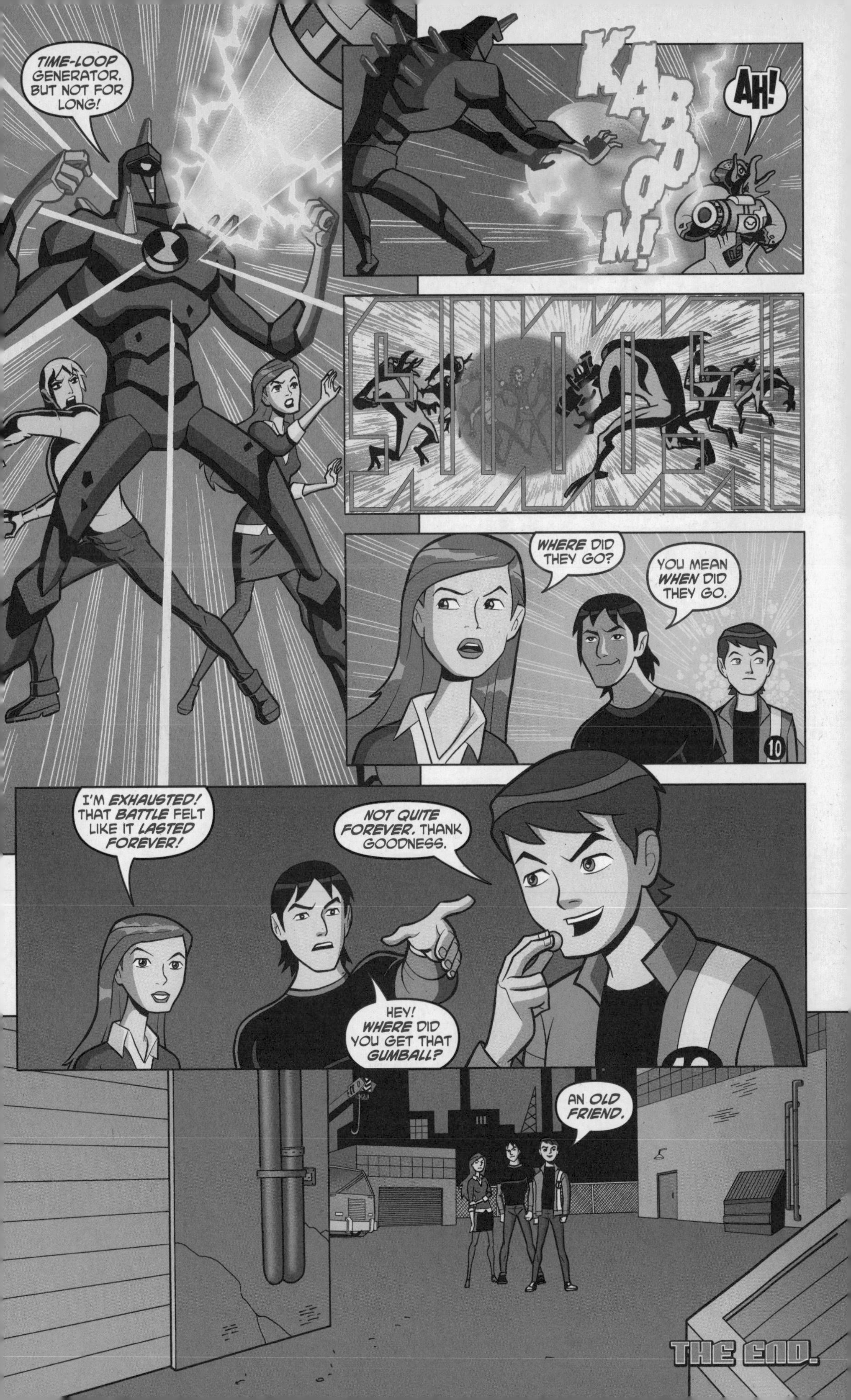
TIME-LOOP GENERATOR. BUT NOT FOR LONG!
KABOOOM!
AH!
WHERE DID THEY GO?
YOU MEAN WHEN DID THEY GO.
I'M EXHAUSTED! THAT BATTLE FELT LIKE IT LASTED FOREVER!
NOT QUITE FOREVER. THANK GOODNESS.
HEY! WHERE DID YOU GET THAT GUMBALL?
AN OLD FRIEND.
THE END.

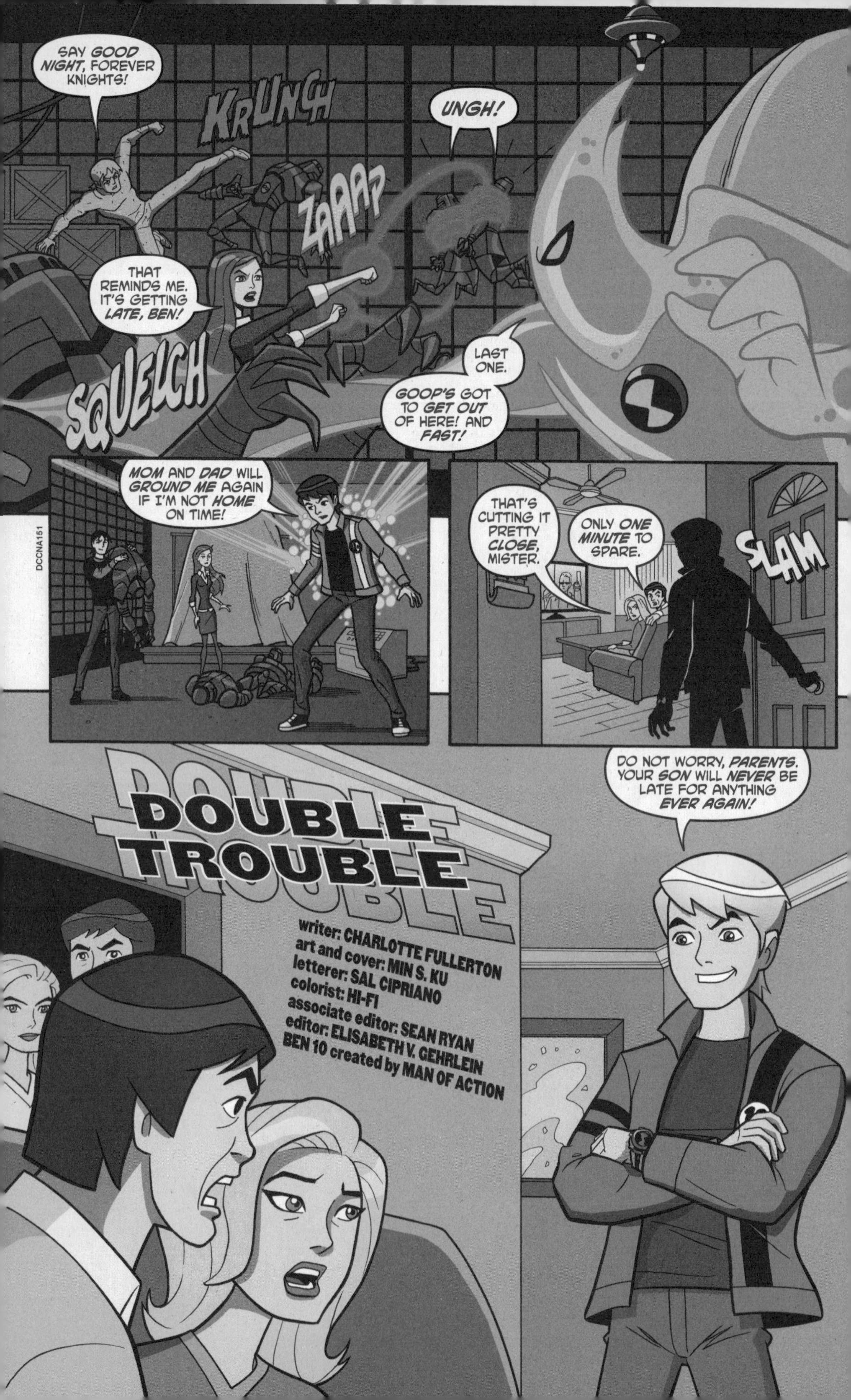

SAY GOOD NIGHT, FOREVER KNIGHTS!
KRUNCH
UNGH!
ZAAAP
THAT REMINDS ME. IT'S GETTING LATE, BEN!
SQUELCH
LAST ONE.
GOOP'S GOT TO GET OUT OF HERE! AND FAST!
MOM AND DAD WILL GROUND ME AGAIN IF I'M NOT HOME ON TIME!
DCCNA151
THAT'S CUTTING IT PRETTY CLOSE, MISTER.
ONLY ONE MINUTE TO SPARE.
SLAM
DOUBLE TROUBLE
DO NOT WORRY, PARENTS. YOUR SON WILL NEVER BE LATE FOR ANYTHING EVER AGAIN!
writer: CHARLOTTE FULLERTON
art and cover: MIN S. KU
letterer: SAL CIPRIANO
colorist: HI-FI
associate editor: SEAN RYAN
editor: ELISABETH V. GEHRLEIN
BEN 10 created by MAN OF ACTION

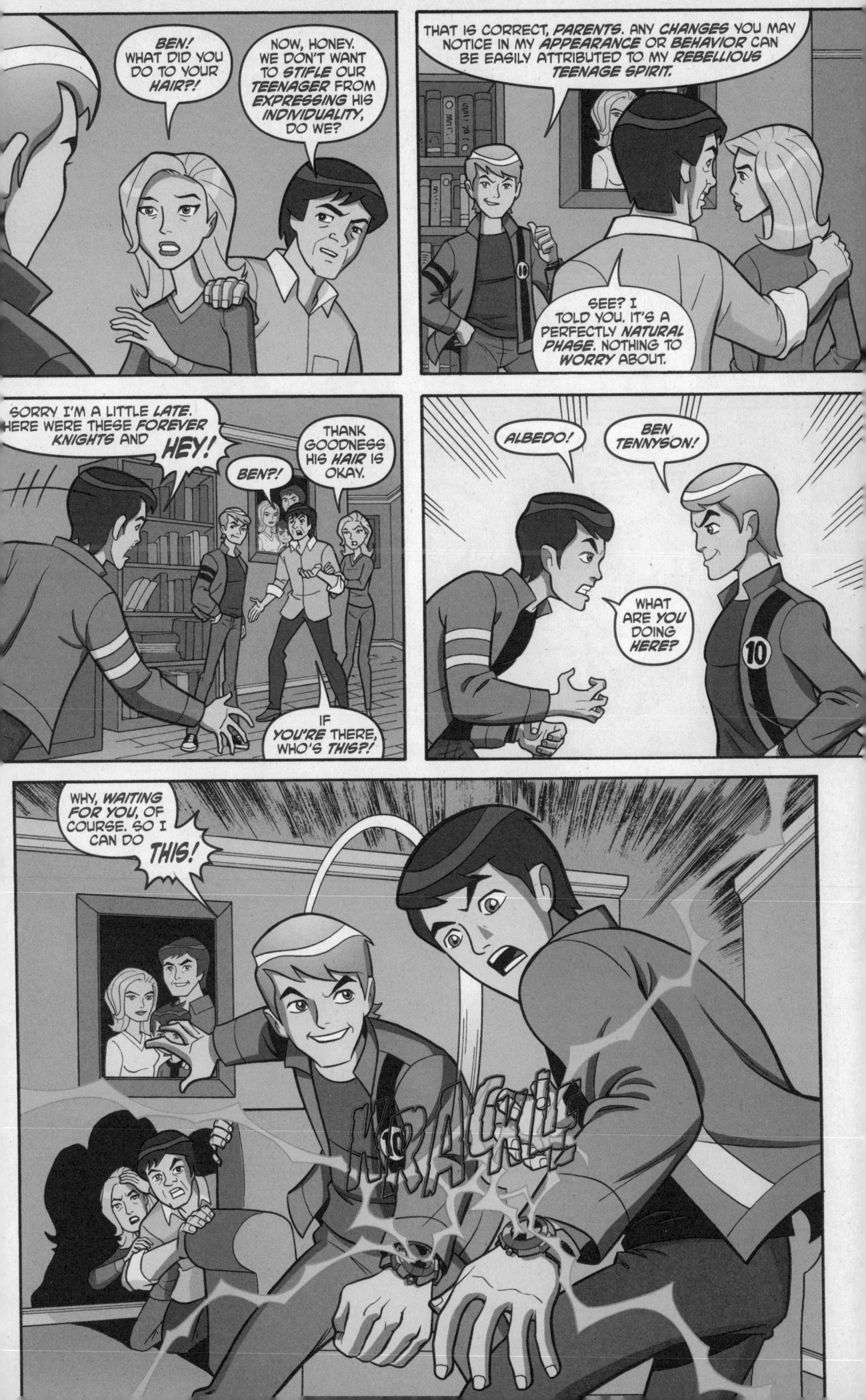
BEN! WHAT DID YOU DO TO YOUR HAIR?!
NOW, HONEY. WE DON'T WANT TO STIFLE OUR TEENAGER FROM EXPRESSING HIS INDIVIDUALITY, DO WE?
THAT IS CORRECT, PARENTS. ANY CHANGES YOU MAY NOTICE IN MY APPEARANCE OR BEHAVIOR CAN BE EASILY ATTRIBUTED TO MY REBELLIOUS TEENAGE SPIRIT.
SEE? I TOLD YOU. IT'S A PERFECTLY NATURAL PHASE. NOTHING TO WORRY ABOUT.
SORRY I'M A LITTLE LATE. HERE WERE THESE FOREVER KNIGHTS AND
HEY!
BEN?!
THANK GOODNESS HIS HAIR IS OKAY.
IF YOU'RE THERE, WHO'S THIS?!
ALBEDO!
BEN TENNYSON!
WHAT ARE YOU DOING HERE?
WHY, WAITING FOR YOU, OF COURSE. SO I CAN DO
THIS!

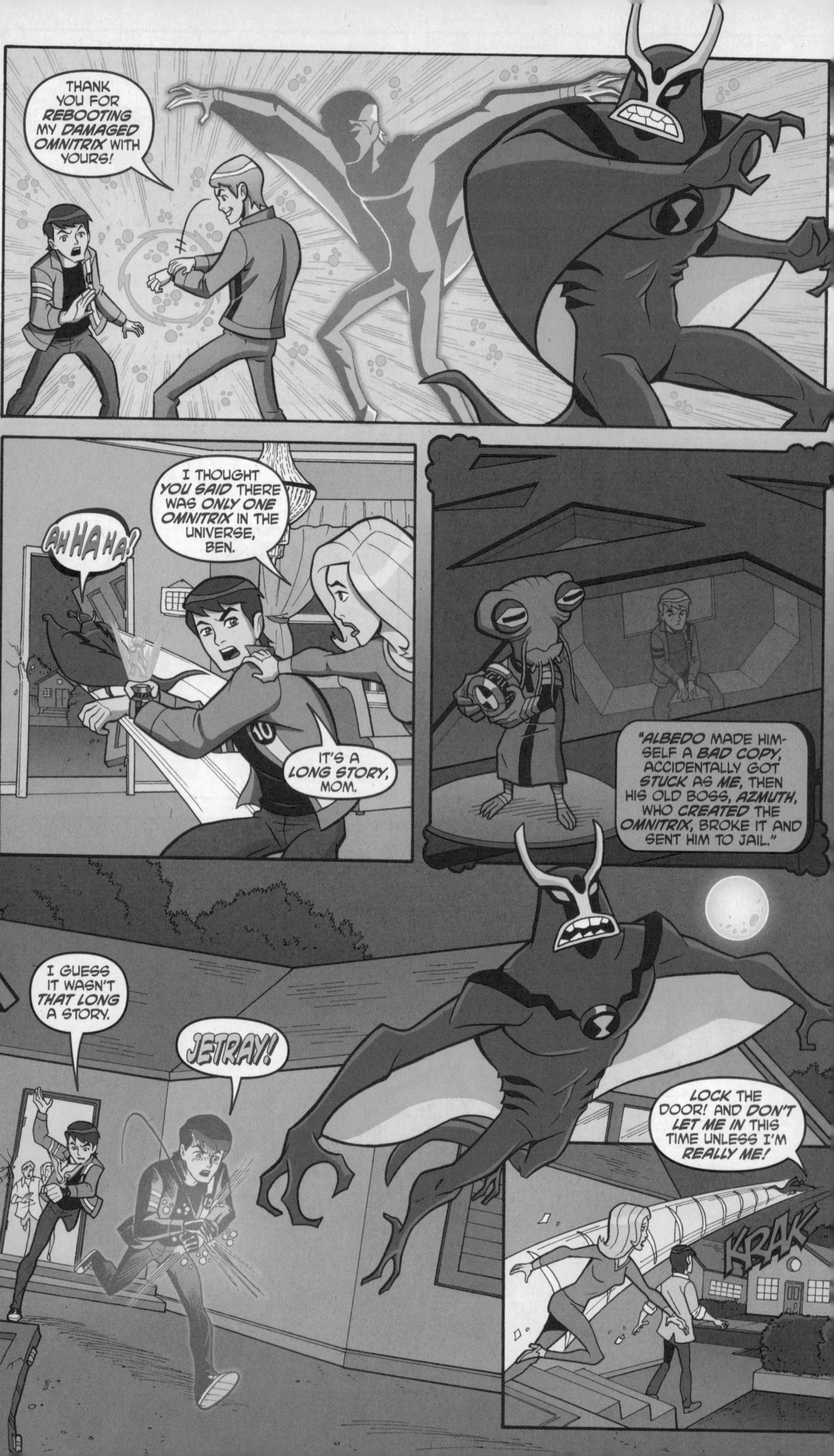
THANK YOU FOR REBOOTING MY DAMAGED OMNITRIX WITH YOURS!
I THOUGHT YOU SAID THERE WAS ONLY ONE OMNITRIX IN THE UNIVERSE, BEN.
AH HA HA!
IT'S A LONG STORY, MOM.
"ALBEDO MADE HIMSELF A BAD COPY, ACCIDENTALLY GOT STUCK AS ME, THEN HIS OLD BOSS, AZMUTH, WHO CREATED THE OMNITRIX, BROKE IT AND SENT HIM TO JAIL."
I GUESS IT WASN'T THAT LONG A STORY.
JETRAY!
LOCK THE DOOR! AND DON'T LET ME IN THIS TIME UNLESS I'M REALLY ME!
KRAK

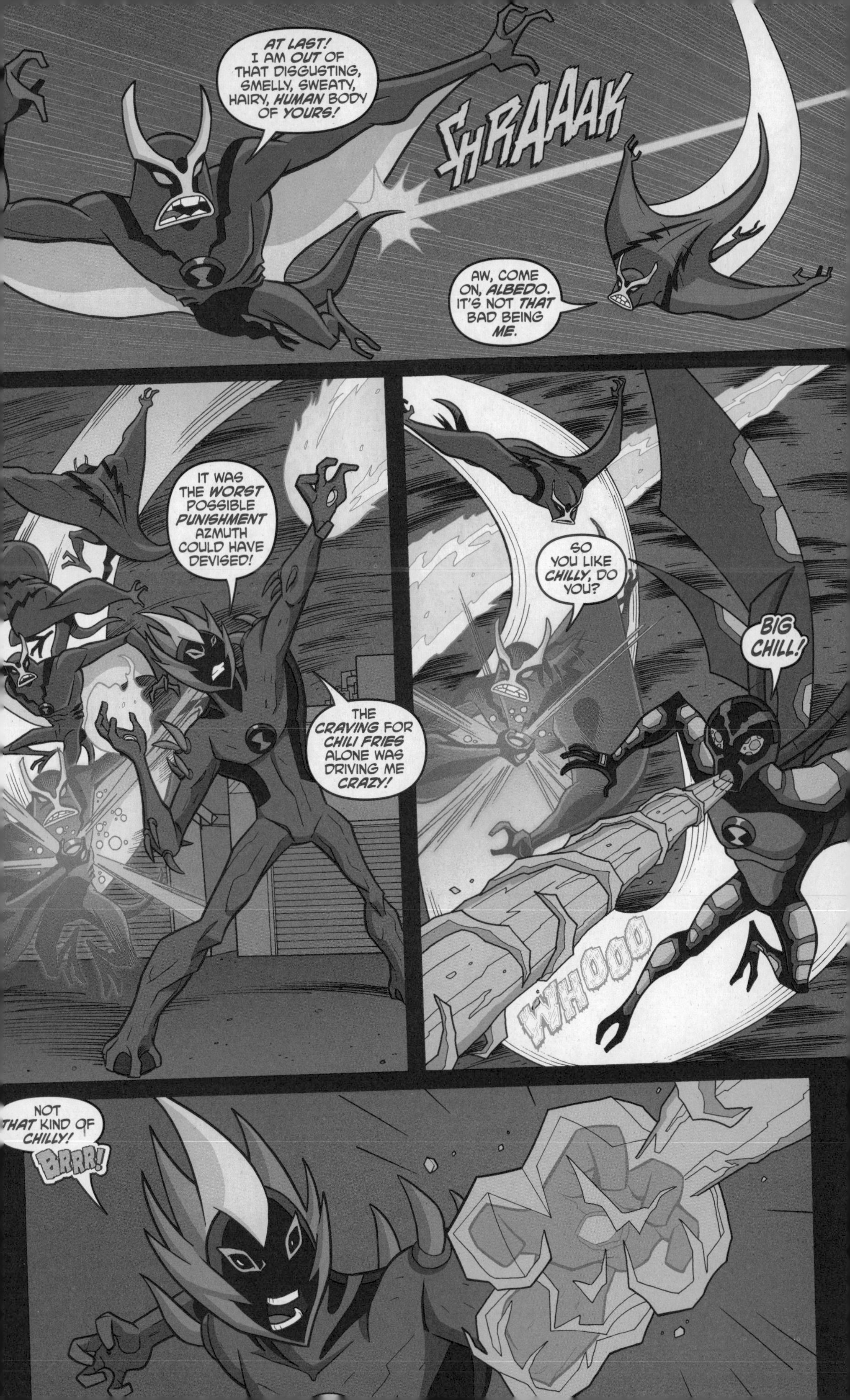
AT LAST! I AM OUT OF THAT DISGUSTING, SMELLY, SWEATY, HAIRY, HUMAN BODY OF YOURS!
SHRAAAK
AW, COME ON, ALBEDO. IT'S NOT THAT BAD BEING ME.
IT WAS THE WORST POSSIBLE PUNISHMENT AZMUTH COULD HAVE DEVISED!
THE CRAVING FOR CHILI FRIES ALONE WAS DRIVING ME CRAZY!
SO YOU LIKE CHILLY, DO YOU?
BIG CHILL!
WHOOO
NOT THAT KIND OF CHILLY!
BRRR!

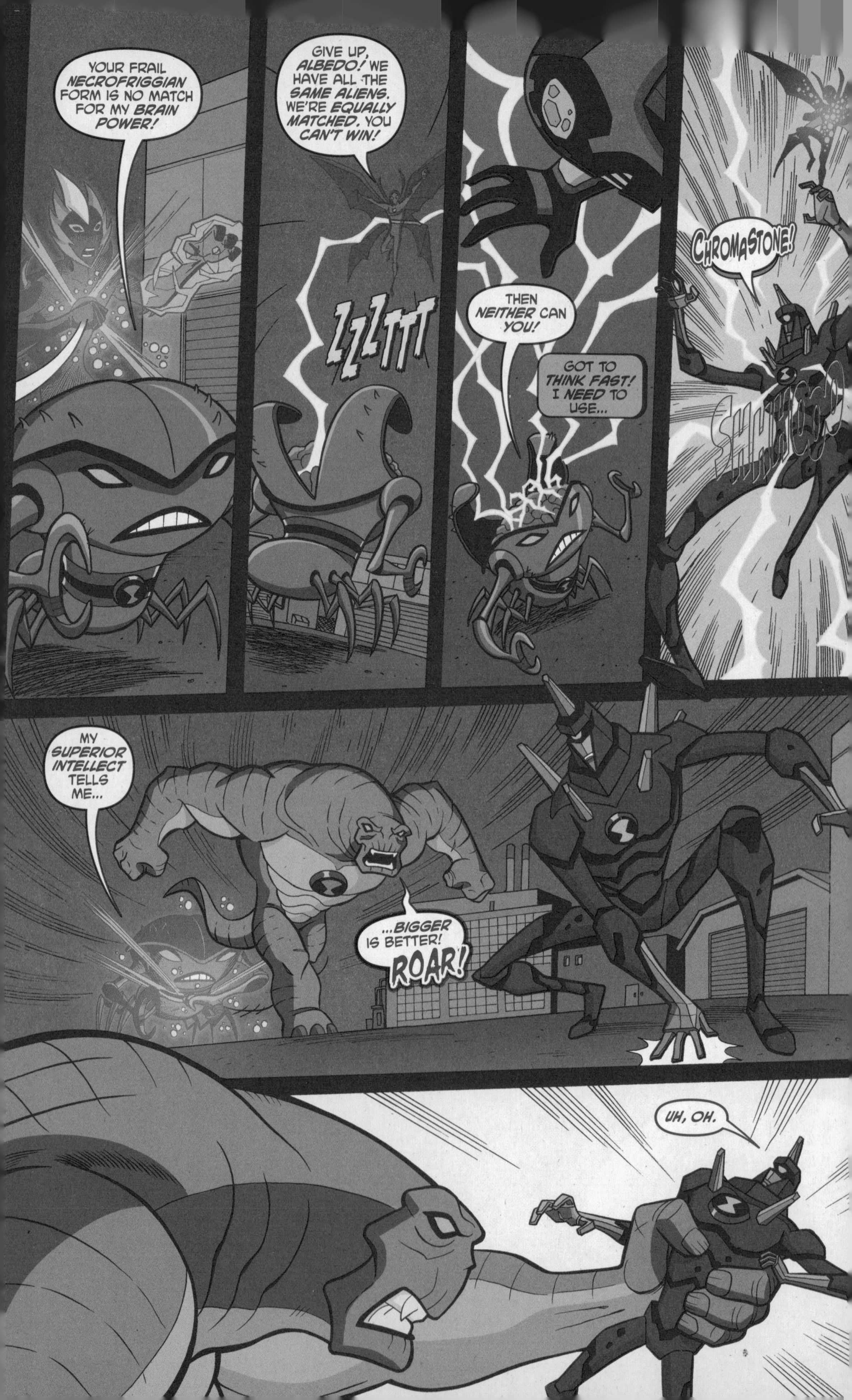
YOUR FRAIL NECROFRIGGIAN FORM IS NO MATCH FOR MY BRAIN POWER!
GIVE UP, ALBEDO! WE HAVE ALL THE SAME ALIENS. WE'RE EQUALLY MATCHED. YOU CAN'T WIN!
ZZZTTT
THEN NEITHER CAN YOU!
GOT TO THINK FAST! I NEED TO USE...
CHROMASTONE!
MY SUPERIOR INTELLECT TELLS ME...
...BIGGER IS BETTER!
ROAR!
UH, OH.

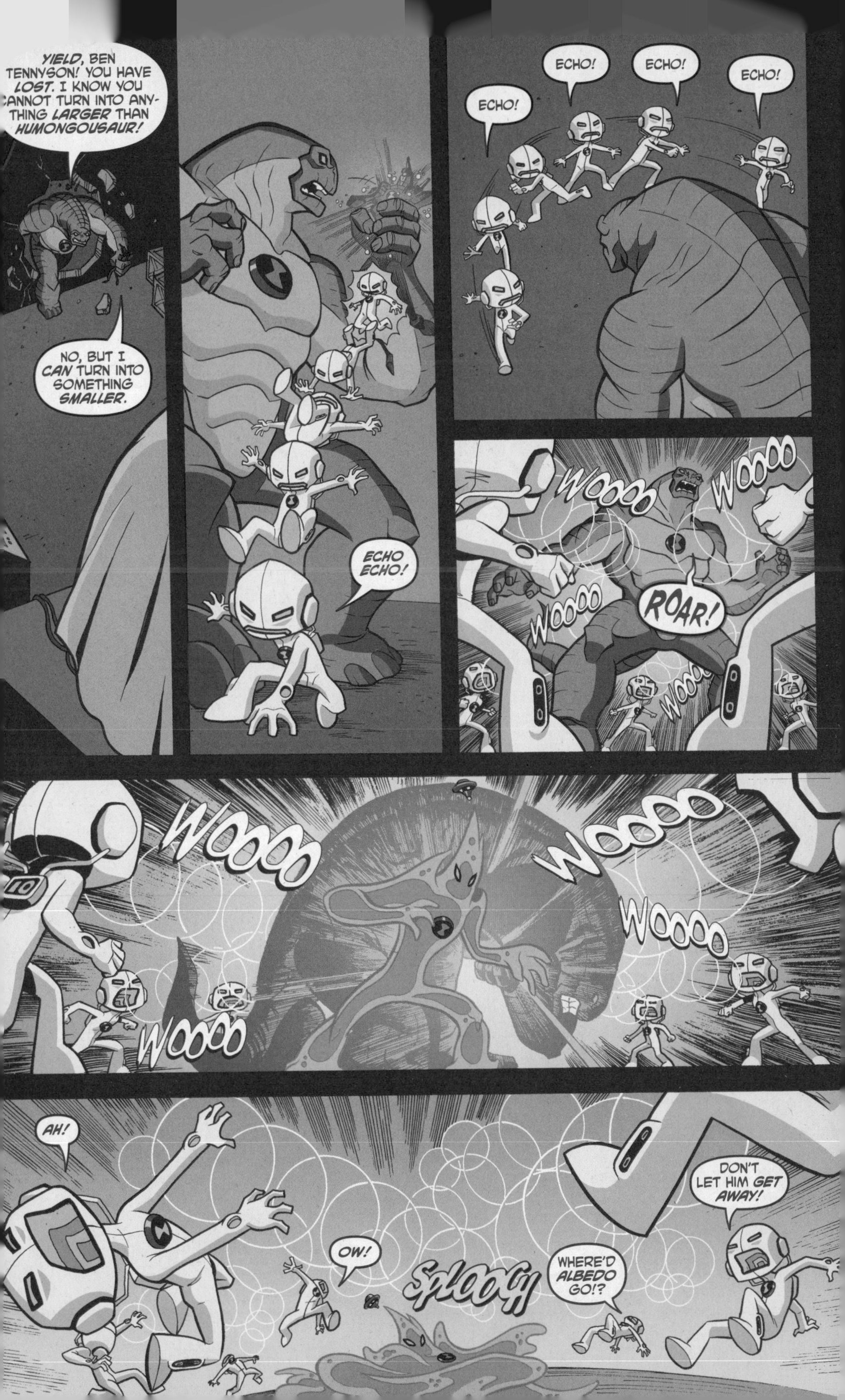
YIELD, BEN TENNYSON! YOU HAVE LOST. I KNOW YOU CANNOT TURN INTO ANYTHING LARGER THAN HUMONGOUSAUR!
NO, BUT I CAN TURN INTO SOMETHING SMALLER.
ECHO ECHO!
ECHO!
ECHO!
ECHO!
ECHO!
WOOOO
WOOOO
ROAR!
WOOOO
WOOOO
WOOOO
WOOOO
WOOOO
WOOOO
AH!
DON'T LET HIM GET AWAY!
OW!
SPLOOGH
WHERE'D ALBEDO GO!?

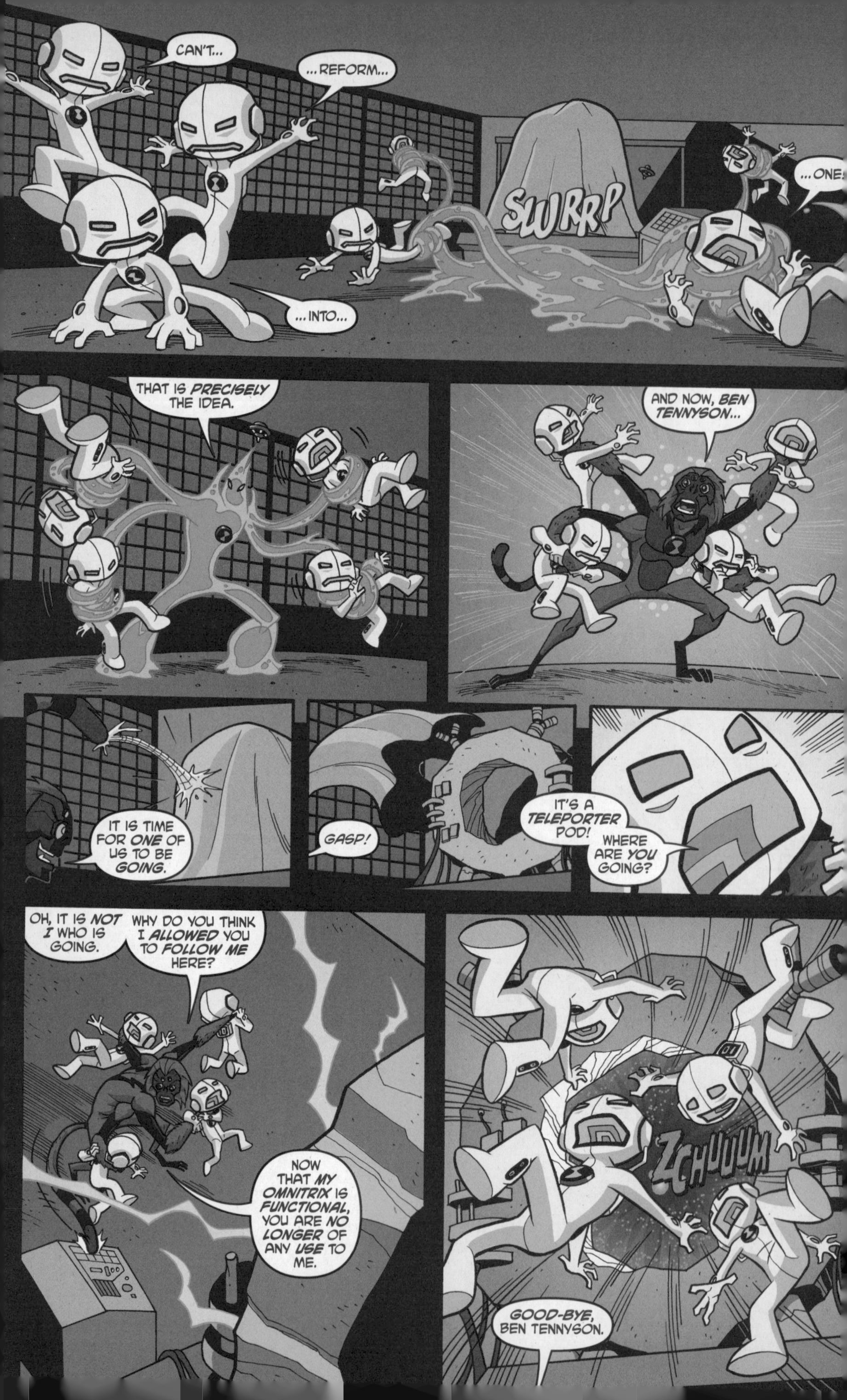
CAN'T...
...REFORM...
...INTO...
SLURRP
...ONE!
THAT IS PRECISELY THE IDEA.
AND NOW, BEN TENNYSON...
IT IS TIME FOR ONE OF US TO BE GOING.
GASP!
IT'S A TELEPORTER POD!
WHERE ARE YOU GOING?
OH, IT IS NOT I WHO IS GOING.
WHY DO YOU THINK I ALLOWED YOU TO FOLLOW ME HERE?
NOW THAT MY OMNITRIX IS FUNCTIONAL, YOU ARE NO LONGER OF ANY USE TO ME.
ZCHUUUM
GOOD-BYE, BEN TENNYSON.

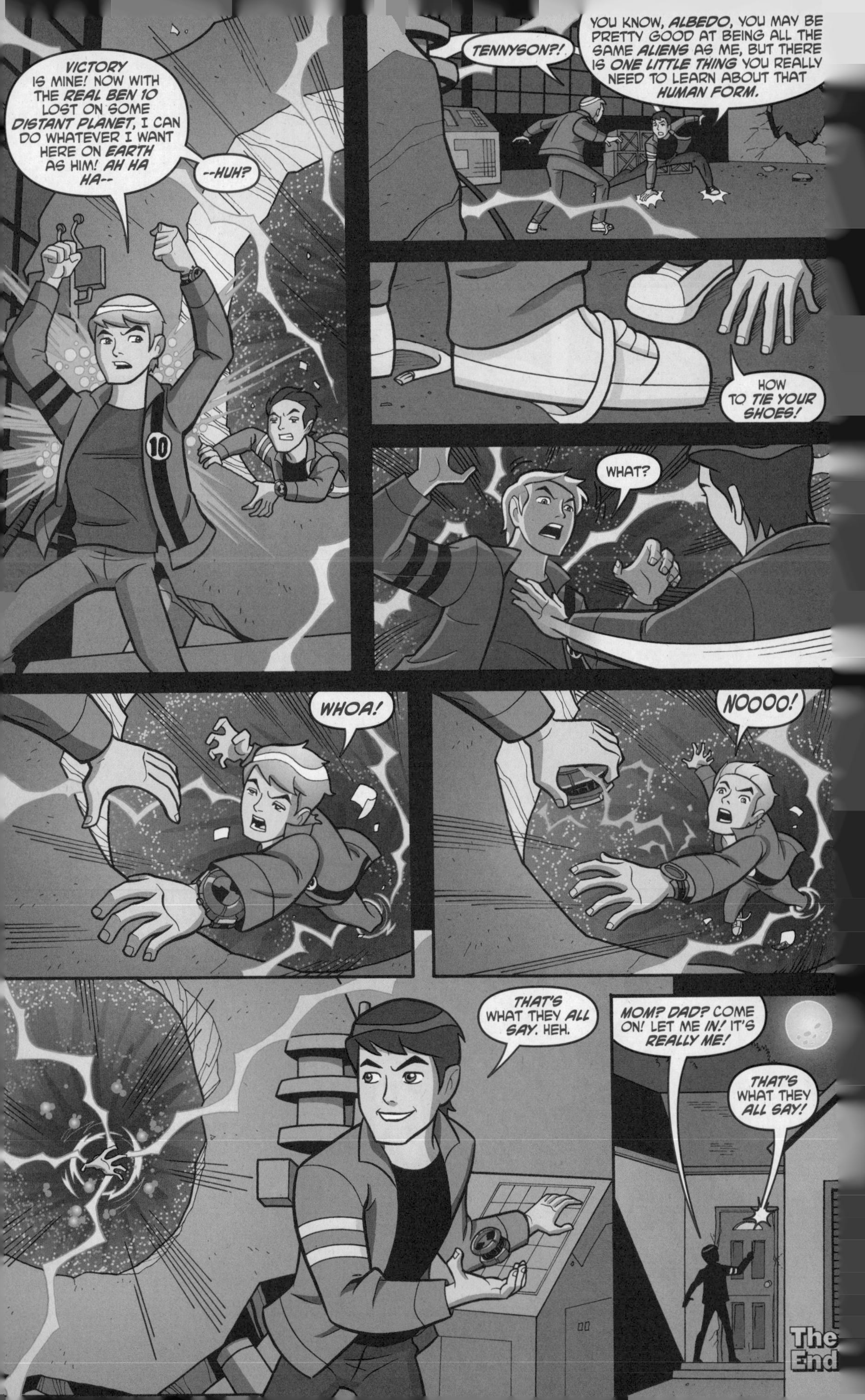
VICTORY IS MINE! NOW WITH THE REAL BEN 10 LOST ON SOME DISTANT PLANET, I CAN DO WHATEVER I WANT HERE ON EARTH AS HIM! AH HA HA--
--HUH?
TENNYSON?!
YOU KNOW, ALBEDO, YOU MAY BE PRETTY GOOD AT BEING ALL THE SAME ALIENS AS ME, BUT THERE IS ONE LITTLE THING YOU REALLY NEED TO LEARN ABOUT THAT HUMAN FORM.
HOW TO TIE YOUR SHOES!
WHAT?
WHOA!
NOOOO!
THAT'S WHAT THEY ALL SAY. HEH.
MOM? DAD? COME ON! LET ME IN! IT'S REALLY ME!
THAT'S WHAT THEY ALL SAY!
The End

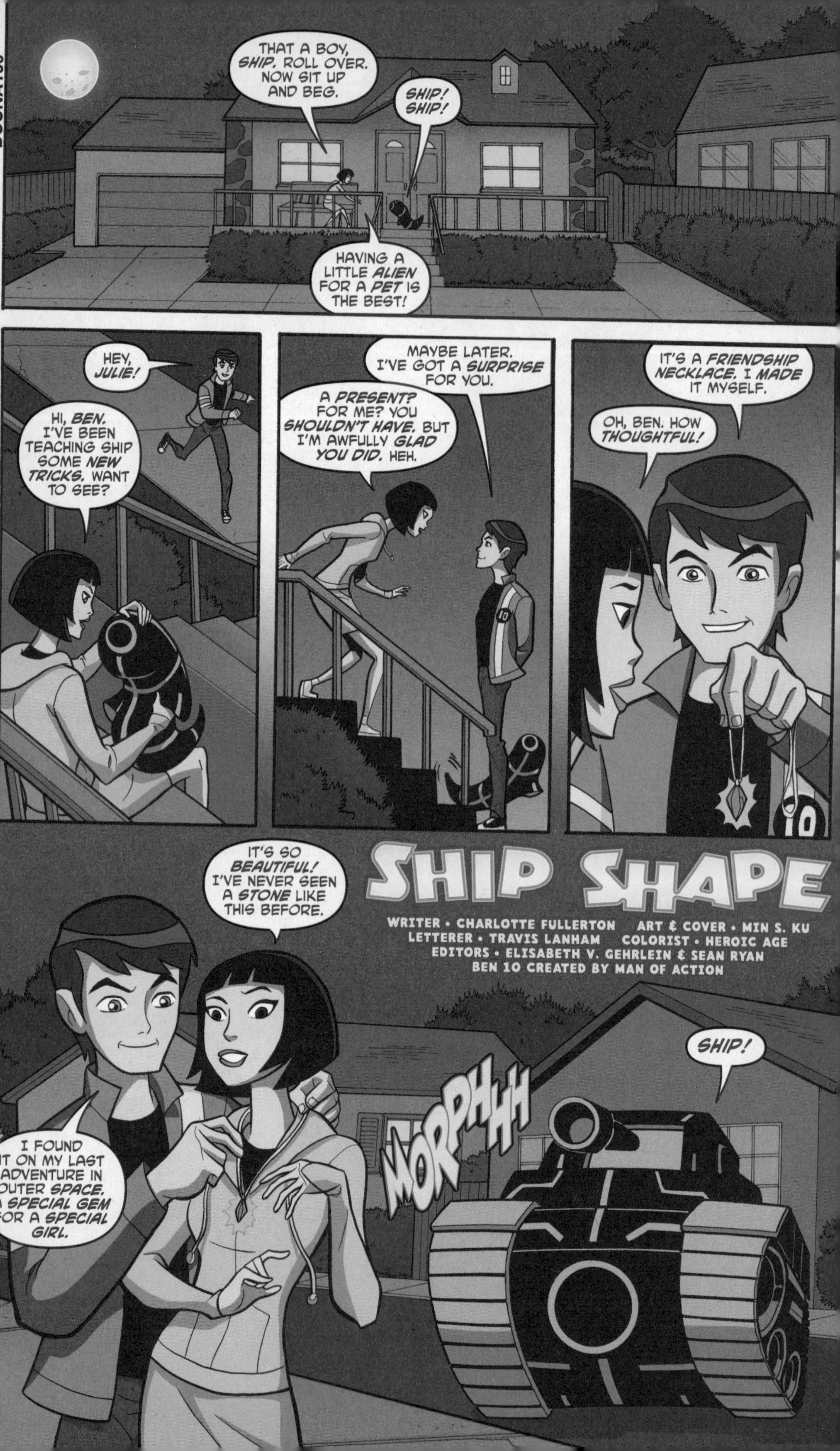
THAT A BOY, SHIP. ROLL OVER. NOW SIT UP AND BEG.
SHIP! SHIP!
HAVING A LITTLE ALIEN FOR A PET IS THE BEST!
HEY, JULIE!
HI, BEN. I'VE BEEN TEACHING SHIP SOME NEW TRICKS. WANT TO SEE?
MAYBE LATER. I'VE GOT A SURPRISE FOR YOU.
A PRESENT? FOR ME? YOU SHOULDN'T HAVE. BUT I'M AWFULLY GLAD YOU DID. HEH.
IT'S A FRIENDSHIP NECKLACE. I MADE IT MYSELF.
OH, BEN. HOW THOUGHTFUL!
SHIP SHAPE
WRITER • CHARLOTTE FULLERTON ART & COVER • MIN S. KU
LETTERER • TRAVIS LANHAM COLORIST • HEROIC AGE
EDITORS • ELISABETH V. GEHRLEIN & SEAN RYAN
BEN 10 CREATED BY MAN OF ACTION
IT'S SO BEAUTIFUL! I'VE NEVER SEEN A STONE LIKE THIS BEFORE.
I FOUND IT ON MY LAST ADVENTURE IN OUTER SPACE. A SPECIAL GEM FOR A SPECIAL GIRL.
MORPHHH
SHIP!

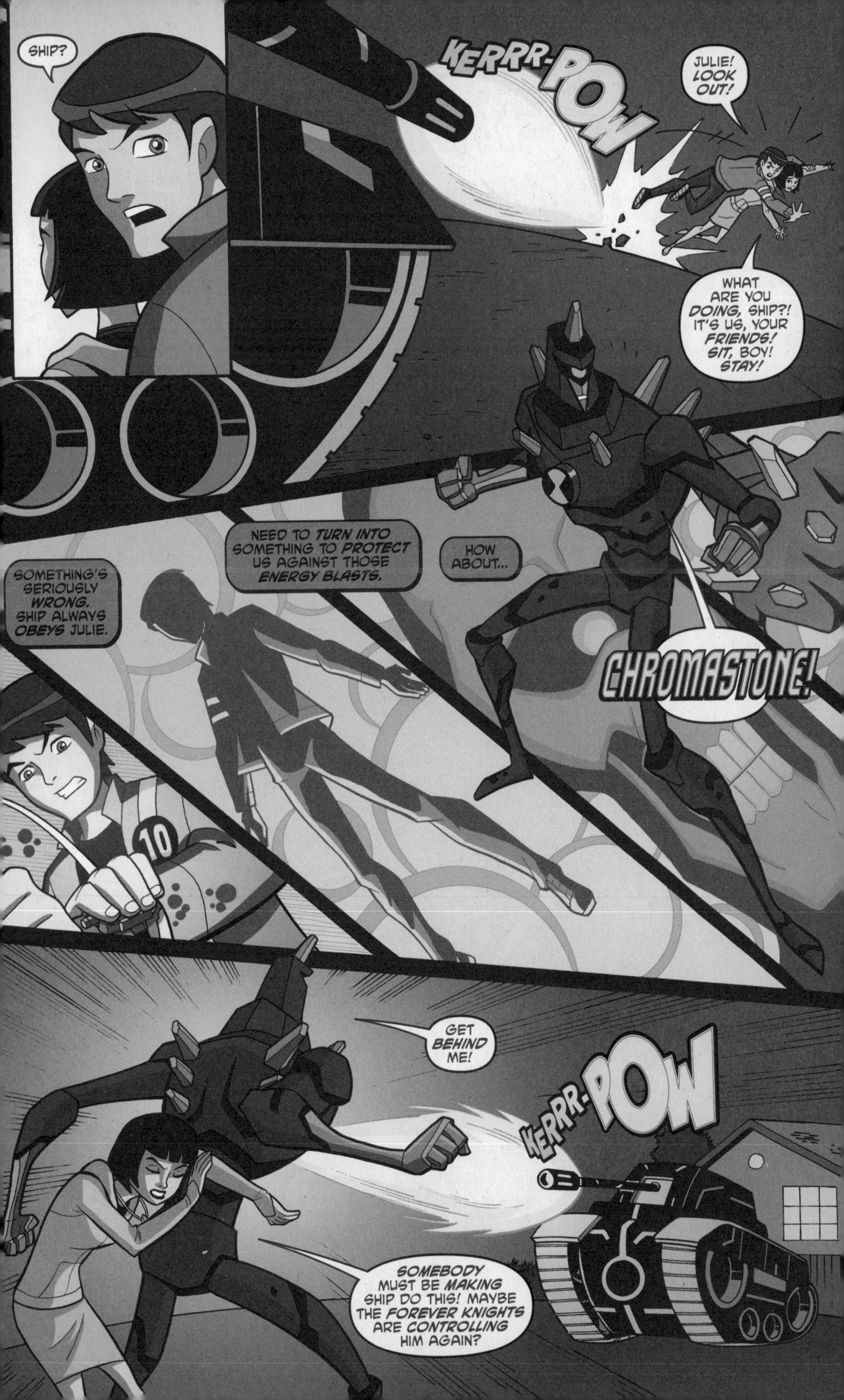
SHIP?
KERRR-POW
JULIE! LOOK OUT!
WHAT ARE YOU DOING, SHIP?! IT'S US, YOUR FRIENDS! SIT, BOY! STAY!
SOMETHING'S SERIOUSLY WRONG. SHIP ALWAYS OBEYS JULIE.
NEED TO TURN INTO SOMETHING TO PROTECT US AGAINST THOSE ENERGY BLASTS.
HOW ABOUT...
CHROMASTONE!
10
GET BEHIND ME!
KERRR-POW
SOMEBODY MUST BE MAKING SHIP DO THIS! MAYBE THE FOREVER KNIGHTS ARE CONTROLLING HIM AGAIN?

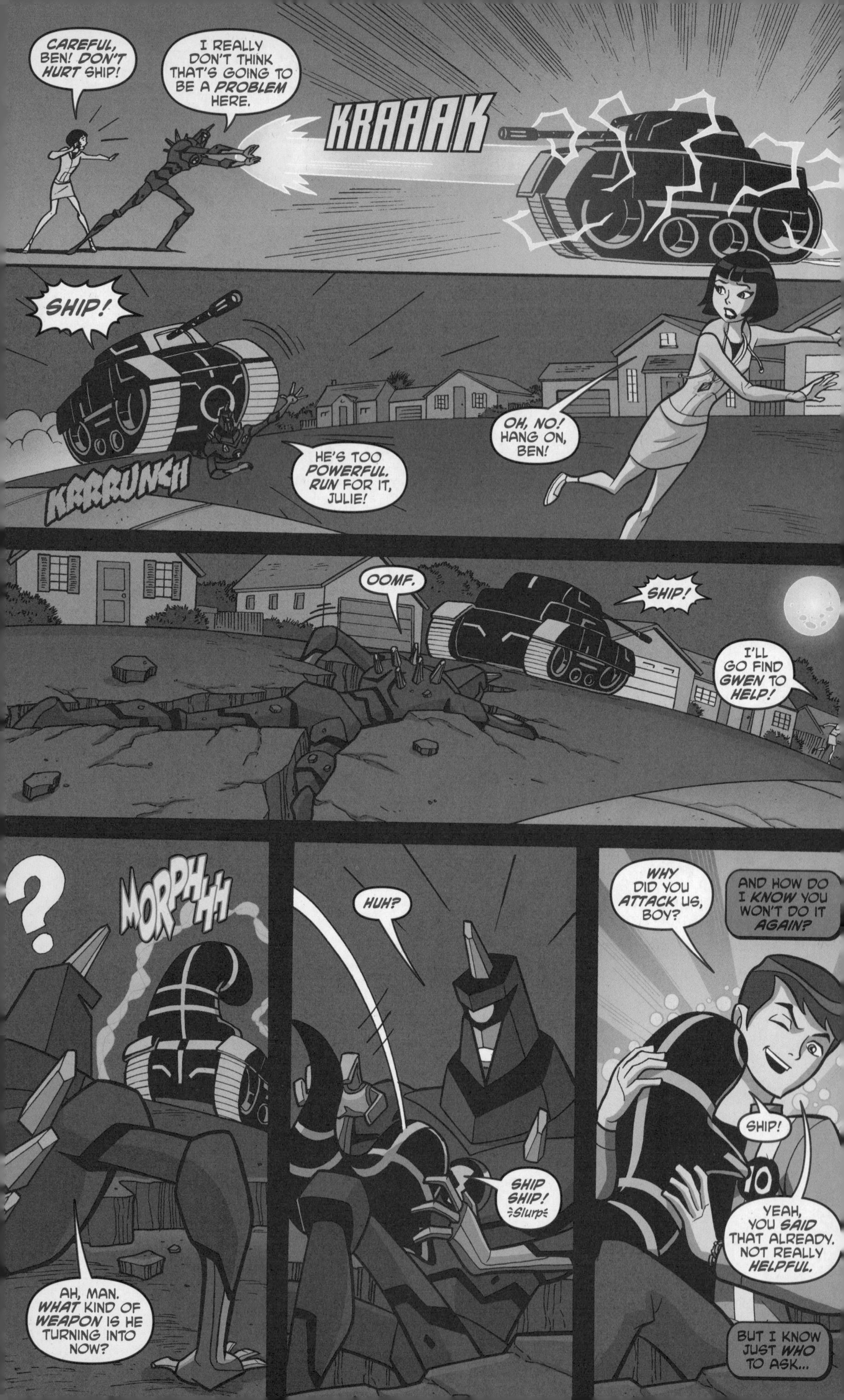
CAREFUL, BEN! DON'T HURT SHIP!
I REALLY DON'T THINK THAT'S GOING TO BE A PROBLEM HERE.
KRAAAK
SHIP!
KRRRUNCH
HE'S TOO POWERFUL. RUN FOR IT, JULIE!
OH, NO! HANG ON, BEN!
OOMF.
SHIP!
I'LL GO FIND GWEN TO HELP!
?
MORPHHH
AH, MAN. WHAT KIND OF WEAPON IS HE TURNING INTO NOW?
HUH?
SHIP SHIP!
Slurp
WHY DID YOU ATTACK US, BOY?
AND HOW DO I KNOW YOU WON'T DO IT AGAIN?
SHIP!
YEAH, YOU SAID THAT ALREADY. NOT REALLY HELPFUL.
BUT I KNOW JUST WHO TO ASK...

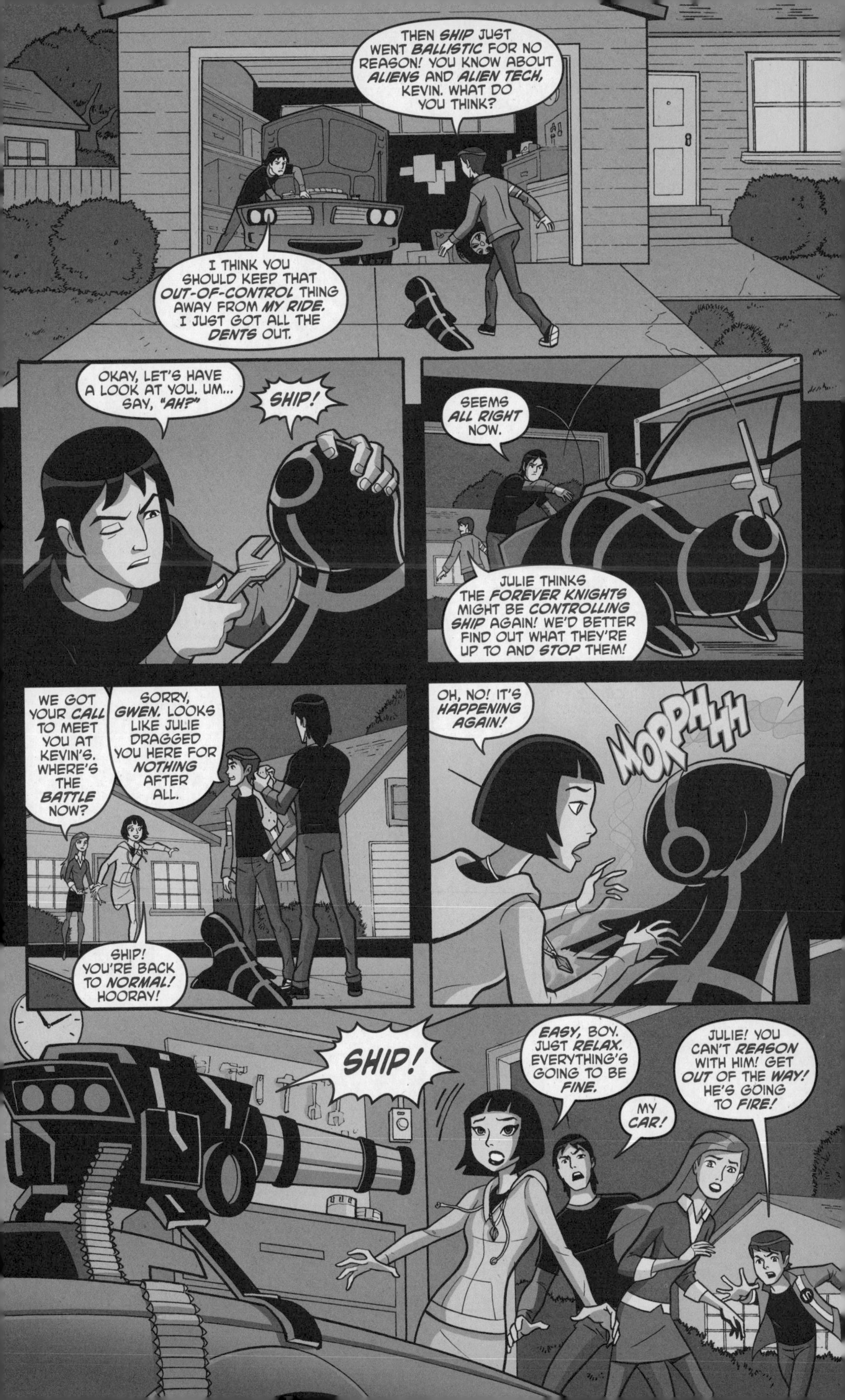
THEN SHIP JUST WENT BALLISTIC FOR NO REASON! YOU KNOW ABOUT ALIENS AND ALIEN TECH, KEVIN. WHAT DO YOU THINK?
I THINK YOU SHOULD KEEP THAT OUT-OF-CONTROL THING AWAY FROM MY RIDE. I JUST GOT ALL THE DENTS OUT.
OKAY, LET'S HAVE A LOOK AT YOU. UM... SAY, "AH?"
SHIP!
SEEMS ALL RIGHT NOW.
JULIE THINKS THE FOREVER KNIGHTS MIGHT BE CONTROLLING SHIP AGAIN! WE'D BETTER FIND OUT WHAT THEY'RE UP TO AND STOP THEM!
WE GOT YOUR CALL TO MEET YOU AT KEVIN'S. WHERE'S THE BATTLE NOW?
SORRY, GWEN. LOOKS LIKE JULIE DRAGGED YOU HERE FOR NOTHING AFTER ALL.
SHIP! YOU'RE BACK TO NORMAL! HOORAY!
OH, NO! IT'S HAPPENING AGAIN!
MORPHHH
SHIP!
EASY, BOY. JUST RELAX. EVERYTHING'S GOING TO BE FINE.
MY CAR!
JULIE! YOU CAN'T REASON WITH HIM! GET OUT OF THE WAY! HE'S GOING TO FIRE!

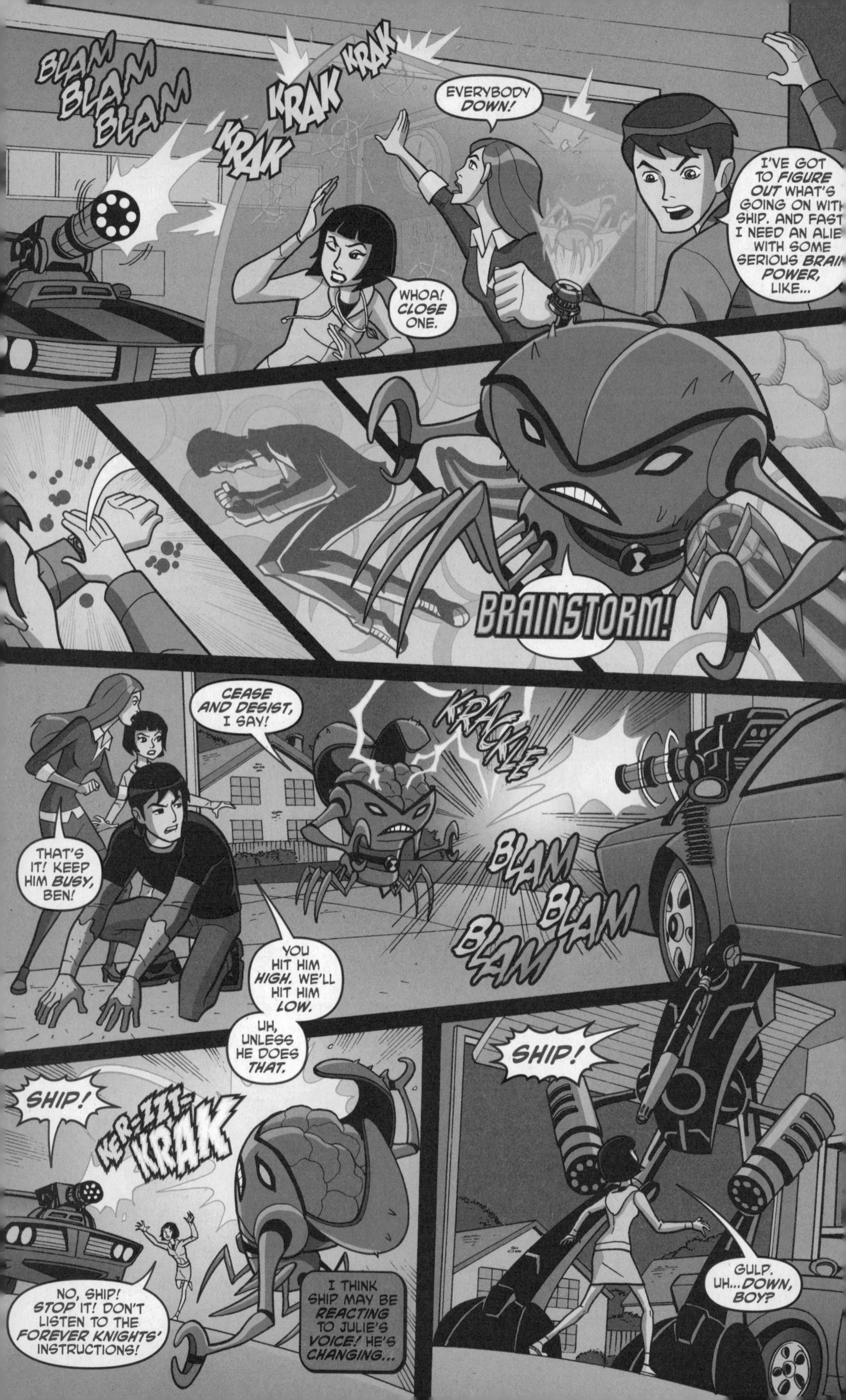
BLAM BLAM BLAM
KRAK KRAK KRAK
EVERYBODY DOWN!
WHOA! CLOSE ONE.
I'VE GOT TO FIGURE OUT WHAT'S GOING ON WIT SHIP. AND FAST I NEED AN ALIE WITH SOME SERIOUS BRAI POWER, LIKE...
BRAINSTORM!
CEASE AND DESIST, I SAY!
KRACKLE
BLAM BLAM BLAM
THAT'S IT! KEEP HIM BUSY, BEN!
YOU HIT HIM HIGH. WE'LL HIT HIM LOW.
UH, UNLESS HE DOES THAT.
SHIP!
KER-ZZT-KRAK
NO, SHIP! STOP IT! DON'T LISTEN TO THE FOREVER KNIGHTS' INSTRUCTIONS!
I THINK SHIP MAY BE REACTING TO JULIE'S VOICE! HE'S CHANGING...
SHIP!
GULP. UH...DOWN, BOY?

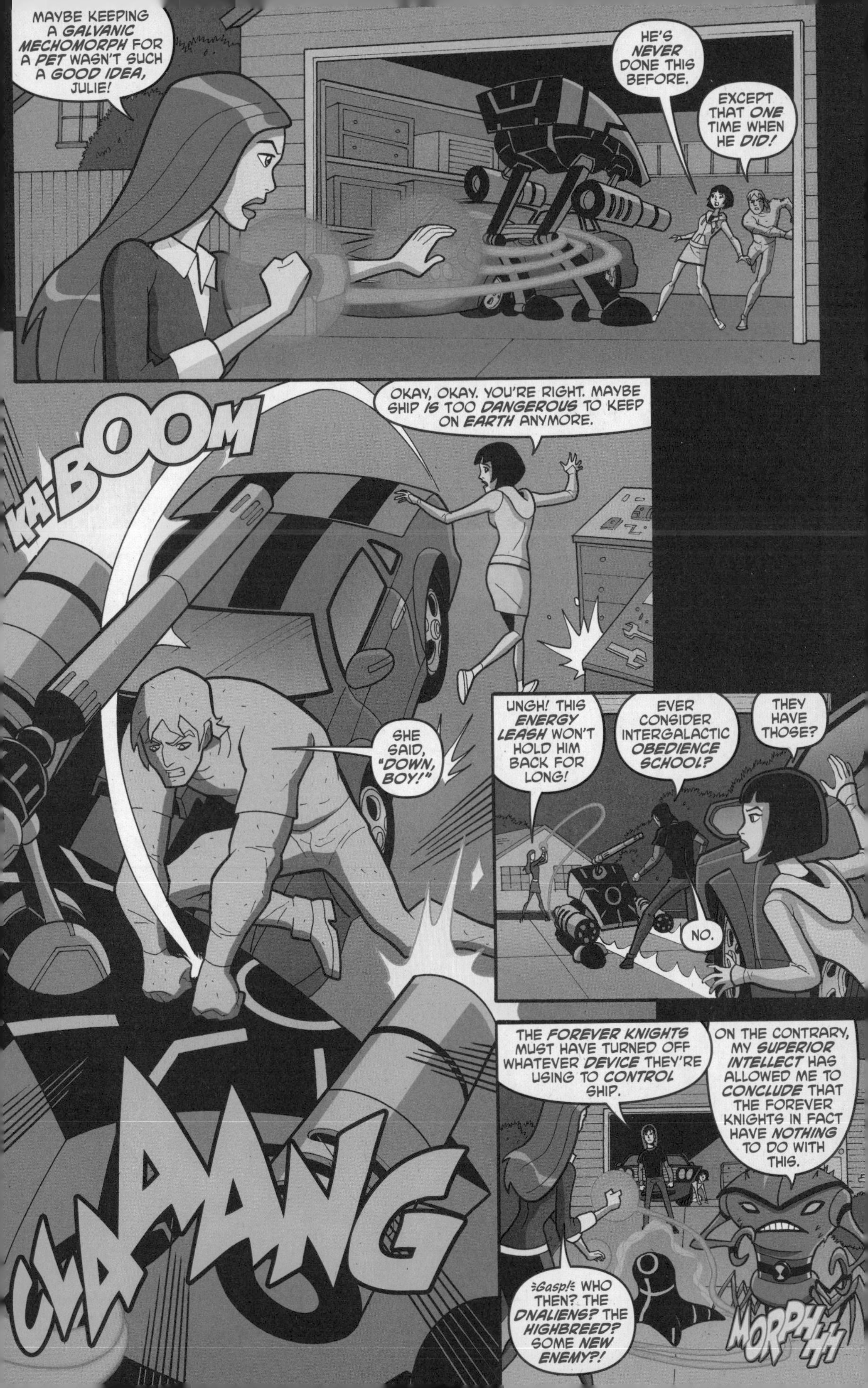

MAYBE KEEPING A GALVANIC MECHOMORPH FOR A PET WASN'T SUCH A GOOD IDEA, JULIE!
HE'S NEVER DONE THIS BEFORE.
EXCEPT THAT ONE TIME WHEN HE DID!
KA-BOOOM
OKAY, OKAY. YOU'RE RIGHT. MAYBE SHIP IS TOO DANGEROUS TO KEEP ON EARTH ANYMORE.
SHE SAID, "DOWN, BOY!"
UNGH! THIS ENERGY LEASH WON'T HOLD HIM BACK FOR LONG!
EVER CONSIDER INTERGALACTIC OBEDIENCE SCHOOL?
THEY HAVE THOSE?
NO.
THE FOREVER KNIGHTS MUST HAVE TURNED OFF WHATEVER DEVICE THEY'RE USING TO CONTROL SHIP.
ON THE CONTRARY, MY SUPERIOR INTELLECT HAS ALLOWED ME TO CONCLUDE THAT THE FOREVER KNIGHTS IN FACT HAVE NOTHING TO DO WITH THIS.
Gasp! WHO THEN? THE DNALIENS? THE HIGHBREED? SOME NEW ENEMY?!
MORPHHH

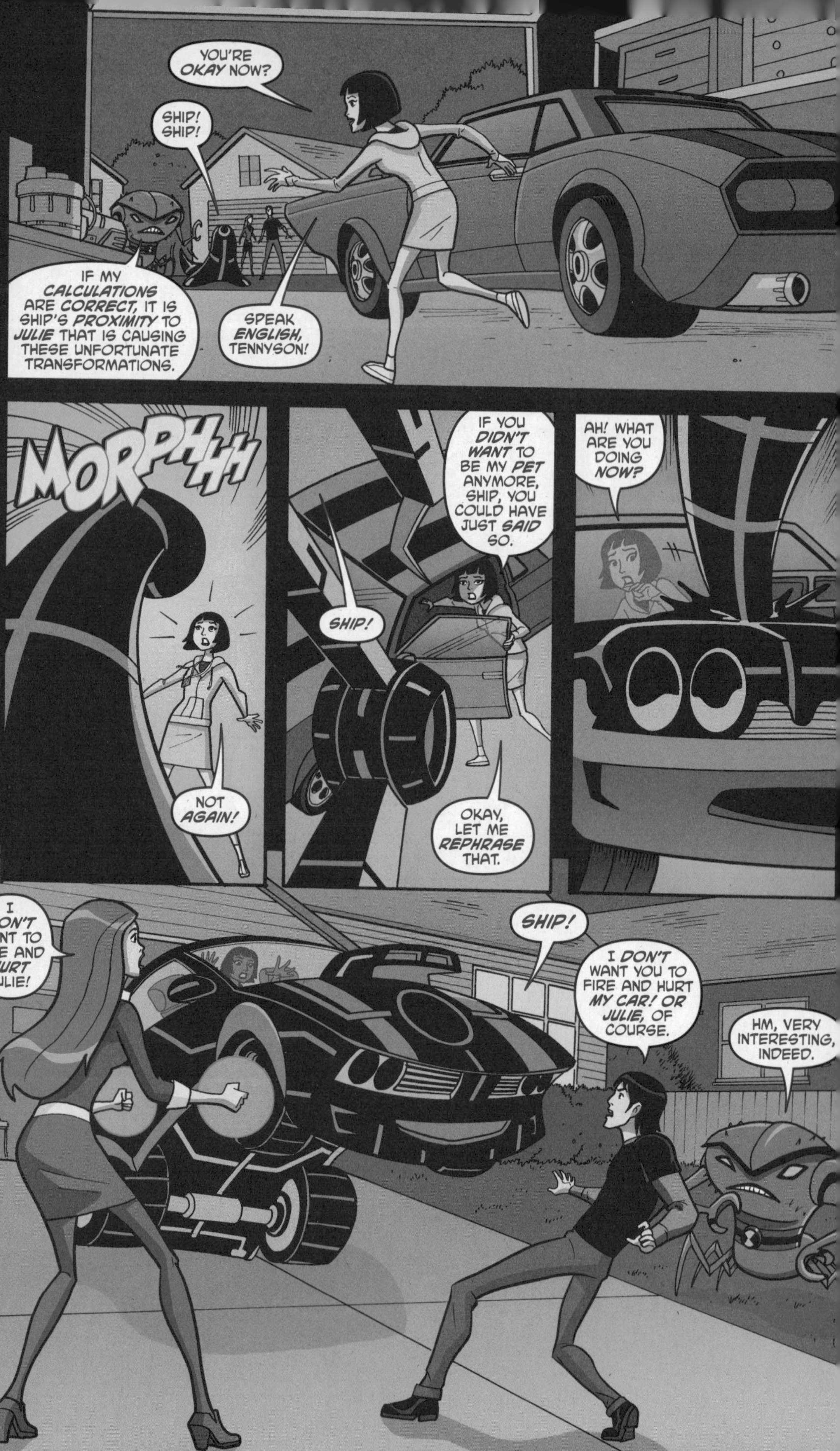
YOU'RE OKAY NOW?
SHIP! SHIP!
IF MY CALCULATIONS ARE CORRECT, IT IS SHIP'S PROXIMITY TO JULIE THAT IS CAUSING THESE UNFORTUNATE TRANSFORMATIONS.
SPEAK ENGLISH, TENNYSON!
MORPHHH
NOT AGAIN!
IF YOU DIDN'T WANT TO BE MY PET ANYMORE, SHIP, YOU COULD HAVE JUST SAID SO.
SHIP!
OKAY, LET ME REPHRASE THAT.
AH! WHAT ARE YOU DOING NOW?
I DON'T WANT TO FIRE AND HURT JULIE!
SHIP!
I DON'T WANT YOU TO FIRE AND HURT MY CAR! OR JULIE, OF COURSE.
HM, VERY INTERESTING, INDEED.

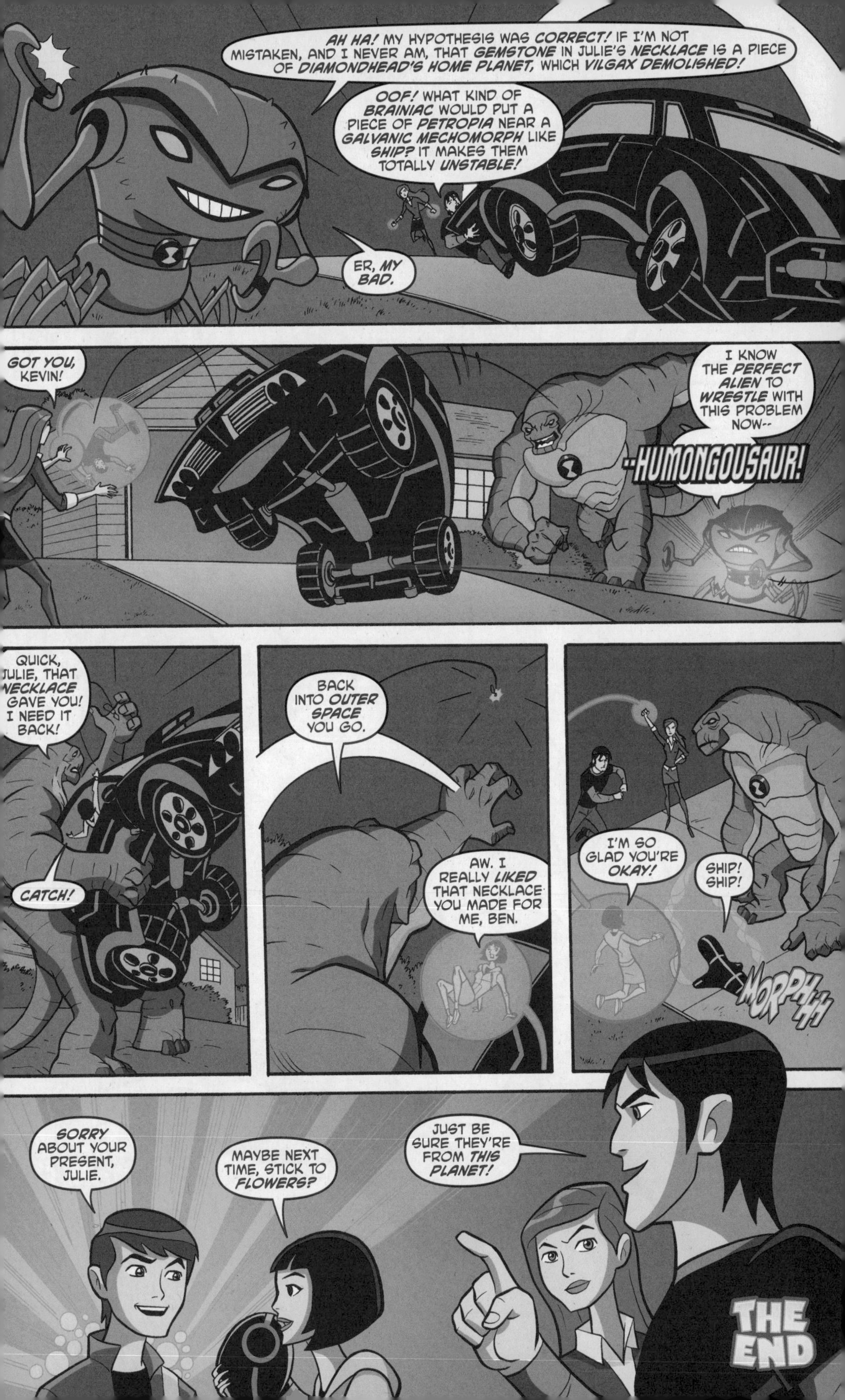
AH HA! MY HYPOTHESIS WAS CORRECT! IF I'M NOT MISTAKEN, AND I NEVER AM, THAT GEMSTONE IN JULIE'S NECKLACE IS A PIECE OF DIAMONDHEAD'S HOME PLANET, WHICH VILGAX DEMOLISHED!
OOF! WHAT KIND OF BRAINIAC WOULD PUT A PIECE OF PETROPIA NEAR A GALVANIC MECHOMORPH LIKE SHIP? IT MAKES THEM TOTALLY UNSTABLE!
ER, MY BAD.
GOT YOU, KEVIN!
I KNOW THE PERFECT ALIEN TO WRESTLE WITH THIS PROBLEM NOW--
--HUMONGOUSAUR!
QUICK, JULIE, THAT NECKLACE GAVE YOU! I NEED IT BACK!
CATCH!
BACK INTO OUTER SPACE YOU GO.
AW. I REALLY LIKED THAT NECKLACE YOU MADE FOR ME, BEN.
I'M SO GLAD YOU'RE OKAY!
SHIP! SHIP!
MORPHHH
SORRY ABOUT YOUR PRESENT, JULIE.
MAYBE NEXT TIME, STICK TO FLOWERS?
JUST BE SURE THEY'RE FROM THIS PLANET!
THE END

DCCNA168

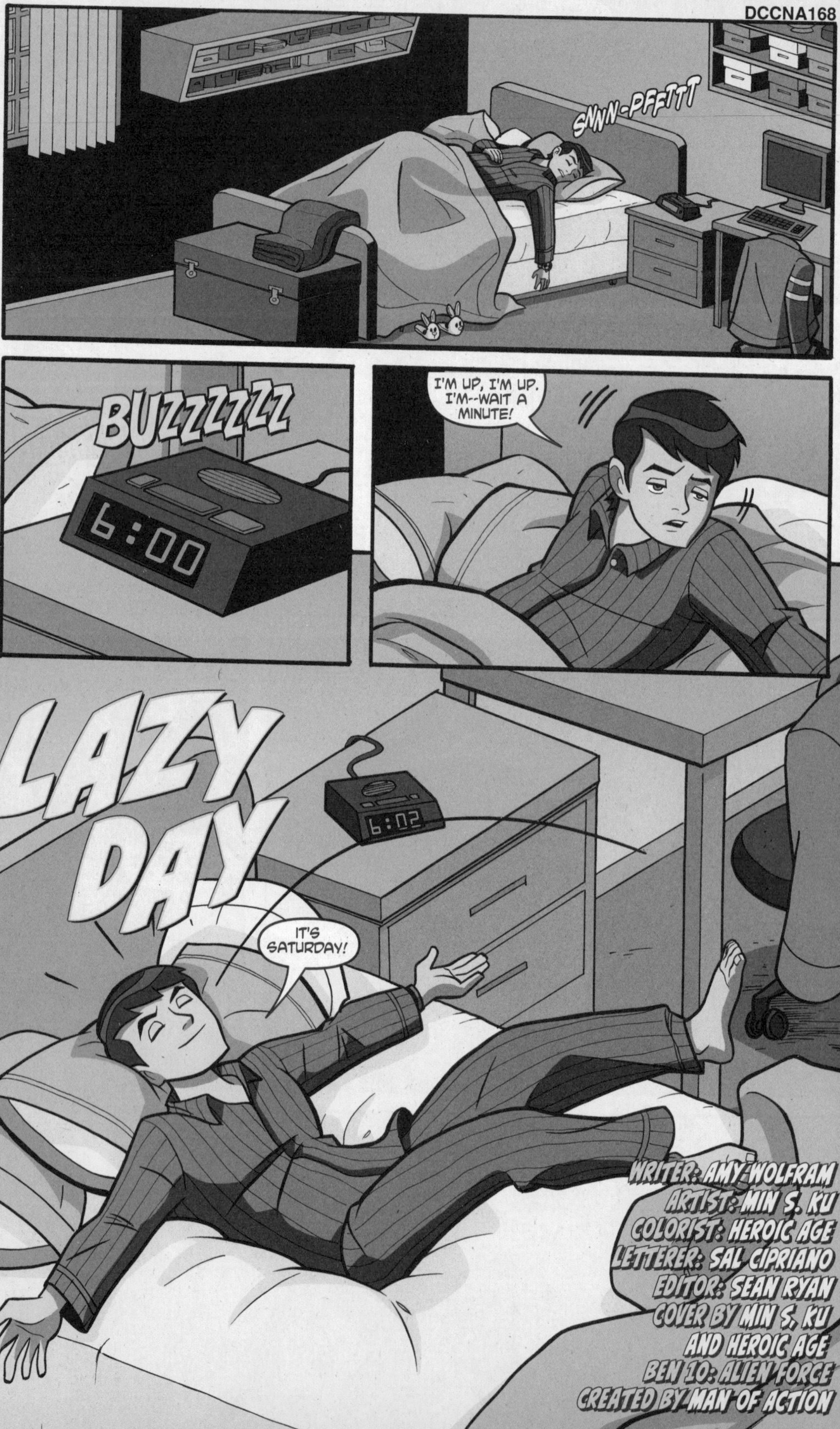
SNNN-PFFTTT
BUZZZZZZ
6:00
I'M UP, I'M UP. I'M--WAIT A MINUTE!
LAZY DAY
6:02
IT'S SATURDAY!
WRITER: AMY WOLFRAM
ARTIST: MIN S. KU
COLORIST: HEROIC AGE
LETTERER: SAL CIPRIANO
EDITOR: SEAN RYAN
COVER BY MIN S. KU
AND HEROIC AGE
BEN 10: ALIEN FORCE
CREATED BY MAN OF ACTION

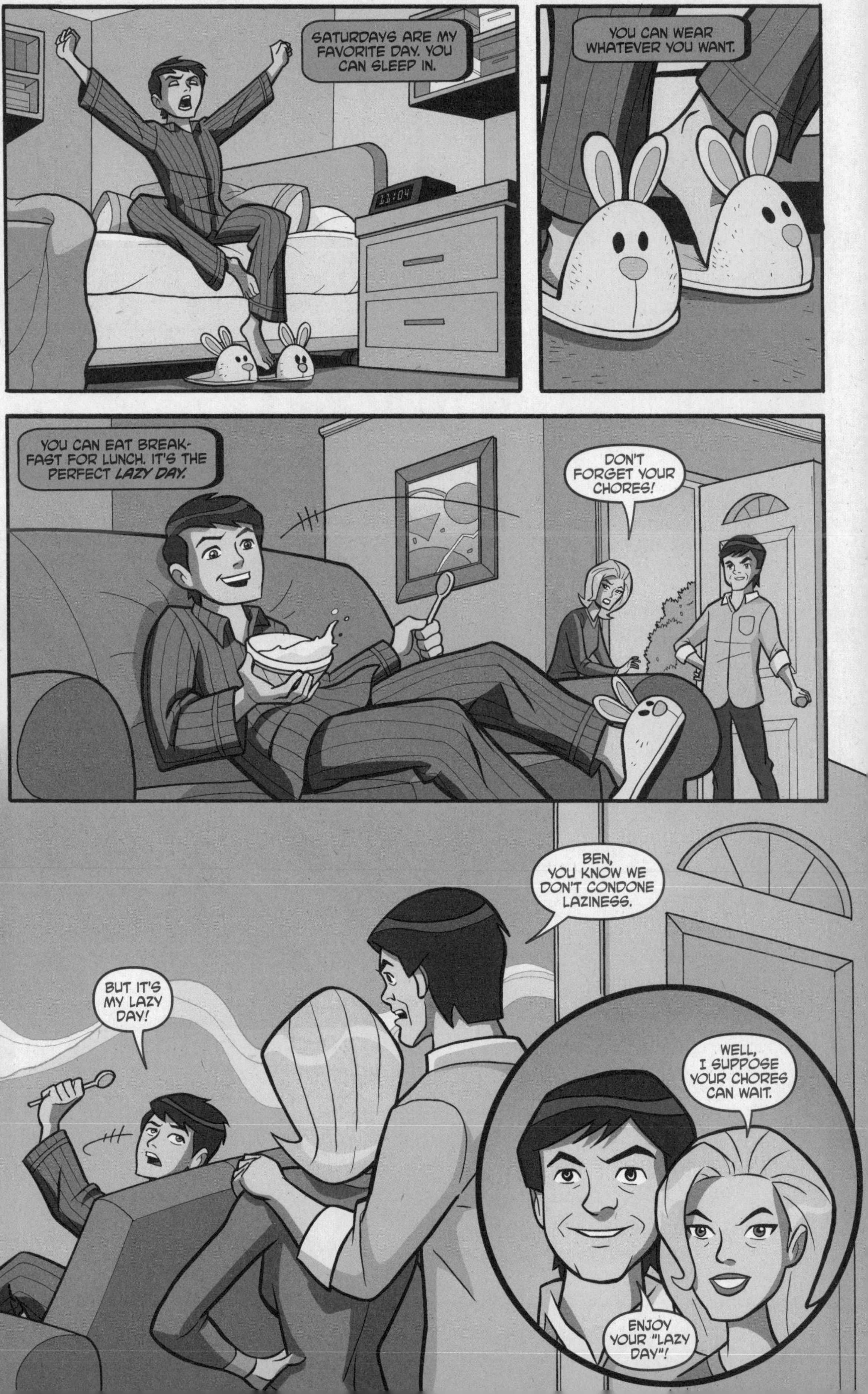
SATURDAYS ARE MY FAVORITE DAY. YOU CAN SLEEP IN.
11:04
YOU CAN WEAR WHATEVER YOU WANT.
YOU CAN EAT BREAK-FAST FOR LUNCH. IT'S THE PERFECT *LAZY DAY.*
DON'T FORGET YOUR CHORES!
BEN, YOU KNOW WE DON'T CONDONE LAZINESS.
BUT IT'S MY LAZY DAY!
WELL, I SUPPOSE YOUR CHORES CAN WAIT.
ENJOY YOUR "LAZY DAY"!

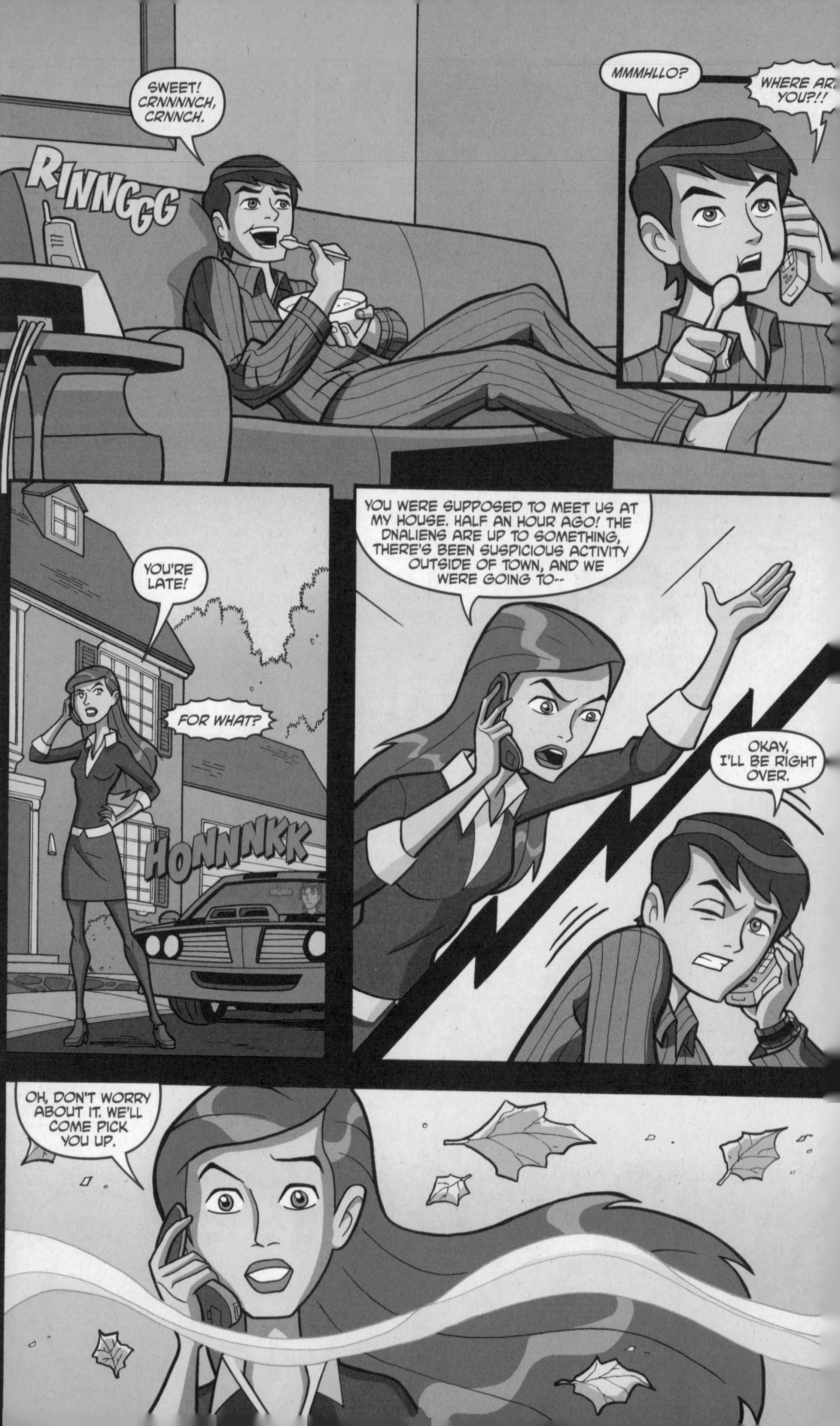
SWEET! CRNNNNCH, CRNNCH.
RINNGGG
MMMHLLO?
WHERE AR YOU?!!
YOU'RE LATE!
FOR WHAT?
HONNNKK
YOU WERE SUPPOSED TO MEET US AT MY HOUSE. HALF AN HOUR AGO! THE DNALIENS ARE UP TO SOMETHING, THERE'S BEEN SUSPICIOUS ACTIVITY OUTSIDE OF TOWN, AND WE WERE GOING TO--
OKAY, I'LL BE RIGHT OVER.
OH, DON'T WORRY ABOUT IT. WE'LL COME PICK YOU UP.

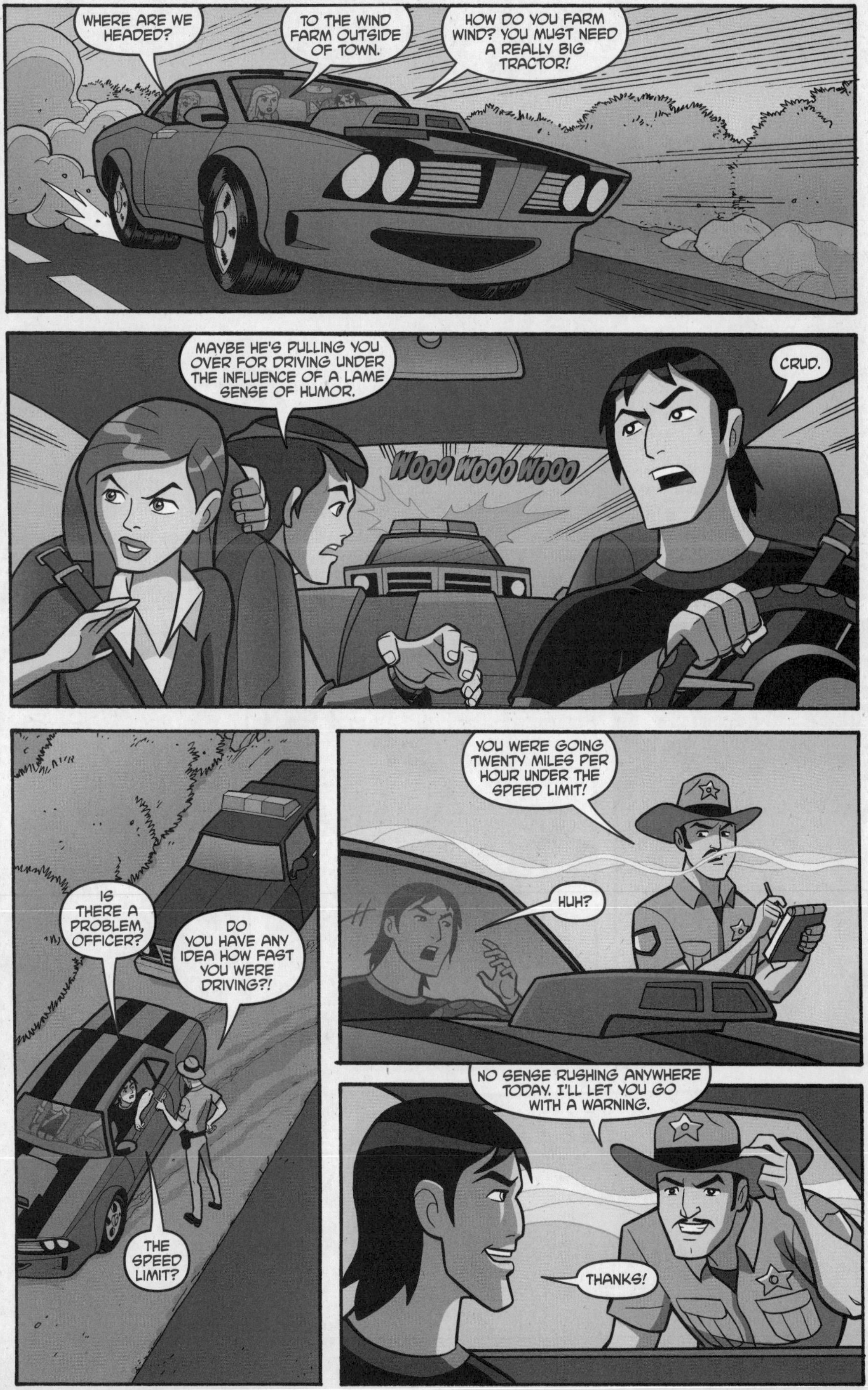
WHERE ARE WE HEADED?
TO THE WIND FARM OUTSIDE OF TOWN.
HOW DO YOU FARM WIND? YOU MUST NEED A REALLY BIG TRACTOR!
MAYBE HE'S PULLING YOU OVER FOR DRIVING UNDER THE INFLUENCE OF A LAME SENSE OF HUMOR.
WOOO WOOO WOOO
CRUD.
IS THERE A PROBLEM, OFFICER?
DO YOU HAVE ANY IDEA HOW FAST YOU WERE DRIVING?!
THE SPEED LIMIT?
YOU WERE GOING TWENTY MILES PER HOUR UNDER THE SPEED LIMIT!
HUH?
NO SENSE RUSHING ANYWHERE TODAY. I'LL LET YOU GO WITH A WARNING.
THANKS!

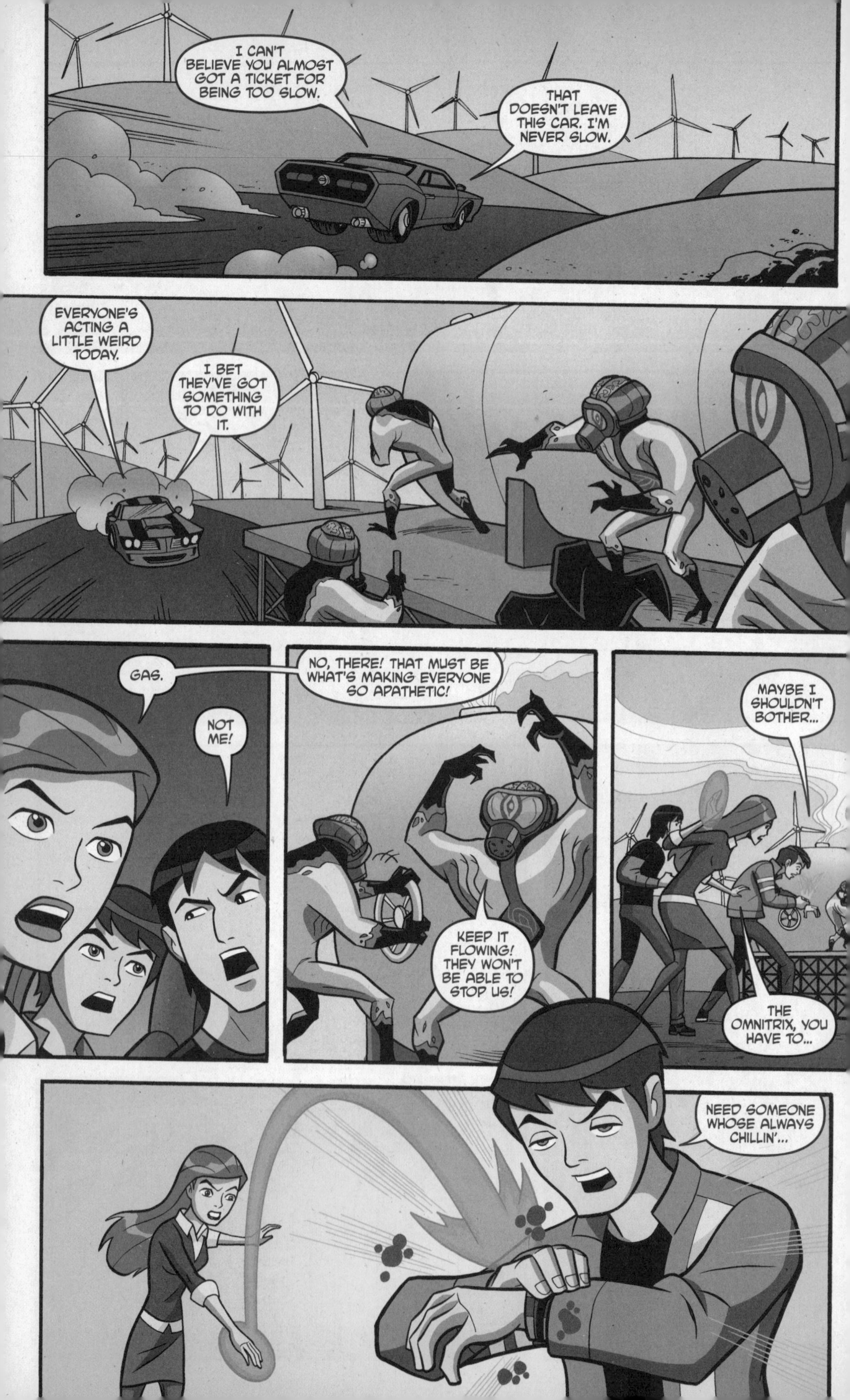
I CAN'T BELIEVE YOU ALMOST GOT A TICKET FOR BEING TOO SLOW.
THAT DOESN'T LEAVE THIS CAR. I'M NEVER SLOW.
EVERYONE'S ACTING A LITTLE WEIRD TODAY.
I BET THEY'VE GOT SOMETHING TO DO WITH IT.
GAS.
NOT ME!
NO, THERE! THAT MUST BE WHAT'S MAKING EVERYONE SO APATHETIC!
KEEP IT FLOWING! THEY WON'T BE ABLE TO STOP US!
MAYBE I SHOULDN'T BOTHER...
THE OMNITRIX, YOU HAVE TO...
NEED SOMEONE WHOSE ALWAYS CHILLIN'...

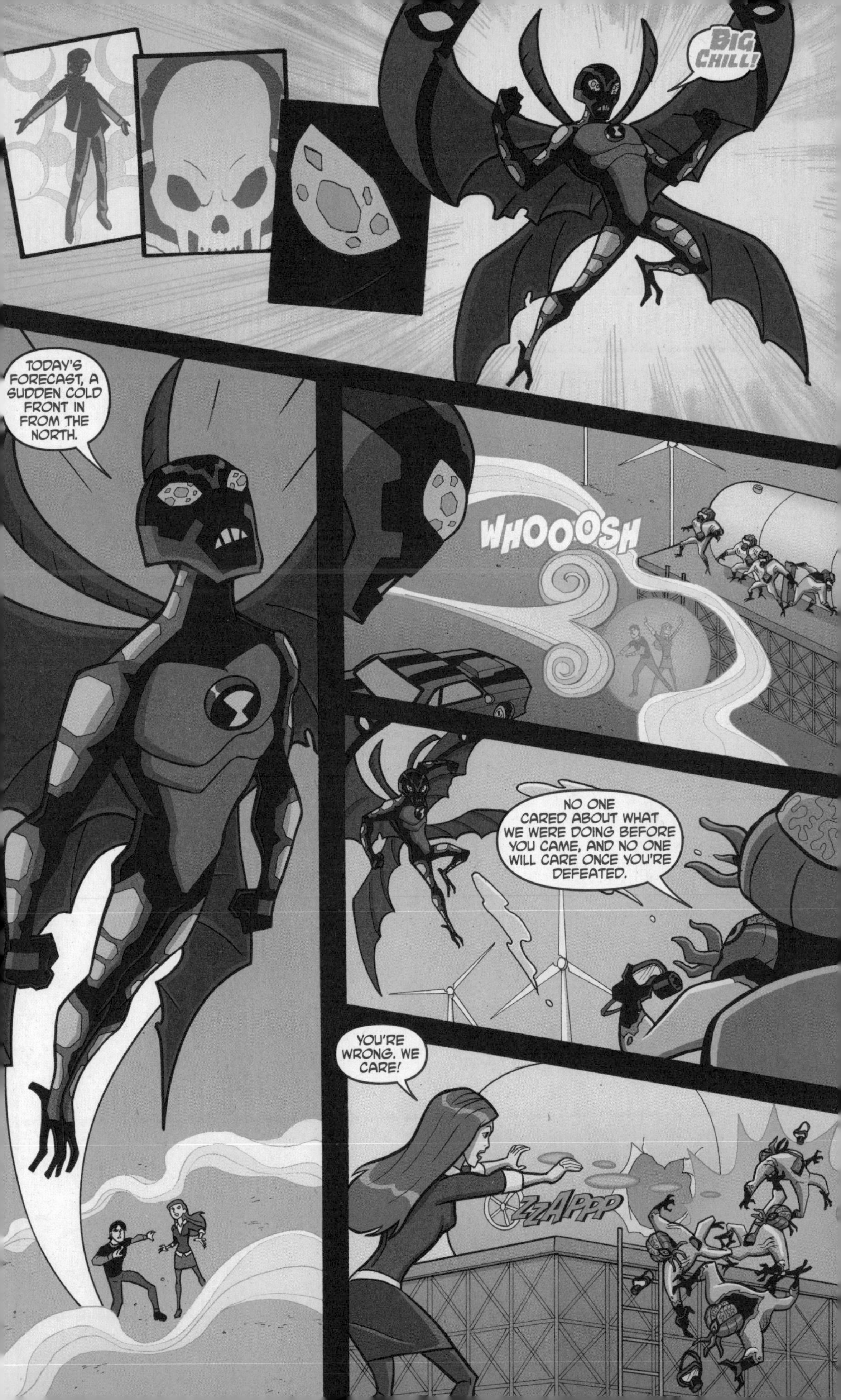
BIG CHILL!
TODAY'S FORECAST, A SUDDEN COLD FRONT IN FROM THE NORTH.
WHOOOSH
NO ONE CARED ABOUT WHAT WE WERE DOING BEFORE YOU CAME, AND NO ONE WILL CARE ONCE YOU'RE DEFEATED.
YOU'RE WRONG. WE CARE!
ZZAPPP

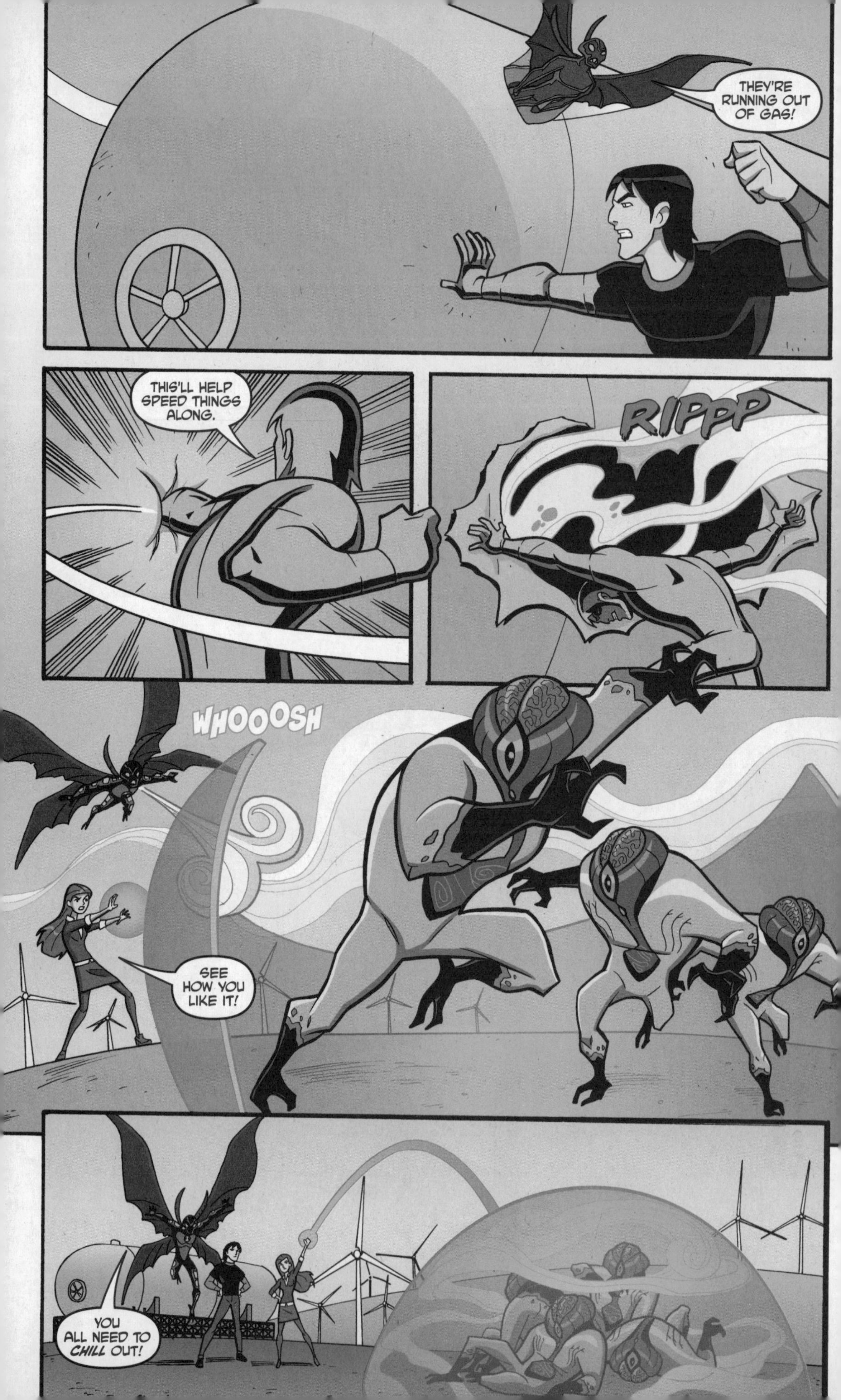

THEY'RE RUNNING OUT OF GAS!
THIS'LL HELP SPEED THINGS ALONG.
RIPPP
WHOOOSH
SEE HOW YOU LIKE IT!
YOU ALL NEED TO CHILL OUT!

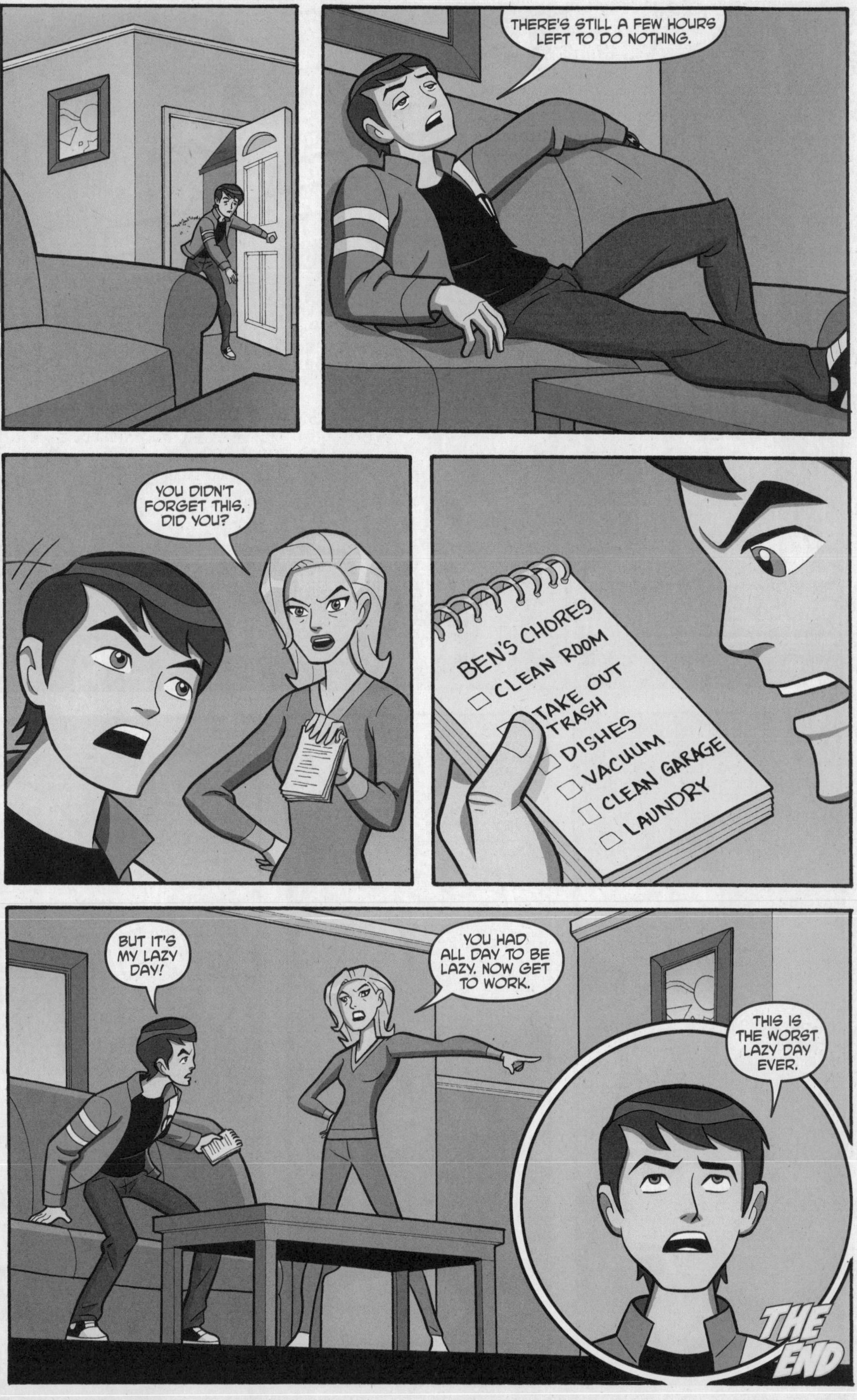
THERE'S STILL A FEW HOURS LEFT TO DO NOTHING.
YOU DIDN'T FORGET THIS, DID YOU?
BEN'S CHORES
CLEAN ROOM
TAKE OUT TRASH
DISHES
VACUUM
CLEAN GARAGE
LAUNDRY
BUT IT'S MY LAZY DAY!
YOU HAD ALL DAY TO BE LAZY. NOW GET TO WORK.
THIS IS THE WORST LAZY DAY EVER.
THE END

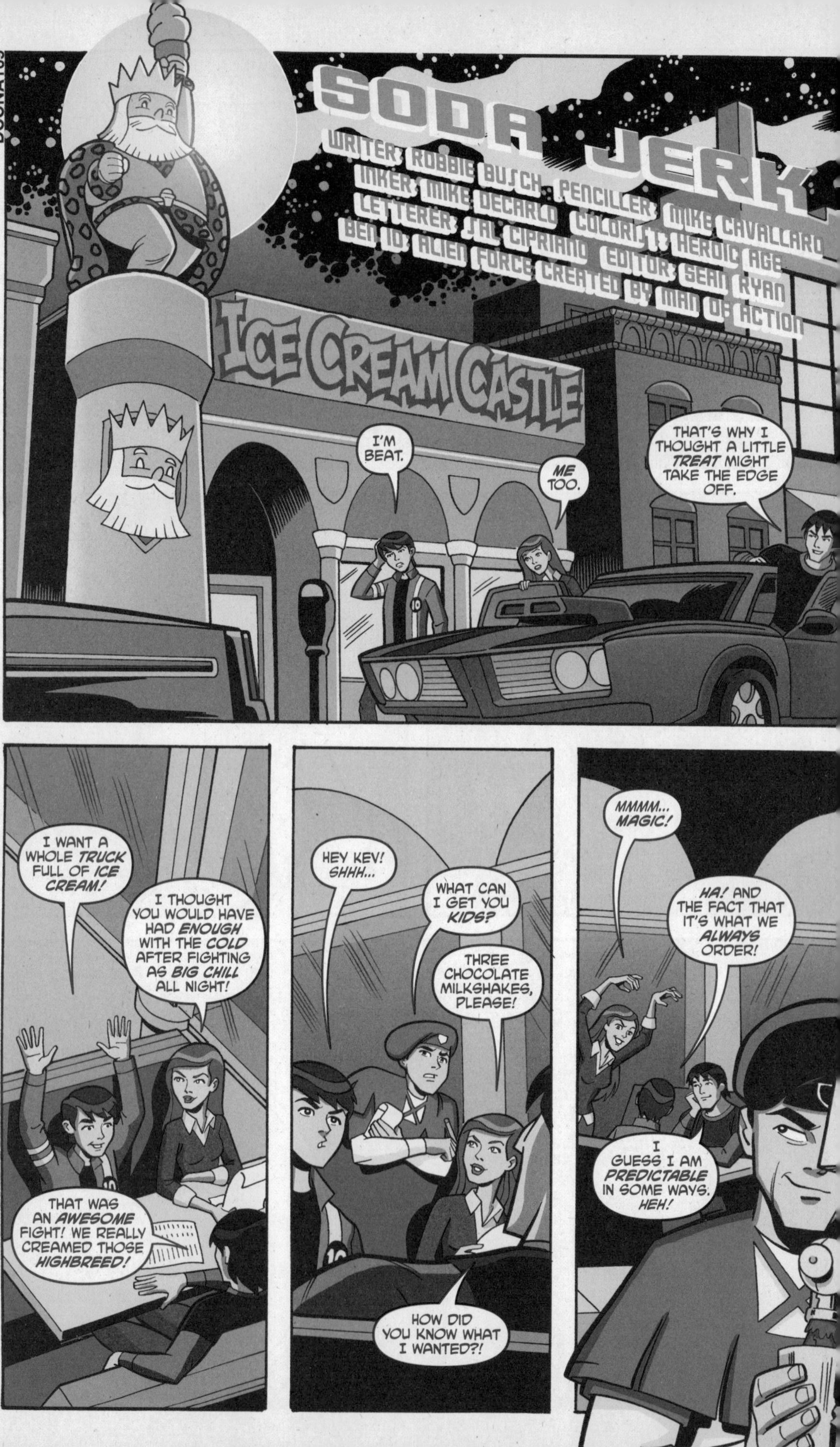
SODA JERK
WRITER: ROBBIE BUSCH
INKER: MIKE DECARLO PENCILLER: MIKE CAVALLARO
LETTERER: SAL CIPRIANO COLORIST: HEROIC AGE
EDITOR: SEAN RYAN
BEN 10: ALIEN FORCE CREATED BY MAN OF ACTION
ICE CREAM CASTLE
I'M BEAT.
ME TOO.
THAT'S WHY I THOUGHT A LITTLE TREAT MIGHT TAKE THE EDGE OFF.
I WANT A WHOLE TRUCK FULL OF ICE CREAM!
I THOUGHT YOU WOULD HAVE HAD ENOUGH WITH THE COLD AFTER FIGHTING AS BIG CHILL ALL NIGHT!
THAT WAS AN AWESOME FIGHT! WE REALLY CREAMED THOSE HIGHBREED!
HEY KEV! SHHH...
WHAT CAN I GET YOU KIDS?
THREE CHOCOLATE MILKSHAKES, PLEASE!
HOW DID YOU KNOW WHAT I WANTED?!
MMMM... MAGIC!
HA! AND THE FACT THAT IT'S WHAT WE ALWAYS ORDER!
I GUESS I AM PREDICTABLE IN SOME WAYS. HEH!

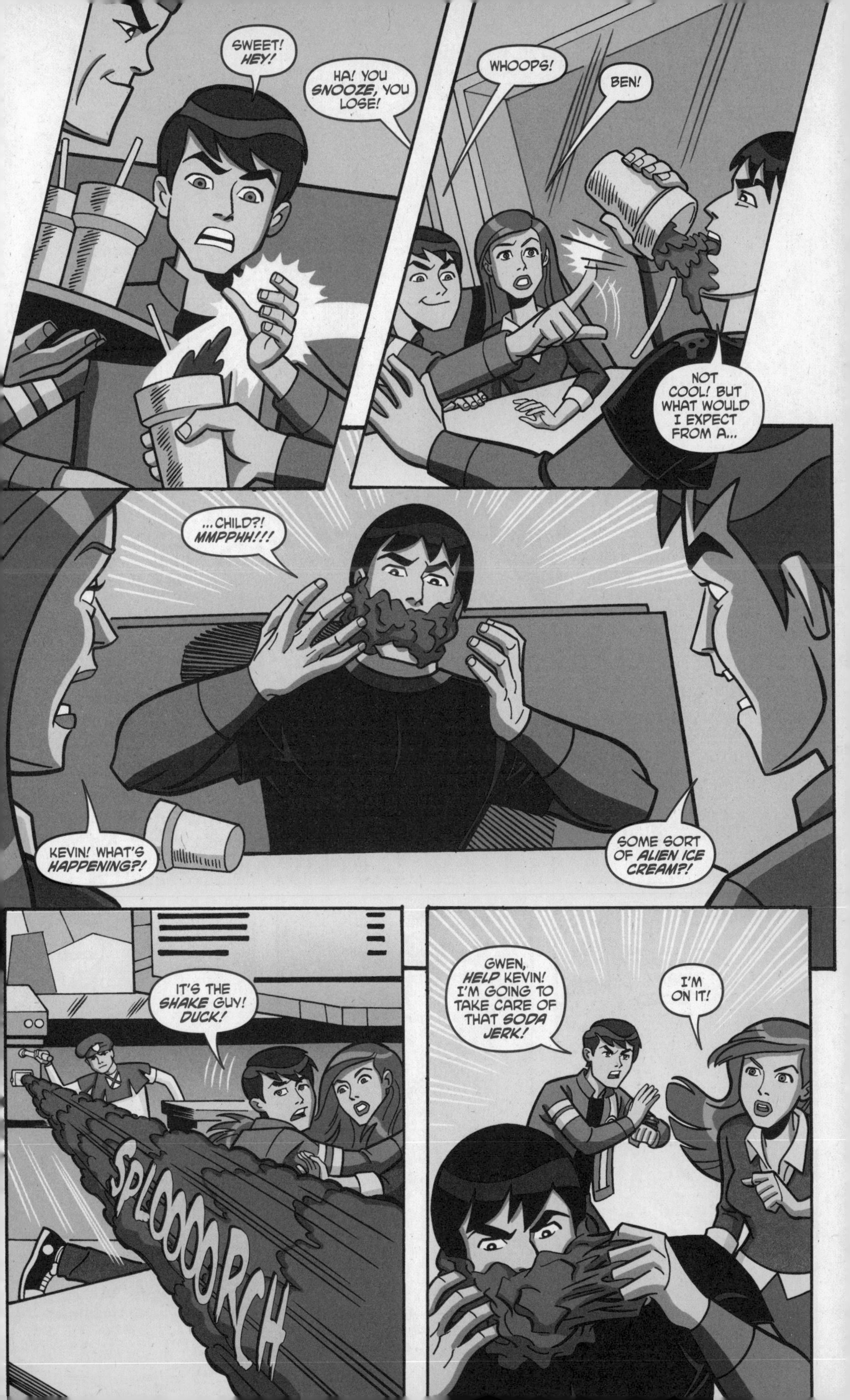

SWEET! *HEY!*
HA! YOU *SNOOZE,* YOU LOSE!
WHOOPS!
BEN!
NOT COOL! BUT WHAT WOULD I EXPECT FROM A...
...CHILD?! *MMPPHH!!!*
KEVIN! WHAT'S *HAPPENING?!*
SOME SORT OF *ALIEN ICE CREAM?!*
IT'S THE *SHAKE* GUY! *DUCK!*
SPLOOOORCH
GWEN, *HELP* KEVIN! I'M GOING TO TAKE CARE OF THAT *SODA JERK!*
I'M ON IT!

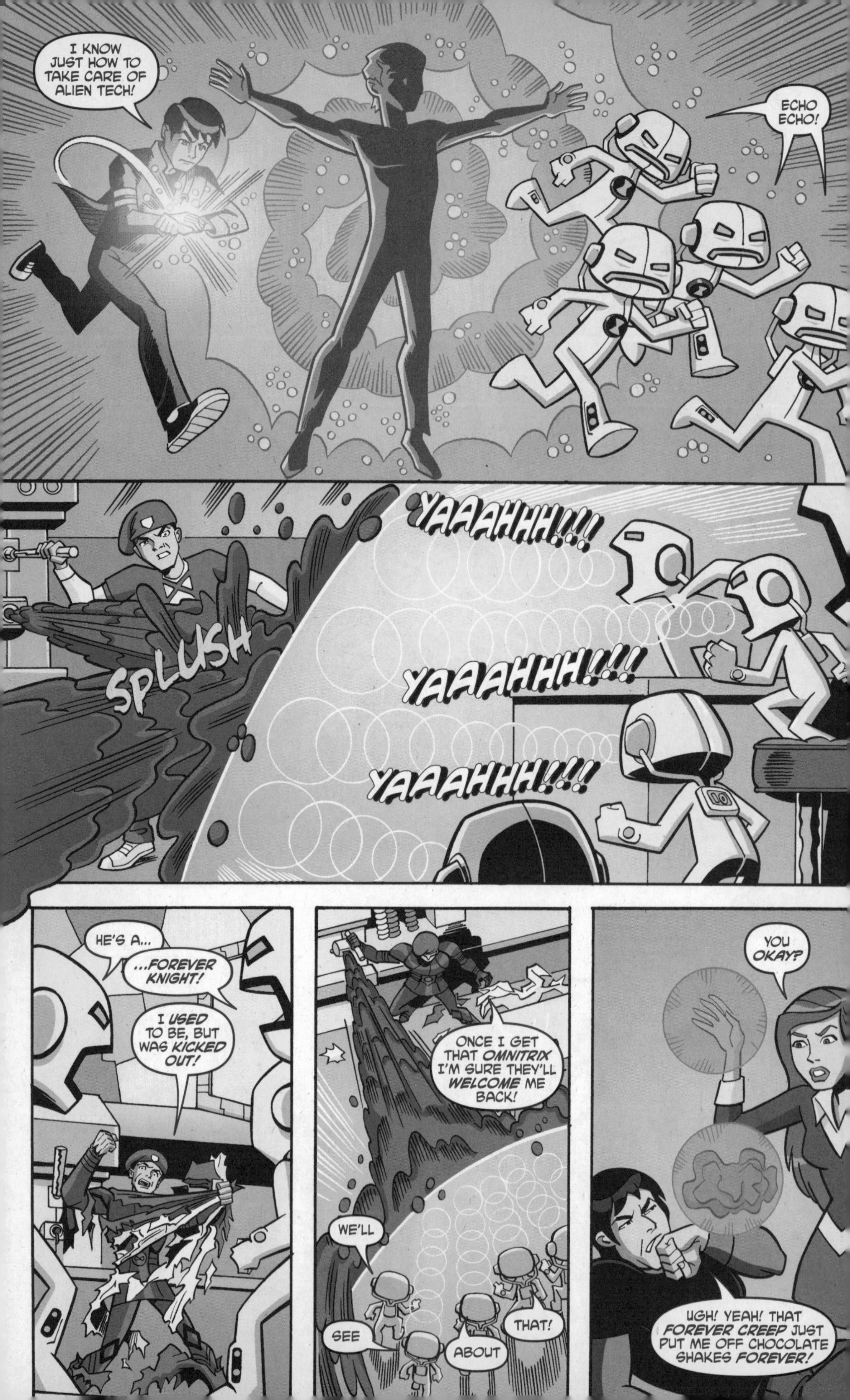
I KNOW JUST HOW TO TAKE CARE OF ALIEN TECH!
ECHO ECHO!
YAAAHHH!!!!
SPLUSH
YAAAHHH!!!!
YAAAHHH!!!!
HE'S A...
...FOREVER KNIGHT!
I USED TO BE, BUT WAS KICKED OUT!
ONCE I GET THAT OMNITRIX I'M SURE THEY'LL WELCOME ME BACK!
WE'LL
SEE
ABOUT
THAT!
YOU OKAY?
UGH! YEAH! THAT FOREVER CREEP JUST PUT ME OFF CHOCOLATE SHAKES FOREVER!

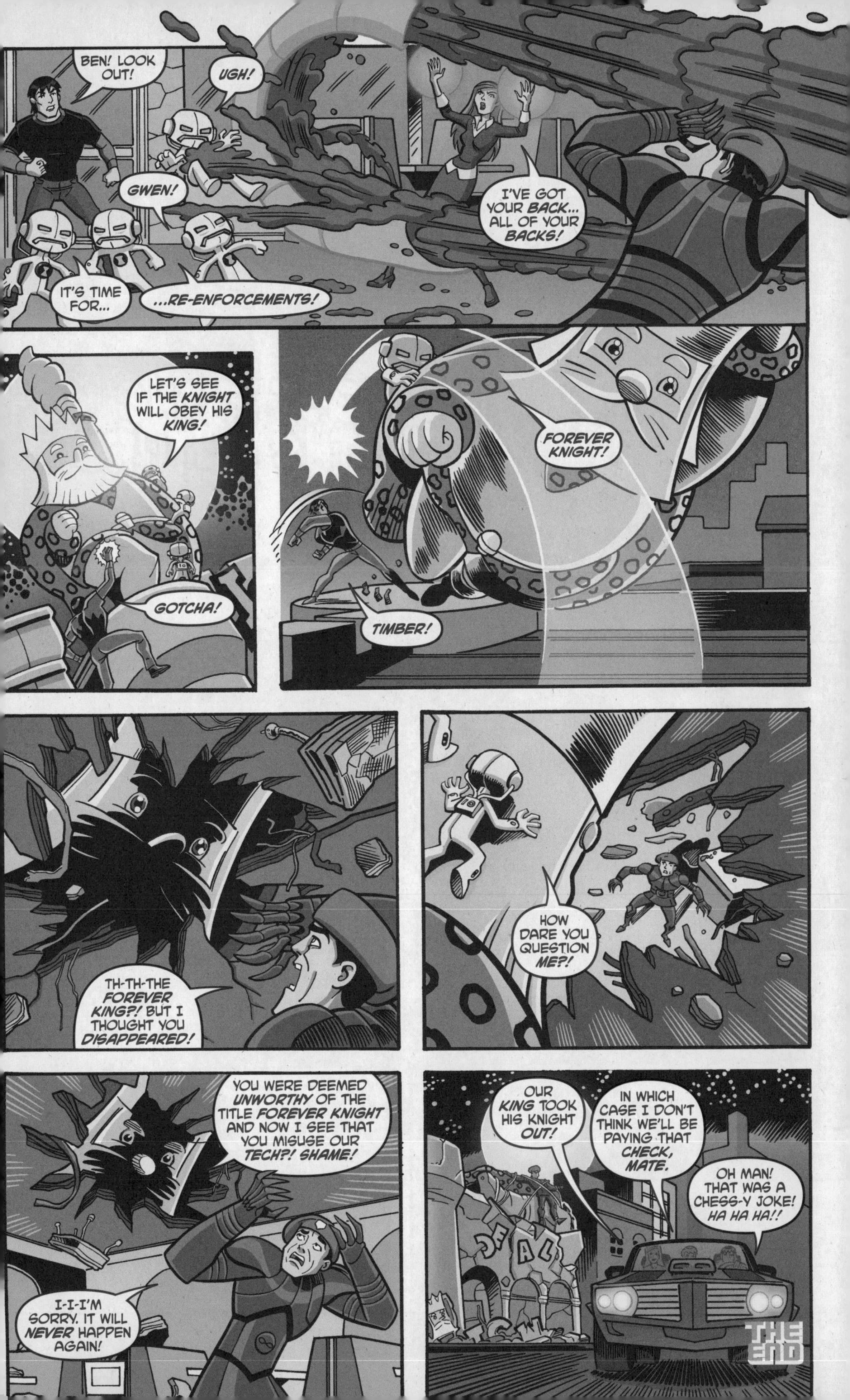

BEN! LOOK OUT!
UGH!
GWEN!
I'VE GOT YOUR BACK... ALL OF YOUR BACKS!
IT'S TIME FOR...
...RE-ENFORCEMENTS!
LET'S SEE IF THE KNIGHT WILL OBEY HIS KING!
GOTCHA!
FOREVER KNIGHT!
TIMBER!
TH-TH-THE FOREVER KING?! BUT I THOUGHT YOU DISAPPEARED!
HOW DARE YOU QUESTION ME?!
YOU WERE DEEMED UNWORTHY OF THE TITLE FOREVER KNIGHT AND NOW I SEE THAT YOU MISUSE OUR TECH?! SHAME!
I-I-I'M SORRY. IT WILL NEVER HAPPEN AGAIN!
OUR KING TOOK HIS KNIGHT OUT!
IN WHICH CASE I DON'T THINK WE'LL BE PAYING THAT CHECK, MATE.
OH MAN! THAT WAS A CHESS-Y JOKE! HA HA HA!!
THE END

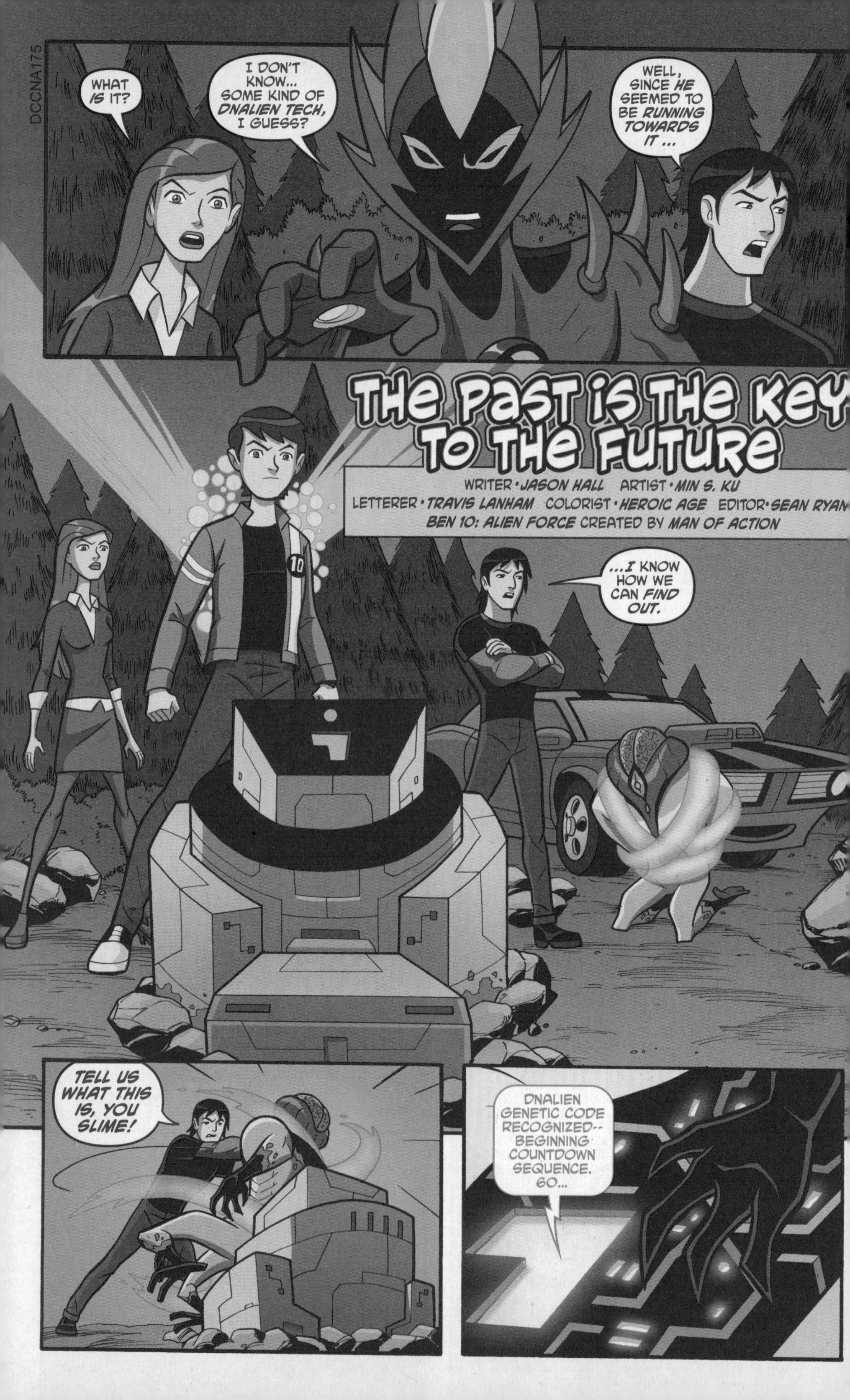
DCCNA175
WHAT IS IT?
I DON'T KNOW... SOME KIND OF DNALIEN TECH, I GUESS?
WELL, SINCE HE SEEMED TO BE RUNNING TOWARDS IT ...
THE PAST IS THE KEY TO THE FUTURE
WRITER • JASON HALL ARTIST • MIN S. KU
LETTERER • TRAVIS LANHAM COLORIST • HEROIC AGE EDITOR • SEAN RYAN
BEN 10: ALIEN FORCE CREATED BY MAN OF ACTION
...I KNOW HOW WE CAN FIND OUT.
TELL US WHAT THIS IS, YOU SLIME!
DNALIEN GENETIC CODE RECOGNIZED-- BEGINNING COUNTDOWN SEQUENCE. 60...

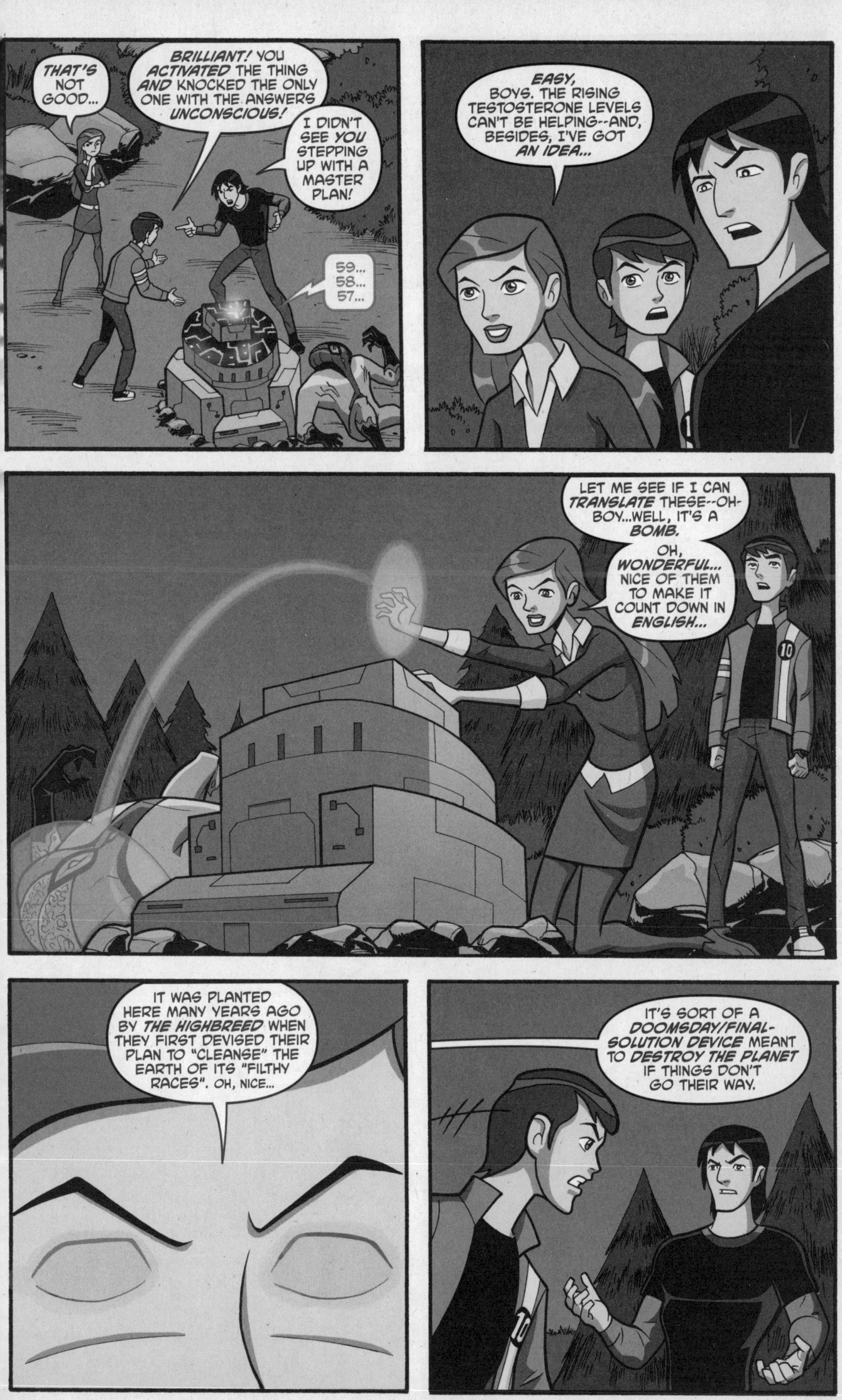
THAT'S NOT GOOD...
BRILLIANT! YOU ACTIVATED THE THING AND KNOCKED THE ONLY ONE WITH THE ANSWERS UNCONSCIOUS!
I DIDN'T SEE YOU STEPPING UP WITH A MASTER PLAN!
59... 58... 57...
EASY, BOYS. THE RISING TESTOSTERONE LEVELS CAN'T BE HELPING--AND, BESIDES, I'VE GOT AN IDEA...
LET ME SEE IF I CAN TRANSLATE THESE--OH-BOY...WELL, IT'S A BOMB.
OH, WONDERFUL... NICE OF THEM TO MAKE IT COUNT DOWN IN ENGLISH...
IT WAS PLANTED HERE MANY YEARS AGO BY THE HIGHBREED WHEN THEY FIRST DEVISED THEIR PLAN TO "CLEANSE" THE EARTH OF ITS "FILTHY RACES". OH, NICE...
IT'S SORT OF A DOOMSDAY/FINAL-SOLUTION DEVICE MEANT TO DESTROY THE PLANET IF THINGS DON'T GO THEIR WAY.

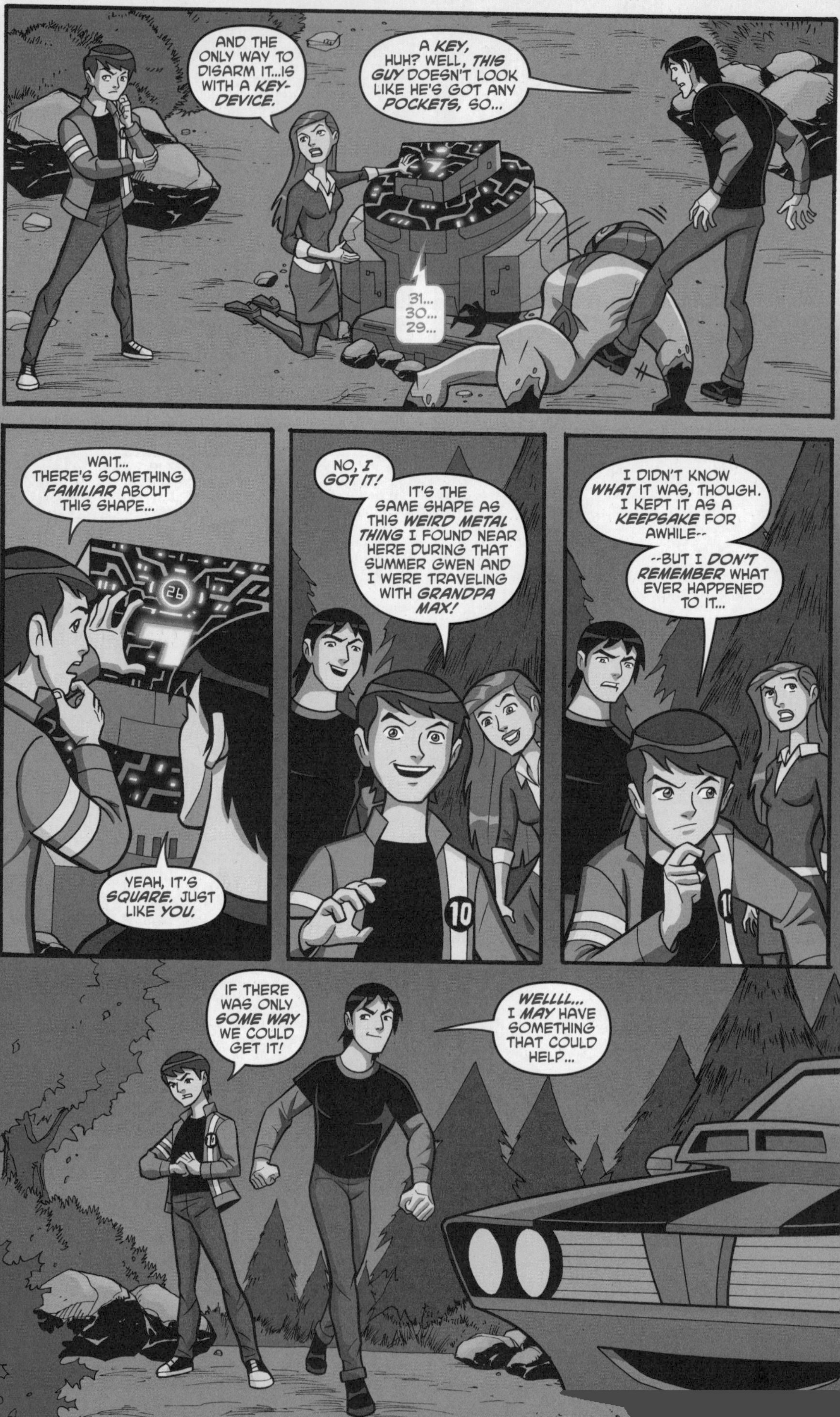
AND THE ONLY WAY TO DISARM IT...IS WITH A KEY-DEVICE.
A KEY, HUH? WELL, THIS GUY DOESN'T LOOK LIKE HE'S GOT ANY POCKETS, SO...
31... 30... 29...
WAIT... THERE'S SOMETHING FAMILIAR ABOUT THIS SHAPE...
26
YEAH, IT'S SQUARE. JUST LIKE YOU.
NO, I GOT IT!
IT'S THE SAME SHAPE AS THIS WEIRD METAL THING I FOUND NEAR HERE DURING THAT SUMMER GWEN AND I WERE TRAVELING WITH GRANDPA MAX!
I DIDN'T KNOW WHAT IT WAS, THOUGH. I KEPT IT AS A KEEPSAKE FOR AWHILE--
--BUT I DON'T REMEMBER WHAT EVER HAPPENED TO IT...
IF THERE WAS ONLY SOME WAY WE COULD GET IT!
WELLLL... I MAY HAVE SOMETHING THAT COULD HELP...

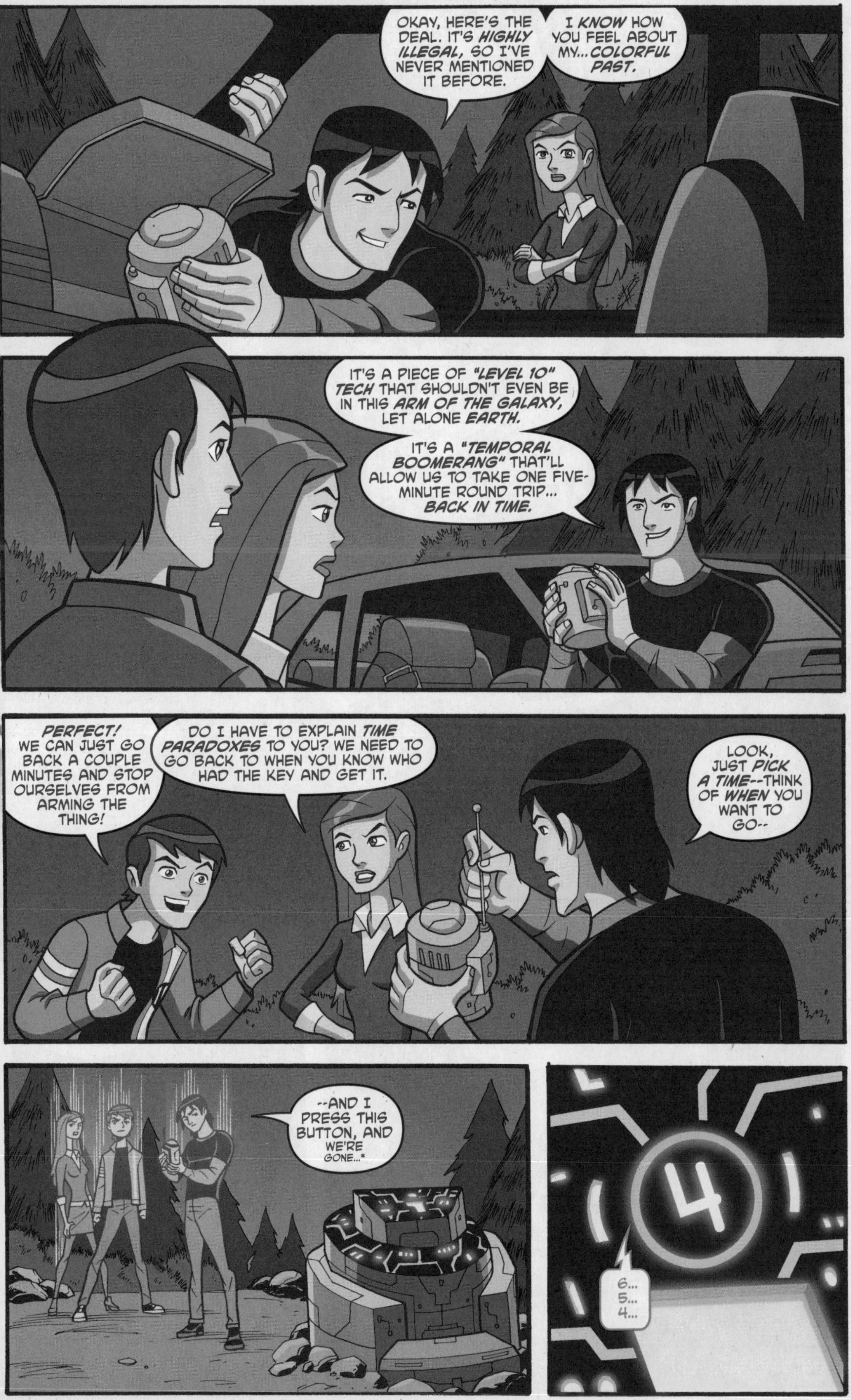
OKAY, HERE'S THE DEAL. IT'S HIGHLY ILLEGAL, SO I'VE NEVER MENTIONED IT BEFORE.
I KNOW HOW YOU FEEL ABOUT MY...COLORFUL PAST.
IT'S A PIECE OF "LEVEL 10" TECH THAT SHOULDN'T EVEN BE IN THIS ARM OF THE GALAXY, LET ALONE EARTH.
IT'S A "TEMPORAL BOOMERANG" THAT'LL ALLOW US TO TAKE ONE FIVE-MINUTE ROUND TRIP... BACK IN TIME.
PERFECT! WE CAN JUST GO BACK A COUPLE MINUTES AND STOP OURSELVES FROM ARMING THE THING!
DO I HAVE TO EXPLAIN TIME PARADOXES TO YOU? WE NEED TO GO BACK TO WHEN YOU KNOW WHO HAD THE KEY AND GET IT.
LOOK, JUST PICK A TIME--THINK OF WHEN YOU WANT TO GO--
--AND I PRESS THIS BUTTON, AND WE'RE GONE...*
4
6... 5... 4...

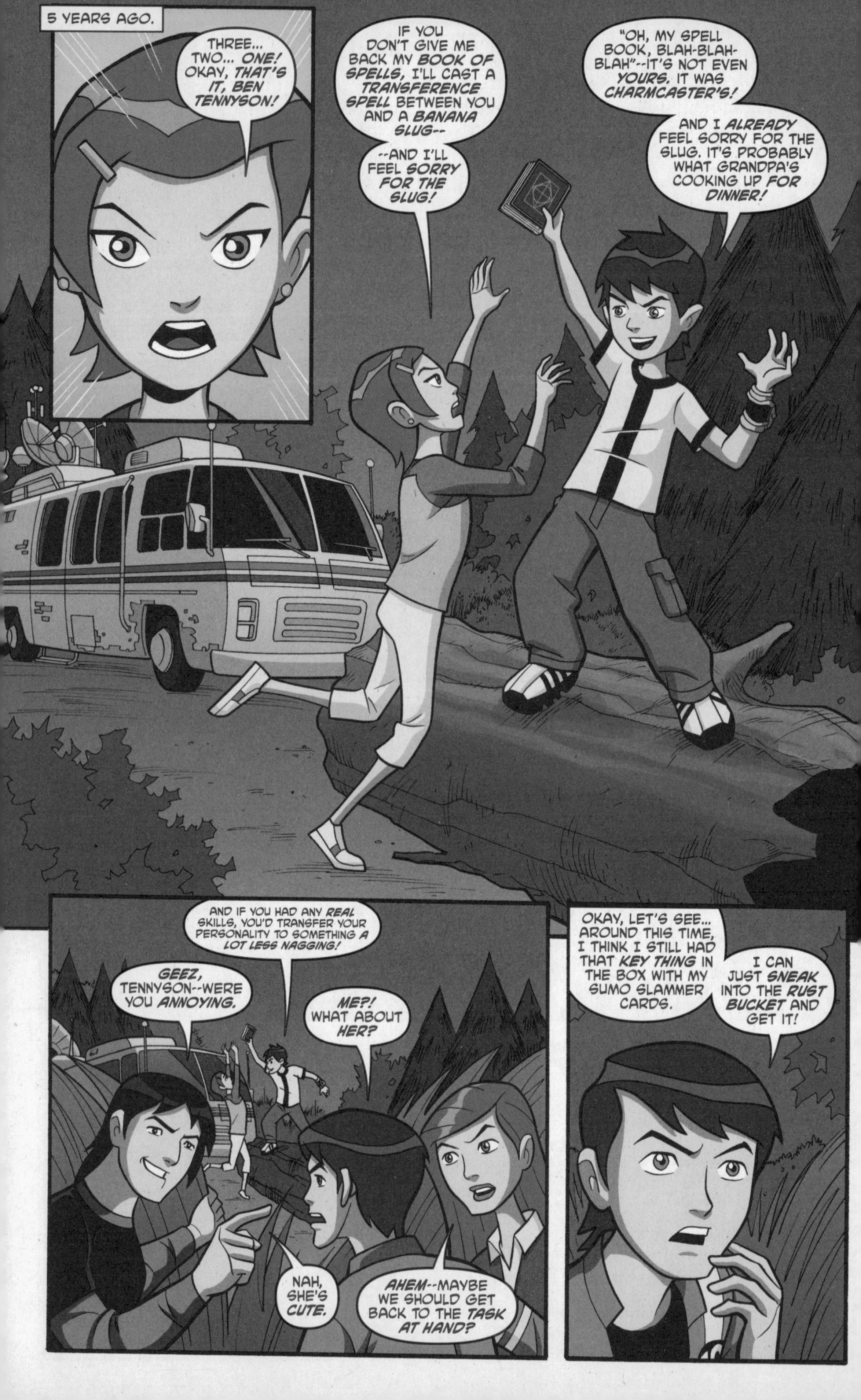
5 YEARS AGO.
THREE... TWO... ONE! OKAY, THAT'S IT, BEN TENNYSON!
IF YOU DON'T GIVE ME BACK MY BOOK OF SPELLS, I'LL CAST A TRANSFERENCE SPELL BETWEEN YOU AND A BANANA SLUG--
--AND I'LL FEEL SORRY FOR THE SLUG!
"OH, MY SPELL BOOK, BLAH-BLAH-BLAH"--IT'S NOT EVEN YOURS. IT WAS CHARMCASTER'S!
AND I ALREADY FEEL SORRY FOR THE SLUG. IT'S PROBABLY WHAT GRANDPA'S COOKING UP FOR DINNER!
AND IF YOU HAD ANY REAL SKILLS, YOU'D TRANSFER YOUR PERSONALITY TO SOMETHING A LOT LESS NAGGING!
GEEZ, TENNYSON--WERE YOU ANNOYING.
ME?! WHAT ABOUT HER?
NAH, SHE'S CUTE.
AHEM--MAYBE WE SHOULD GET BACK TO THE TASK AT HAND?
OKAY, LET'S SEE... AROUND THIS TIME, I THINK I STILL HAD THAT KEY THING IN THE BOX WITH MY SUMO SLAMMER CARDS.
I CAN JUST SNEAK INTO THE RUST BUCKET AND GET IT!

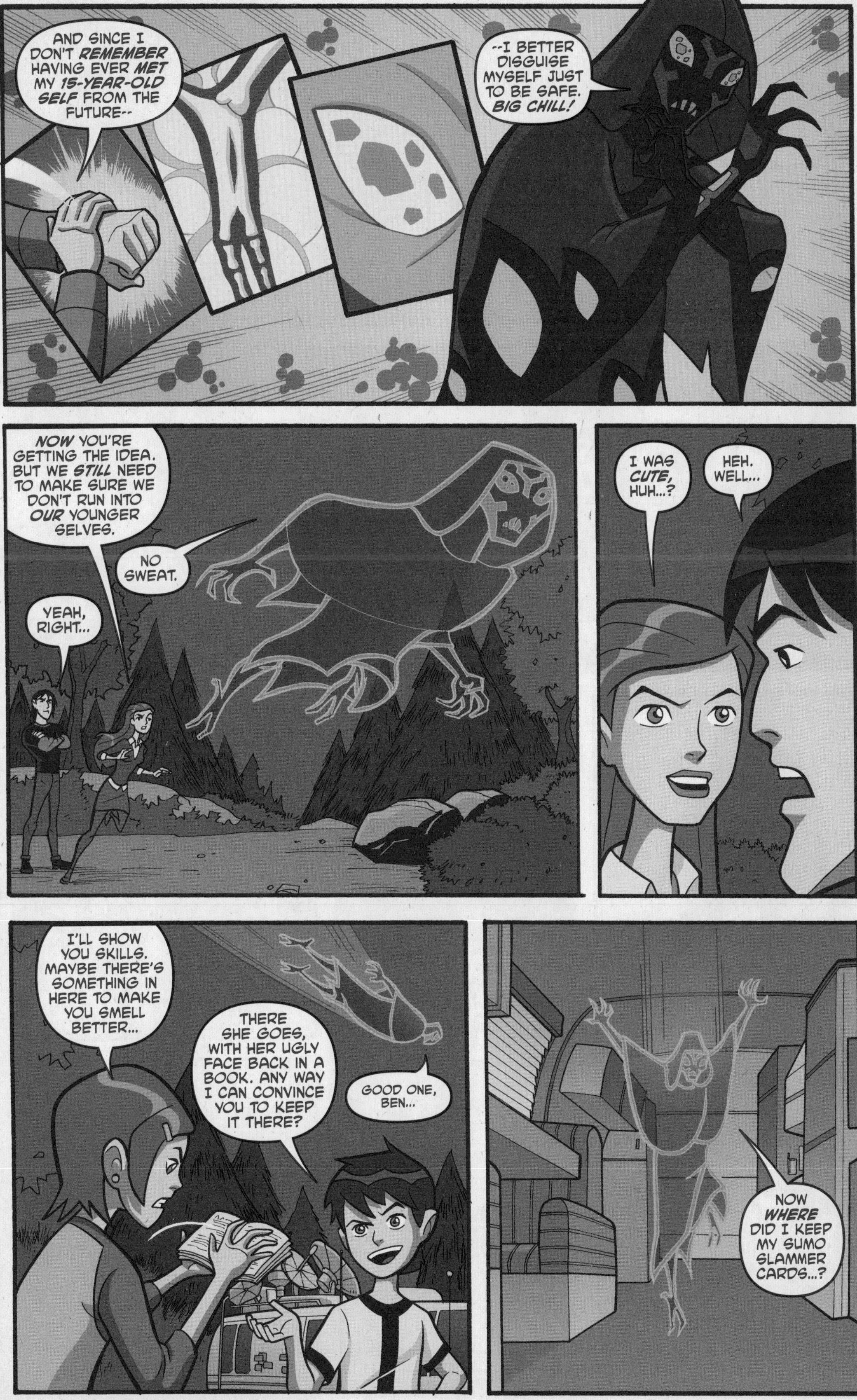
AND SINCE I DON'T REMEMBER HAVING EVER MET MY 15-YEAR-OLD SELF FROM THE FUTURE--
--I BETTER DISGUISE MYSELF JUST TO BE SAFE. BIG CHILL!
NOW YOU'RE GETTING THE IDEA. BUT WE STILL NEED TO MAKE SURE WE DON'T RUN INTO OUR YOUNGER SELVES.
NO SWEAT.
YEAH, RIGHT...
I WAS CUTE, HUH...?
HEH. WELL...
I'LL SHOW YOU SKILLS. MAYBE THERE'S SOMETHING IN HERE TO MAKE YOU SMELL BETTER...
THERE SHE GOES, WITH HER UGLY FACE BACK IN A BOOK. ANY WAY I CAN CONVINCE YOU TO KEEP IT THERE?
GOOD ONE, BEN...
NOW WHERE DID I KEEP MY SUMO SLAMMER CARDS...?

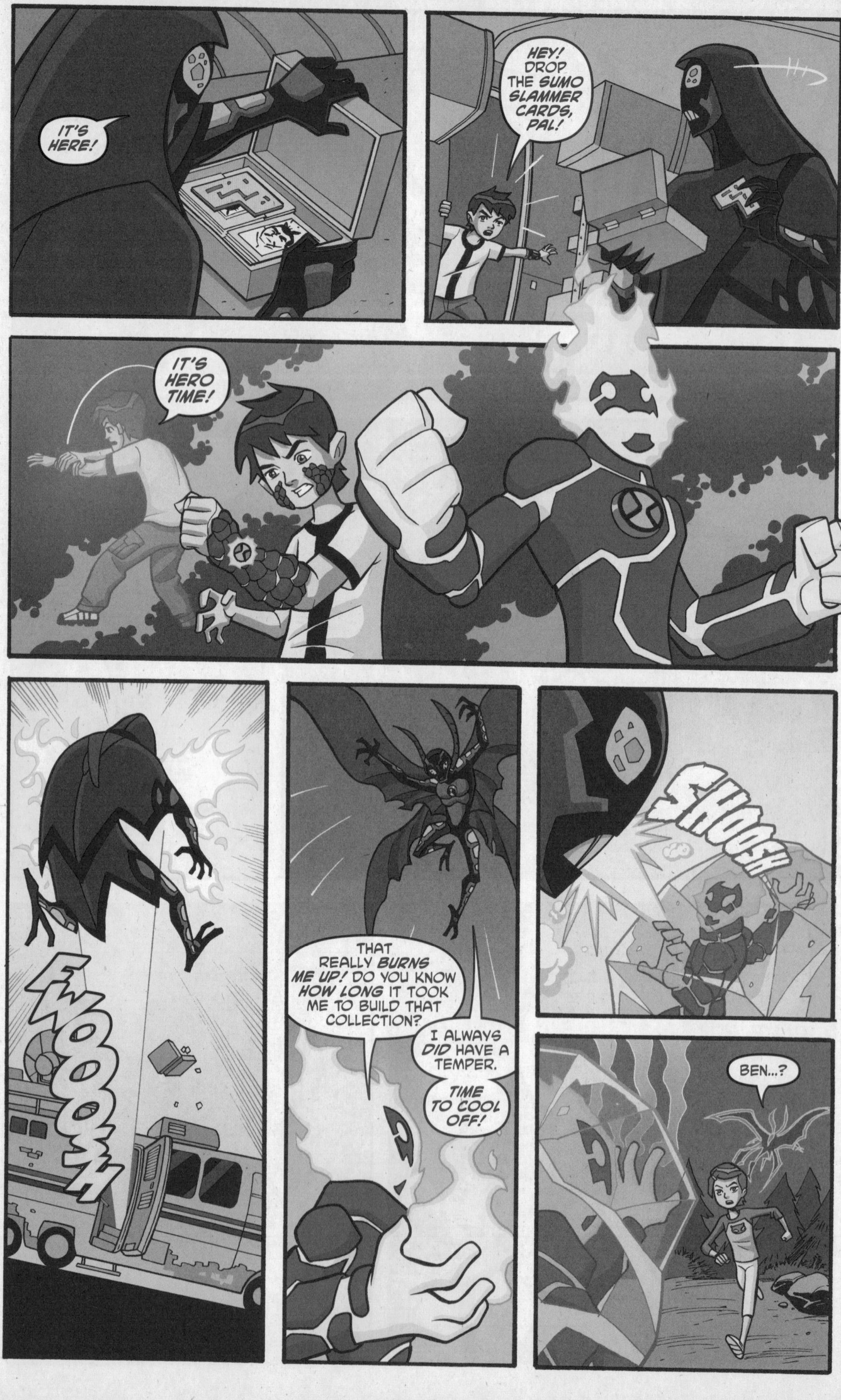
IT'S HERE!
HEY! DROP THE SUMO SLAMMER CARDS, PAL!
IT'S HERO TIME!
FWOOOOMH
THAT REALLY BURNS ME UP! DO YOU KNOW HOW LONG IT TOOK ME TO BUILD THAT COLLECTION?
I ALWAYS DID HAVE A TEMPER.
TIME TO COOL OFF!
SHOOSH
BEN...?

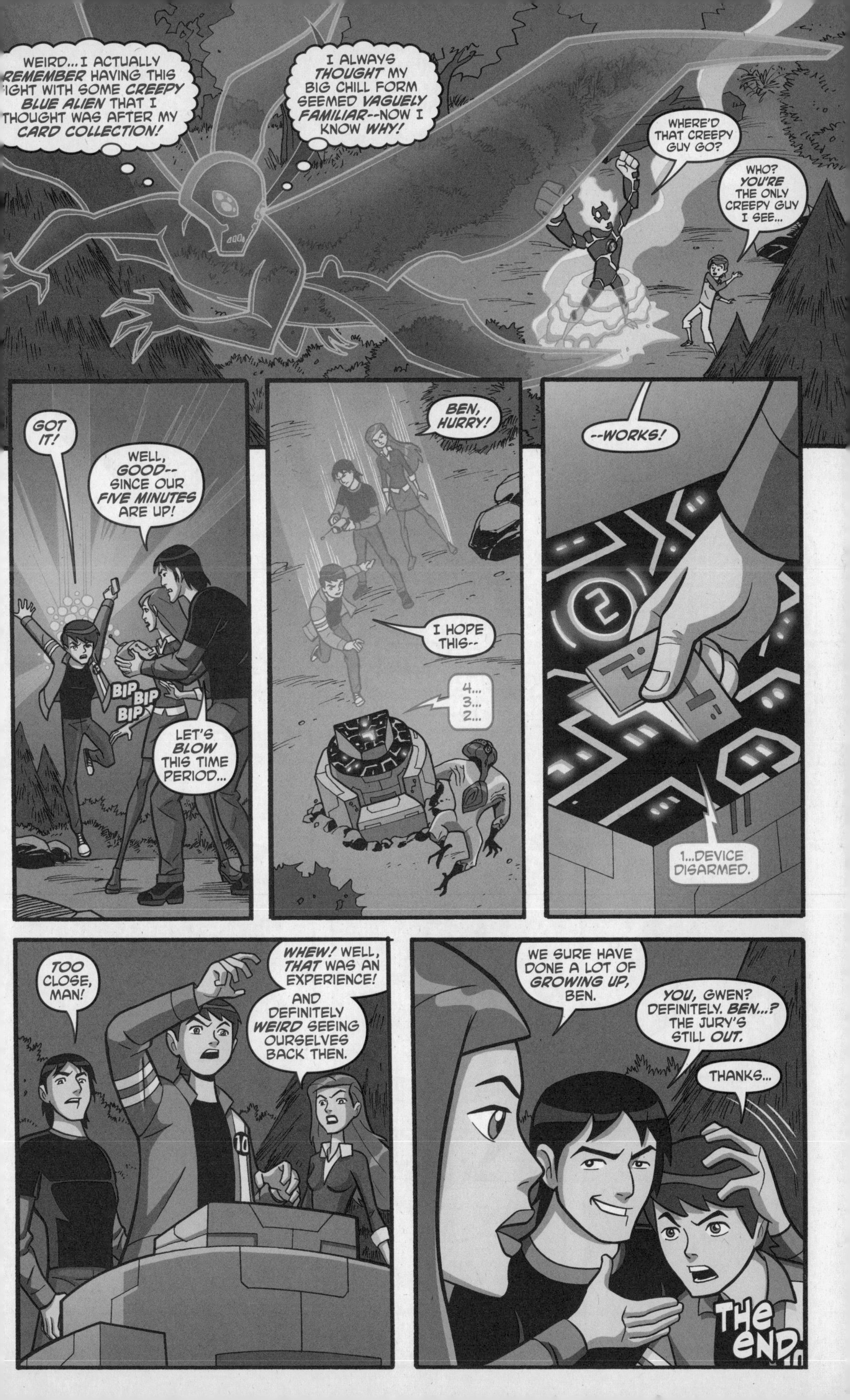
WEIRD... I ACTUALLY REMEMBER HAVING THIS FIGHT WITH SOME CREEPY BLUE ALIEN THAT I THOUGHT WAS AFTER MY CARD COLLECTION!
I ALWAYS THOUGHT MY BIG CHILL FORM SEEMED VAGUELY FAMILIAR--NOW I KNOW WHY!
WHERE'D THAT CREEPY GUY GO?
WHO? YOU'RE THE ONLY CREEPY GUY I SEE...
GOT IT!
WELL, GOOD-- SINCE OUR FIVE MINUTES ARE UP!
BIP BIP BIP
LET'S BLOW THIS TIME PERIOD...
BEN, HURRY!
I HOPE THIS--
4... 3... 2...
--WORKS!
1...DEVICE DISARMED.
TOO CLOSE, MAN!
WHEW! WELL, THAT WAS AN EXPERIENCE!
AND DEFINITELY WEIRD SEEING OURSELVES BACK THEN.
WE SURE HAVE DONE A LOT OF GROWING UP, BEN.
YOU, GWEN? DEFINITELY. BEN...? THE JURY'S STILL OUT.
THANKS...
THE END

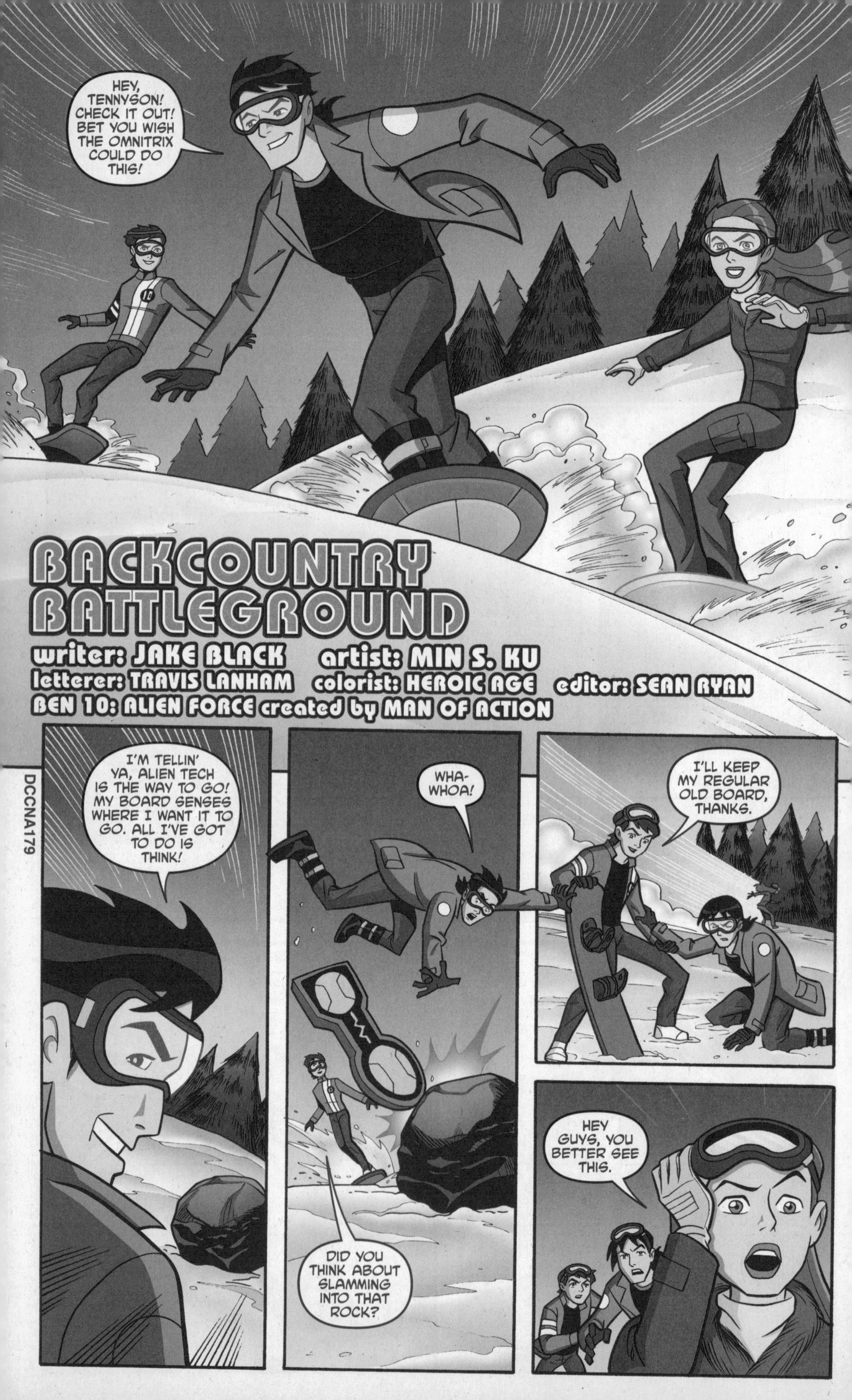
HEY, TENNYSON! CHECK IT OUT! BET YOU WISH THE OMNITRIX COULD DO THIS!
BACKCOUNTRY BATTLEGROUND
writer: JAKE BLACK artist: MIN S. KU
letterer: TRAVIS LANHAM colorist: HEROIC AGE editor: SEAN RYAN
BEN 10: ALIEN FORCE created by MAN OF ACTION
I'M TELLIN' YA, ALIEN TECH IS THE WAY TO GO! MY BOARD SENSES WHERE I WANT IT TO GO. ALL I'VE GOT TO DO IS THINK!
WHA-WHOA!
DID YOU THINK ABOUT SLAMMING INTO THAT ROCK?
I'LL KEEP MY REGULAR OLD BOARD, THANKS.
HEY GUYS, YOU BETTER SEE THIS.
DCCNA179

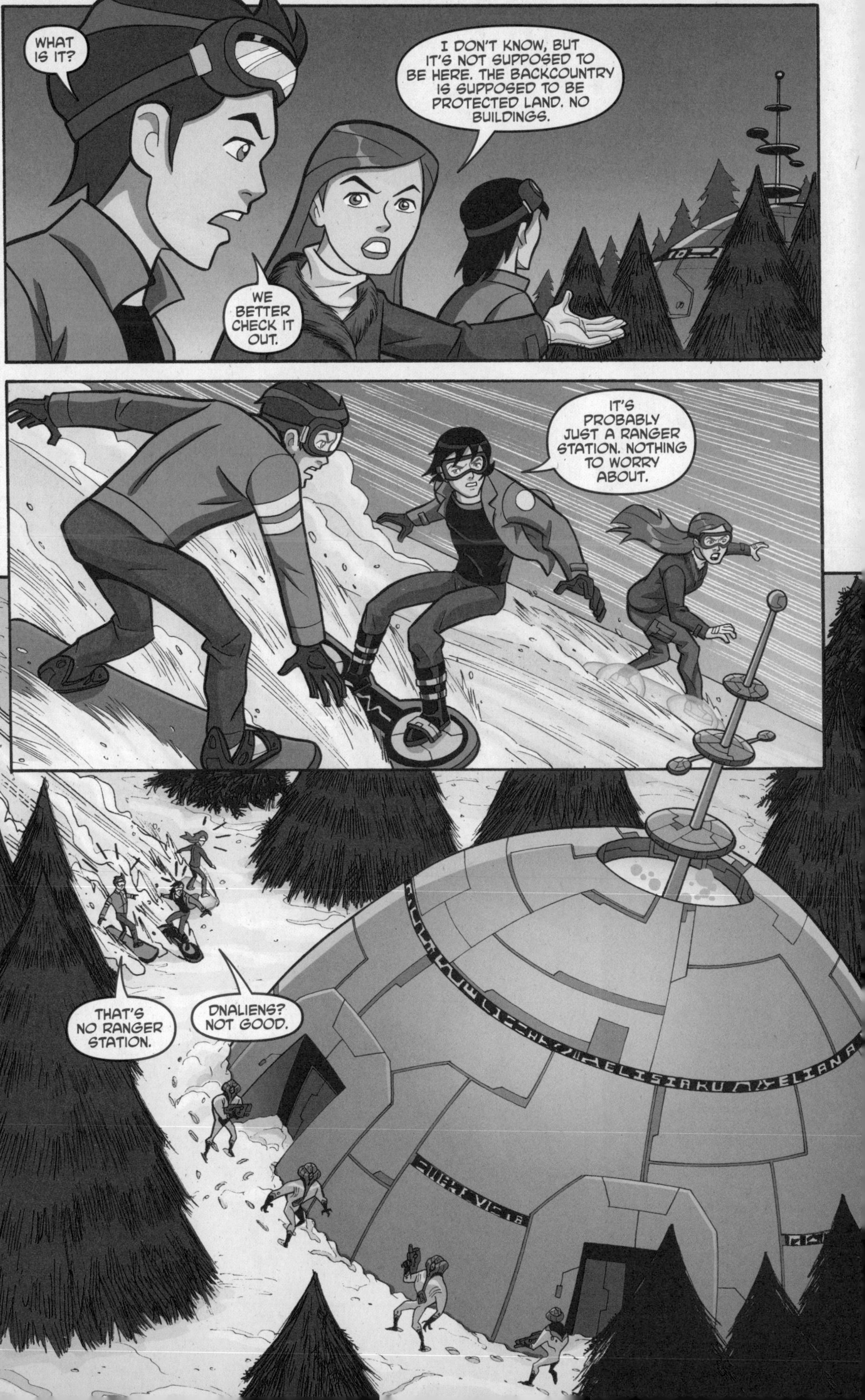
WHAT IS IT?
I DON'T KNOW, BUT IT'S NOT SUPPOSED TO BE HERE. THE BACKCOUNTRY IS SUPPOSED TO BE PROTECTED LAND. NO BUILDINGS.
WE BETTER CHECK IT OUT.
IT'S PROBABLY JUST A RANGER STATION. NOTHING TO WORRY ABOUT.
THAT'S NO RANGER STATION.
DNALIENS? NOT GOOD.

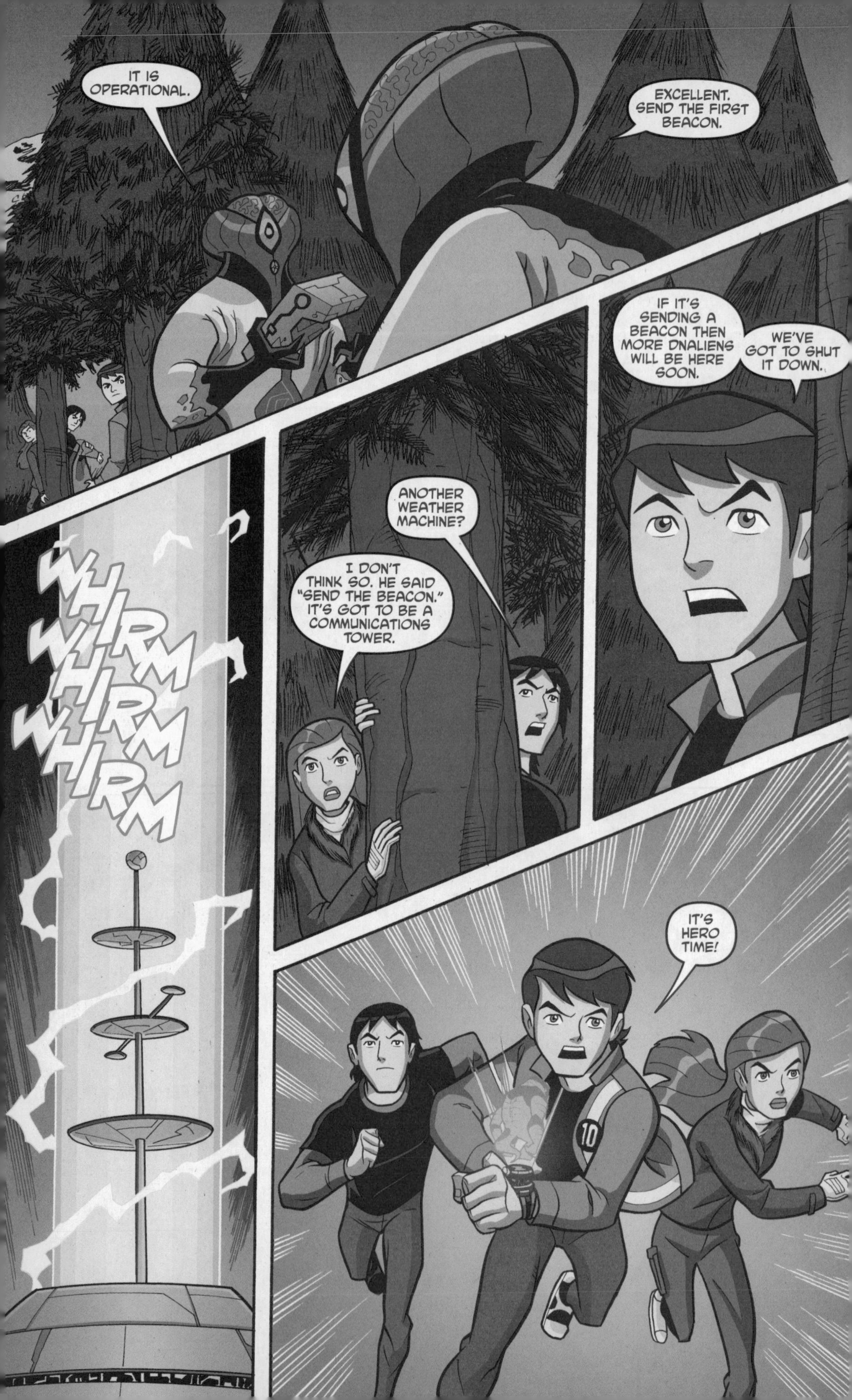
IT IS OPERATIONAL.
EXCELLENT. SEND THE FIRST BEACON.
IF IT'S SENDING A BEACON THEN MORE DNALIENS WILL BE HERE SOON.
WE'VE GOT TO SHUT IT DOWN.
ANOTHER WEATHER MACHINE?
I DON'T THINK SO. HE SAID "SEND THE BEACON." IT'S GOT TO BE A COMMUNICATIONS TOWER.
WHIRM WHIRM WHIRM
IT'S HERO TIME!

BEN TENNYSON!

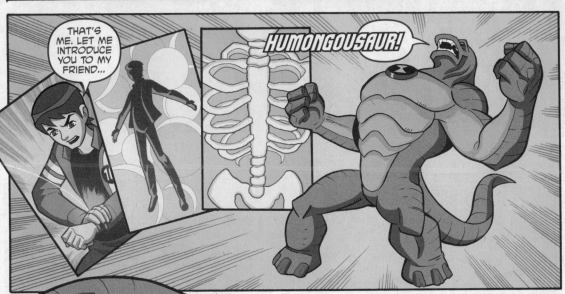

THAT'S ME. LET ME INTRODUCE YOU TO MY FRIEND...

HUMONGOUSAUR!

TURN OFF THE BEACON!

IT'S TOO LATE.

WHAT DO YOU MEAN IT'S TOO LATE?

ONCE THE BEACON HAS BEEN ACTIVATED, IT CANNOT BE TURNED OFF!

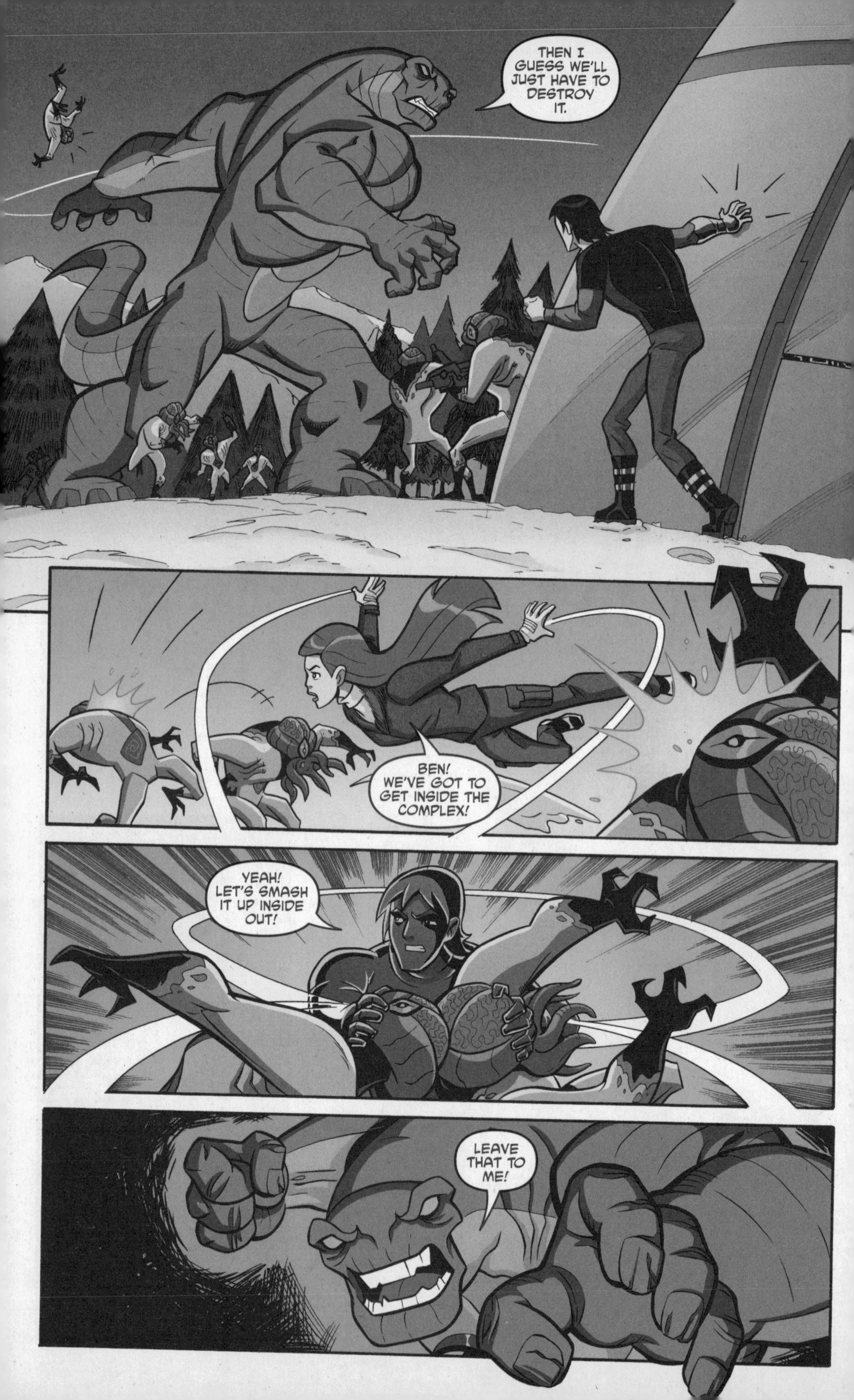
THEN I GUESS WE'LL JUST HAVE TO DESTROY IT.
BEN! WE'VE GOT TO GET INSIDE THE COMPLEX!
YEAH! LET'S SMASH IT UP INSIDE OUT!
LEAVE THAT TO ME!

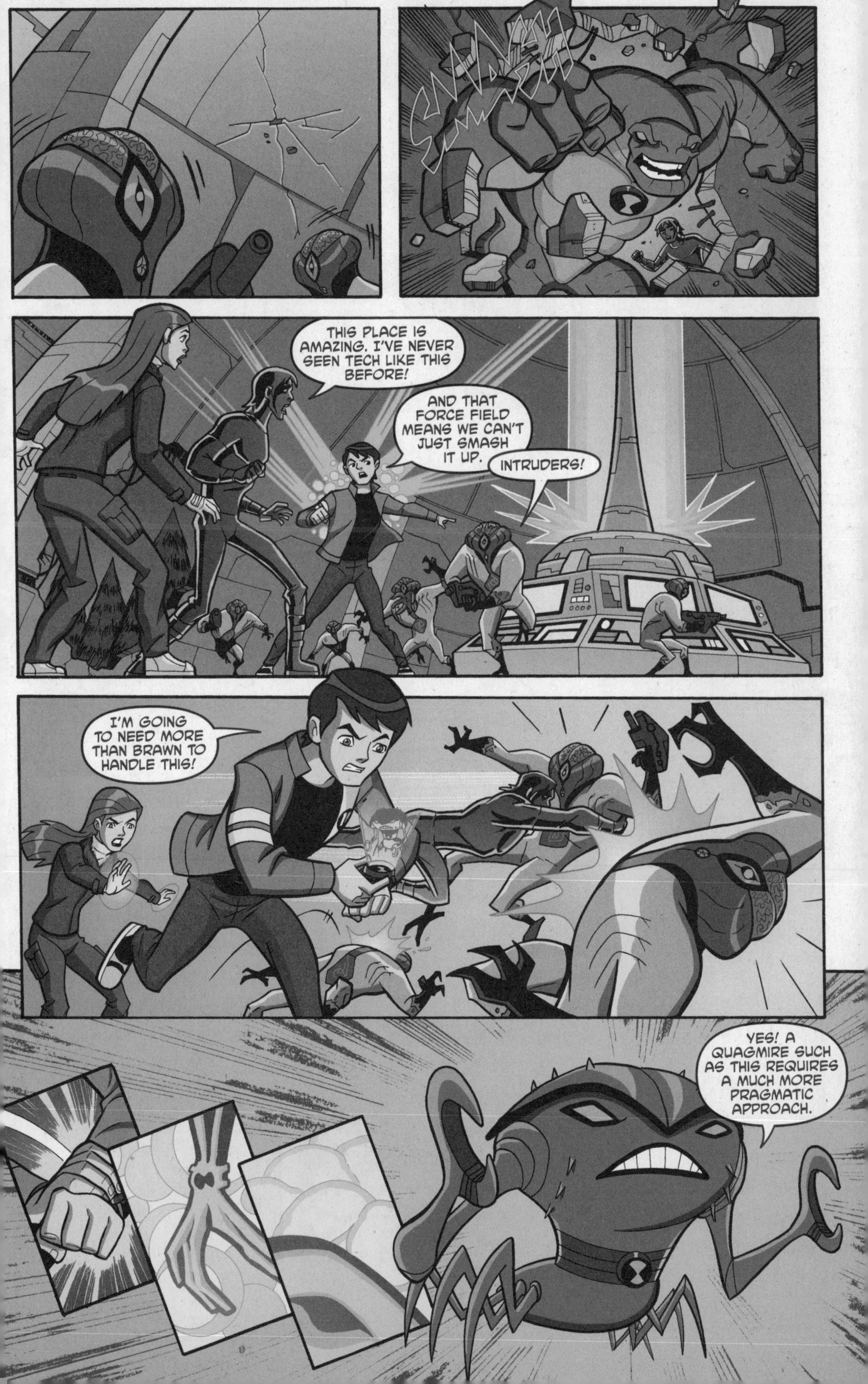
THIS PLACE IS AMAZING. I'VE NEVER SEEN TECH LIKE THIS BEFORE!
AND THAT FORCE FIELD MEANS WE CAN'T JUST SMASH IT UP.
INTRUDERS!
I'M GOING TO NEED MORE THAN BRAWN TO HANDLE THIS!
YES! A QUAGMIRE SUCH AS THIS REQUIRES A MUCH MORE PRAGMATIC APPROACH.

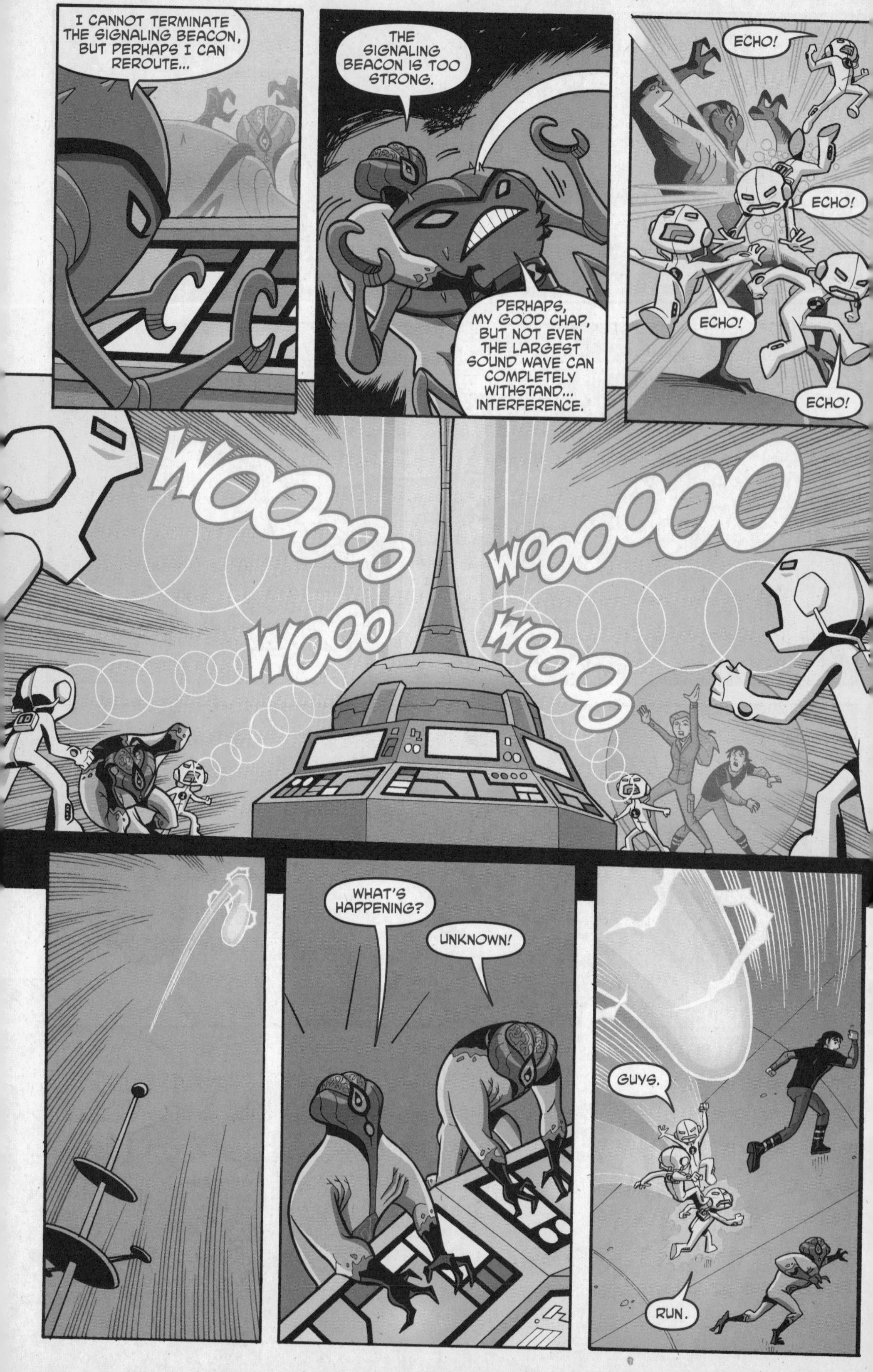
I CANNOT TERMINATE THE SIGNALING BEACON, BUT PERHAPS I CAN REROUTE...
THE SIGNALING BEACON IS TOO STRONG.
PERHAPS, MY GOOD CHAP, BUT NOT EVEN THE LARGEST SOUND WAVE CAN COMPLETELY WITHSTAND... INTERFERENCE.
ECHO!
ECHO!
ECHO!
ECHO!
WOOOOO
WOOOOOOO
WOOO
WOOOO
WHAT'S HAPPENING?
UNKNOWN!
GUYS.
RUN.

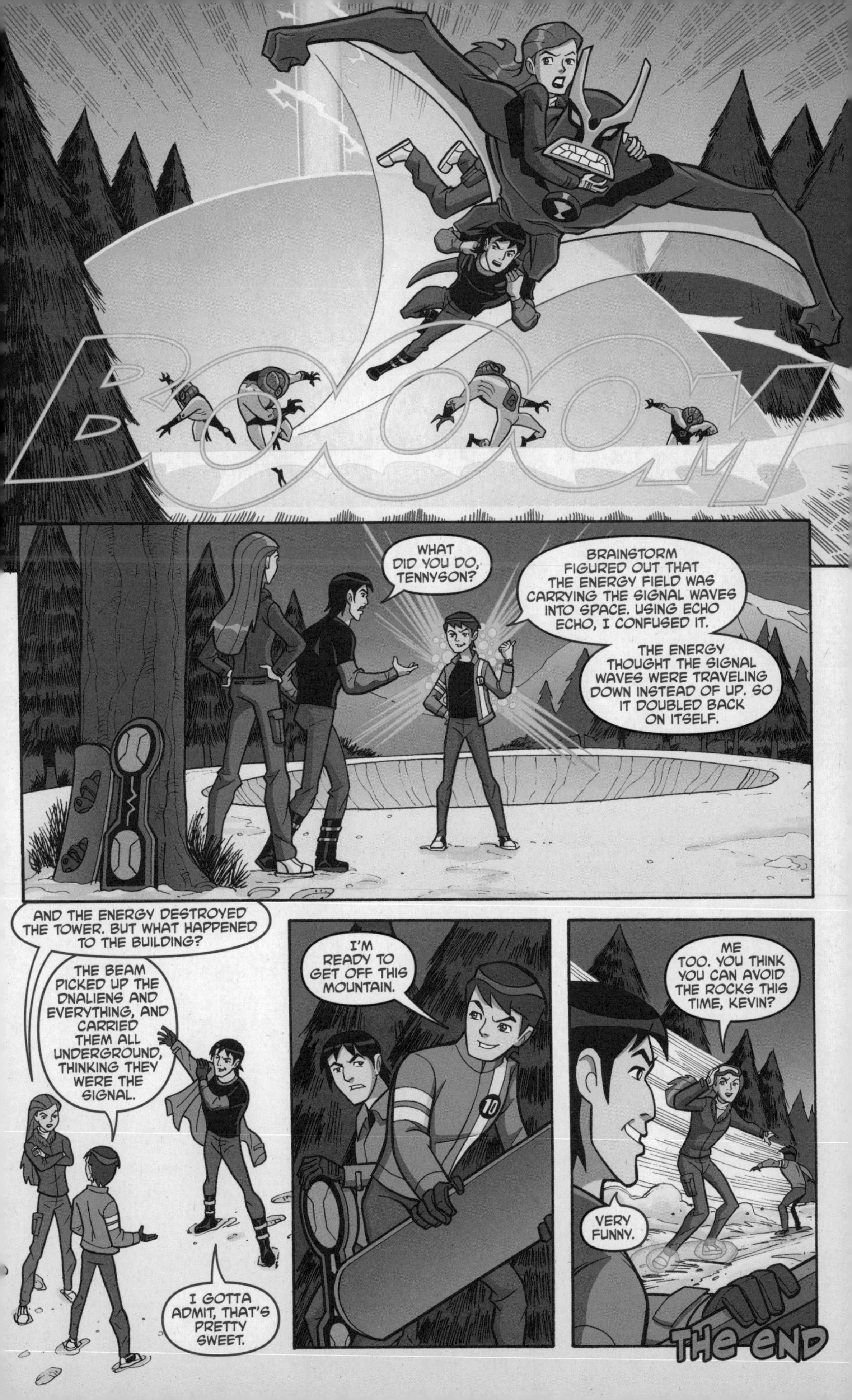
BOOOOM
WHAT DID YOU DO, TENNYSON?
BRAINSTORM FIGURED OUT THAT THE ENERGY FIELD WAS CARRYING THE SIGNAL WAVES INTO SPACE. USING ECHO ECHO, I CONFUSED IT.
THE ENERGY THOUGHT THE SIGNAL WAVES WERE TRAVELING DOWN INSTEAD OF UP. SO IT DOUBLED BACK ON ITSELF.
AND THE ENERGY DESTROYED THE TOWER. BUT WHAT HAPPENED TO THE BUILDING?
THE BEAM PICKED UP THE DNALIENS AND EVERYTHING, AND CARRIED THEM ALL UNDERGROUND, THINKING THEY WERE THE SIGNAL.
I GOTTA ADMIT, THAT'S PRETTY SWEET.
I'M READY TO GET OFF THIS MOUNTAIN.
ME TOO. YOU THINK YOU CAN AVOID THE ROCKS THIS TIME, KEVIN?
VERY FUNNY.
THE END

THE SECRET SATURDAYS ™

JAY STEPHENS BRANDON SAWYER JOHN ROZUM
WRITERS

SCOTT JERALDS MIKE MANLEY WILL SWEENEY
PENCILLERS

JAY STEPHENS MIKE MANLEY
INKERS

JAY STEPHENS HEROIC AGE
COLORISTS

Travis Lanham Sal Cipriano Randy Gentile John J. Hill
Letterers

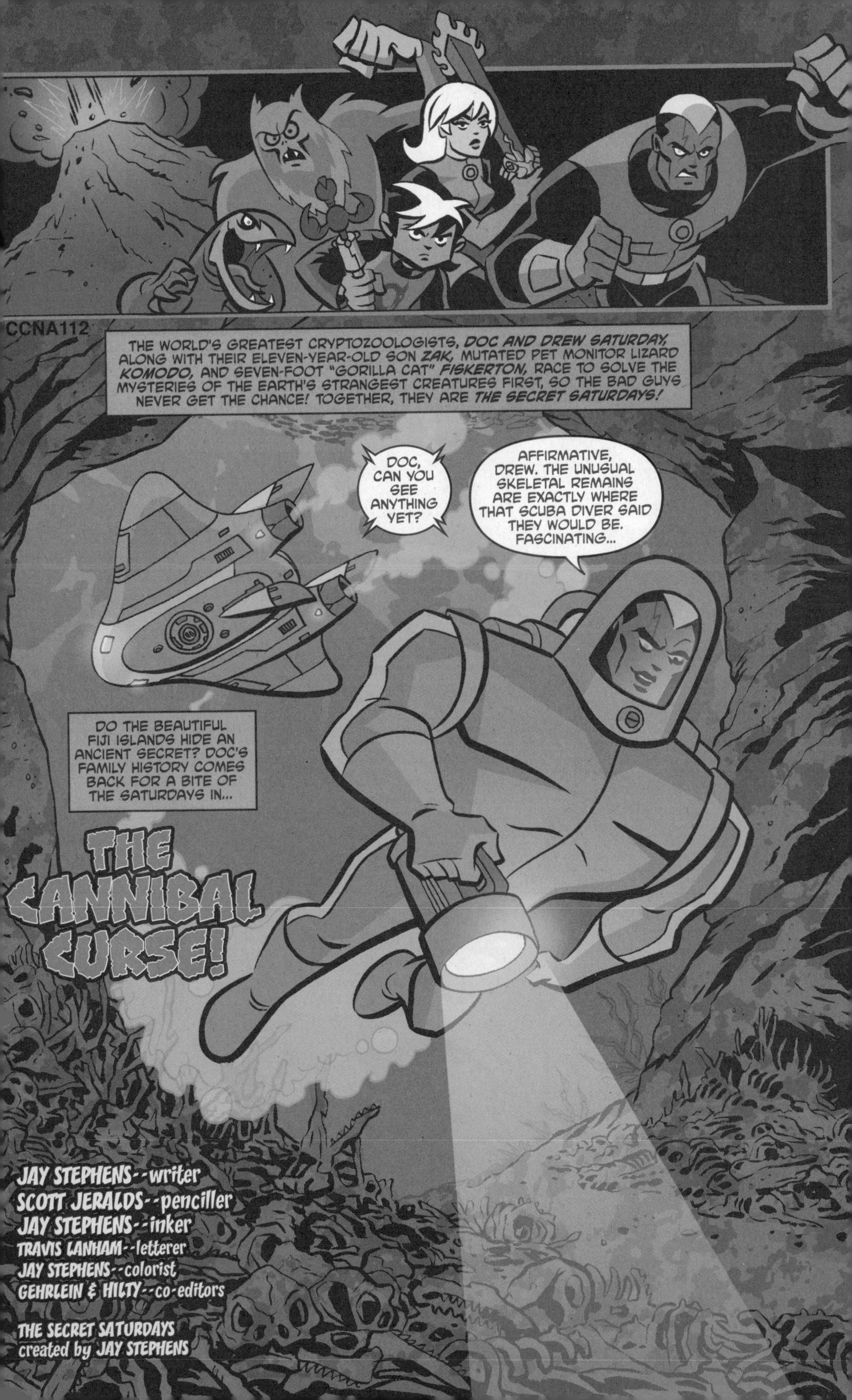
CCNA112
THE WORLD'S GREATEST CRYPTOZOOLOGISTS, DOC AND DREW SATURDAY, ALONG WITH THEIR ELEVEN-YEAR-OLD SON ZAK, MUTATED PET MONITOR LIZARD KOMODO, AND SEVEN-FOOT "GORILLA CAT" FISKERTON, RACE TO SOLVE THE MYSTERIES OF THE EARTH'S STRANGEST CREATURES FIRST, SO THE BAD GUYS NEVER GET THE CHANCE! TOGETHER, THEY ARE THE SECRET SATURDAYS!
DOC, CAN YOU SEE ANYTHING YET?
AFFIRMATIVE, DREW. THE UNUSUAL SKELETAL REMAINS ARE EXACTLY WHERE THAT SCUBA DIVER SAID THEY WOULD BE. FASCINATING...
DO THE BEAUTIFUL FIJI ISLANDS HIDE AN ANCIENT SECRET? DOC'S FAMILY HISTORY COMES BACK FOR A BITE OF THE SATURDAYS IN...
THE CANNIBAL CURSE!
JAY STEPHENS--writer
SCOTT JERALDS--penciller
JAY STEPHENS--inker
TRAVIS LANHAM--letterer
JAY STEPHENS--colorist
GEHRLEIN & HILTY--co-editors
THE SECRET SATURDAYS created by JAY STEPHENS

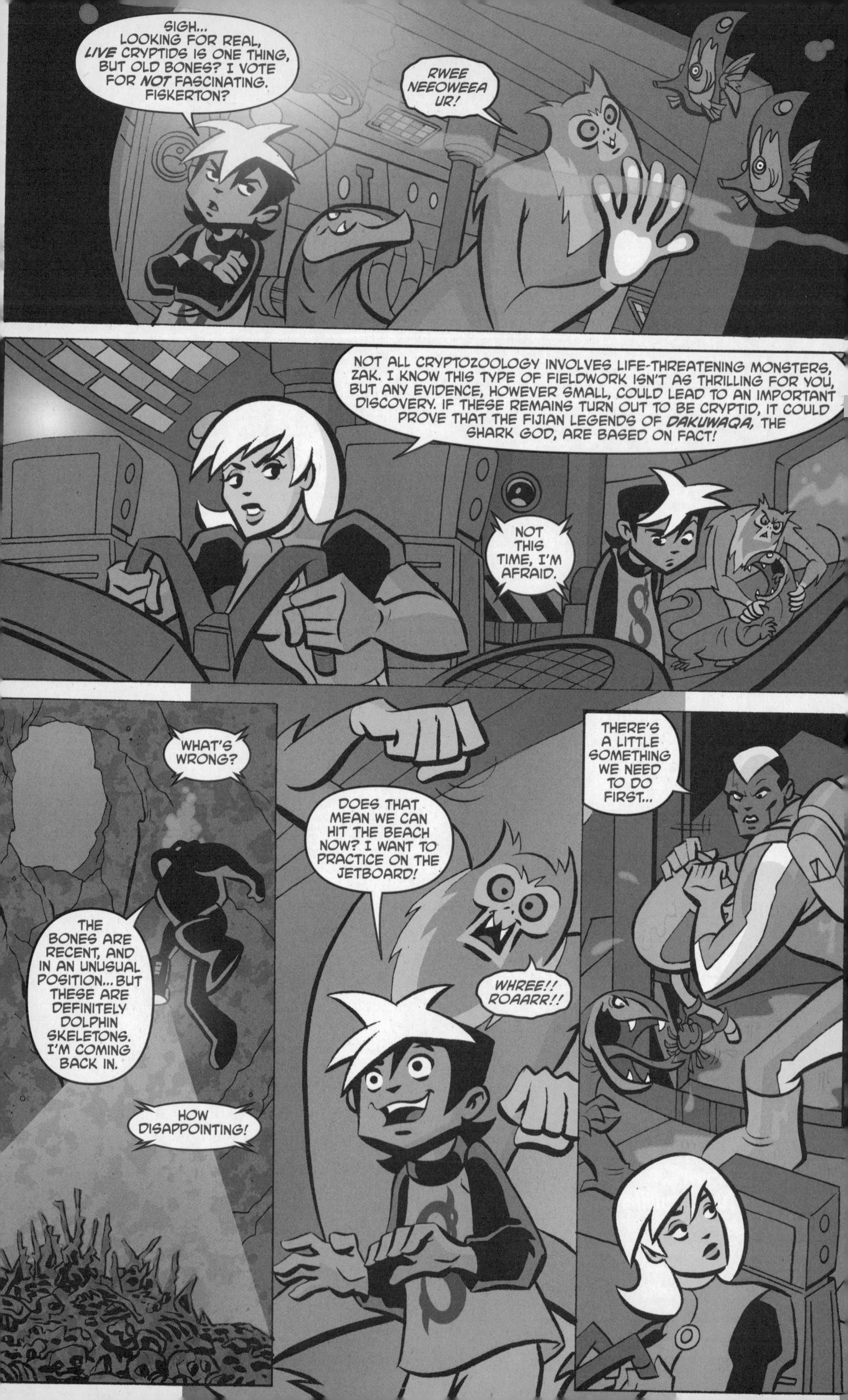
SIGH... LOOKING FOR REAL, LIVE CRYPTIDS IS ONE THING, BUT OLD BONES? I VOTE FOR NOT FASCINATING. FISKERTON?
RWEE NEEOWEEA UR!
NOT ALL CRYPTOZOOLOGY INVOLVES LIFE-THREATENING MONSTERS, ZAK. I KNOW THIS TYPE OF FIELDWORK ISN'T AS THRILLING FOR YOU, BUT ANY EVIDENCE, HOWEVER SMALL, COULD LEAD TO AN IMPORTANT DISCOVERY. IF THESE REMAINS TURN OUT TO BE CRYPTID, IT COULD PROVE THAT THE FIJIAN LEGENDS OF DAKUWAQA, THE SHARK GOD, ARE BASED ON FACT!
NOT THIS TIME, I'M AFRAID.
WHAT'S WRONG?
THE BONES ARE RECENT, AND IN AN UNUSUAL POSITION... BUT THESE ARE DEFINITELY DOLPHIN SKELETONS. I'M COMING BACK IN.
HOW DISAPPOINTING!
DOES THAT MEAN WE CAN HIT THE BEACH NOW? I WANT TO PRACTICE ON THE JETBOARD!
WHREE!! ROAARR!!
THERE'S A LITTLE SOMETHING WE NEED TO DO FIRST...

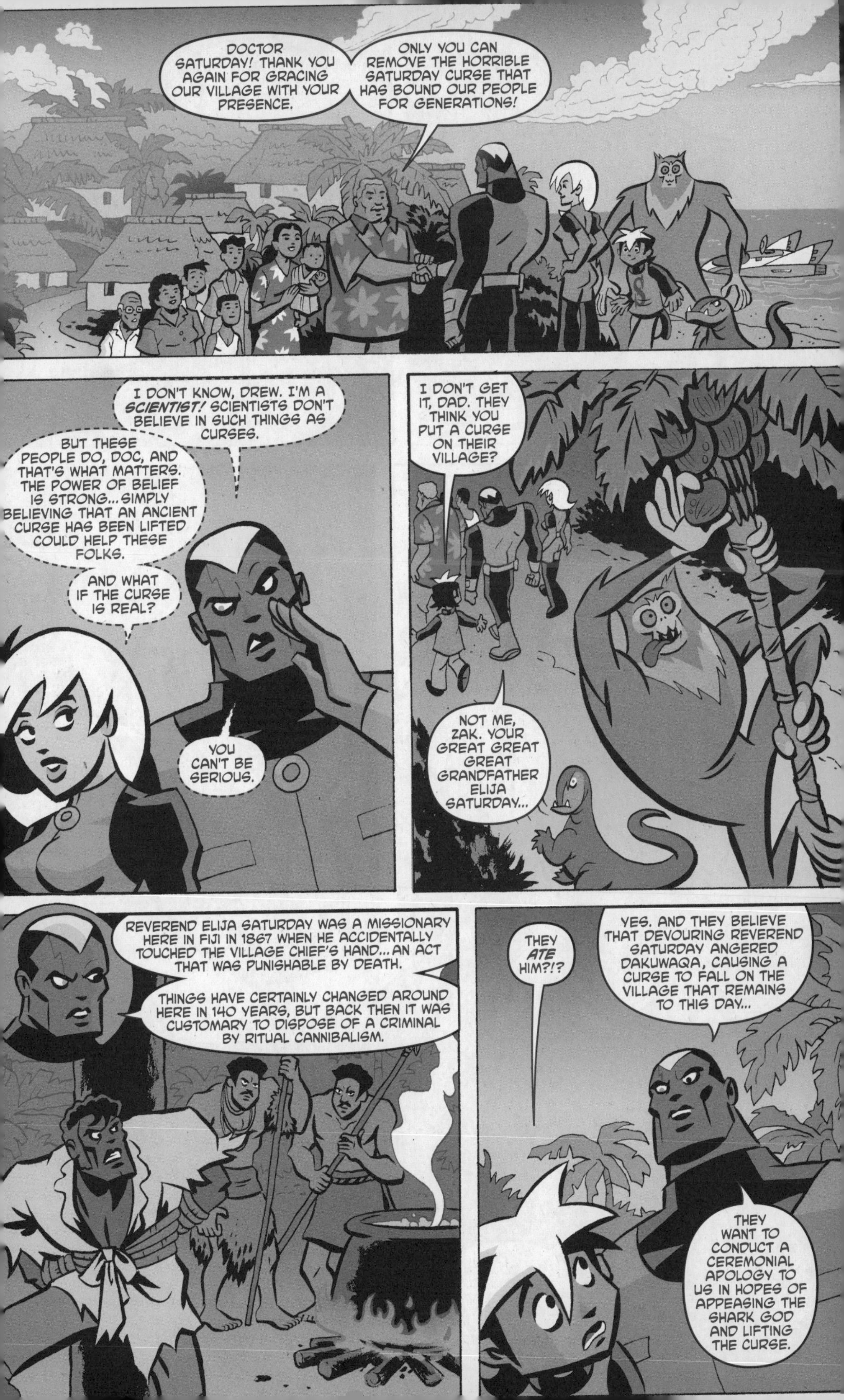
DOCTOR SATURDAY! THANK YOU AGAIN FOR GRACING OUR VILLAGE WITH YOUR PRESENCE.
ONLY YOU CAN REMOVE THE HORRIBLE SATURDAY CURSE THAT HAS BOUND OUR PEOPLE FOR GENERATIONS!
I DON'T KNOW, DREW. I'M A *SCIENTIST!* SCIENTISTS DON'T BELIEVE IN SUCH THINGS AS CURSES.
BUT THESE PEOPLE DO, DOC, AND THAT'S WHAT MATTERS. THE POWER OF BELIEF IS STRONG... SIMPLY BELIEVING THAT AN ANCIENT CURSE HAS BEEN LIFTED COULD HELP THESE FOLKS.
AND WHAT IF THE CURSE IS REAL?
YOU CAN'T BE SERIOUS.
I DON'T GET IT, DAD. THEY THINK YOU PUT A CURSE ON THEIR VILLAGE?
NOT ME, ZAK. YOUR GREAT GREAT GREAT GRANDFATHER ELIJA SATURDAY...
REVEREND ELIJA SATURDAY WAS A MISSIONARY HERE IN FIJI IN 1867 WHEN HE ACCIDENTALLY TOUCHED THE VILLAGE CHIEF'S HAND... AN ACT THAT WAS PUNISHABLE BY DEATH.
THINGS HAVE CERTAINLY CHANGED AROUND HERE IN 140 YEARS, BUT BACK THEN IT WAS CUSTOMARY TO DISPOSE OF A CRIMINAL BY RITUAL CANNIBALISM.
THEY *ATE* HIM?!?
YES. AND THEY BELIEVE THAT DEVOURING REVEREND SATURDAY ANGERED DAKUWAQA, CAUSING A CURSE TO FALL ON THE VILLAGE THAT REMAINS TO THIS DAY...
THEY WANT TO CONDUCT A CEREMONIAL APOLOGY TO US IN HOPES OF APPEASING THE SHARK GOD AND LIFTING THE CURSE.

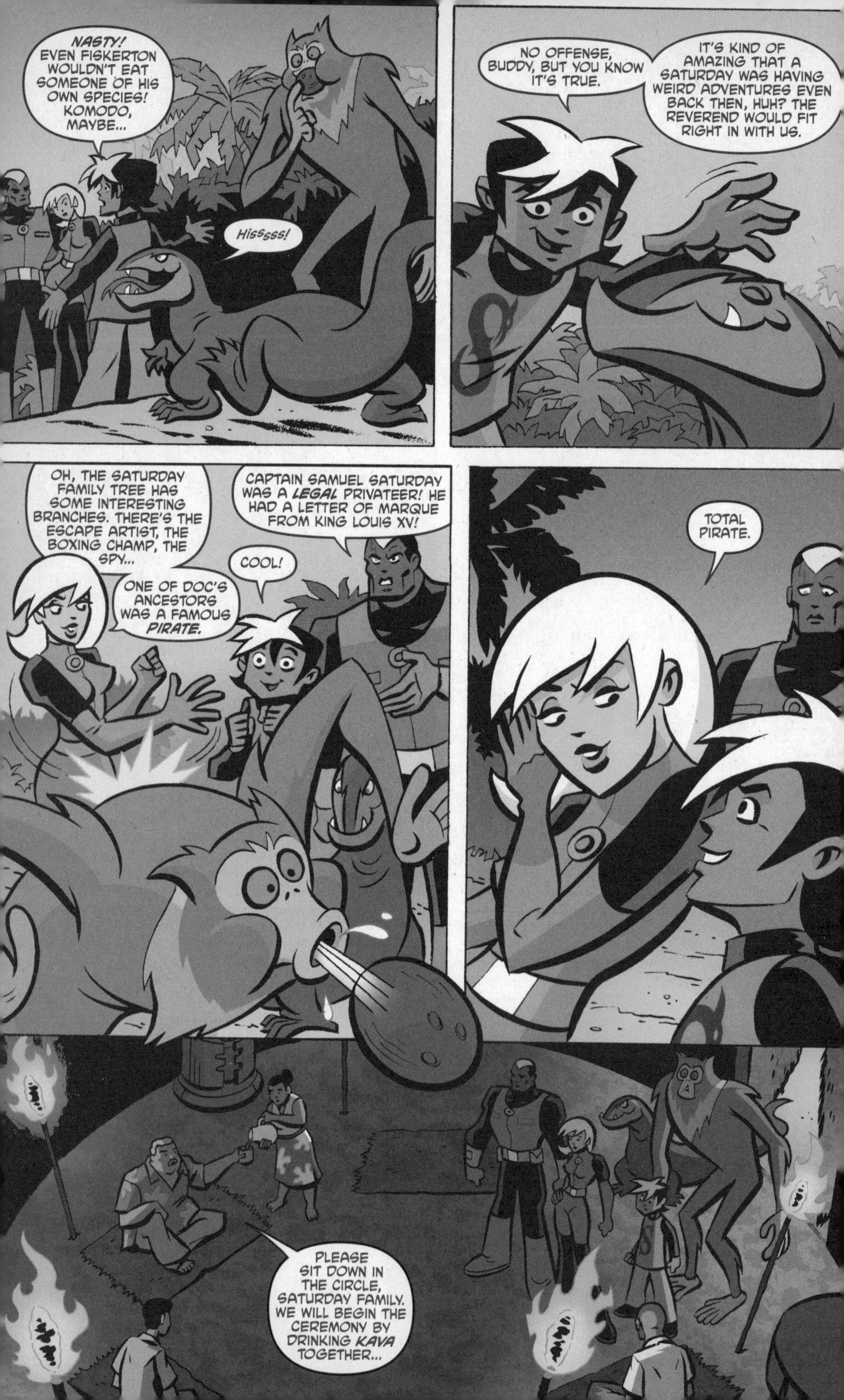
NASTY! EVEN FISKERTON WOULDN'T EAT SOMEONE OF HIS OWN SPECIES! KOMODO, MAYBE...
HISSSSS!
NO OFFENSE, BUDDY, BUT YOU KNOW IT'S TRUE.
IT'S KIND OF AMAZING THAT A SATURDAY WAS HAVING WEIRD ADVENTURES EVEN BACK THEN, HUH? THE REVEREND WOULD FIT RIGHT IN WITH US.
ONE OF DOC'S ANCESTORS WAS A FAMOUS PIRATE.
COOL!
CAPTAIN SAMUEL SATURDAY WAS A LEGAL PRIVATEER! HE HAD A LETTER OF MARQUE FROM KING LOUIS XV!
OH, THE SATURDAY FAMILY TREE HAS SOME INTERESTING BRANCHES. THERE'S THE ESCAPE ARTIST, THE BOXING CHAMP, THE SPY...
TOTAL PIRATE.
PLEASE SIT DOWN IN THE CIRCLE, SATURDAY FAMILY. WE WILL BEGIN THE CEREMONY BY DRINKING KAVA TOGETHER...

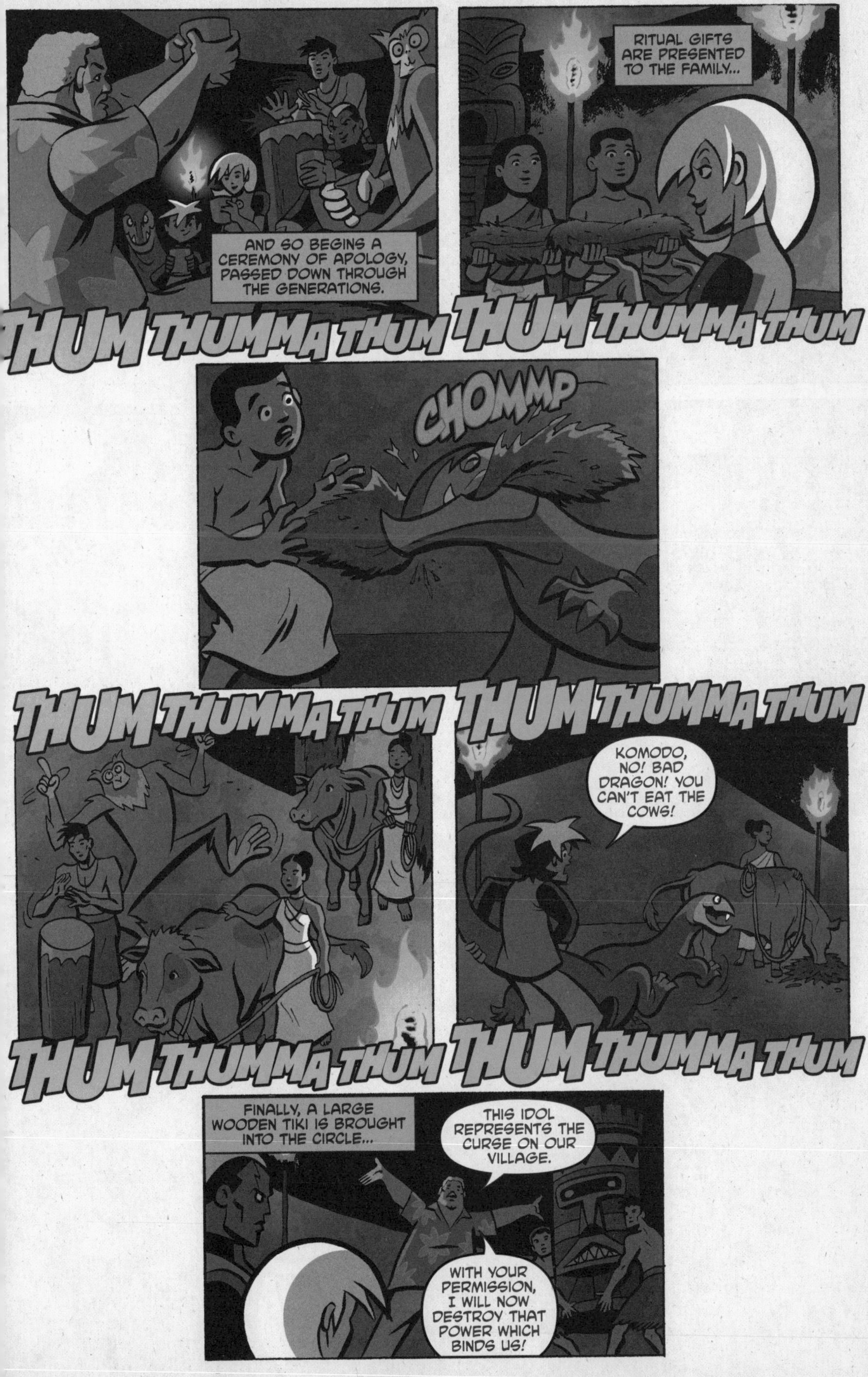
AND SO BEGINS A CEREMONY OF APOLOGY, PASSED DOWN THROUGH THE GENERATIONS.
RITUAL GIFTS ARE PRESENTED TO THE FAMILY...
THUM THUMMA THUM THUM THUMMA THUM
CHOMMP
THUM THUMMA THUM THUM THUMMA THUM
KOMODO, NO! BAD DRAGON! YOU CAN'T EAT THE COWS!
THUM THUMMA THUM THUM THUMMA THUM
FINALLY, A LARGE WOODEN TIKI IS BROUGHT INTO THE CIRCLE...
THIS IDOL REPRESENTS THE CURSE ON OUR VILLAGE.
WITH YOUR PERMISSION, I WILL NOW DESTROY THAT POWER WHICH BINDS US!

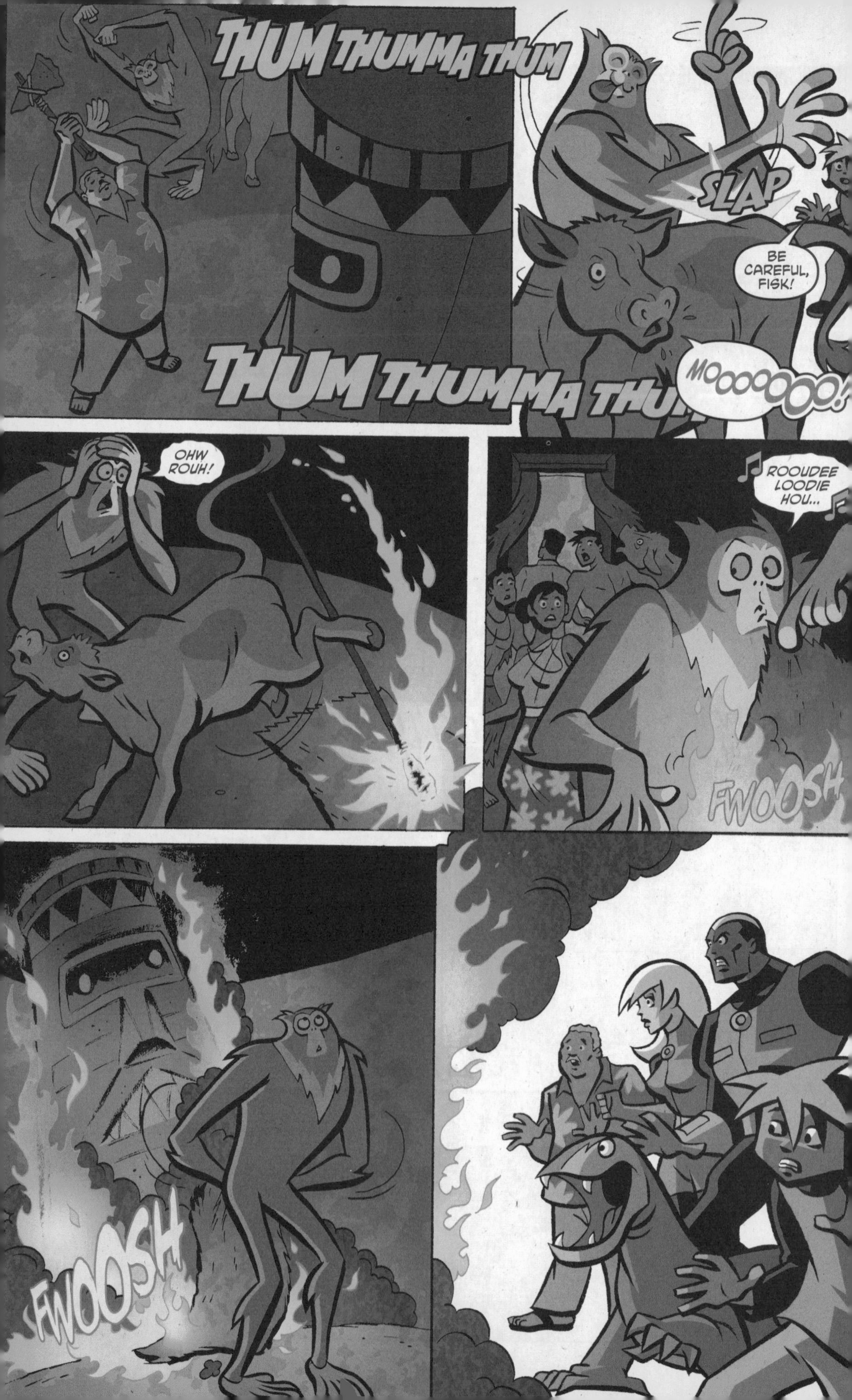
THUM THUMMA THUM
THUM THUMMA THUM
SLAP
BE CAREFUL, FISK!
MOOOOOOOO!
OHW ROUH!
ROOUDEE LOODIE HOU...
FWOOSH
FWOOSH

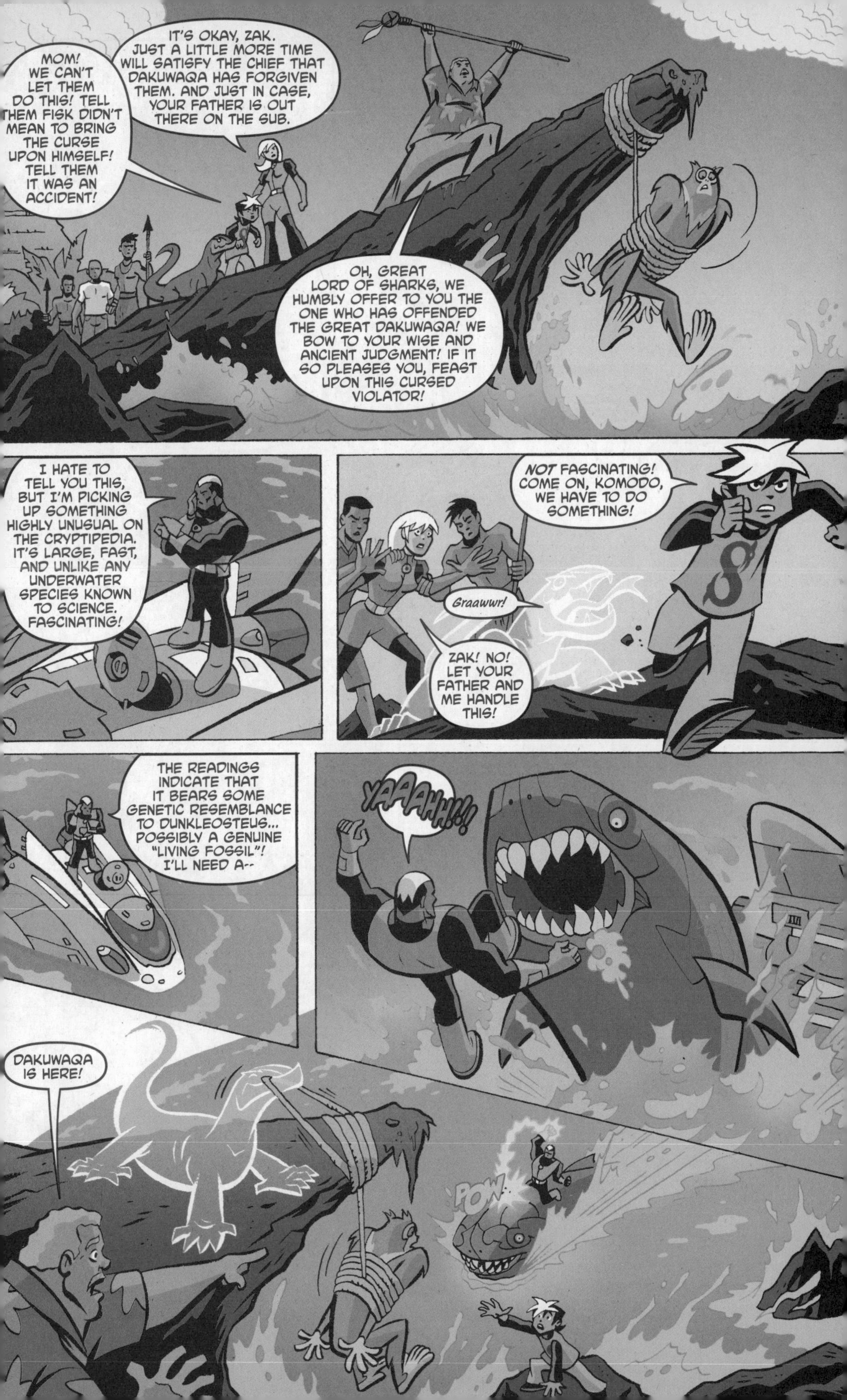
MOM! WE CAN'T LET THEM DO THIS! TELL THEM FISK DIDN'T MEAN TO BRING THE CURSE UPON HIMSELF! TELL THEM IT WAS AN ACCIDENT!
IT'S OKAY, ZAK. JUST A LITTLE MORE TIME WILL SATISFY THE CHIEF THAT DAKUWAQA HAS FORGIVEN THEM. AND JUST IN CASE, YOUR FATHER IS OUT THERE ON THE SUB.
OH, GREAT LORD OF SHARKS, WE HUMBLY OFFER TO YOU THE ONE WHO HAS OFFENDED THE GREAT DAKUWAQA! WE BOW TO YOUR WISE AND ANCIENT JUDGMENT! IF IT SO PLEASES YOU, FEAST UPON THIS CURSED VIOLATOR!
I HATE TO TELL YOU THIS, BUT I'M PICKING UP SOMETHING HIGHLY UNUSUAL ON THE CRYPTIPEDIA. IT'S LARGE, FAST, AND UNLIKE ANY UNDERWATER SPECIES KNOWN TO SCIENCE. FASCINATING!
NOT FASCINATING! COME ON, KOMODO, WE HAVE TO DO SOMETHING!
Graawwr!
ZAK! NO! LET YOUR FATHER AND ME HANDLE THIS!
THE READINGS INDICATE THAT IT BEARS SOME GENETIC RESEMBLANCE TO DUNKLEOSTEUS... POSSIBLY A GENUINE "LIVING FOSSIL"! I'LL NEED A--
YAAAHH!!!
DAKUWAQA IS HERE!
POW

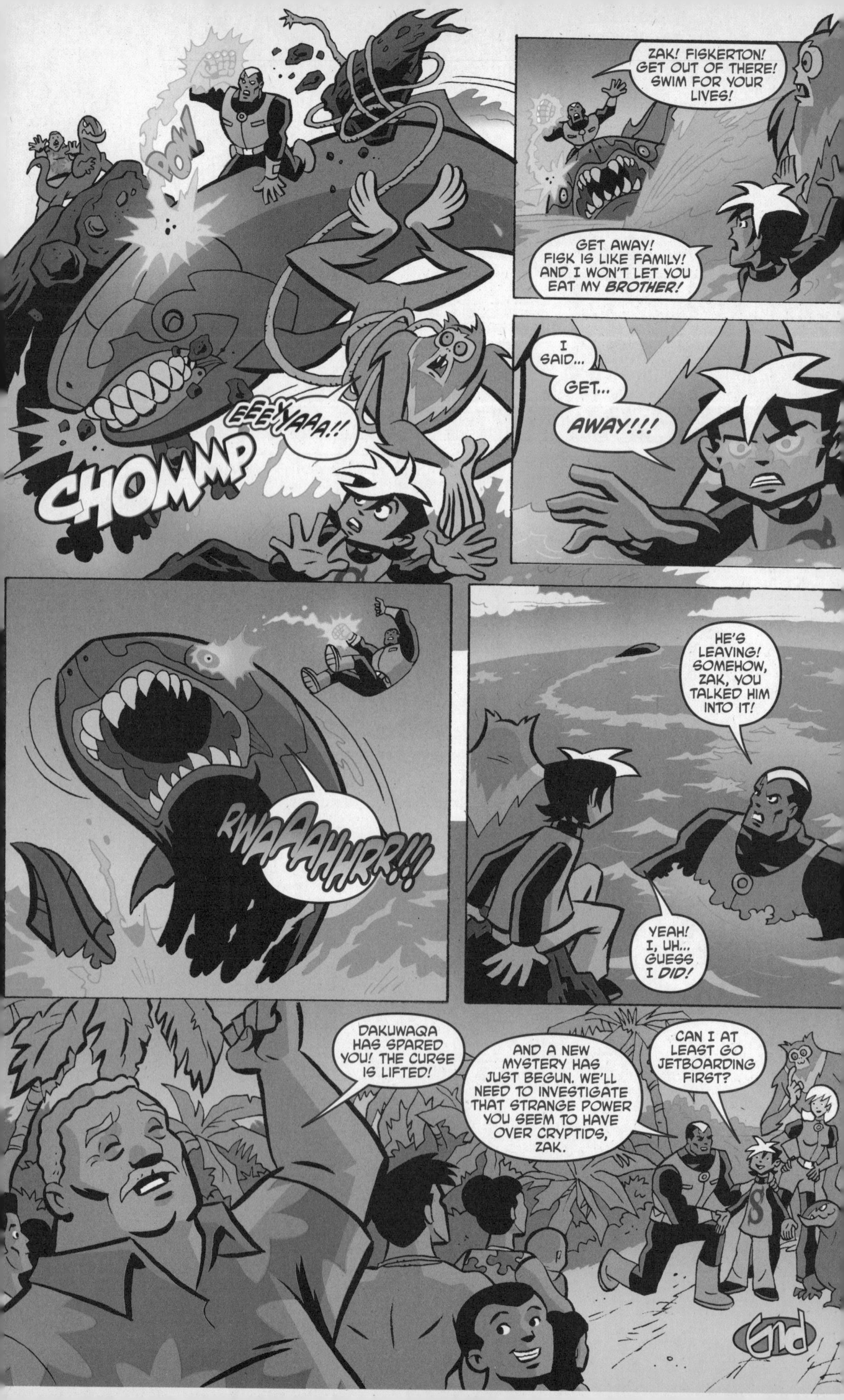
POW
ZAK! FISKERTON! GET OUT OF THERE! SWIM FOR YOUR LIVES!
GET AWAY! FISK IS LIKE FAMILY! AND I WON'T LET YOU EAT MY BROTHER!
EEEYAAA!!
CHOMMP
I SAID...
GET...
AWAY!!!
RWAAAAHHRR!!!
HE'S LEAVING! SOMEHOW, ZAK, YOU TALKED HIM INTO IT!
YEAH! I, UH... GUESS I DID!
DAKUWAQA HAS SPARED YOU! THE CURSE IS LIFTED!
AND A NEW MYSTERY HAS JUST BEGUN. WE'LL NEED TO INVESTIGATE THAT STRANGE POWER YOU SEEM TO HAVE OVER CRYPTIDS, ZAK.
CAN I AT LEAST GO JETBOARDING FIRST?
End

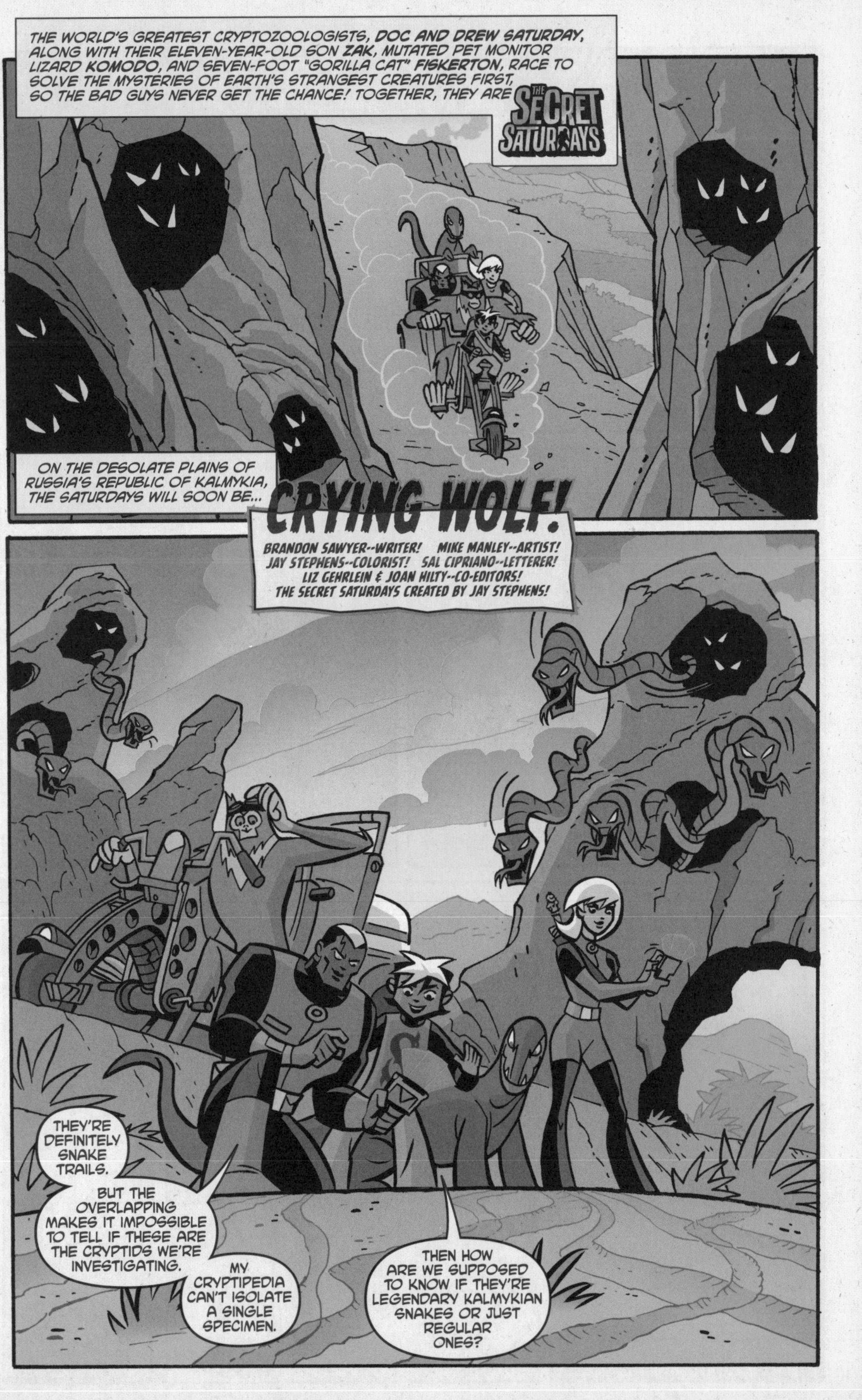
THE WORLD'S GREATEST CRYPTOZOOLOGISTS, DOC AND DREW SATURDAY, ALONG WITH THEIR ELEVEN-YEAR-OLD SON ZAK, MUTATED PET MONITOR LIZARD KOMODO, AND SEVEN-FOOT "GORILLA CAT" FISKERTON, RACE TO SOLVE THE MYSTERIES OF EARTH'S STRANGEST CREATURES FIRST, SO THE BAD GUYS NEVER GET THE CHANCE! TOGETHER, THEY ARE
THE SECRET SATURDAYS
ON THE DESOLATE PLAINS OF RUSSIA'S REPUBLIC OF KALMYKIA, THE SATURDAYS WILL SOON BE...
CRYING WOLF!
BRANDON SAWYER--WRITER! MIKE MANLEY--ARTIST! JAY STEPHENS--COLORIST! SAL CIPRIANO--LETTERER! LIZ GEHRLEIN & JOAN HILTY--CO-EDITORS! THE SECRET SATURDAYS CREATED BY JAY STEPHENS!
THEY'RE DEFINITELY SNAKE TRAILS.
BUT THE OVERLAPPING MAKES IT IMPOSSIBLE TO TELL IF THESE ARE THE CRYPTIDS WE'RE INVESTIGATING.
MY CRYPTIPEDIA CAN'T ISOLATE A SINGLE SPECIMEN.
THEN HOW ARE WE SUPPOSED TO KNOW IF THEY'RE LEGENDARY KALMYKIAN SNAKES OR JUST REGULAR ONES?

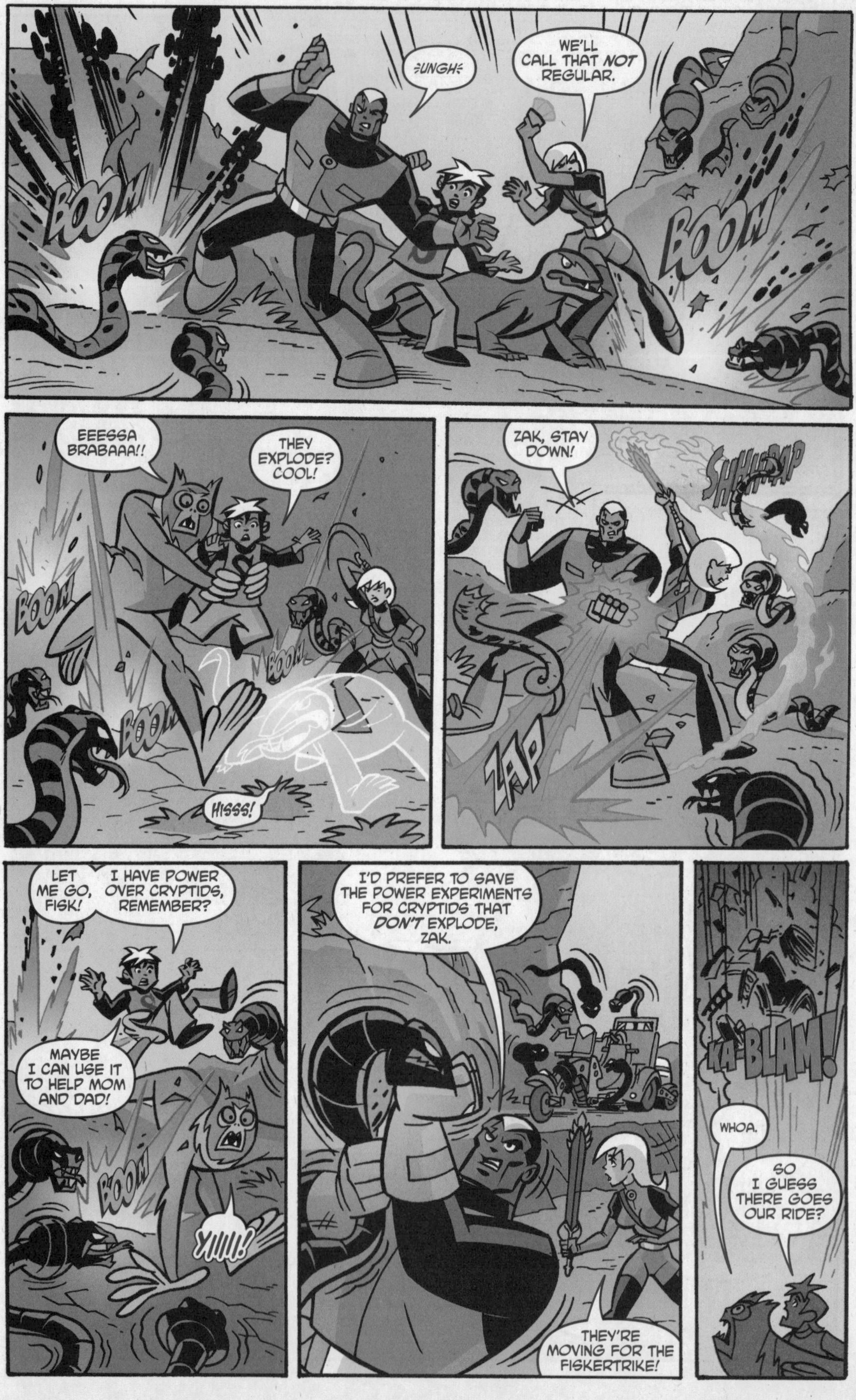
BOOM!
UNGH
WE'LL CALL THAT NOT REGULAR.
BOOM!
EEESSA BRABAAA!!
THEY EXPLODE? COOL!
BOOM
BOOM
BOOM
HISSS!
ZAK, STAY DOWN!
SHHHRAP
ZAP
LET ME GO, FISK!
I HAVE POWER OVER CRYPTIDS, REMEMBER?
MAYBE I CAN USE IT TO HELP MOM AND DAD!
BOOM
YIIIII!
I'D PREFER TO SAVE THE POWER EXPERIMENTS FOR CRYPTIDS THAT DON'T EXPLODE, ZAK.
THEY'RE MOVING FOR THE FISKERTRIKE!
KA-BLAM!
WHOA.
SO I GUESS THERE GOES OUR RIDE?

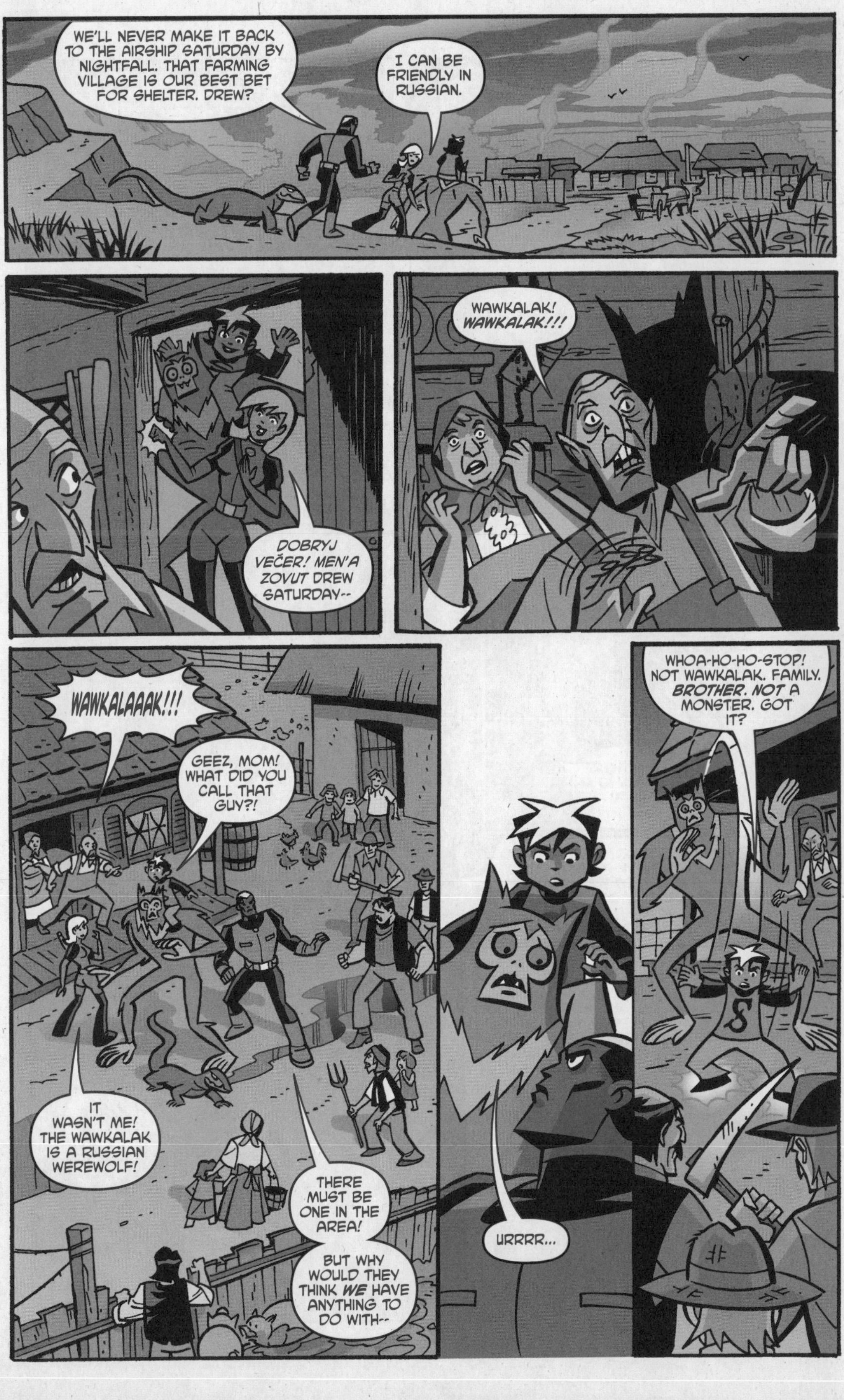
WE'LL NEVER MAKE IT BACK TO THE AIRSHIP SATURDAY BY NIGHTFALL. THAT FARMING VILLAGE IS OUR BEST BET FOR SHELTER. DREW?
I CAN BE FRIENDLY IN RUSSIAN.
DOBRYJ VEČER! MEN'A ZOVUT DREW SATURDAY--
WAWKALAK! WAWKALAK!!!
WAWKALAAAK!!!
GEEZ, MOM! WHAT DID YOU CALL THAT GUY?!
IT WASN'T ME! THE WAWKALAK IS A RUSSIAN WEREWOLF!
THERE MUST BE ONE IN THE AREA!
BUT WHY WOULD THEY THINK WE HAVE ANYTHING TO DO WITH--
URRRR...
WHOA-HO-HO-STOP! NOT WAWKALAK. FAMILY. BROTHER. NOT A MONSTER. GOT IT?

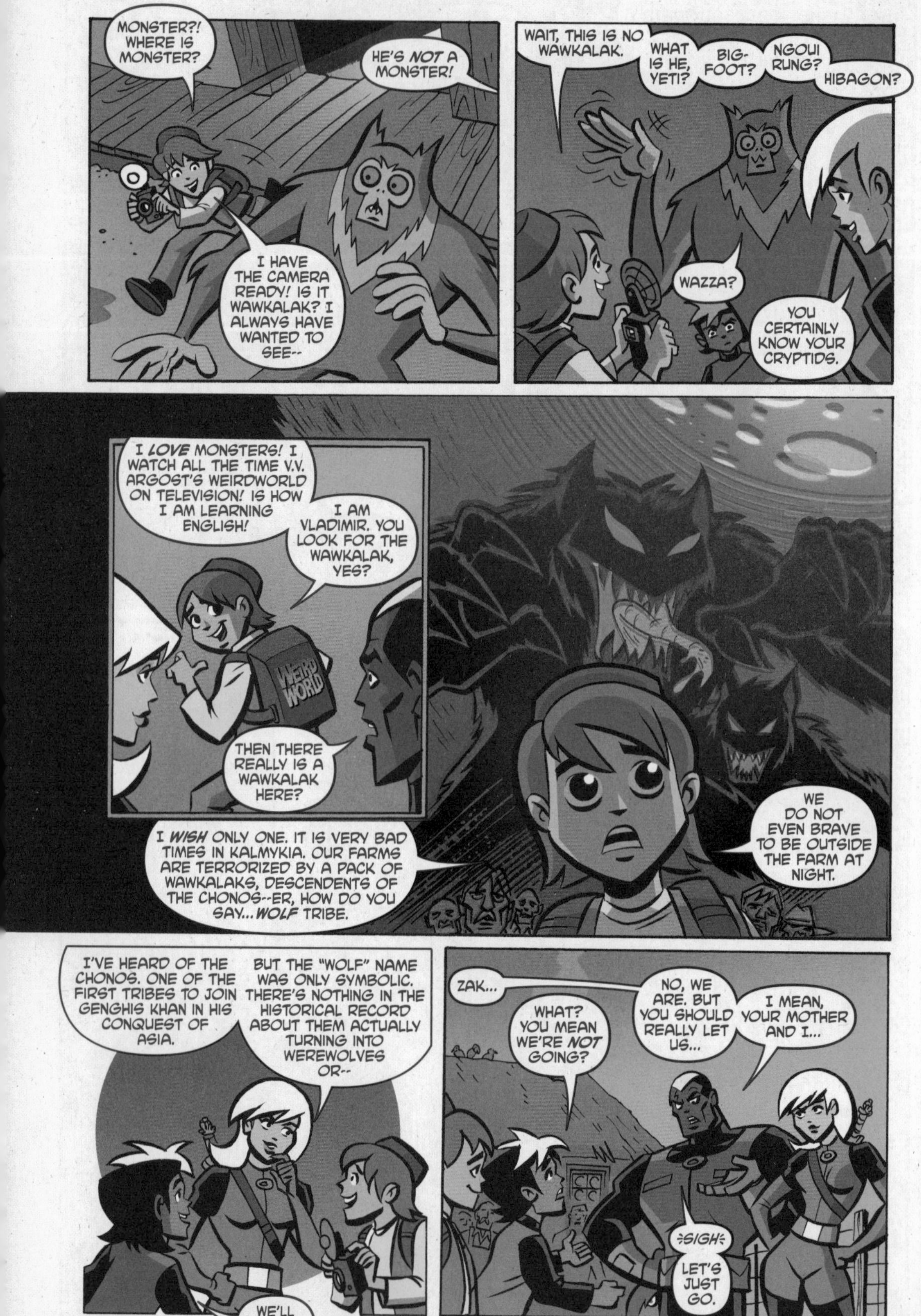
MONSTER?! WHERE IS MONSTER?
HE'S *NOT* A MONSTER!
I HAVE THE CAMERA READY! IS IT WAWKALAK? I ALWAYS HAVE WANTED TO SEE--
WAIT, THIS IS NO WAWKALAK.
WHAT IS HE, YETI?
BIG-FOOT?
NGOUI RUNG?
HIBAGON?
WAZZA?
YOU CERTAINLY KNOW YOUR CRYPTIDS.
I *LOVE* MONSTERS! I WATCH ALL THE TIME V.V. ARGOST'S WEIRDWORLD ON TELEVISION! IS HOW I AM LEARNING ENGLISH!
I AM VLADIMIR. YOU LOOK FOR THE WAWKALAK, YES?
WEIRD WORLD
THEN THERE REALLY IS A WAWKALAK HERE?
I *WISH* ONLY ONE. IT IS VERY BAD TIMES IN KALMYKIA. OUR FARMS ARE TERRORIZED BY A PACK OF WAWKALAKS, DESCENDENTS OF THE CHONOS--ER, HOW DO YOU SAY... *WOLF* TRIBE.
WE DO NOT EVEN BRAVE TO BE OUTSIDE THE FARM AT NIGHT.
I'VE HEARD OF THE CHONOS. ONE OF THE FIRST TRIBES TO JOIN GENGHIS KHAN IN HIS CONQUEST OF ASIA.
BUT THE "WOLF" NAME WAS ONLY SYMBOLIC. THERE'S NOTHING IN THE HISTORICAL RECORD ABOUT THEM ACTUALLY TURNING INTO WEREWOLVES OR--
WE'LL CHECK IT OUT!
ZAK...
WHAT? YOU MEAN WE'RE *NOT* GOING?
NO, WE ARE. BUT YOU SHOULD REALLY LET US...
I MEAN, YOUR MOTHER AND I...
SIGH
LET'S JUST GO.

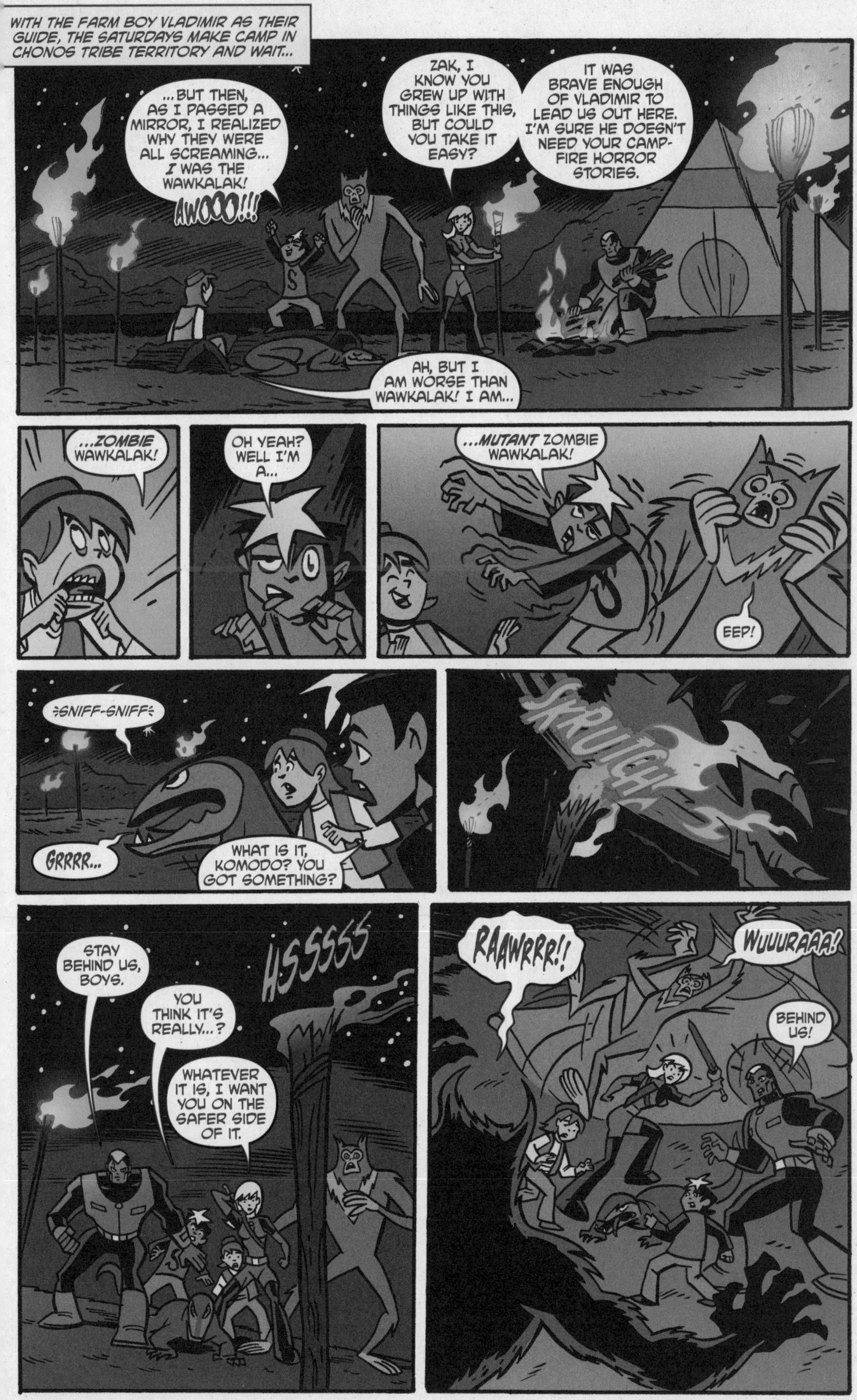
WITH THE FARM BOY VLADIMIR AS THEIR GUIDE, THE SATURDAYS MAKE CAMP IN CHONOS TRIBE TERRITORY AND WAIT...
...BUT THEN, AS I PASSED A MIRROR, I REALIZED WHY THEY WERE ALL SCREAMING... I WAS THE WAWKALAK!
AWOOO!!!
ZAK, I KNOW YOU GREW UP WITH THINGS LIKE THIS, BUT COULD YOU TAKE IT EASY?
IT WAS BRAVE ENOUGH OF VLADIMIR TO LEAD US OUT HERE. I'M SURE HE DOESN'T NEED YOUR CAMP-FIRE HORROR STORIES.
AH, BUT I AM WORSE THAN WAWKALAK! I AM...
...ZOMBIE WAWKALAK!
OH YEAH? WELL I'M A...
...MUTANT ZOMBIE WAWKALAK!
EEP!
SNIFF-SNIFF
GRRRR...
WHAT IS IT, KOMODO? YOU GOT SOMETHING?
SKRUTCH!
STAY BEHIND US, BOYS.
YOU THINK IT'S REALLY...?
WHATEVER IT IS, I WANT YOU ON THE SAFER SIDE OF IT.
HSSSSS
RAAWRRR!!
WUUURAAA!
BEHIND US!

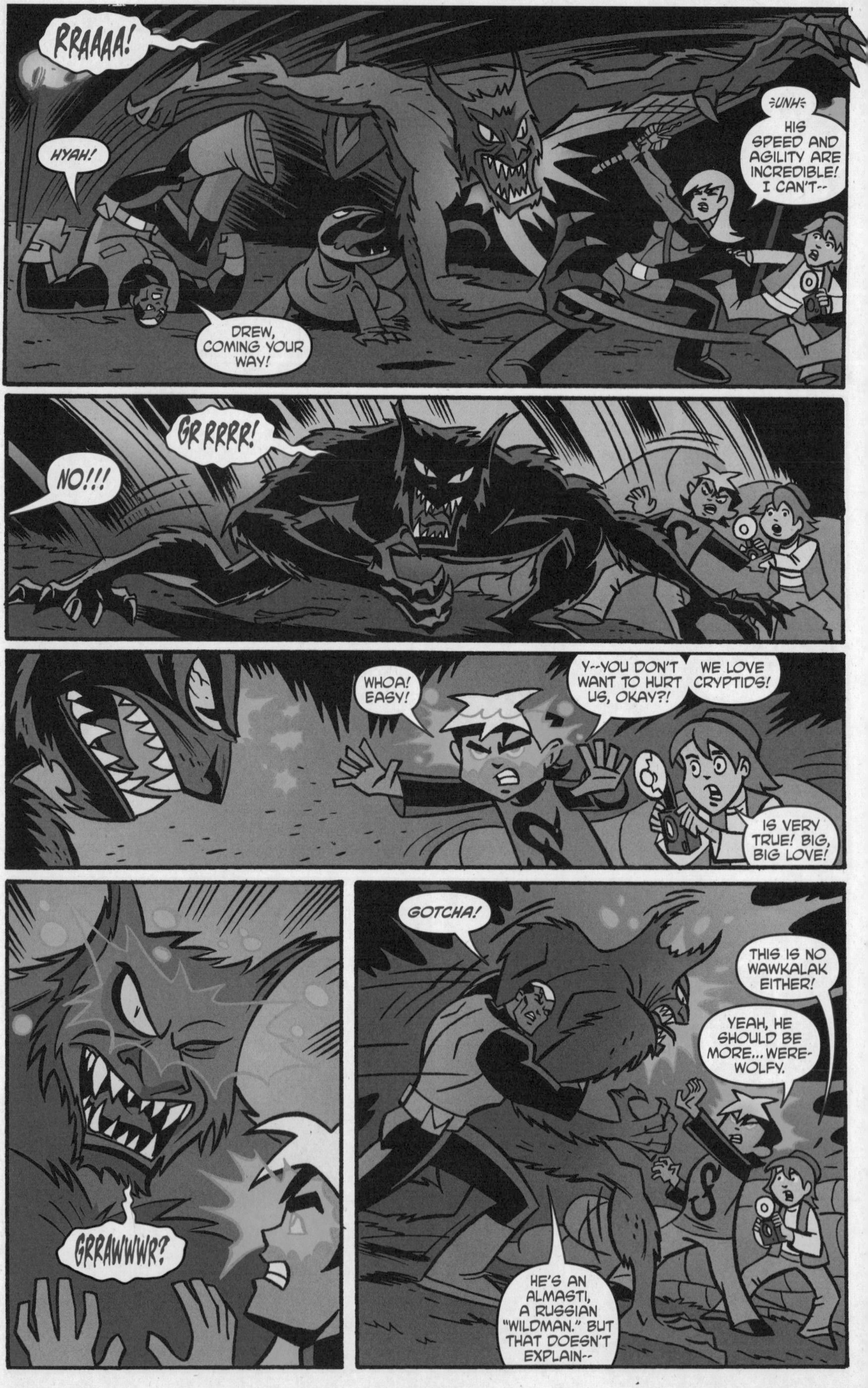
RRAAAA!
HYAH!
UNH
HIS SPEED AND AGILITY ARE INCREDIBLE! I CAN'T--
DREW, COMING YOUR WAY!
GRRRRR!
NO!!!
WHOA! EASY!
Y--YOU DON'T WANT TO HURT US, OKAY?!
WE LOVE CRYPTIDS!
IS VERY TRUE! BIG, BIG LOVE!
GRRAWWWR?
GOTCHA!
THIS IS NO WAWKALAK EITHER!
YEAH, HE SHOULD BE MORE... WERE-WOLFY.
HE'S AN ALMASTI, A RUSSIAN "WILDMAN." BUT THAT DOESN'T EXPLAIN--

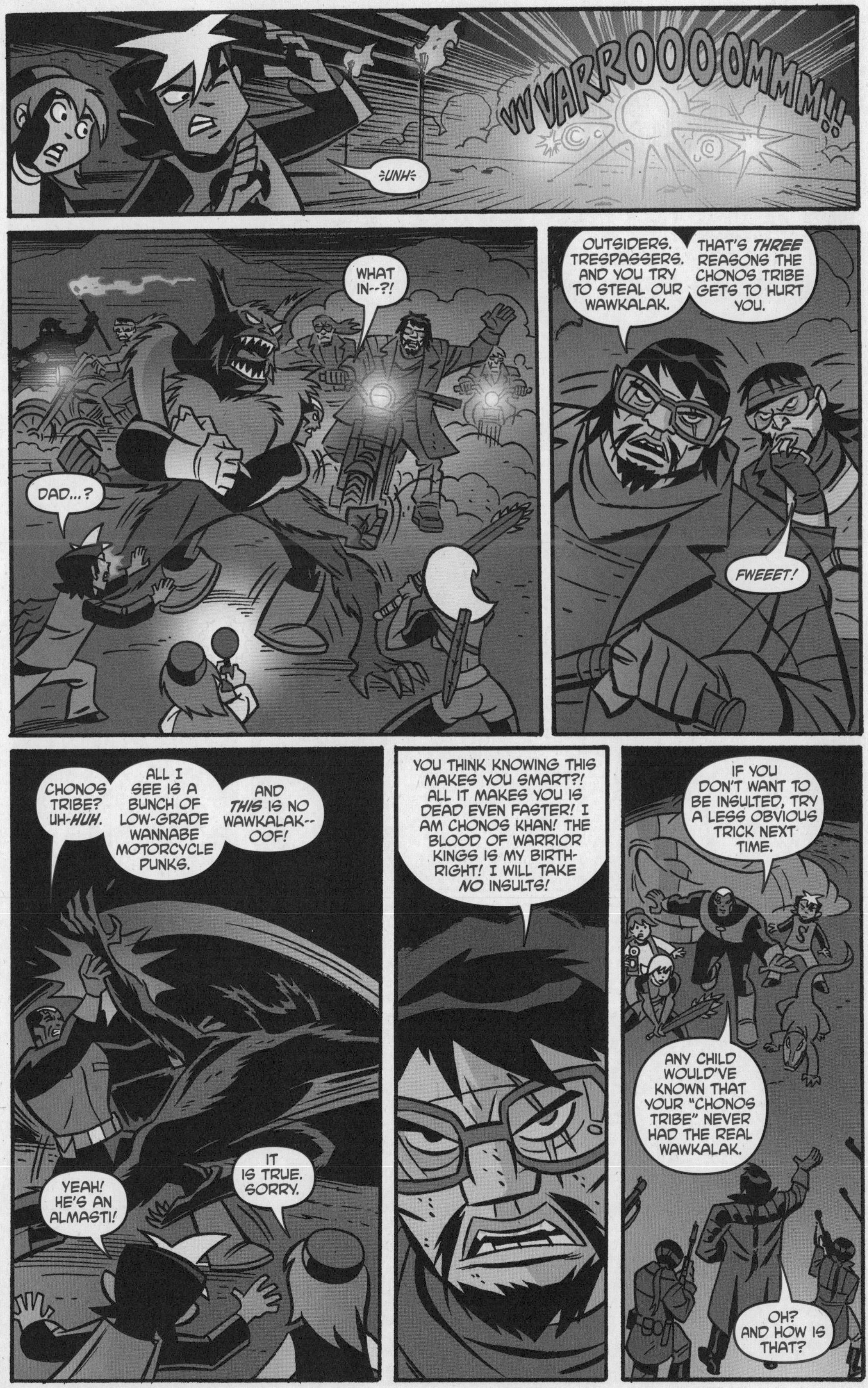
UNH
VVVARROOOOMMMM!!
WHAT IN--?!
DAD...?
OUTSIDERS. TRESPASSERS. AND YOU TRY TO STEAL OUR WAWKALAK.
THAT'S *THREE* REASONS THE CHONOS TRIBE GETS TO HURT YOU.
FWEEET!
CHONOS TRIBE? UH-*HUH*.
ALL I SEE IS A BUNCH OF LOW-GRADE WANNABE MOTORCYCLE PUNKS.
AND *THIS* IS NO WAWKALAK-- OOF!
YEAH! HE'S AN ALMASTI!
IT IS TRUE. SORRY.
YOU THINK KNOWING THIS MAKES YOU SMART?! ALL IT MAKES YOU IS DEAD EVEN FASTER! I AM CHONOS KHAN! THE BLOOD OF WARRIOR KINGS IS MY BIRTH-RIGHT! I WILL TAKE *NO* INSULTS!
IF YOU DON'T WANT TO BE INSULTED, TRY A LESS OBVIOUS TRICK NEXT TIME.
ANY CHILD WOULD'VE KNOWN THAT YOUR "CHONOS TRIBE" NEVER HAD THE REAL WAWKALAK.
OH? AND HOW IS THAT?

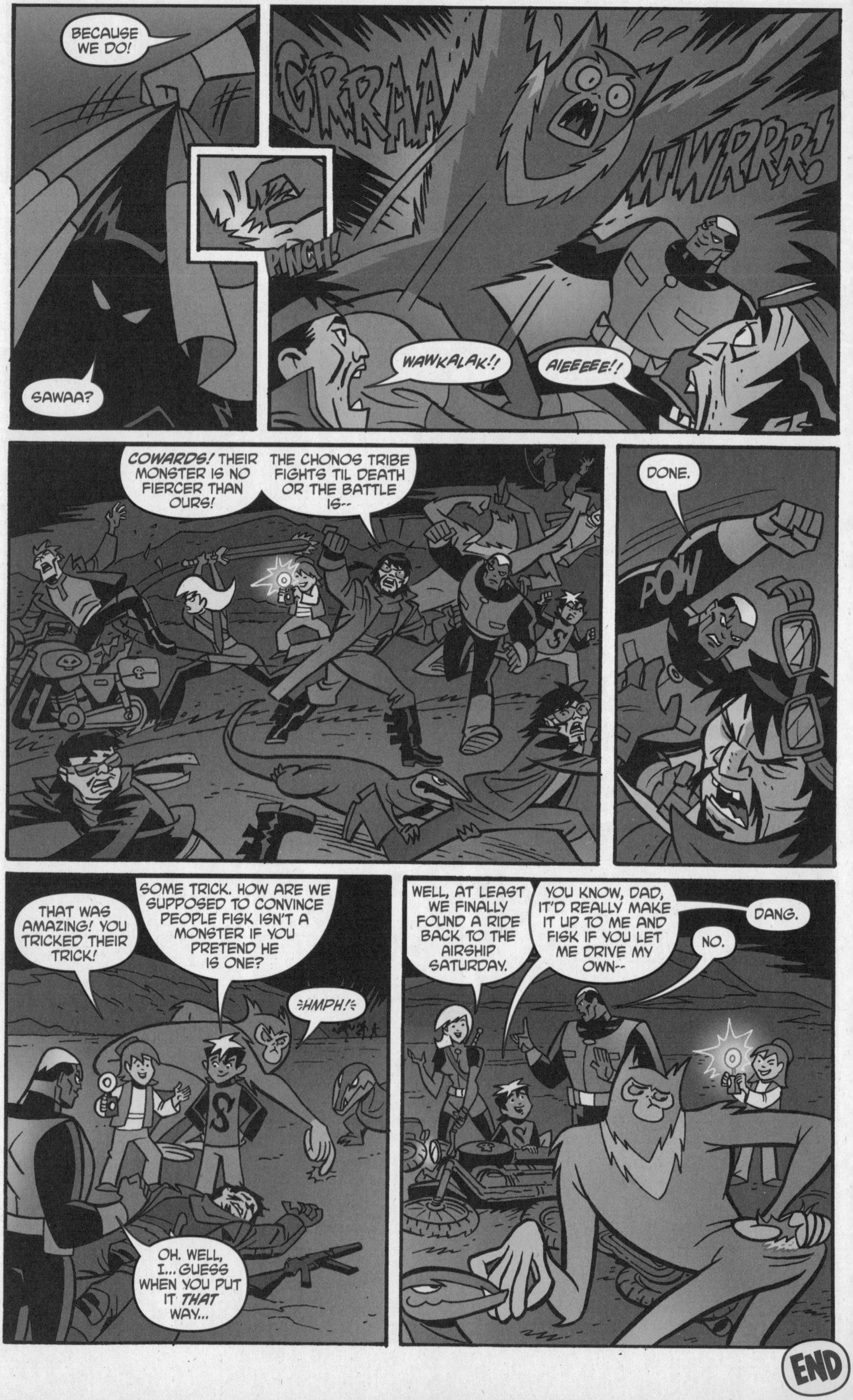
BECAUSE WE DO!
GRRAA
PINCH!
NWRRR!
SAWAA?
WAWKALAK!!
AIEEEEE!!
COWARDS! THEIR MONSTER IS NO FIERCER THAN OURS!
THE CHONOS TRIBE FIGHTS TIL DEATH OR THE BATTLE IS--
DONE.
POW
THAT WAS AMAZING! YOU TRICKED THEIR TRICK!
SOME TRICK. HOW ARE WE SUPPOSED TO CONVINCE PEOPLE FISK ISN'T A MONSTER IF YOU PRETEND HE IS ONE?
HMPH!
OH. WELL, I...GUESS WHEN YOU PUT IT THAT WAY...
WELL, AT LEAST WE FINALLY FOUND A RIDE BACK TO THE AIRSHIP SATURDAY.
YOU KNOW, DAD, IT'D REALLY MAKE IT UP TO ME AND FISK IF YOU LET ME DRIVE MY OWN--
NO.
DANG.
END

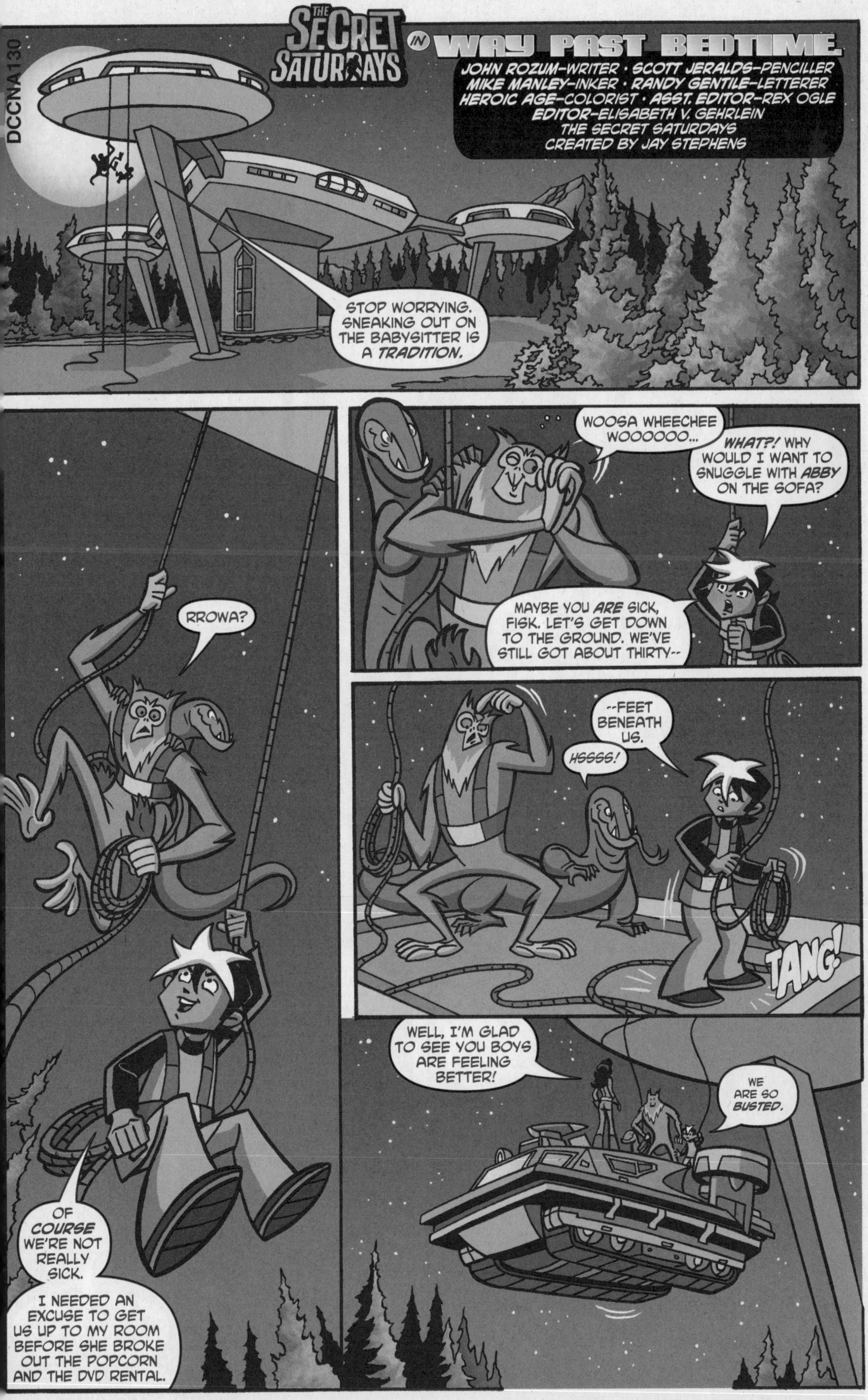

THE SECRET SATURDAYS
IN
WAY PAST BEDTIME.
JOHN ROZUM–WRITER · SCOTT JERALDS–PENCILLER
MIKE MANLEY–INKER · RANDY GENTILE–LETTERER
HEROIC AGE–COLORIST · ASST. EDITOR–REX OGLE
EDITOR–ELISABETH V. GEHRLEIN
THE SECRET SATURDAYS
CREATED BY JAY STEPHENS
DCCNA130
STOP WORRYING. SNEAKING OUT ON THE BABYSITTER IS A *TRADITION.*
RROWA?
OF *COURSE* WE'RE NOT REALLY SICK.
I NEEDED AN EXCUSE TO GET US UP TO MY ROOM BEFORE SHE BROKE OUT THE POPCORN AND THE DVD RENTAL.
WOOSA WHEECHEE WOOOOOO...
WHAT?! WHY WOULD I WANT TO SNUGGLE WITH *ABBY* ON THE SOFA?
MAYBE YOU *ARE* SICK, FISK. LET'S GET DOWN TO THE GROUND. WE'VE STILL GOT ABOUT THIRTY--
--FEET BENEATH US.
HSSSS!
TANG!
WELL, I'M GLAD TO SEE YOU BOYS ARE FEELING BETTER!
WE ARE SO *BUSTED.*

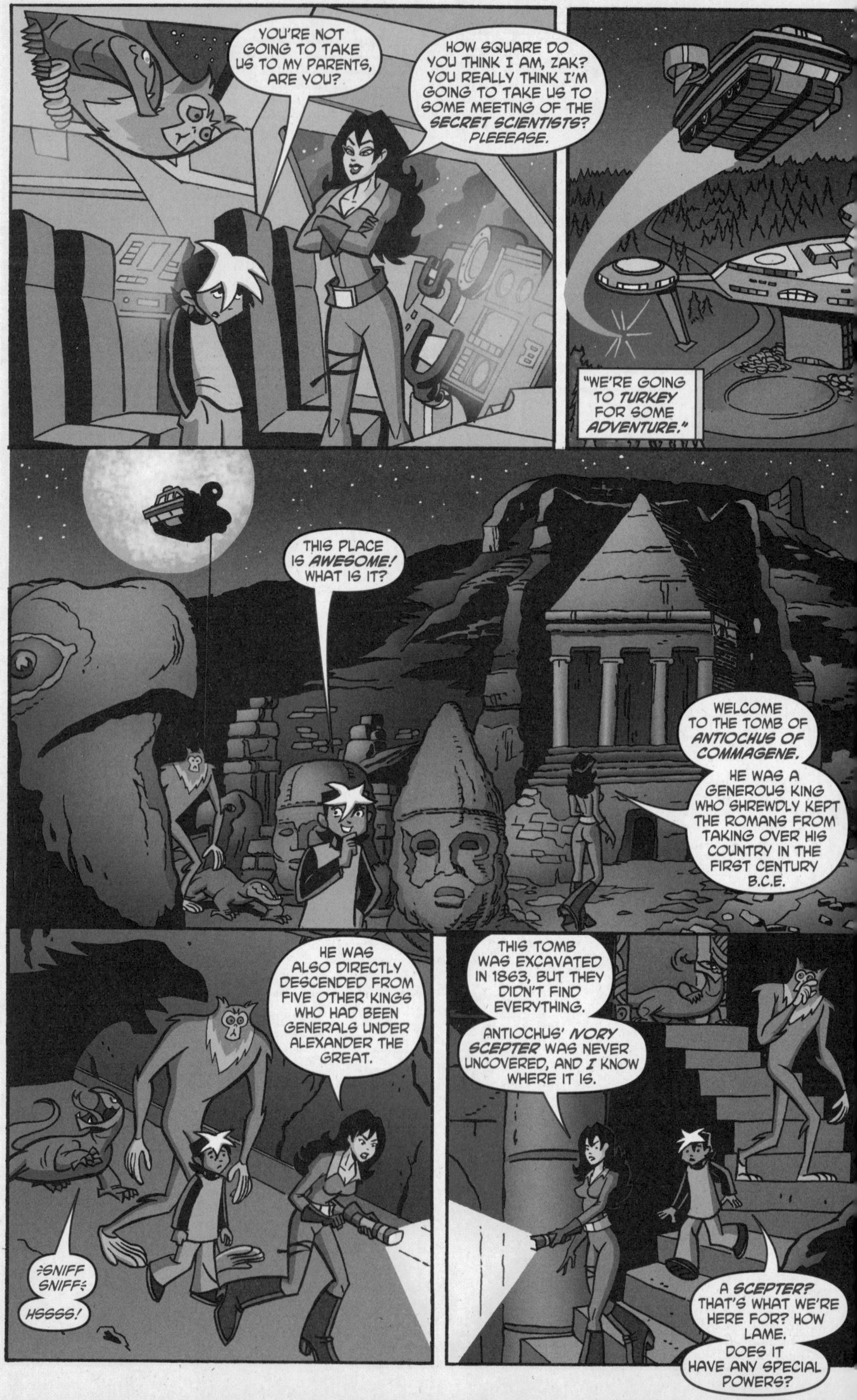
YOU'RE NOT GOING TO TAKE US TO MY PARENTS, ARE YOU?
HOW SQUARE DO YOU THINK I AM, ZAK? YOU REALLY THINK I'M GOING TO TAKE US TO SOME MEETING OF THE SECRET SCIENTISTS? PLEEEASE.
"WE'RE GOING TO TURKEY FOR SOME ADVENTURE."
THIS PLACE IS AWESOME! WHAT IS IT?
WELCOME TO THE TOMB OF ANTIOCHUS OF COMMAGENE.
HE WAS A GENEROUS KING WHO SHREWDLY KEPT THE ROMANS FROM TAKING OVER HIS COUNTRY IN THE FIRST CENTURY B.C.E.
HE WAS ALSO DIRECTLY DESCENDED FROM FIVE OTHER KINGS WHO HAD BEEN GENERALS UNDER ALEXANDER THE GREAT.
SNIFF SNIFF
HSSSS!
THIS TOMB WAS EXCAVATED IN 1863, BUT THEY DIDN'T FIND EVERYTHING.
ANTIOCHUS' IVORY SCEPTER WAS NEVER UNCOVERED, AND I KNOW WHERE IT IS.
A SCEPTER? THAT'S WHAT WE'RE HERE FOR? HOW LAME.
DOES IT HAVE ANY SPECIAL POWERS?

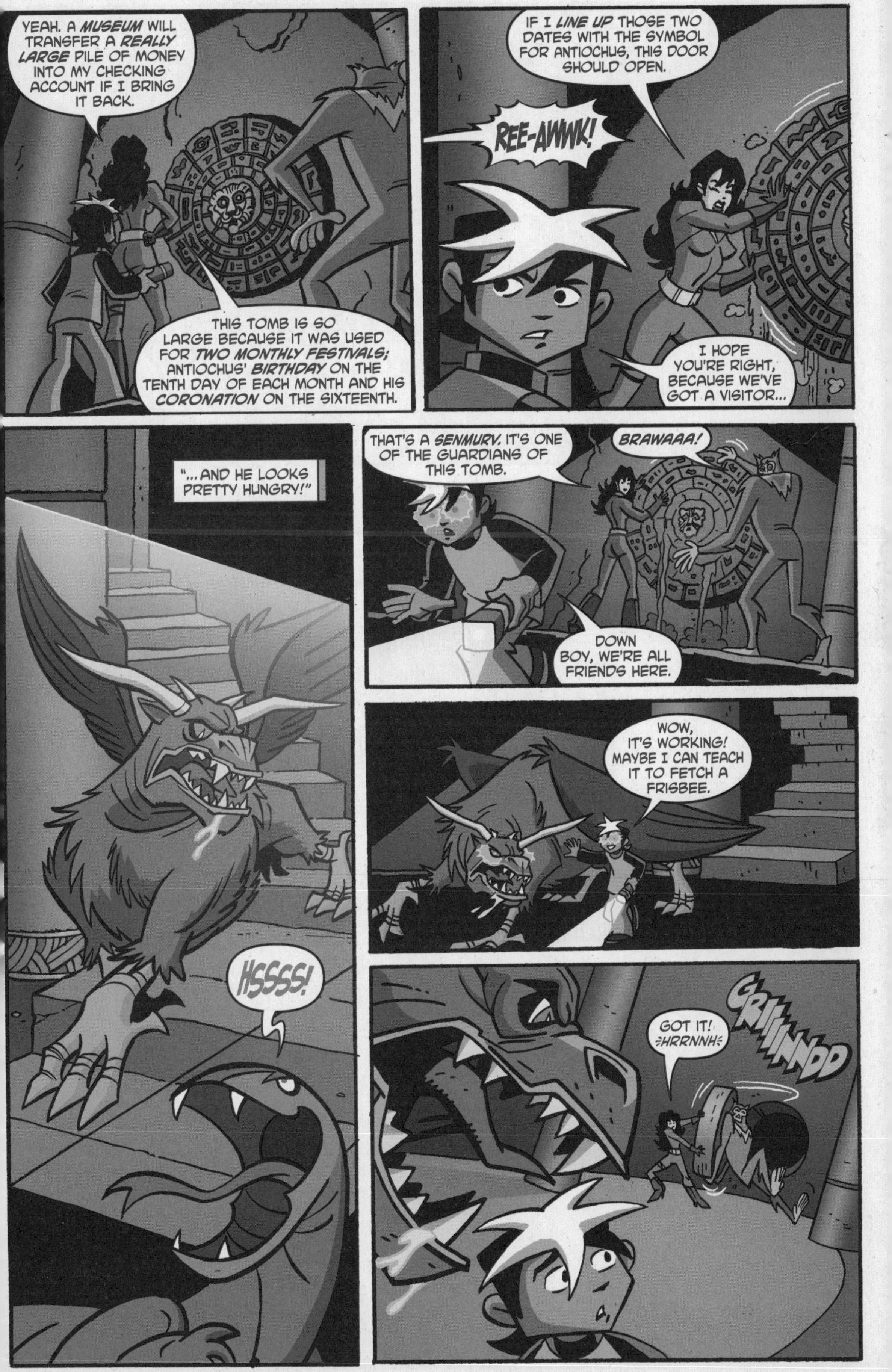
YEAH. A MUSEUM WILL TRANSFER A REALLY LARGE PILE OF MONEY INTO MY CHECKING ACCOUNT IF I BRING IT BACK.
THIS TOMB IS SO LARGE BECAUSE IT WAS USED FOR TWO MONTHLY FESTIVALS; ANTIOCHUS' BIRTHDAY ON THE TENTH DAY OF EACH MONTH AND HIS CORONATION ON THE SIXTEENTH.
IF I LINE UP THOSE TWO DATES WITH THE SYMBOL FOR ANTIOCHUS, THIS DOOR SHOULD OPEN.
REE-AWWK!
I HOPE YOU'RE RIGHT, BECAUSE WE'VE GOT A VISITOR...
"...AND HE LOOKS PRETTY HUNGRY!"
HSSSS!
THAT'S A SENMURV. IT'S ONE OF THE GUARDIANS OF THIS TOMB.
BRAWAAA!
DOWN BOY, WE'RE ALL FRIENDS HERE.
WOW, IT'S WORKING! MAYBE I CAN TEACH IT TO FETCH A FRISBEE.
GOT IT! HRRNNH
GRIIIINNDD

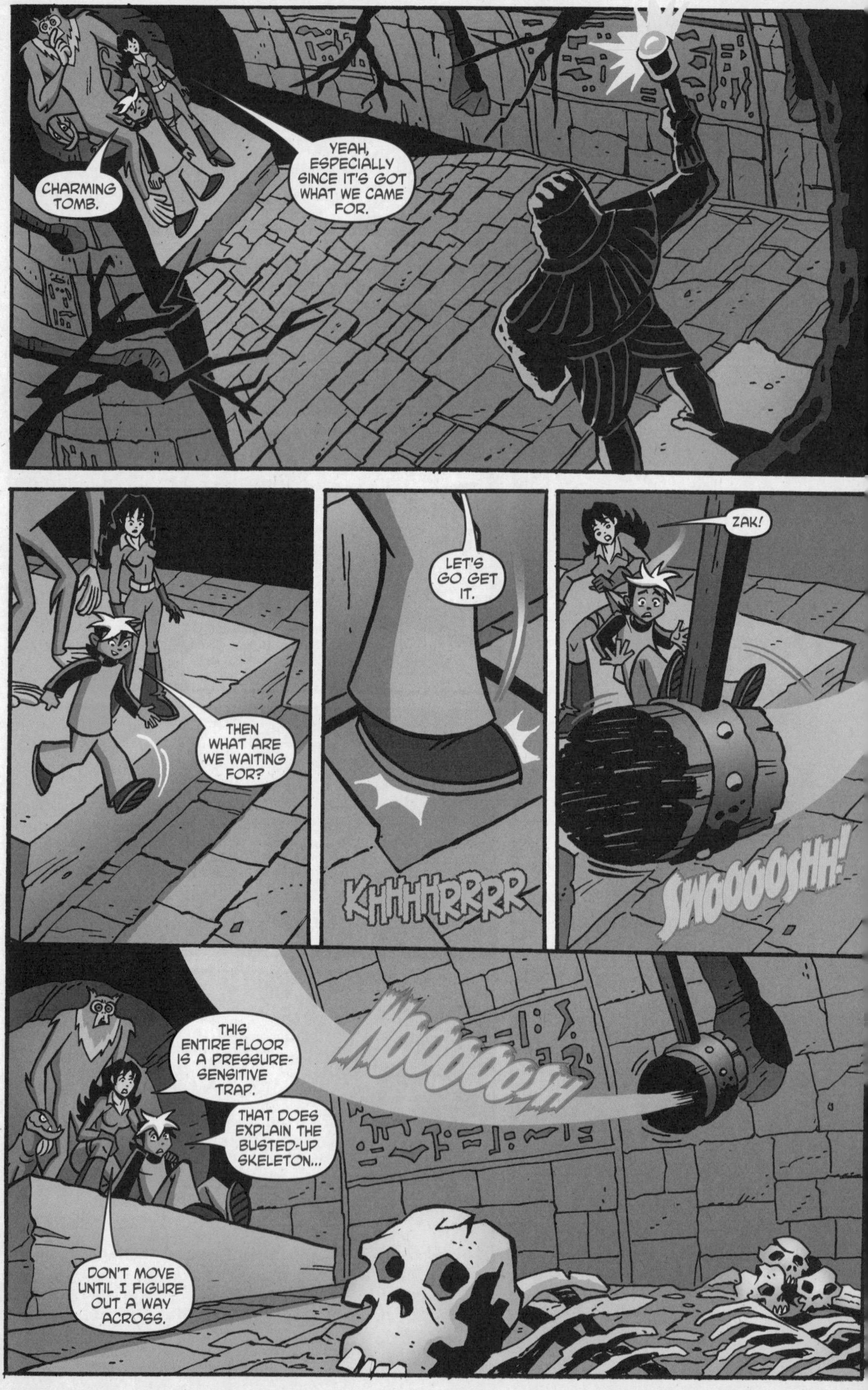
CHARMING TOMB.
YEAH, ESPECIALLY SINCE IT'S GOT WHAT WE CAME FOR.
THEN WHAT ARE WE WAITING FOR?
LET'S GO GET IT.
KHHHRRRR
ZAK!
SWOOOOSHH!
WOOOOOSH
THIS ENTIRE FLOOR IS A PRESSURE-SENSITIVE TRAP.
THAT DOES EXPLAIN THE BUSTED-UP SKELETON...
DON'T MOVE UNTIL I FIGURE OUT A WAY ACROSS.

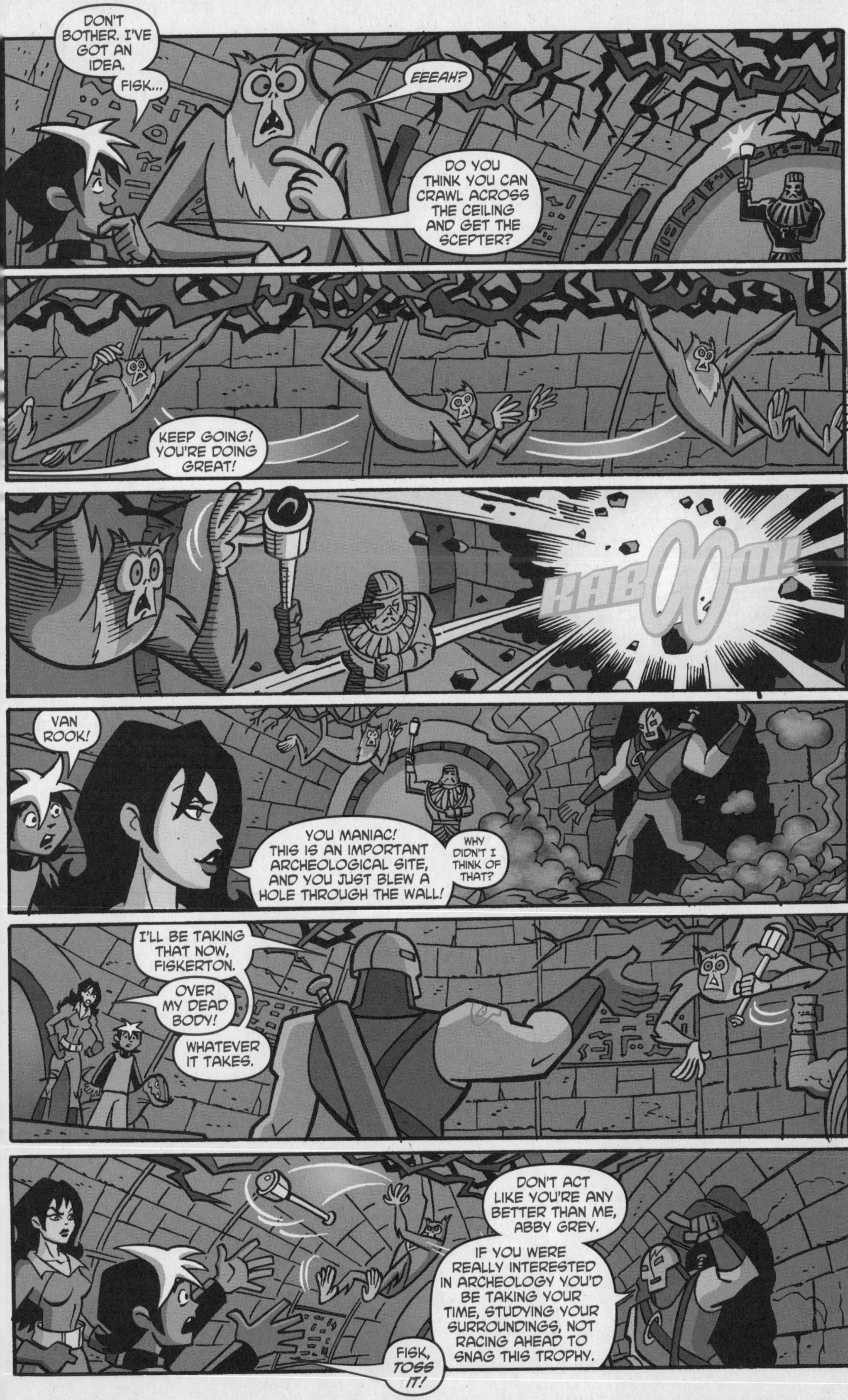
DON'T BOTHER. I'VE GOT AN IDEA.
FISK...
EEEAH?
DO YOU THINK YOU CAN CRAWL ACROSS THE CEILING AND GET THE SCEPTER?
KEEP GOING! YOU'RE DOING GREAT!
KABOOOM!!
VAN ROOK!
YOU MANIAC! THIS IS AN IMPORTANT ARCHEOLOGICAL SITE, AND YOU JUST BLEW A HOLE THROUGH THE WALL!
WHY DIDN'T I THINK OF THAT?
I'LL BE TAKING THAT NOW, FISKERTON.
OVER MY DEAD BODY!
WHATEVER IT TAKES.
DON'T ACT LIKE YOU'RE ANY BETTER THAN ME, ABBY GREY.
IF YOU WERE REALLY INTERESTED IN ARCHEOLOGY YOU'D BE TAKING YOUR TIME, STUDYING YOUR SURROUNDINGS, NOT RACING AHEAD TO SNAG THIS TROPHY.
FISK, TOSS IT!

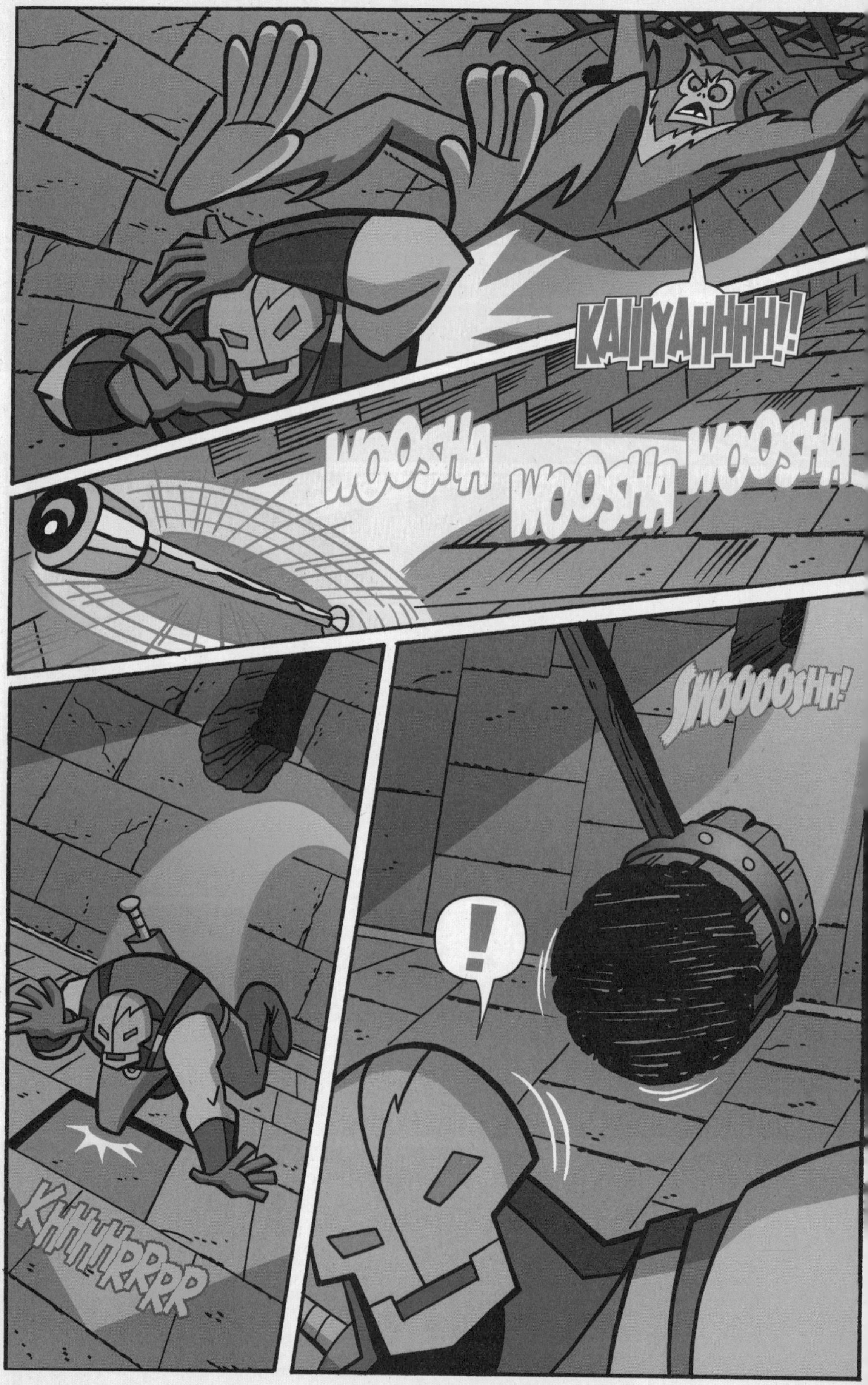
KAIIIYAHHHH!!
WOOSHA
WOOSHA
WOOSHA
SWOOOOSHH!
!
KHHHRRRR

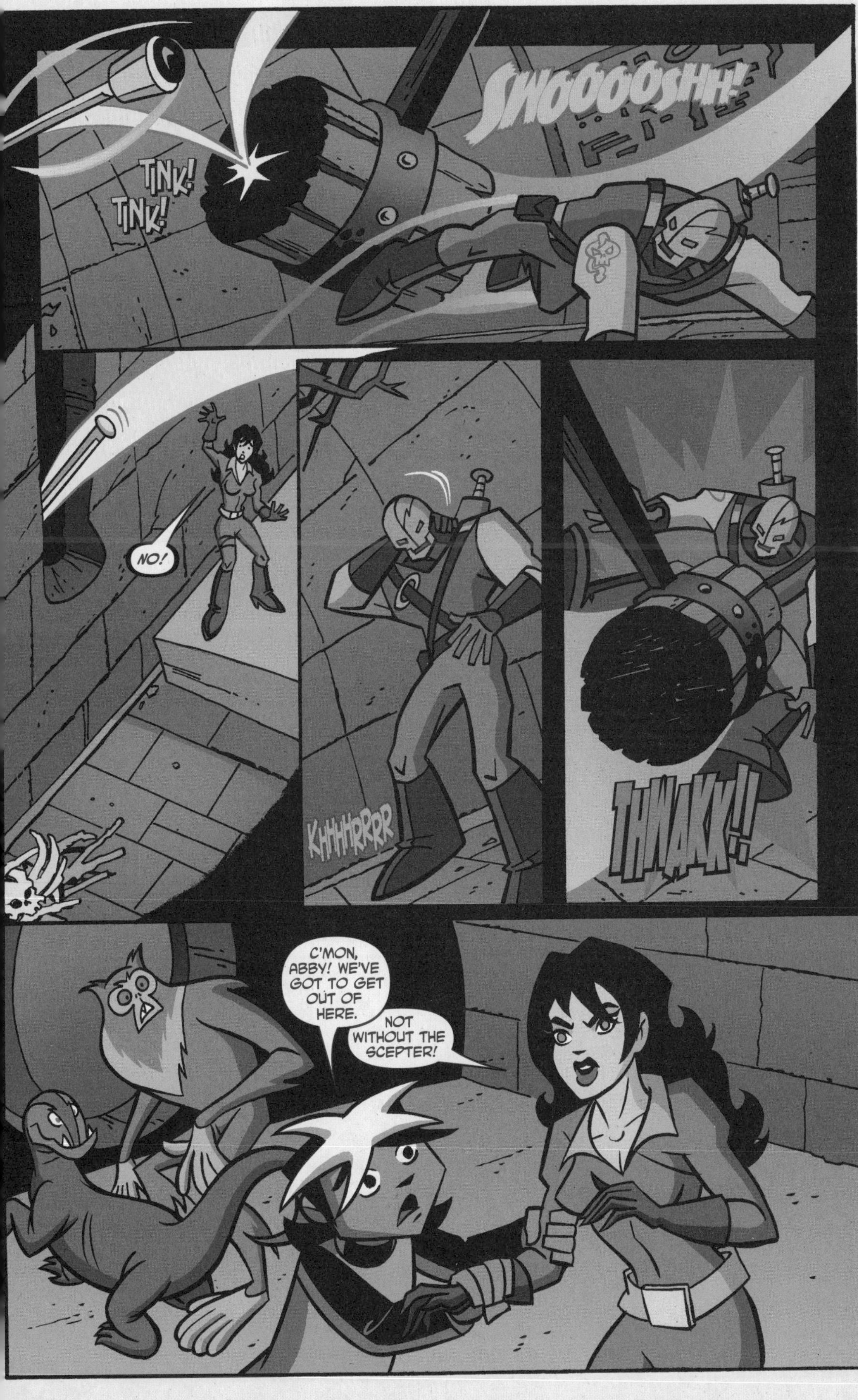
SWOOOOSHH!
TINK!
TINK!
NO!
KHHHHRRRR
THWAKK!!
C'MON, ABBY! WE'VE GOT TO GET OUT OF HERE.
NOT WITHOUT THE SCEPTER!

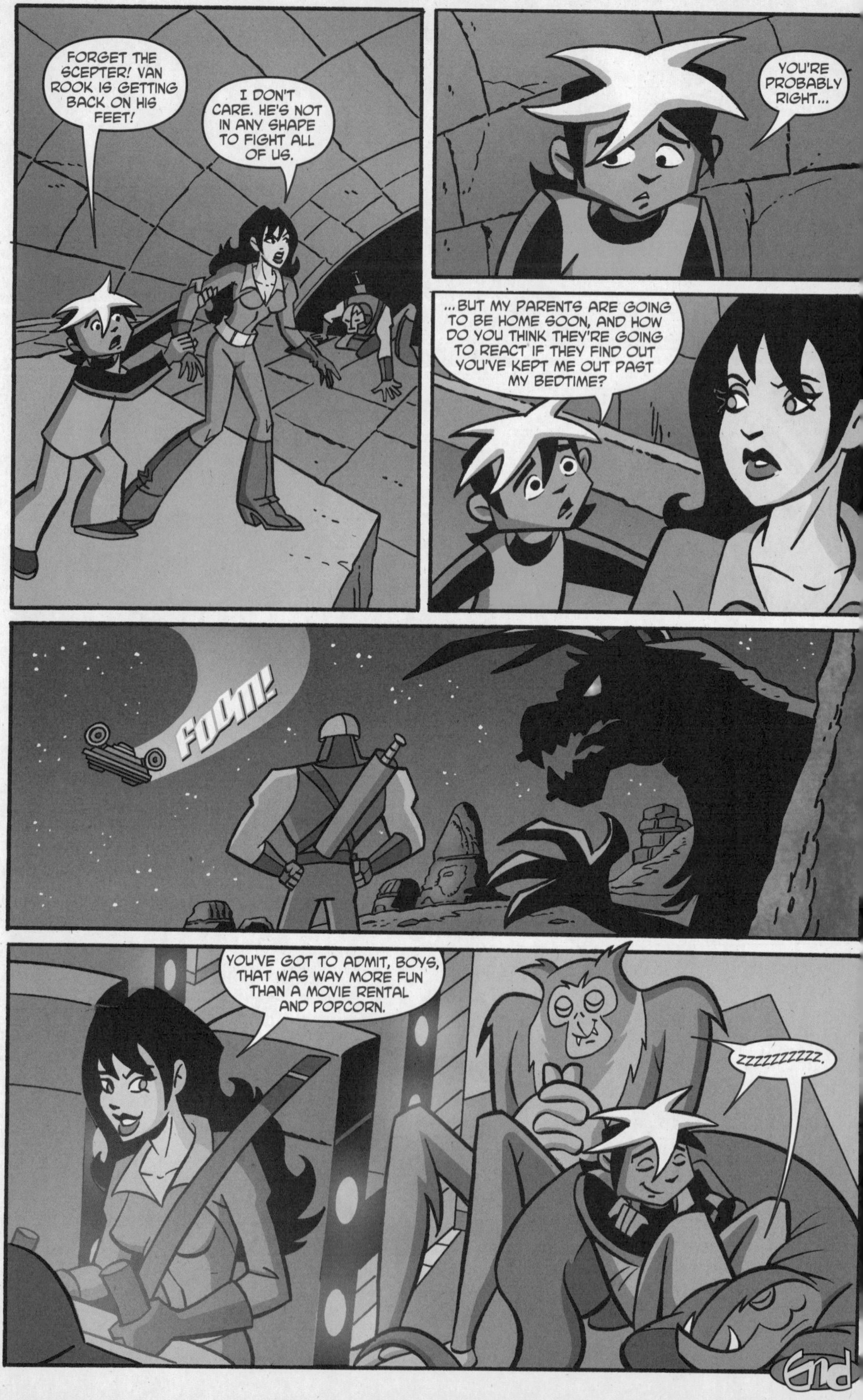
FORGET THE SCEPTER! VAN ROOK IS GETTING BACK ON HIS FEET!
I DON'T CARE. HE'S NOT IN ANY SHAPE TO FIGHT ALL OF US.
YOU'RE PROBABLY RIGHT...
...BUT MY PARENTS ARE GOING TO BE HOME SOON, AND HOW DO YOU THINK THEY'RE GOING TO REACT IF THEY FIND OUT YOU'VE KEPT ME OUT PAST MY BEDTIME?
FOOM!
YOU'VE GOT TO ADMIT, BOYS, THAT WAS WAY MORE FUN THAN A MOVIE RENTAL AND POPCORN.
ZZZZZZZZZZZ.
End

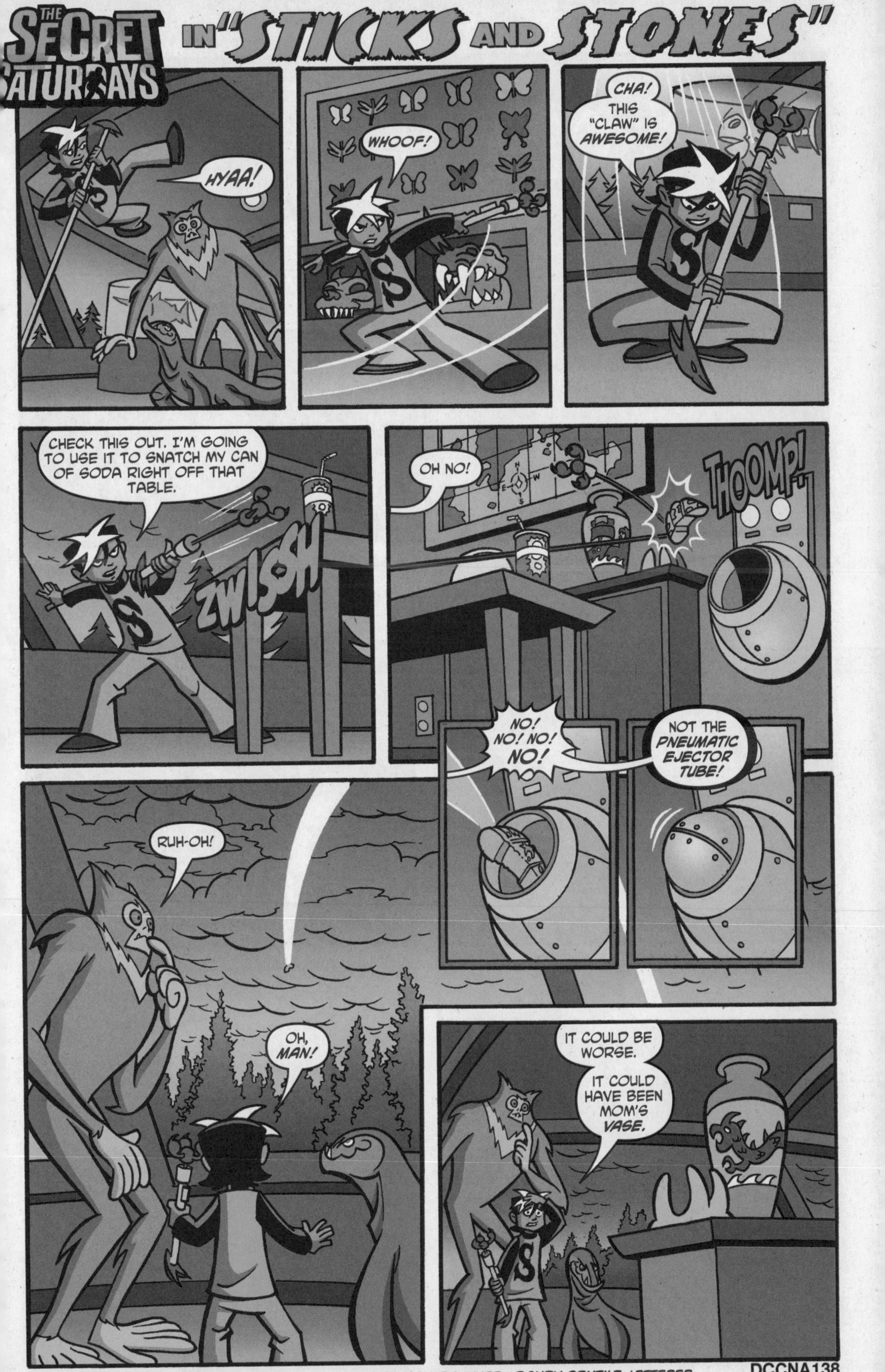
THE SECRET SATURDAYS
IN "STICKS AND STONES"
HYAA!
WHOOF!
CHA! THIS "CLAW" IS AWESOME!
CHECK THIS OUT. I'M GOING TO USE IT TO SNATCH MY CAN OF SODA RIGHT OFF THAT TABLE.
ZWISSH
OH NO!
THOOMP!
NO! NO! NO! NO!
NOT THE PNEUMATIC EJECTOR TUBE!
RUH-OH!
OH, MAN!
IT COULD BE WORSE.
IT COULD HAVE BEEN MOM'S VASE.

JOHN ROZUM–WRITER · WILL SWEENEY–PENCILLER · MIKE MANLEY–INKER · RANDY GENTILE–LETTERER
HEROIC AGE–COLORIST · REX OGLE–ASST. EDITOR · ELISABETH V. GEHRLEIN–EDITOR

DCCNA138

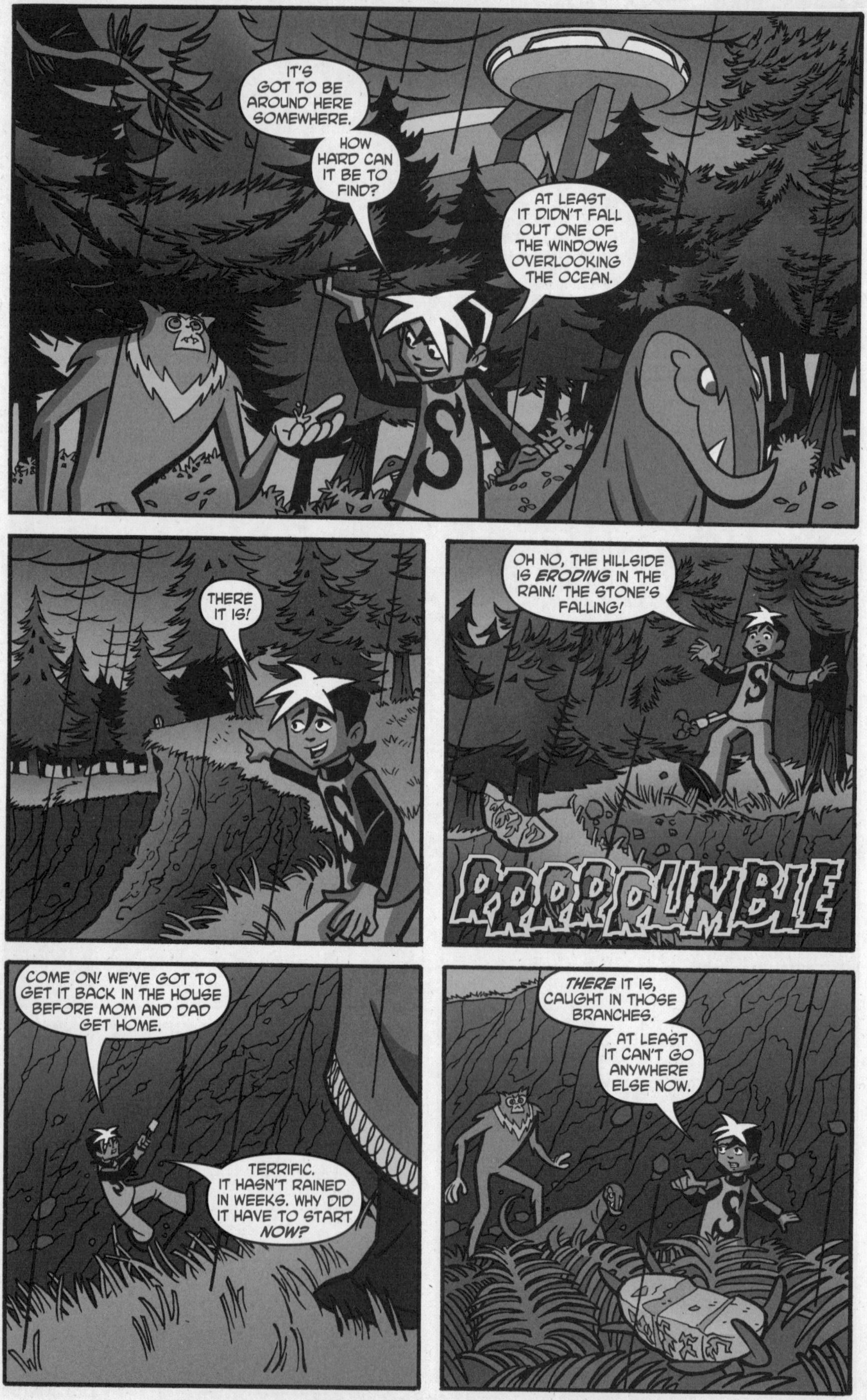
IT'S GOT TO BE AROUND HERE SOMEWHERE.
HOW HARD CAN IT BE TO FIND?
AT LEAST IT DIDN'T FALL OUT ONE OF THE WINDOWS OVERLOOKING THE OCEAN.
THERE IT IS!
OH NO, THE HILLSIDE IS *ERODING* IN THE RAIN! THE STONE'S FALLING!
RRRRRUMBLE
COME ON! WE'VE GOT TO GET IT BACK IN THE HOUSE BEFORE MOM AND DAD GET HOME.
TERRIFIC. IT HASN'T RAINED IN WEEKS. WHY DID IT HAVE TO START *NOW?*
THERE IT IS, CAUGHT IN THOSE BRANCHES.
AT LEAST IT CAN'T GO ANYWHERE ELSE NOW.

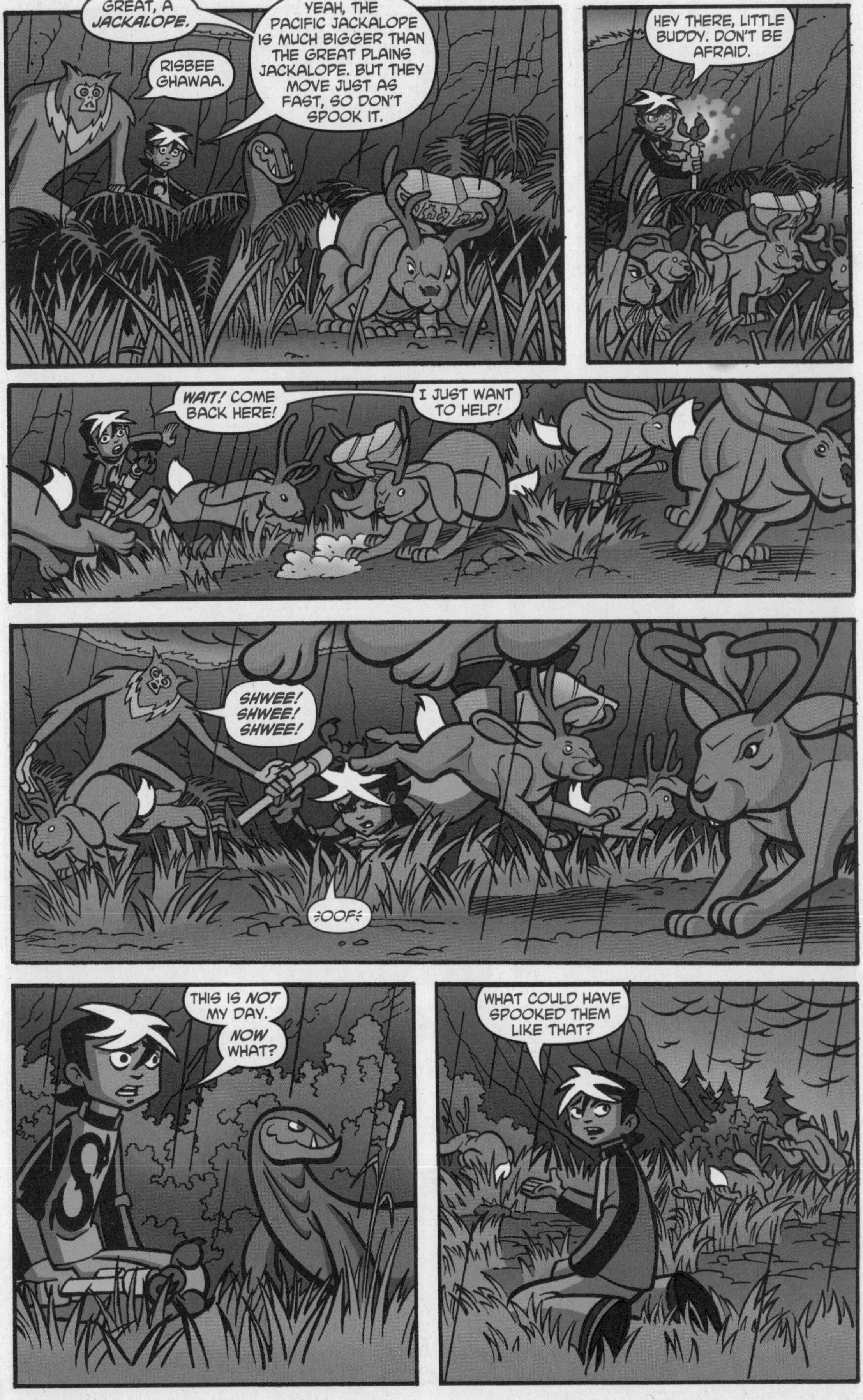
GREAT, A *JACKALOPE.*
RISBEE GHAWAA.
YEAH, THE PACIFIC JACKALOPE IS MUCH BIGGER THAN THE GREAT PLAINS JACKALOPE. BUT THEY MOVE JUST AS FAST, SO DON'T SPOOK IT.
HEY THERE, LITTLE BUDDY. DON'T BE AFRAID.
WAIT! COME BACK HERE!
I JUST WANT TO HELP!
SHWEE! SHWEE! SHWEE!
OOF
THIS IS *NOT* MY DAY. *NOW* WHAT?
WHAT COULD HAVE SPOOKED THEM LIKE THAT?

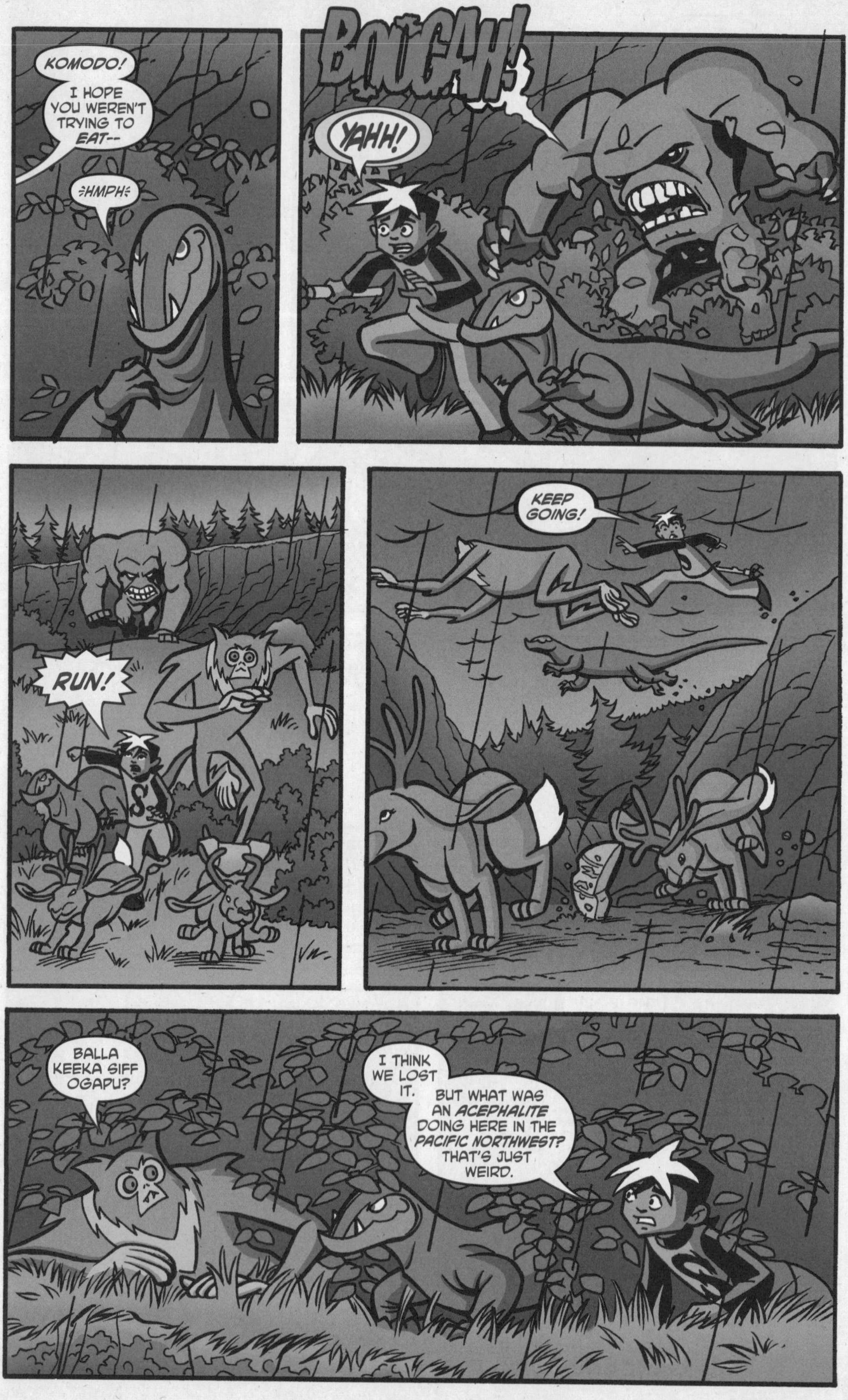
KOMODO!
I HOPE YOU WEREN'T TRYING TO EAT--
HMPH
BOUGAH!
YAHH!
RUN!
KEEP GOING!
BALLA KEEKA SIFF OGAPU?
I THINK WE LOST IT.
BUT WHAT WAS AN ACEPHALITE DOING HERE IN THE PACIFIC NORTHWEST? THAT'S JUST WEIRD.

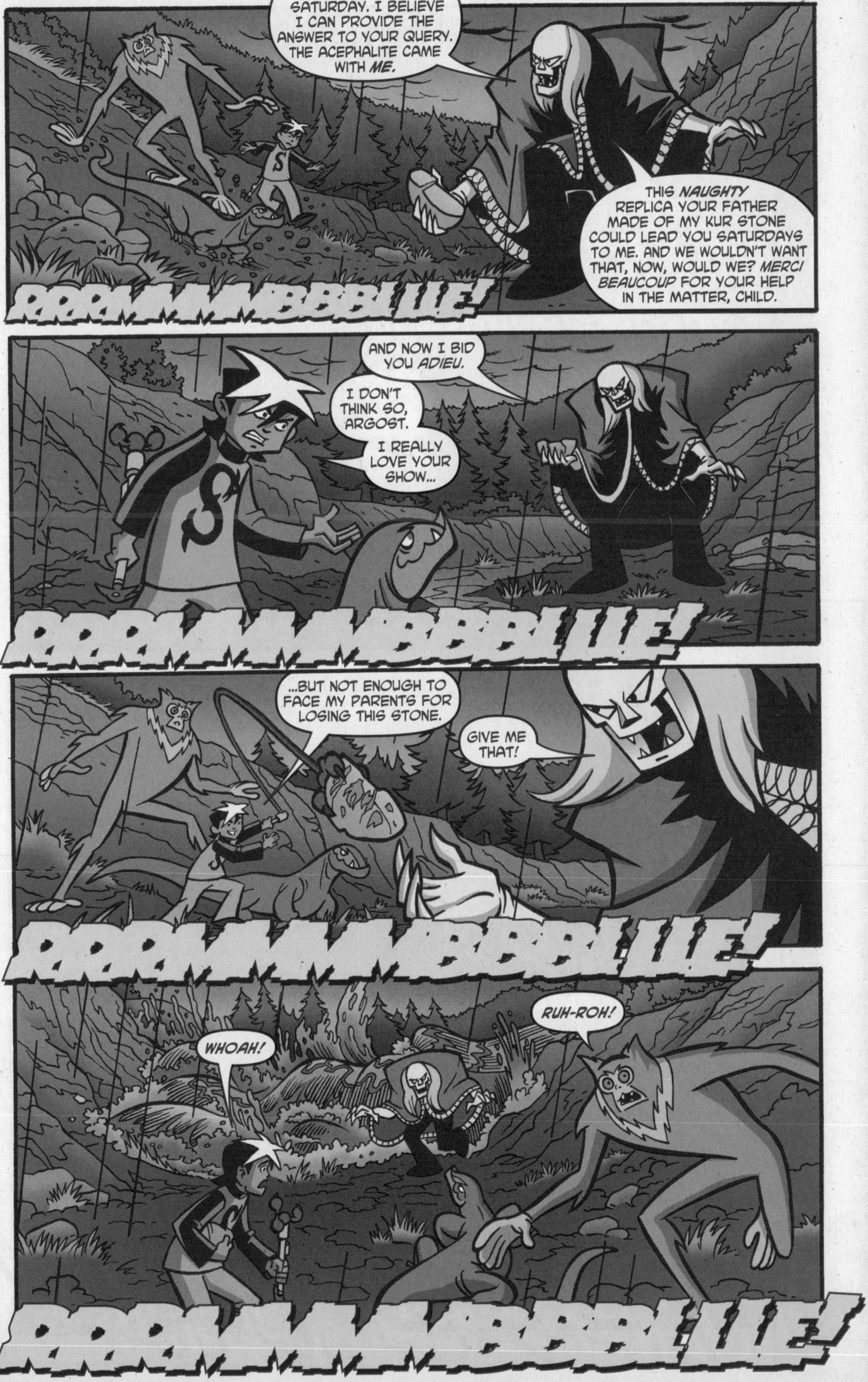
GREETINGS AND BIENVENUE, LITTLE SATURDAY. I BELIEVE I CAN PROVIDE THE ANSWER TO YOUR QUERY. THE ACEPHALITE CAME WITH *ME*.
THIS *NAUGHTY* REPLICA YOUR FATHER MADE OF MY KUR STONE COULD LEAD YOU SATURDAYS TO ME. AND WE WOULDN'T WANT THAT, NOW, WOULD WE? *MERCI BEAUCOUP* FOR YOUR HELP IN THE MATTER, CHILD.
RRRMMMBBBLLE!
AND NOW I BID YOU *ADIEU*.
I DON'T THINK SO, ARGOST.
I REALLY LOVE YOUR SHOW...
RRRMMMBBBLLE!
...BUT NOT ENOUGH TO FACE MY PARENTS FOR LOSING THIS STONE.
GIVE ME THAT!
RRRMMMBBBLLE!
WHOAH!
RUH-ROH!
RRRMMMBBBLLE!

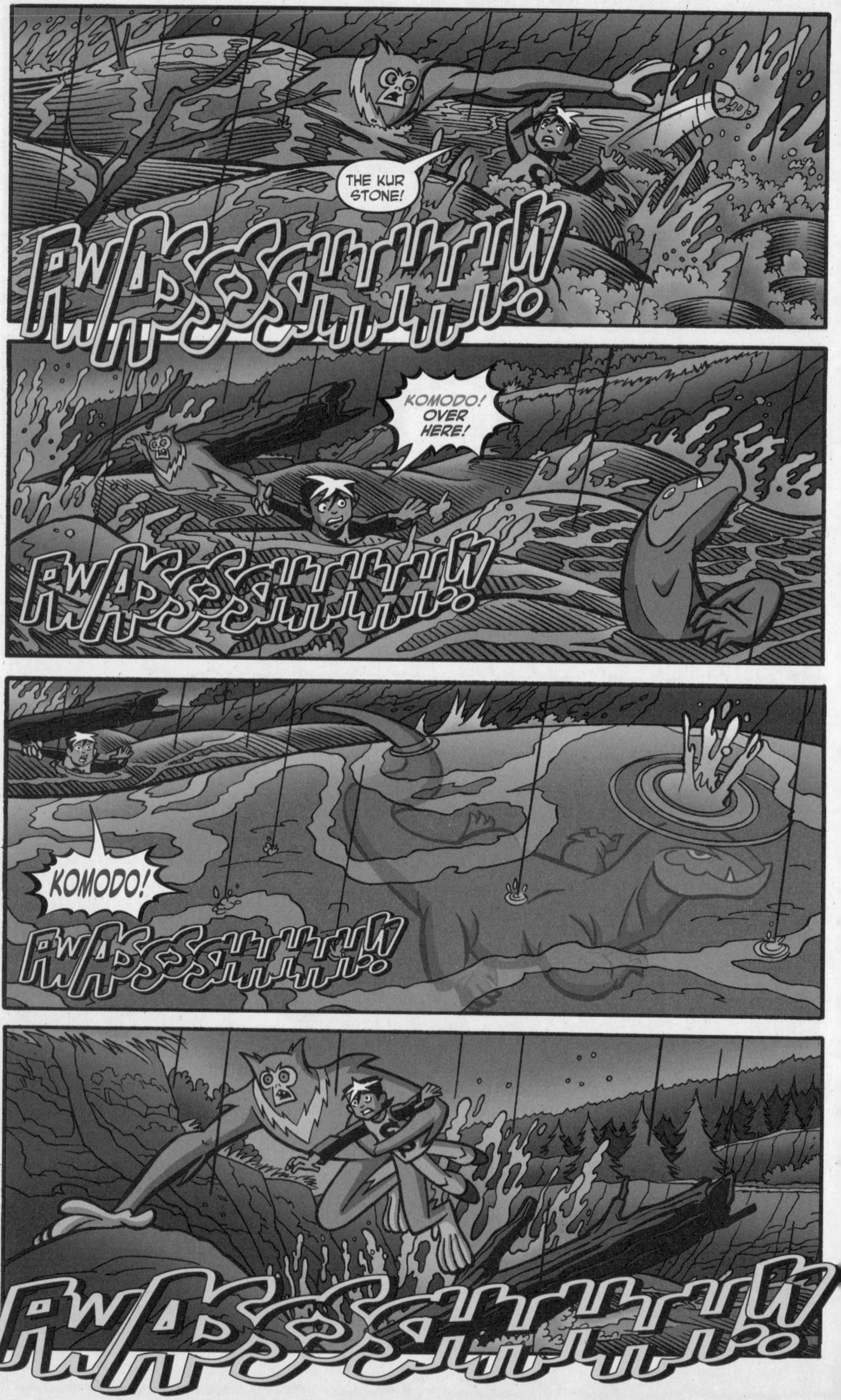
THE KUR STONE!
RWASSSHHHHHH!
KOMODO! OVER HERE!
RWASSSHHHHHH!
KOMODO!
RWASSSHHHHHH!
RWASSSHHHHHH!

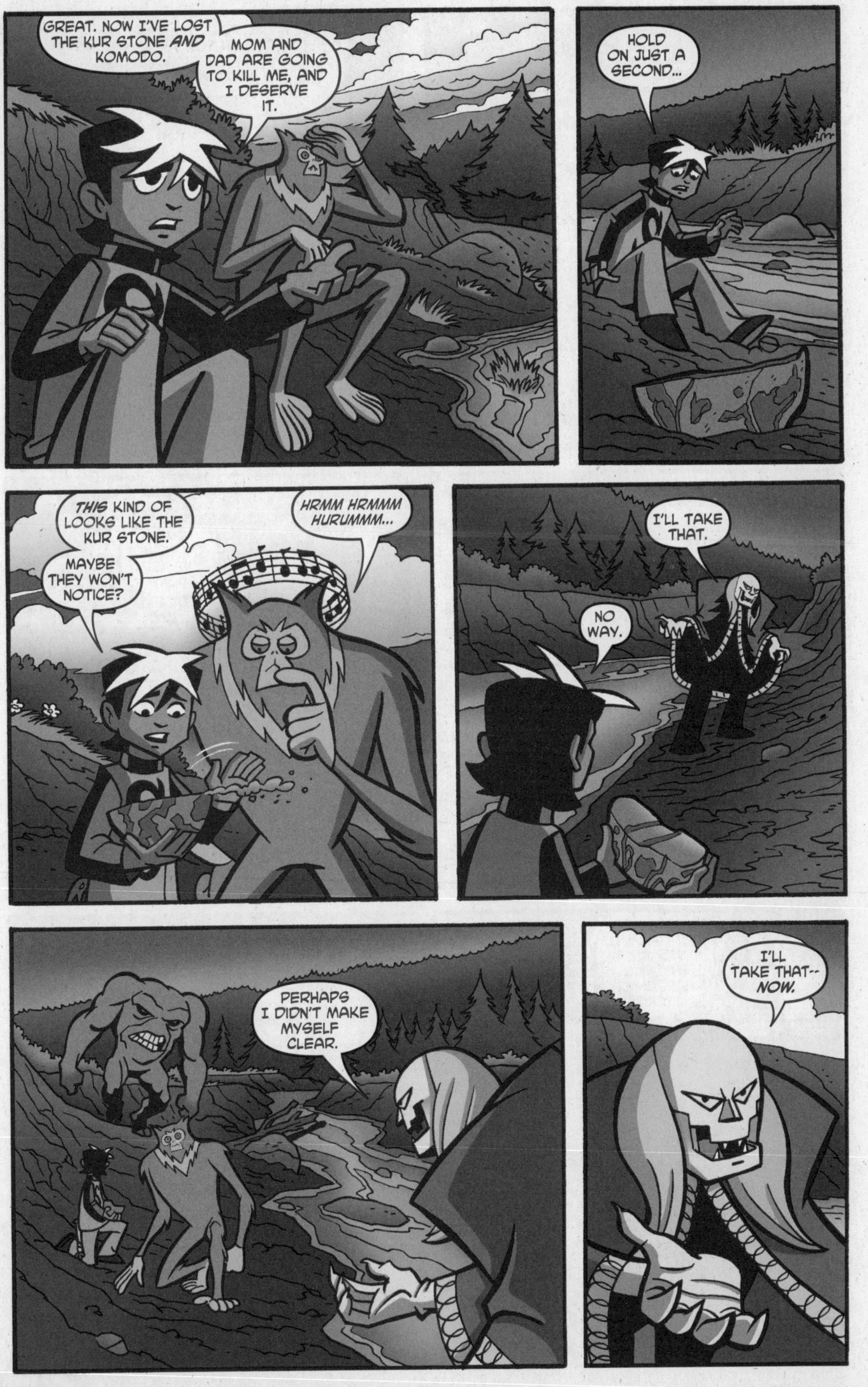
GREAT. NOW I'VE LOST THE KUR STONE *AND* KOMODO.
MOM AND DAD ARE GOING TO KILL ME, AND I DESERVE IT.
HOLD ON JUST A SECOND...
THIS KIND OF LOOKS LIKE THE KUR STONE.
MAYBE THEY WON'T NOTICE?
HRMM HRMMM HURUMMM...
I'LL TAKE THAT.
NO WAY.
PERHAPS I DIDN'T MAKE MYSELF CLEAR.
I'LL TAKE THAT--*NOW.*

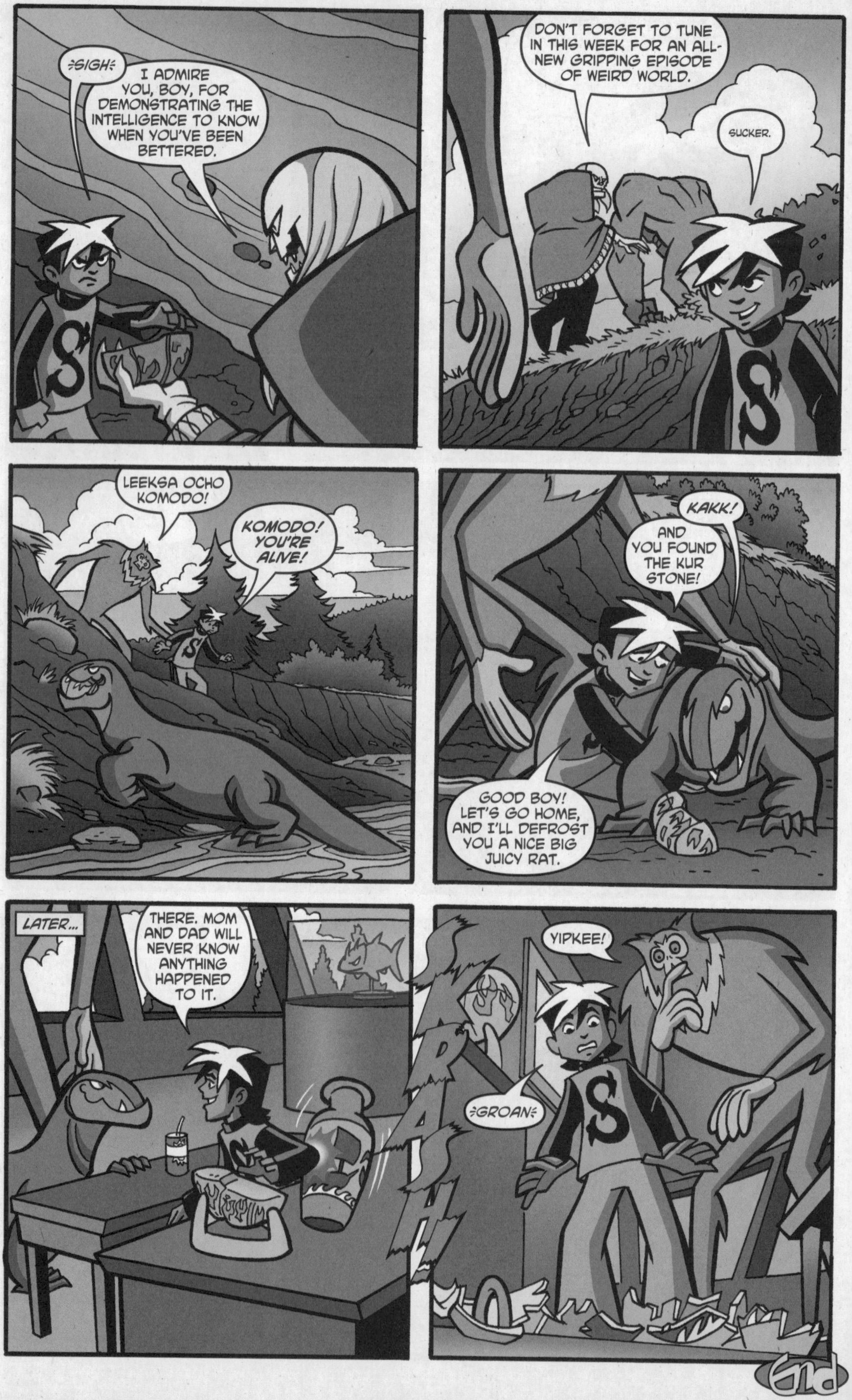

SIGH
I ADMIRE YOU, BOY, FOR DEMONSTRATING THE INTELLIGENCE TO KNOW WHEN YOU'VE BEEN BETTERED.
DON'T FORGET TO TUNE IN THIS WEEK FOR AN ALL-NEW GRIPPING EPISODE OF WEIRD WORLD.
SUCKER.
LEEKSA OCHO KOMODO!
KOMODO! YOU'RE ALIVE!
KAKK!
AND YOU FOUND THE KUR STONE!
GOOD BOY! LET'S GO HOME, AND I'LL DEFROST YOU A NICE BIG JUICY RAT.
LATER...
THERE. MOM AND DAD WILL NEVER KNOW ANYTHING HAPPENED TO IT.
YIPKEE!
GROAN
End

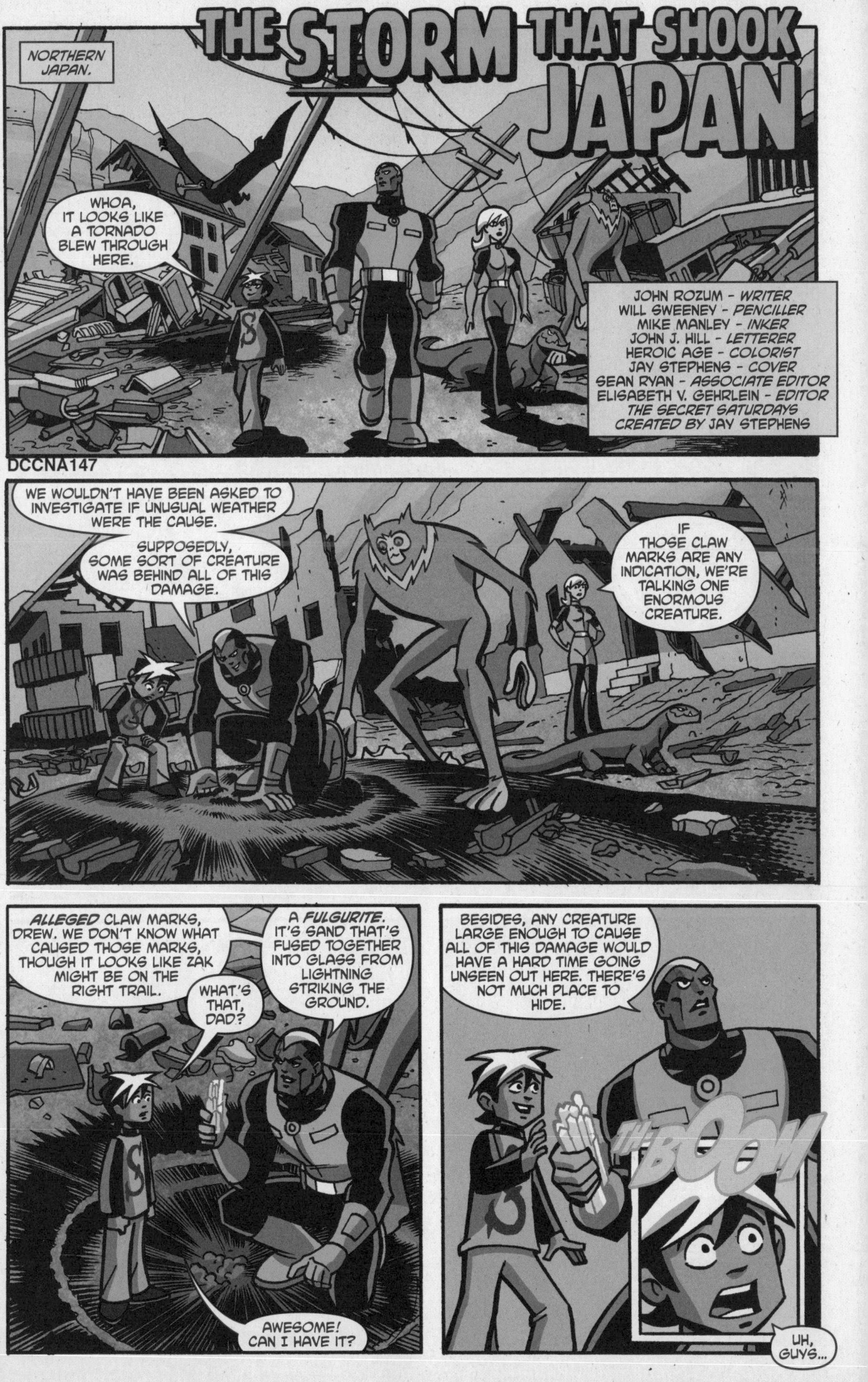
THE STORM THAT SHOOK JAPAN
NORTHERN JAPAN.
WHOA, IT LOOKS LIKE A TORNADO BLEW THROUGH HERE.
JOHN ROZUM - WRITER
WILL SWEENEY - PENCILLER
MIKE MANLEY - INKER
JOHN J. HILL - LETTERER
HEROIC AGE - COLORIST
JAY STEPHENS - COVER
SEAN RYAN - ASSOCIATE EDITOR
ELISABETH V. GEHRLEIN - EDITOR
THE SECRET SATURDAYS CREATED BY JAY STEPHENS
DCCNA147
WE WOULDN'T HAVE BEEN ASKED TO INVESTIGATE IF UNUSUAL WEATHER WERE THE CAUSE.
SUPPOSEDLY, SOME SORT OF CREATURE WAS BEHIND ALL OF THIS DAMAGE.
IF THOSE CLAW MARKS ARE ANY INDICATION, WE'RE TALKING ONE ENORMOUS CREATURE.
ALLEGED CLAW MARKS, DREW. WE DON'T KNOW WHAT CAUSED THOSE MARKS, THOUGH IT LOOKS LIKE ZAK MIGHT BE ON THE RIGHT TRAIL.
WHAT'S THAT, DAD?
A FULGURITE. IT'S SAND THAT'S FUSED TOGETHER INTO GLASS FROM LIGHTNING STRIKING THE GROUND.
AWESOME! CAN I HAVE IT?
BESIDES, ANY CREATURE LARGE ENOUGH TO CAUSE ALL OF THIS DAMAGE WOULD HAVE A HARD TIME GOING UNSEEN OUT HERE. THERE'S NOT MUCH PLACE TO HIDE.
THBOOM
UH, GUYS...

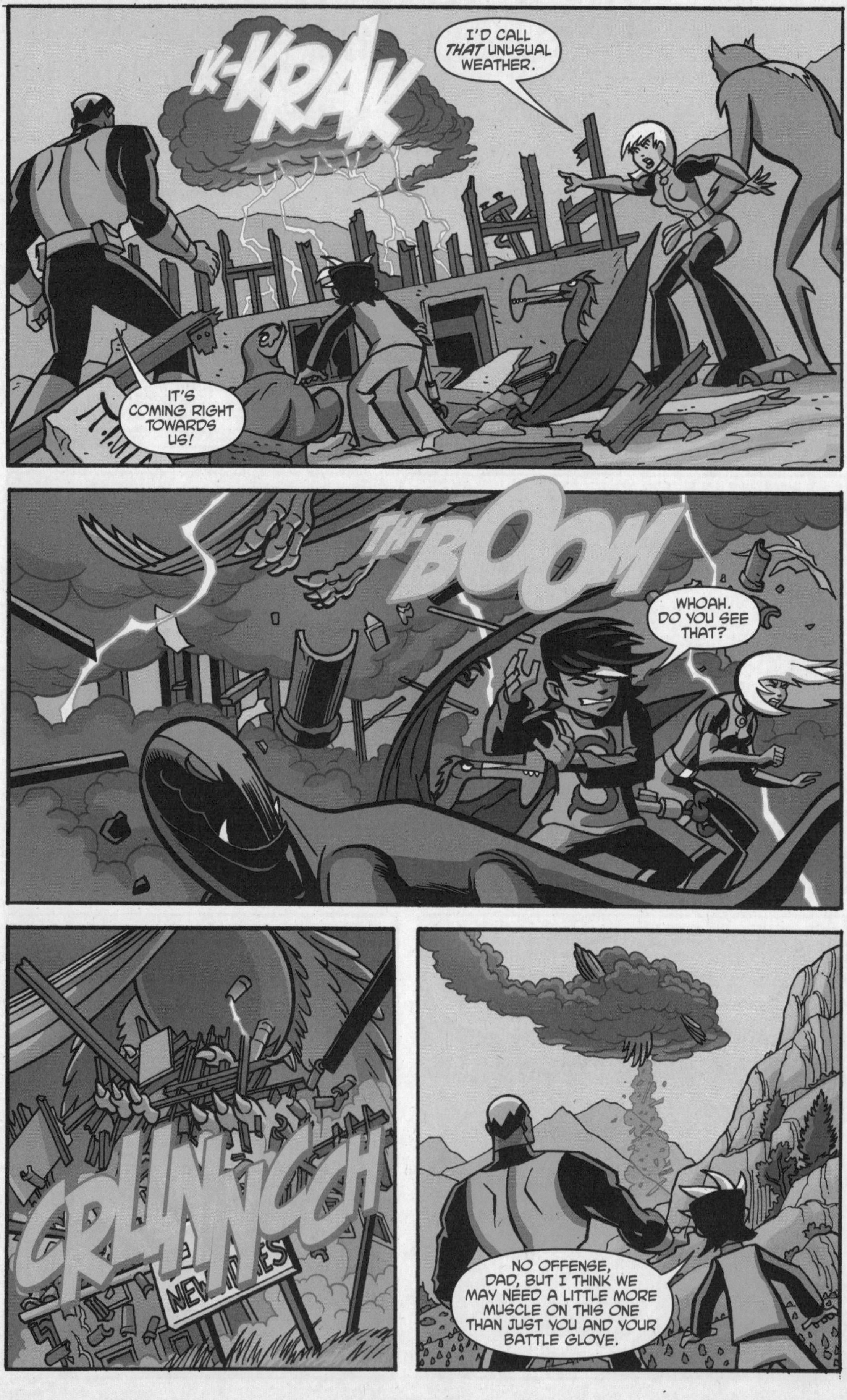
K-KRAK
I'D CALL THAT UNUSUAL WEATHER.
IT'S COMING RIGHT TOWARDS US!
TH-BOOM
WHOAH. DO YOU SEE THAT?
CRUNNCCH
NO OFFENSE, DAD, BUT I THINK WE MAY NEED A LITTLE MORE MUSCLE ON THIS ONE THAN JUST YOU AND YOUR BATTLE GLOVE.

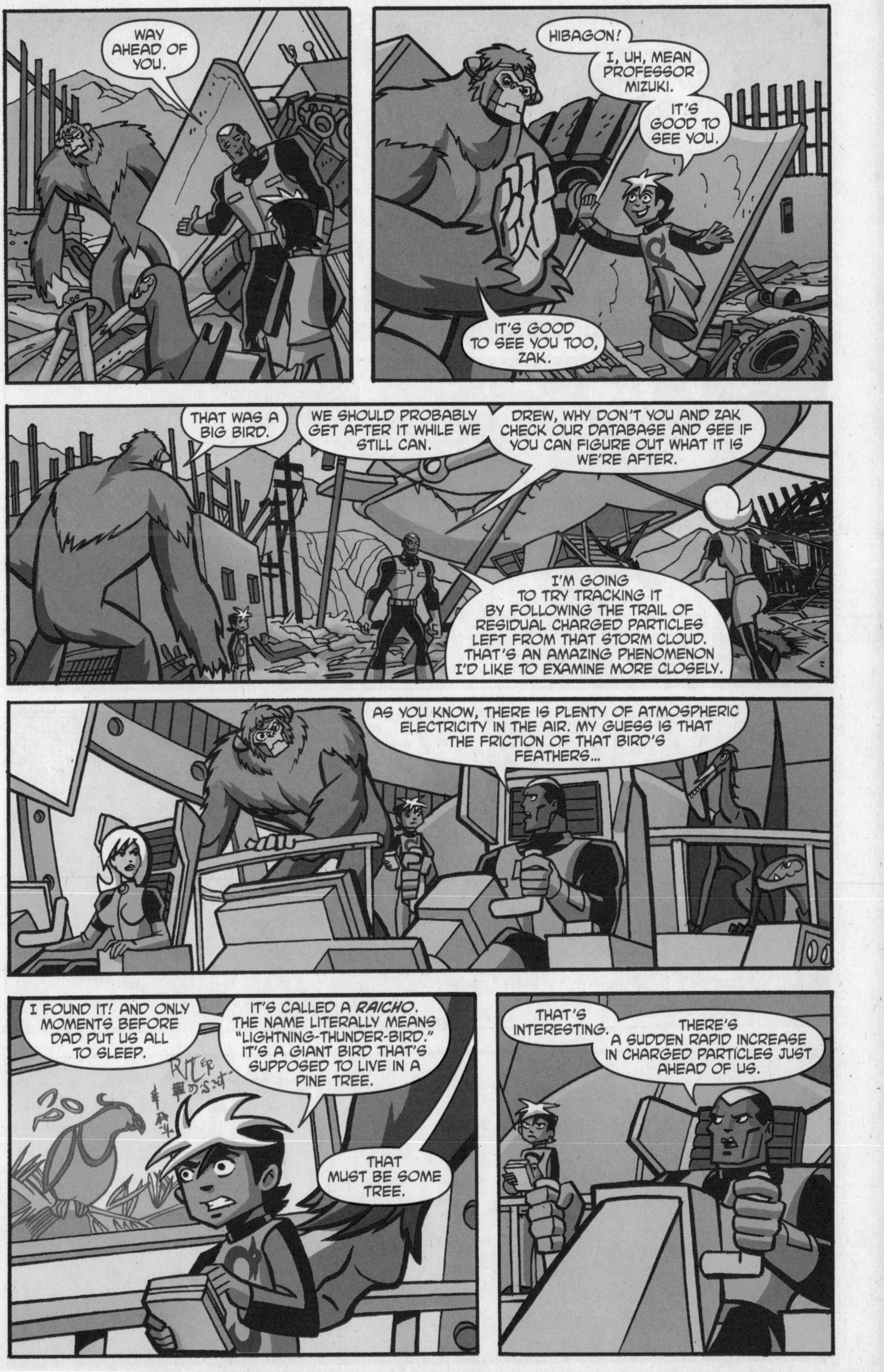
WAY AHEAD OF YOU.
HIBAGON!
I, UH, MEAN PROFESSOR MIZUKI.
IT'S GOOD TO SEE YOU.
IT'S GOOD TO SEE YOU TOO, ZAK.
THAT WAS A BIG BIRD.
WE SHOULD PROBABLY GET AFTER IT WHILE WE STILL CAN.
DREW, WHY DON'T YOU AND ZAK CHECK OUR DATABASE AND SEE IF YOU CAN FIGURE OUT WHAT IT IS WE'RE AFTER.
I'M GOING TO TRY TRACKING IT BY FOLLOWING THE TRAIL OF RESIDUAL CHARGED PARTICLES LEFT FROM THAT STORM CLOUD. THAT'S AN AMAZING PHENOMENON I'D LIKE TO EXAMINE MORE CLOSELY.
AS YOU KNOW, THERE IS PLENTY OF ATMOSPHERIC ELECTRICITY IN THE AIR. MY GUESS IS THAT THE FRICTION OF THAT BIRD'S FEATHERS...
I FOUND IT! AND ONLY MOMENTS BEFORE DAD PUT US ALL TO SLEEP.
IT'S CALLED A *RAICHO*. THE NAME LITERALLY MEANS "LIGHTNING-THUNDER-BIRD." IT'S A GIANT BIRD THAT'S SUPPOSED TO LIVE IN A PINE TREE.
THAT MUST BE SOME TREE.
THAT'S INTERESTING.
THERE'S A SUDDEN RAPID INCREASE IN CHARGED PARTICLES JUST AHEAD OF US.

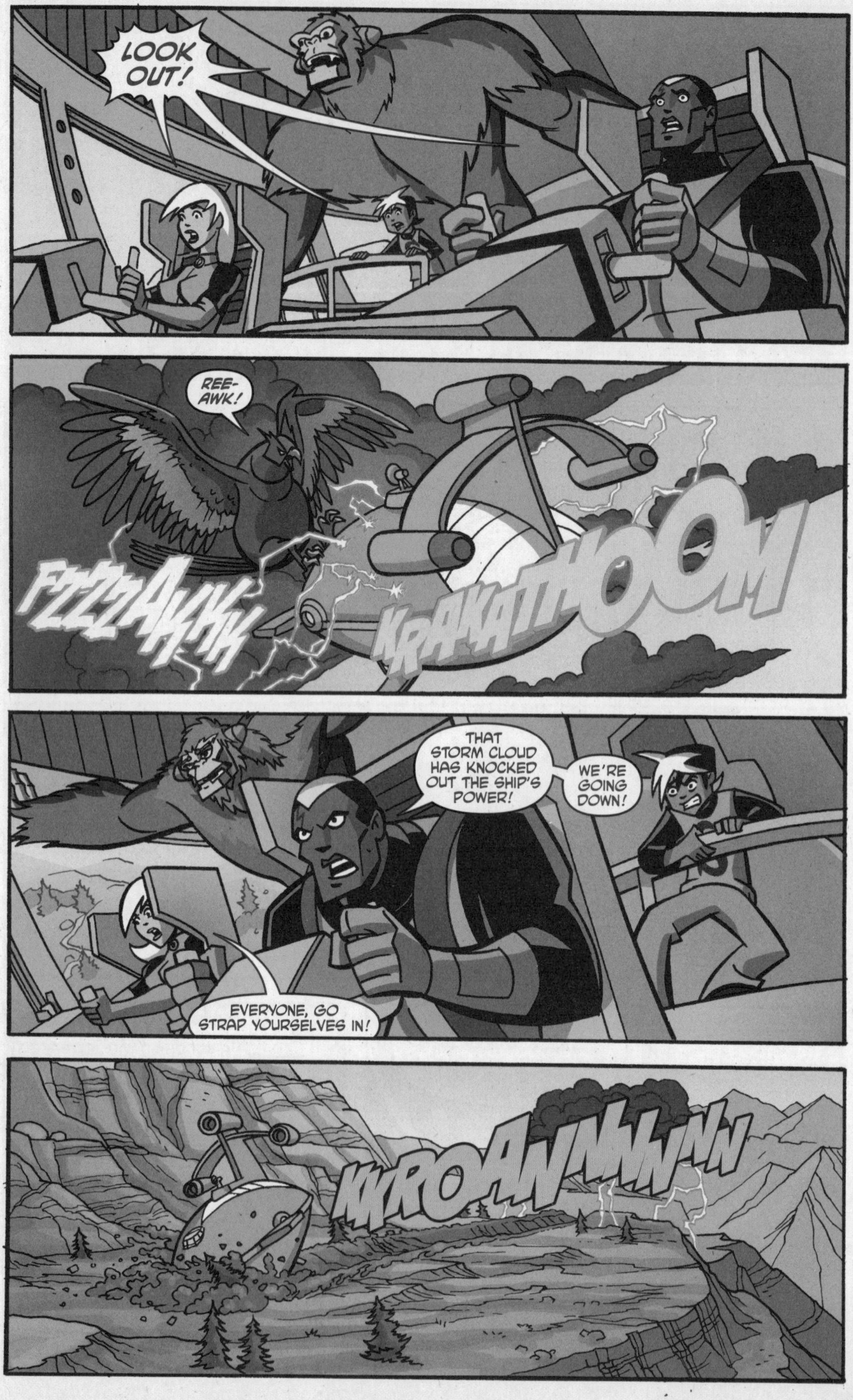
LOOK OUT!
REE-AWK!
FZZZZAKKK
KRAKATHOOM
THAT STORM CLOUD HAS KNOCKED OUT THE SHIP'S POWER!
WE'RE GOING DOWN!
EVERYONE, GO STRAP YOURSELVES IN!
KKROANNNNNN

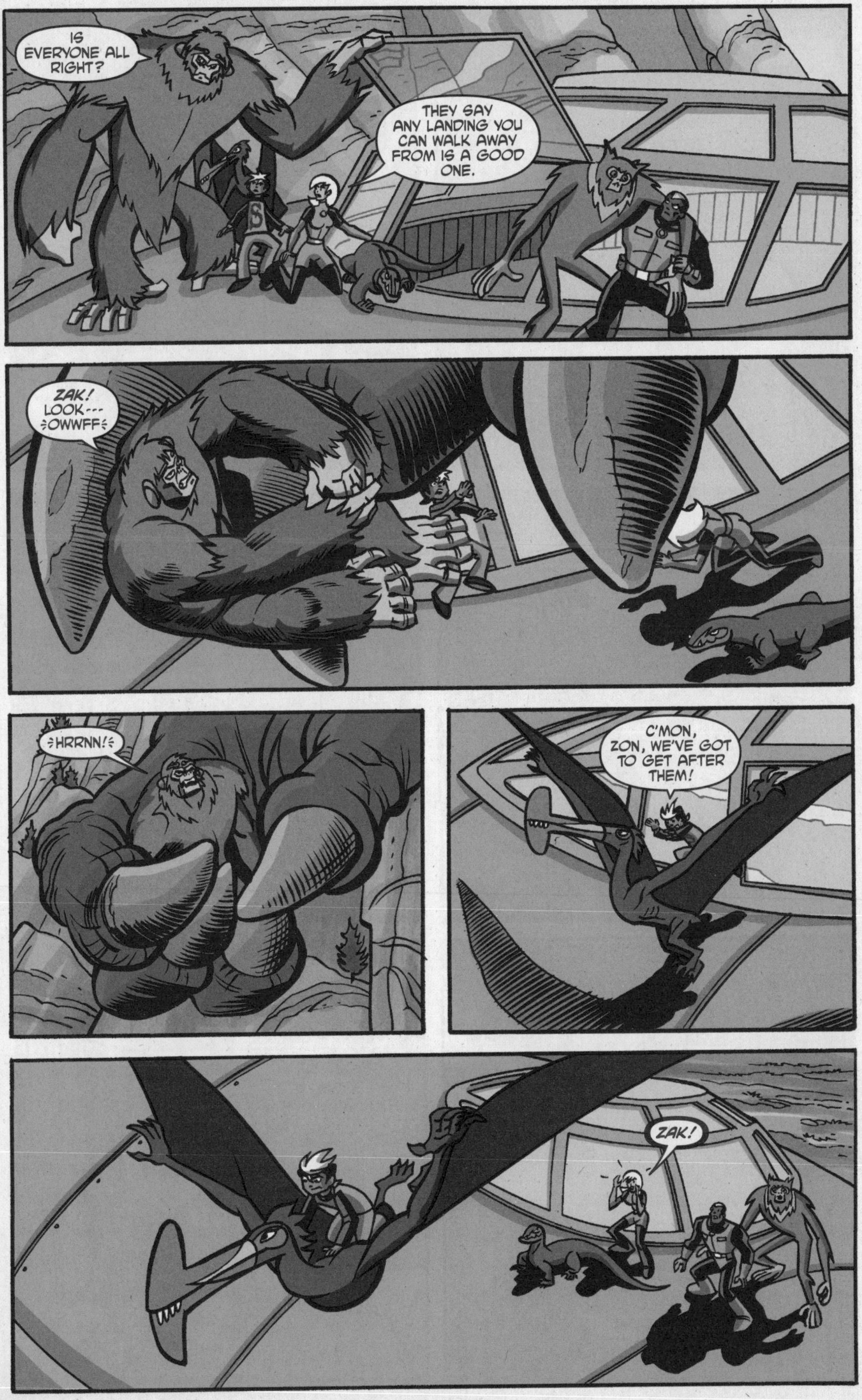
IS EVERYONE ALL RIGHT?
THEY SAY ANY LANDING YOU CAN WALK AWAY FROM IS A GOOD ONE.
ZAK! LOOK--- OWWFF
HRRNN!
C'MON, ZON, WE'VE GOT TO GET AFTER THEM!
ZAK!

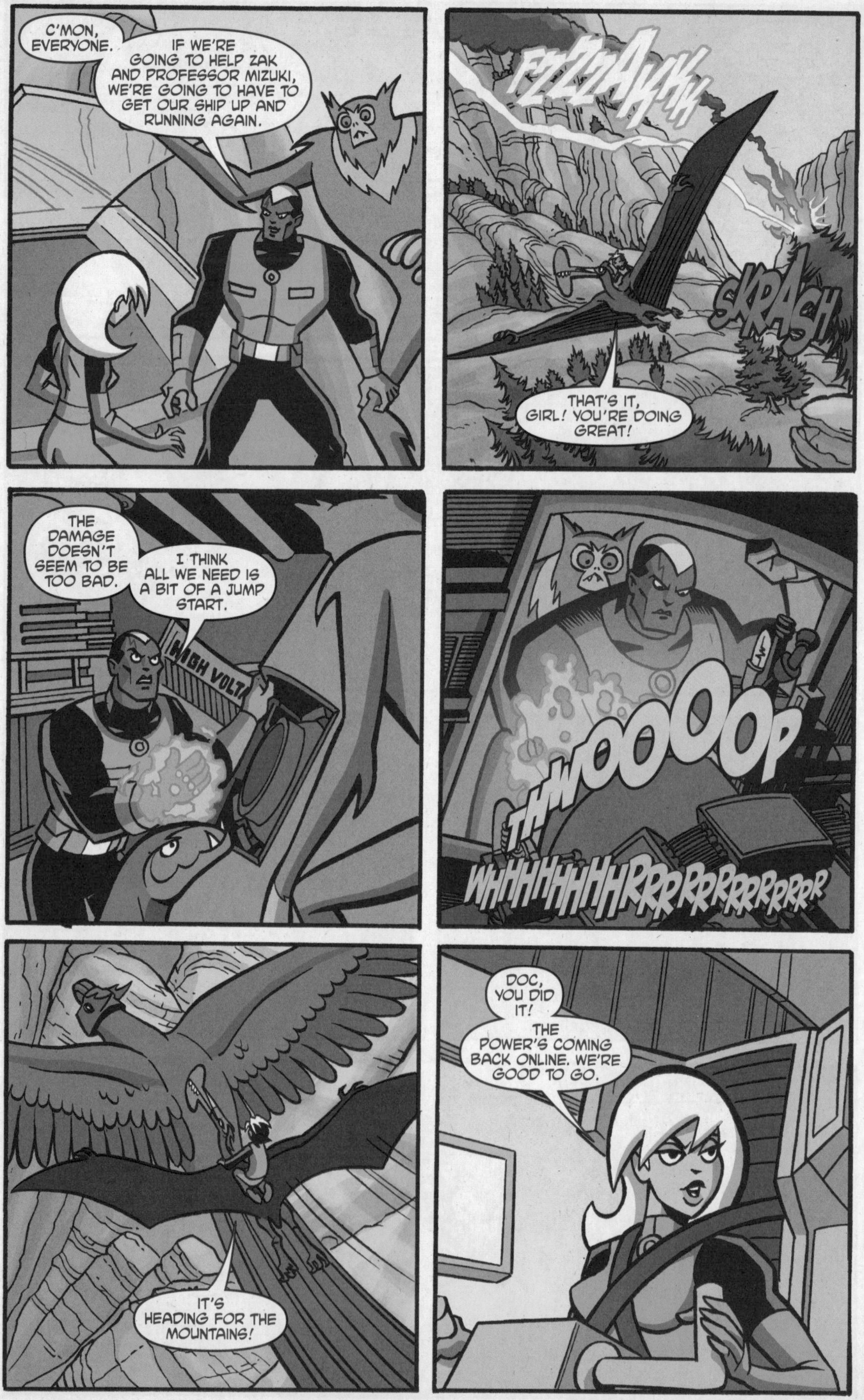
C'MON, EVERYONE.
IF WE'RE GOING TO HELP ZAK AND PROFESSOR MIZUKI, WE'RE GOING TO HAVE TO GET OUR SHIP UP AND RUNNING AGAIN.
FZZZZAKKK
SKRASH
THAT'S IT, GIRL! YOU'RE DOING GREAT!
THE DAMAGE DOESN'T SEEM TO BE TOO BAD.
I THINK ALL WE NEED IS A BIT OF A JUMP START.
THWOOOOP
WHHHHHHHRRRRRRRRRRR
IT'S HEADING FOR THE MOUNTAINS!
DOC, YOU DID IT!
THE POWER'S COMING BACK ONLINE. WE'RE GOOD TO GO.

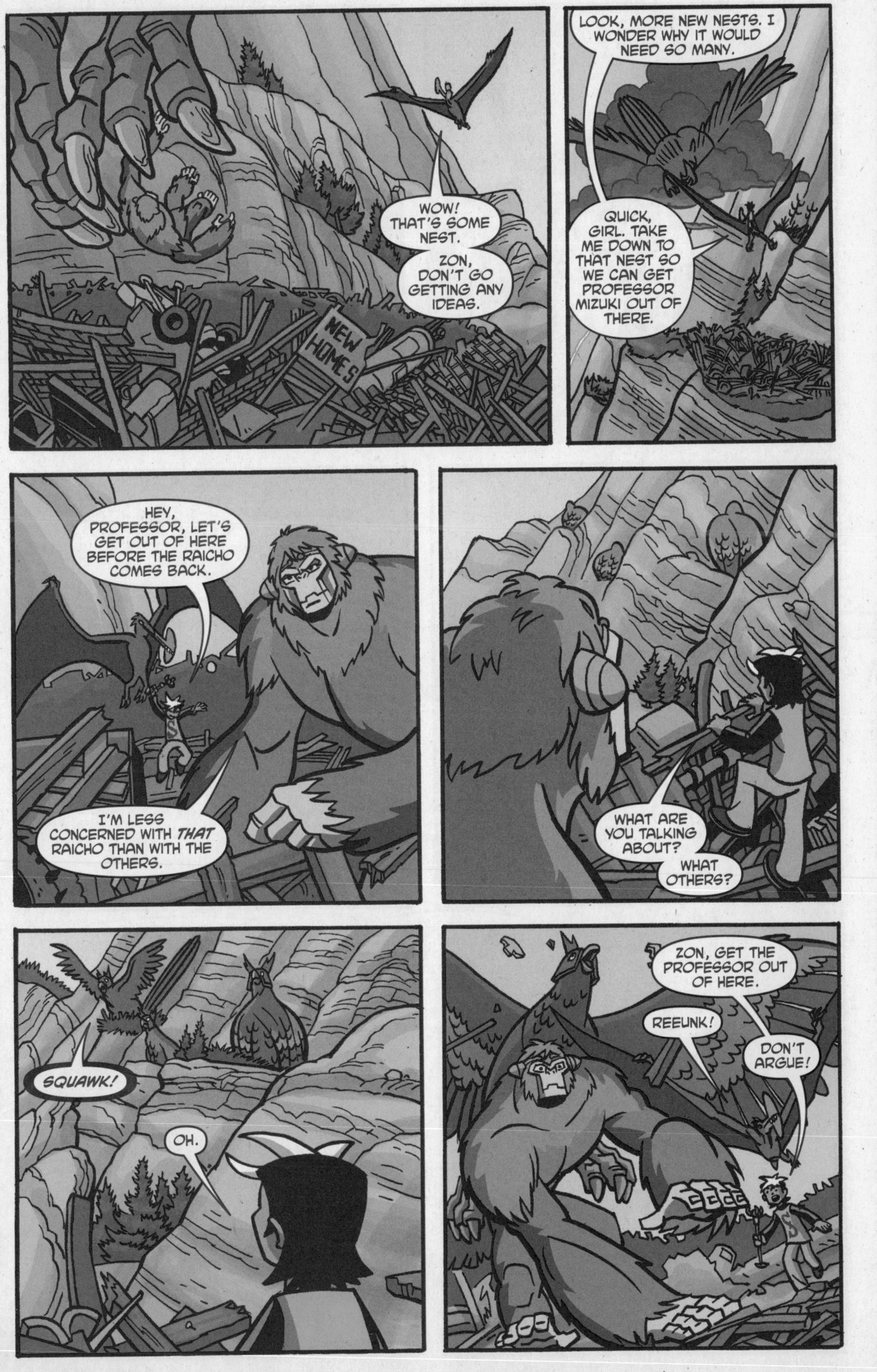
WOW! THAT'S SOME NEST.
ZON, DON'T GO GETTING ANY IDEAS.
NEW HOMES
LOOK, MORE NEW NESTS. I WONDER WHY IT WOULD NEED SO MANY.
QUICK, GIRL. TAKE ME DOWN TO THAT NEST SO WE CAN GET PROFESSOR MIZUKI OUT OF THERE.
HEY, PROFESSOR, LET'S GET OUT OF HERE BEFORE THE RAICHO COMES BACK.
I'M LESS CONCERNED WITH *THAT* RAICHO THAN WITH THE OTHERS.
WHAT ARE YOU TALKING ABOUT?
WHAT OTHERS?
SQUAWK!
OH.
ZON, GET THE PROFESSOR OUT OF HERE.
REEUNK!
DON'T ARGUE!

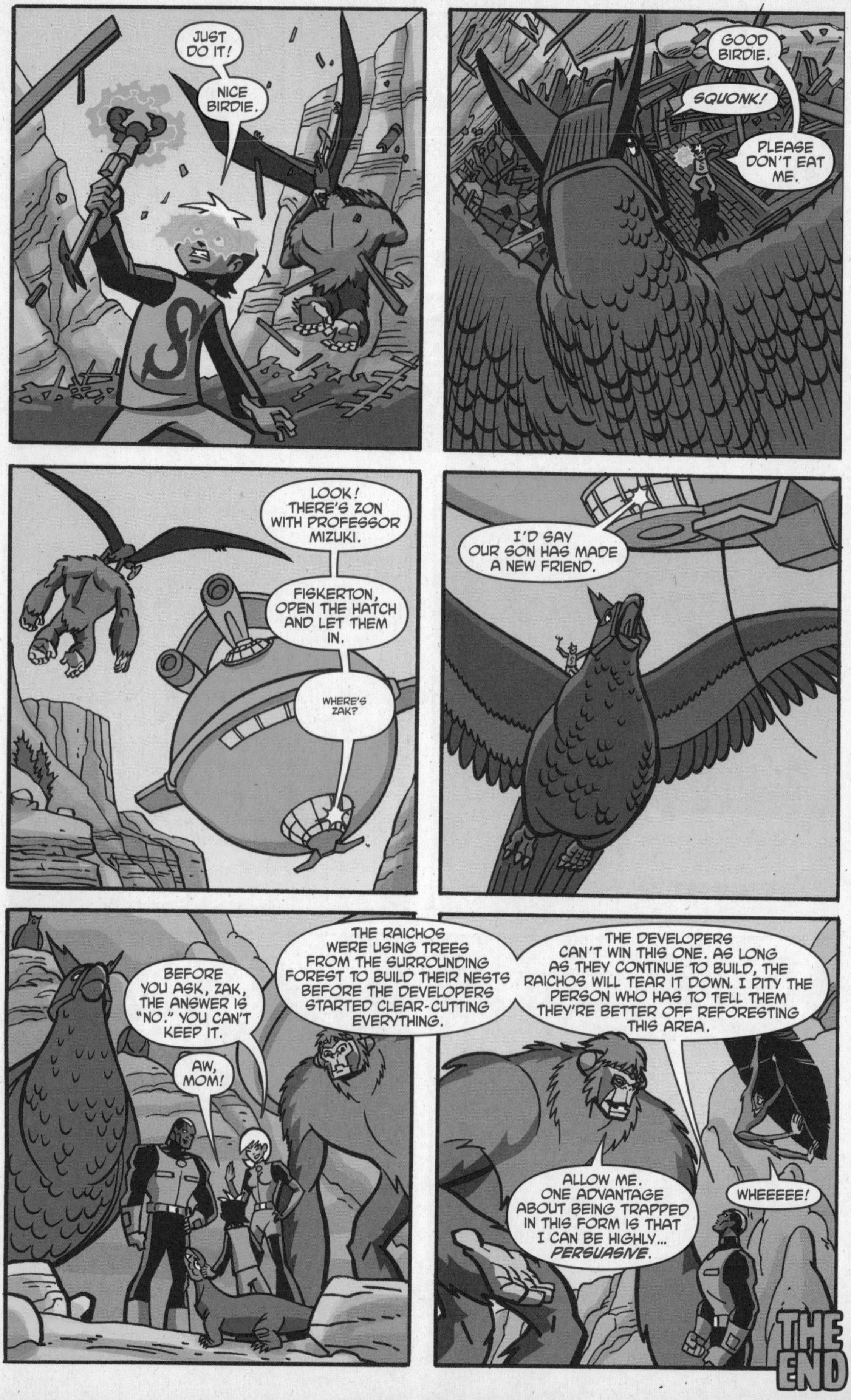
JUST DO IT!
NICE BIRDIE.
GOOD BIRDIE.
SQUONK!
PLEASE DON'T EAT ME.
LOOK! THERE'S ZON WITH PROFESSOR MIZUKI.
FISKERTON, OPEN THE HATCH AND LET THEM IN.
WHERE'S ZAK?
I'D SAY OUR SON HAS MADE A NEW FRIEND.
BEFORE YOU ASK, ZAK, THE ANSWER IS "NO." YOU CAN'T KEEP IT.
AW, MOM!
THE RAICHOS WERE USING TREES FROM THE SURROUNDING FOREST TO BUILD THEIR NESTS BEFORE THE DEVELOPERS STARTED CLEAR-CUTTING EVERYTHING.
THE DEVELOPERS CAN'T WIN THIS ONE. AS LONG AS THEY CONTINUE TO BUILD, THE RAICHOS WILL TEAR IT DOWN. I PITY THE PERSON WHO HAS TO TELL THEM THEY'RE BETTER OFF REFORESTING THIS AREA.
ALLOW ME. ONE ADVANTAGE ABOUT BEING TRAPPED IN THIS FORM IS THAT I CAN BE HIGHLY... PERSUASIVE.
WHEEEEE!
THE END

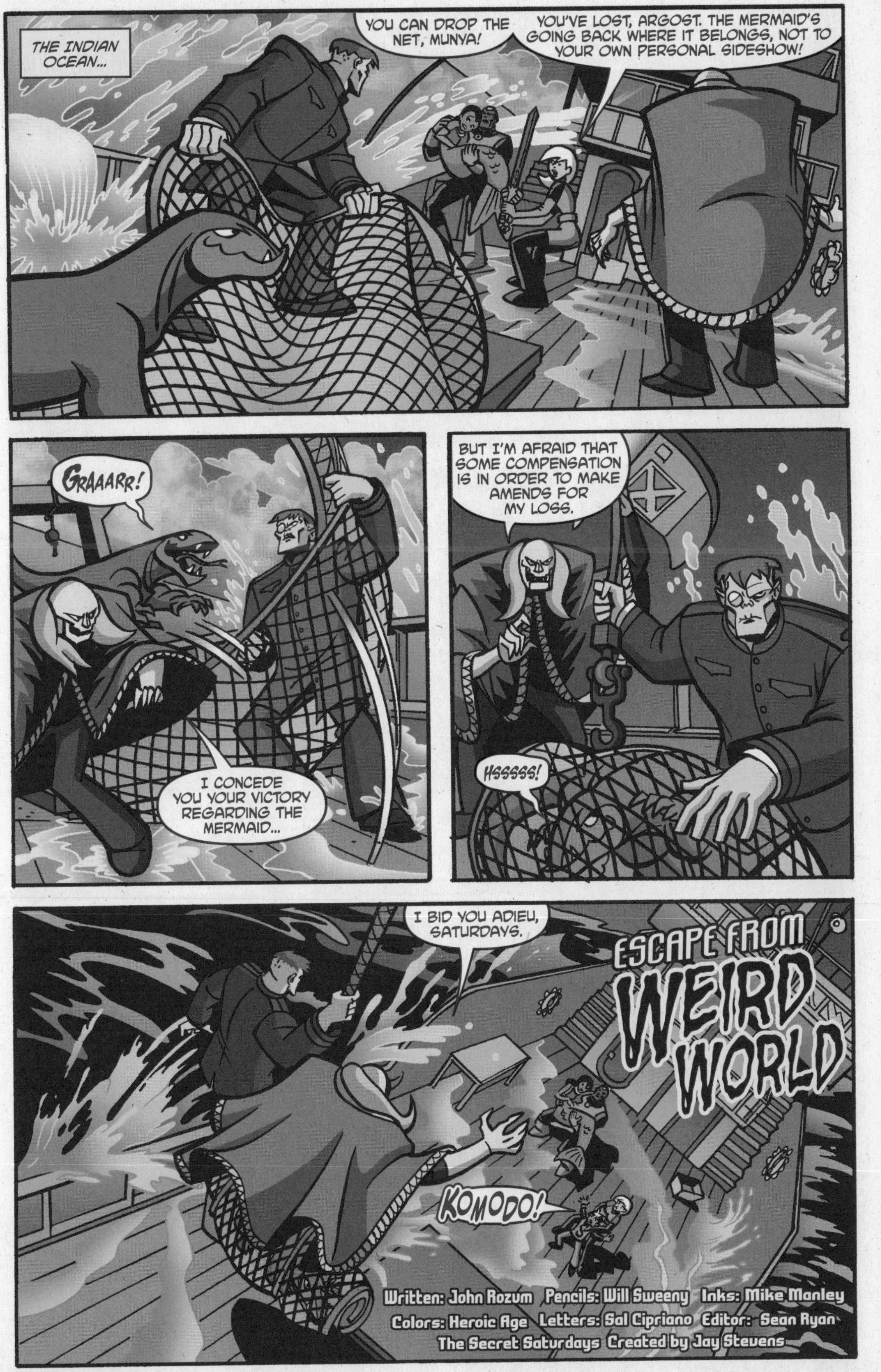
THE INDIAN OCEAN...
YOU CAN DROP THE NET, MUNYA!
YOU'VE LOST, ARGOST. THE MERMAID'S GOING BACK WHERE IT BELONGS, NOT TO YOUR OWN PERSONAL SIDESHOW!
GRAAARR!
I CONCEDE YOU YOUR VICTORY REGARDING THE MERMAID...
BUT I'M AFRAID THAT SOME COMPENSATION IS IN ORDER TO MAKE AMENDS FOR MY LOSS.
HSSSSS!
I BID YOU ADIEU, SATURDAYS.
ESCAPE FROM WEIRD WORLD
KOMODO!
Written: John Rozum Pencils: Will Sweeny Inks: Mike Manley
Colors: Heroic Age Letters: Sal Cipriano Editor: Sean Ryan
The Secret Saturdays Created by Jay Stevens

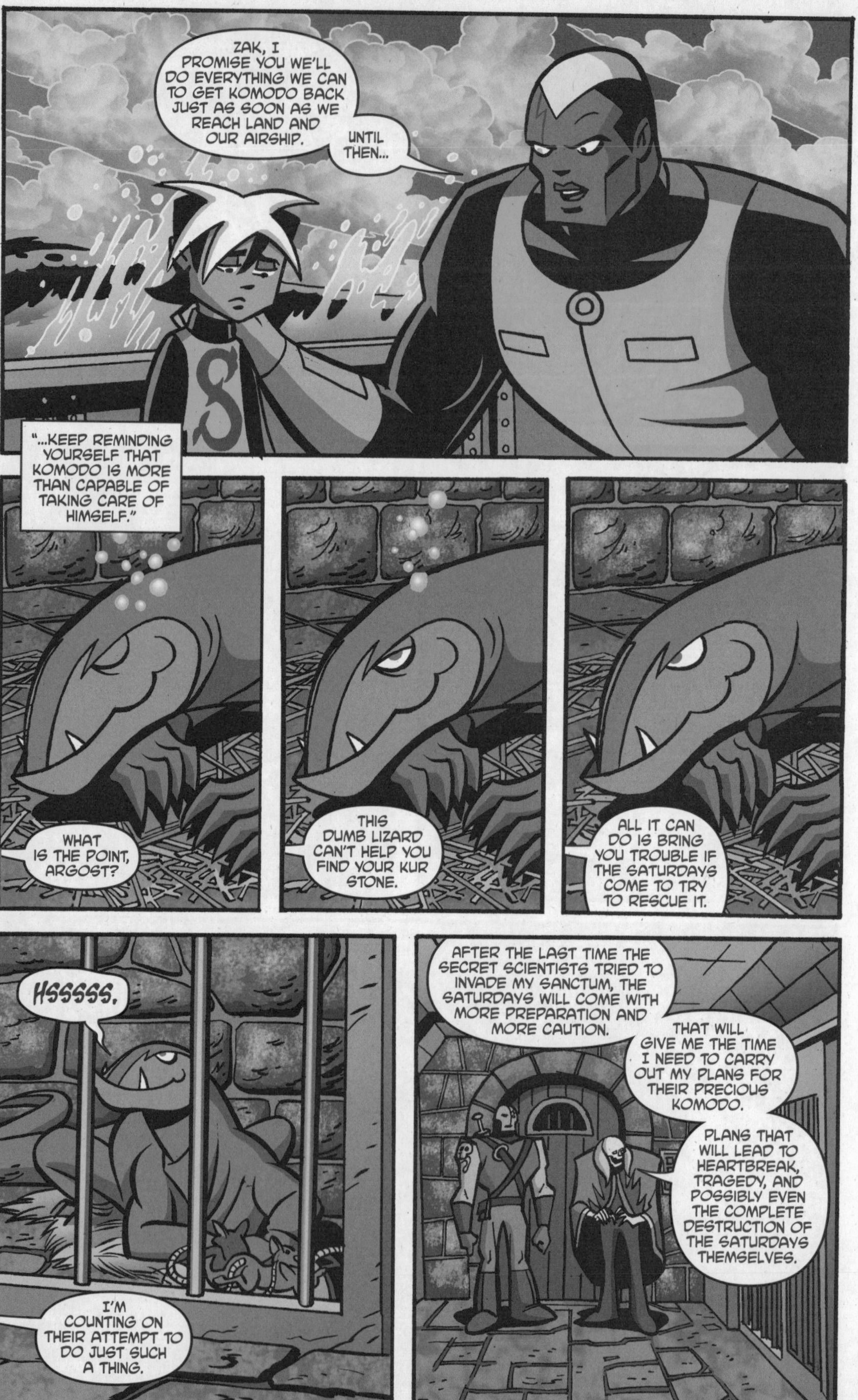
ZAK, I PROMISE YOU WE'LL DO EVERYTHING WE CAN TO GET KOMODO BACK JUST AS SOON AS WE REACH LAND AND OUR AIRSHIP.
UNTIL THEN...
"...KEEP REMINDING YOURSELF THAT KOMODO IS MORE THAN CAPABLE OF TAKING CARE OF HIMSELF."
WHAT IS THE POINT, ARGOST?
THIS DUMB LIZARD CAN'T HELP YOU FIND YOUR KUR STONE.
ALL IT CAN DO IS BRING YOU TROUBLE IF THE SATURDAYS COME TO TRY TO RESCUE IT.
HSSSSS.
I'M COUNTING ON THEIR ATTEMPT TO DO JUST SUCH A THING.
AFTER THE LAST TIME THE SECRET SCIENTISTS TRIED TO INVADE MY SANCTUM, THE SATURDAYS WILL COME WITH MORE PREPARATION AND MORE CAUTION.
THAT WILL GIVE ME THE TIME I NEED TO CARRY OUT MY PLANS FOR THEIR PRECIOUS KOMODO.
PLANS THAT WILL LEAD TO HEARTBREAK, TRAGEDY, AND POSSIBLY EVEN THE COMPLETE DESTRUCTION OF THE SATURDAYS THEMSELVES.

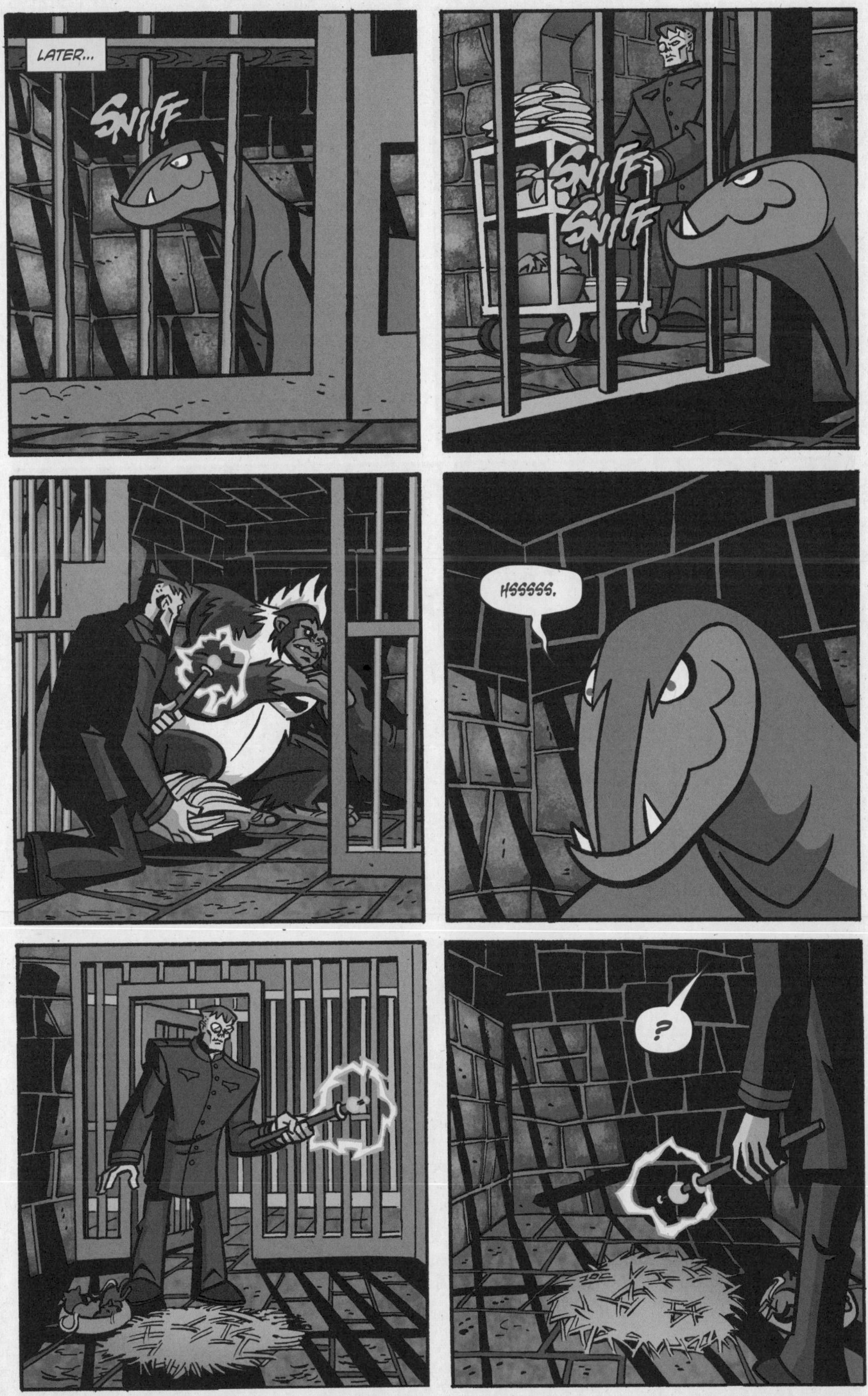
LATER...
SNIFF
SNIFF
SNIFF
HSSSSS.
?

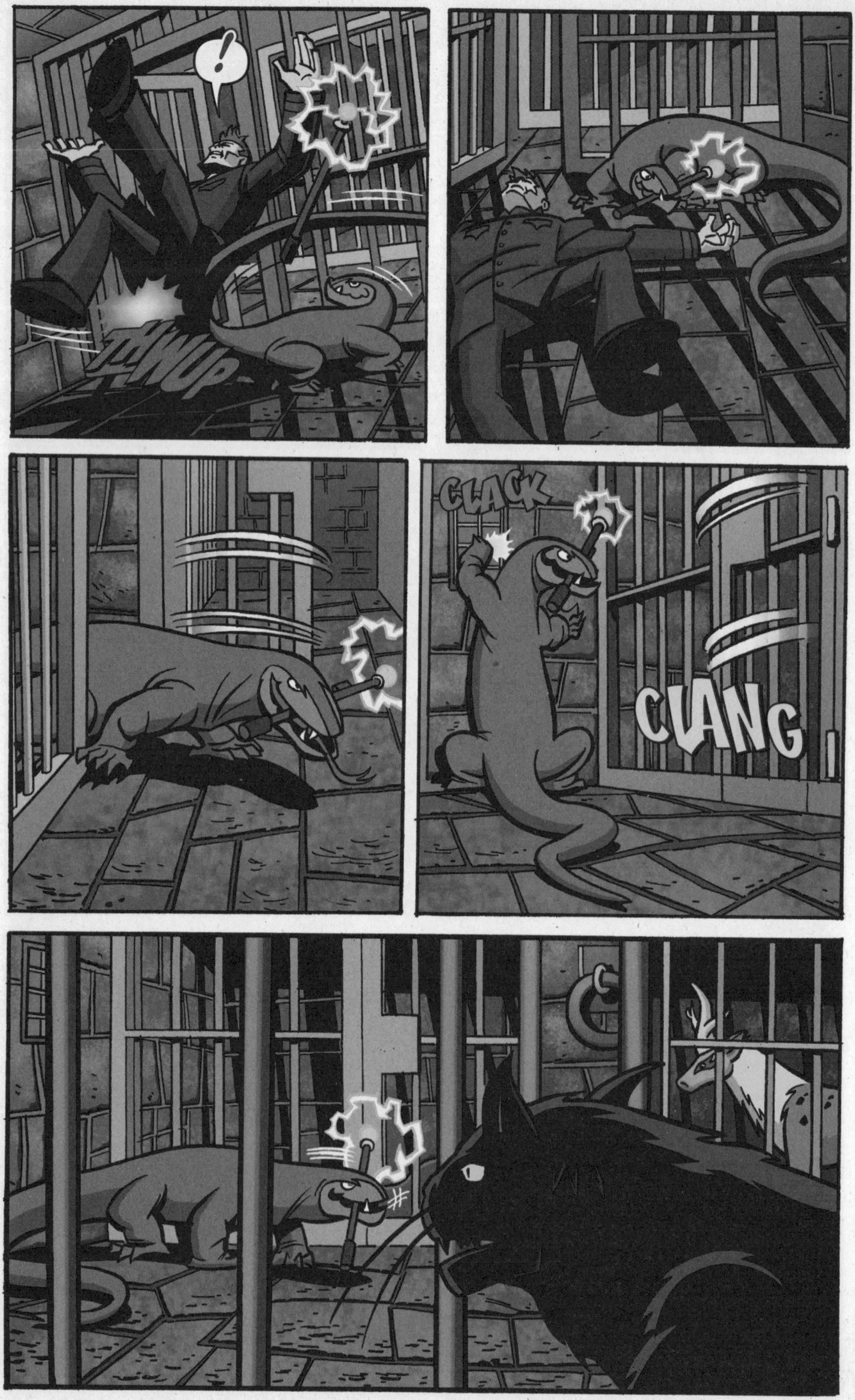
!
THWUP
CLACK
CLANG

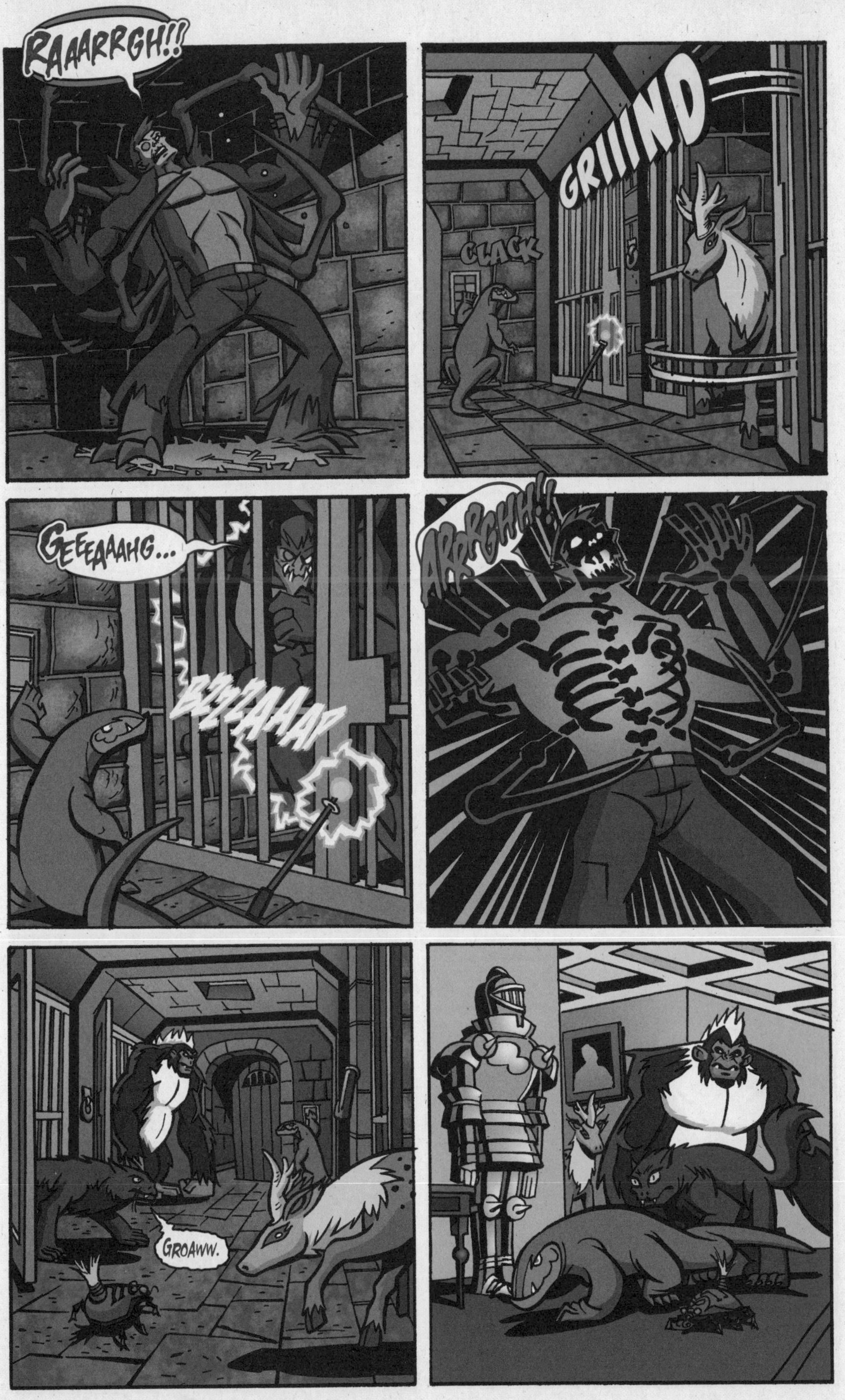
RAAARRGH!!
GRIIIND
CLACK
GEEEAAAHG...
BZZZAAAP
ARRGHH!!
GROAWW.

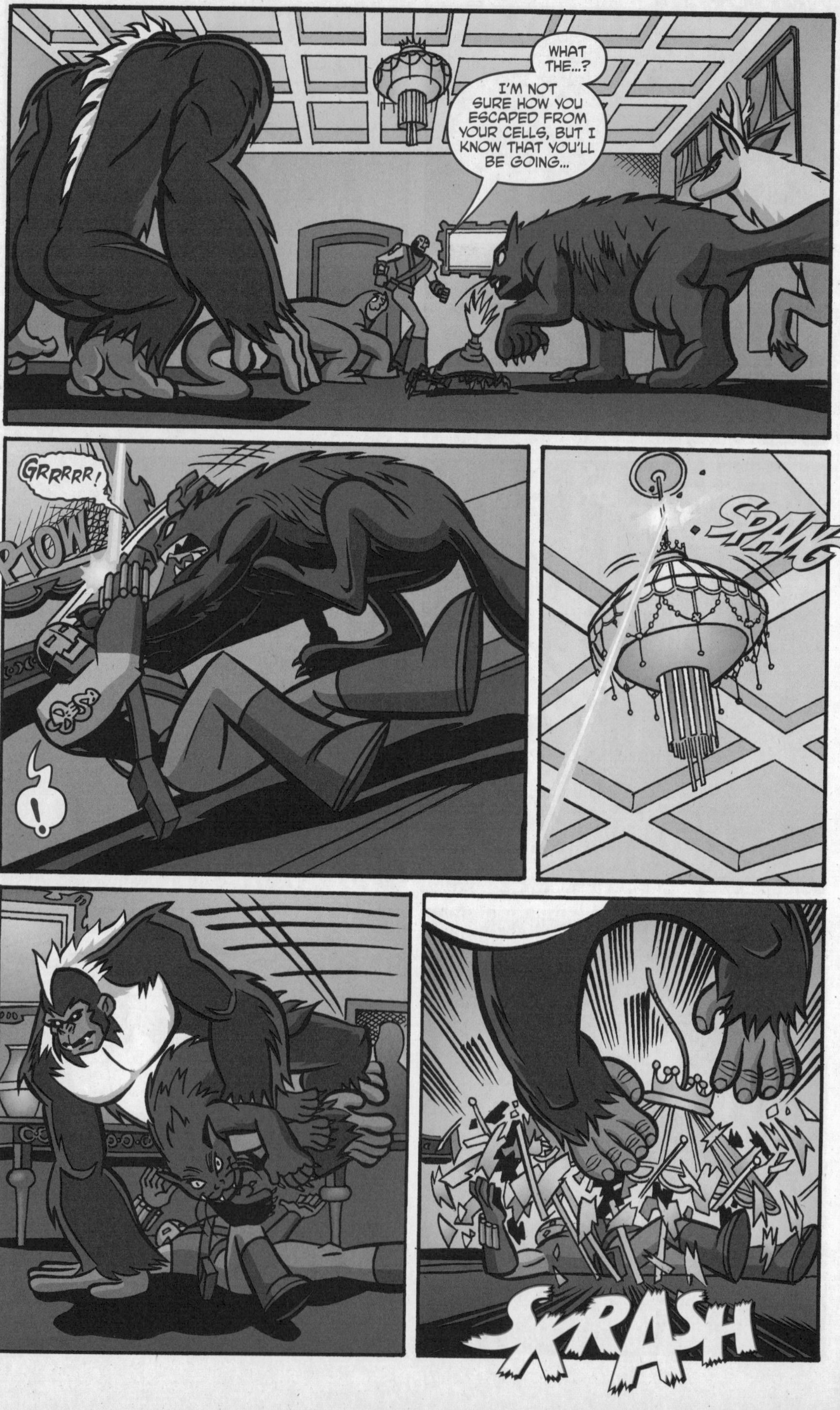
WHAT THE...?
I'M NOT SURE HOW YOU ESCAPED FROM YOUR CELLS, BUT I KNOW THAT YOU'LL BE GOING...
GRRRRR!
PTOW
!
SPANG
SKRASH

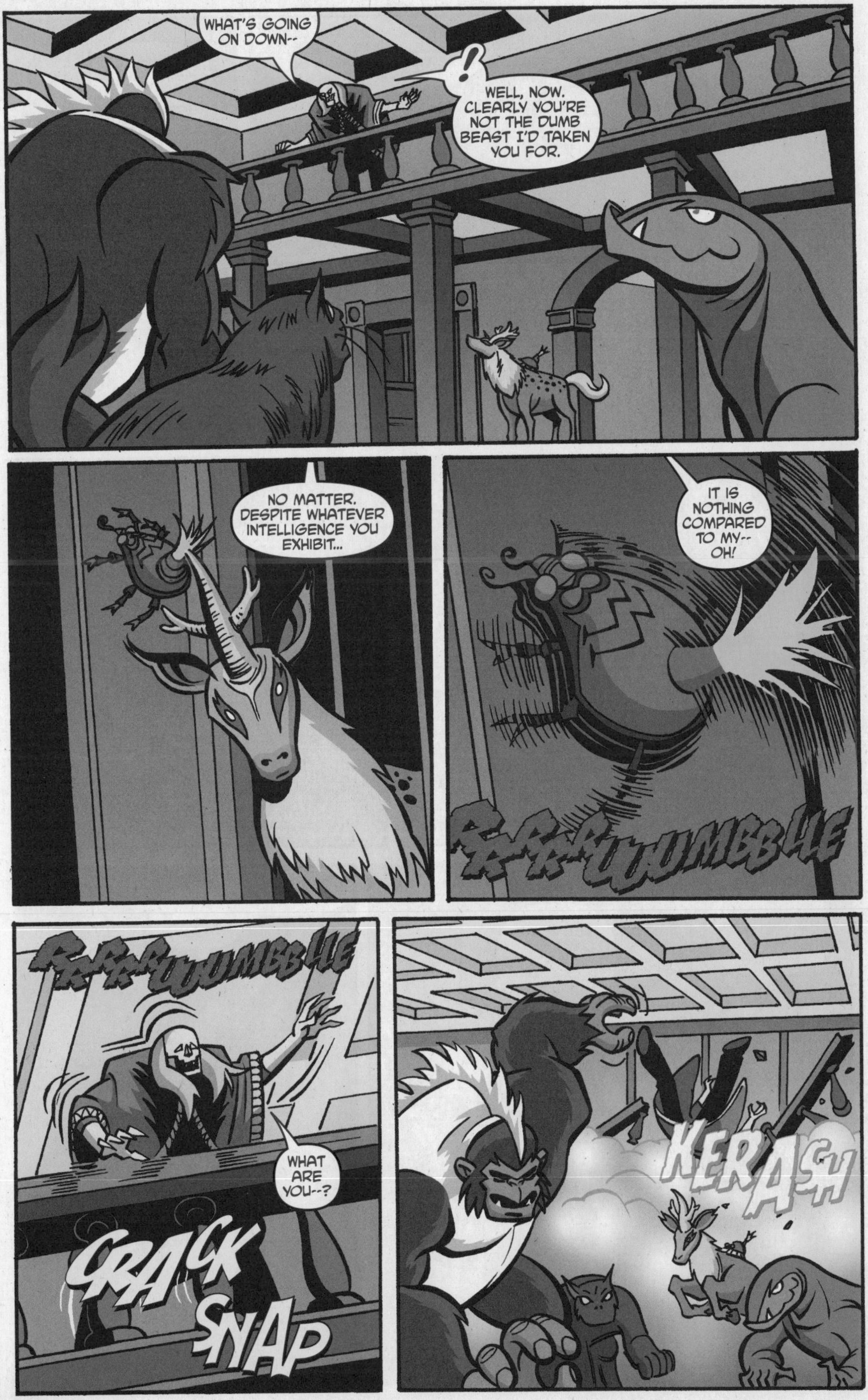
WHAT'S GOING ON DOWN--
!
WELL, NOW. CLEARLY YOU'RE NOT THE DUMB BEAST I'D TAKEN YOU FOR.
NO MATTER. DESPITE WHATEVER INTELLIGENCE YOU EXHIBIT...
IT IS NOTHING COMPARED TO MY-- OH!
RRRRUUUMBBLLE
RRRRUUUMBBLLE
WHAT ARE YOU--?
CRACK
SNAP
KERASH

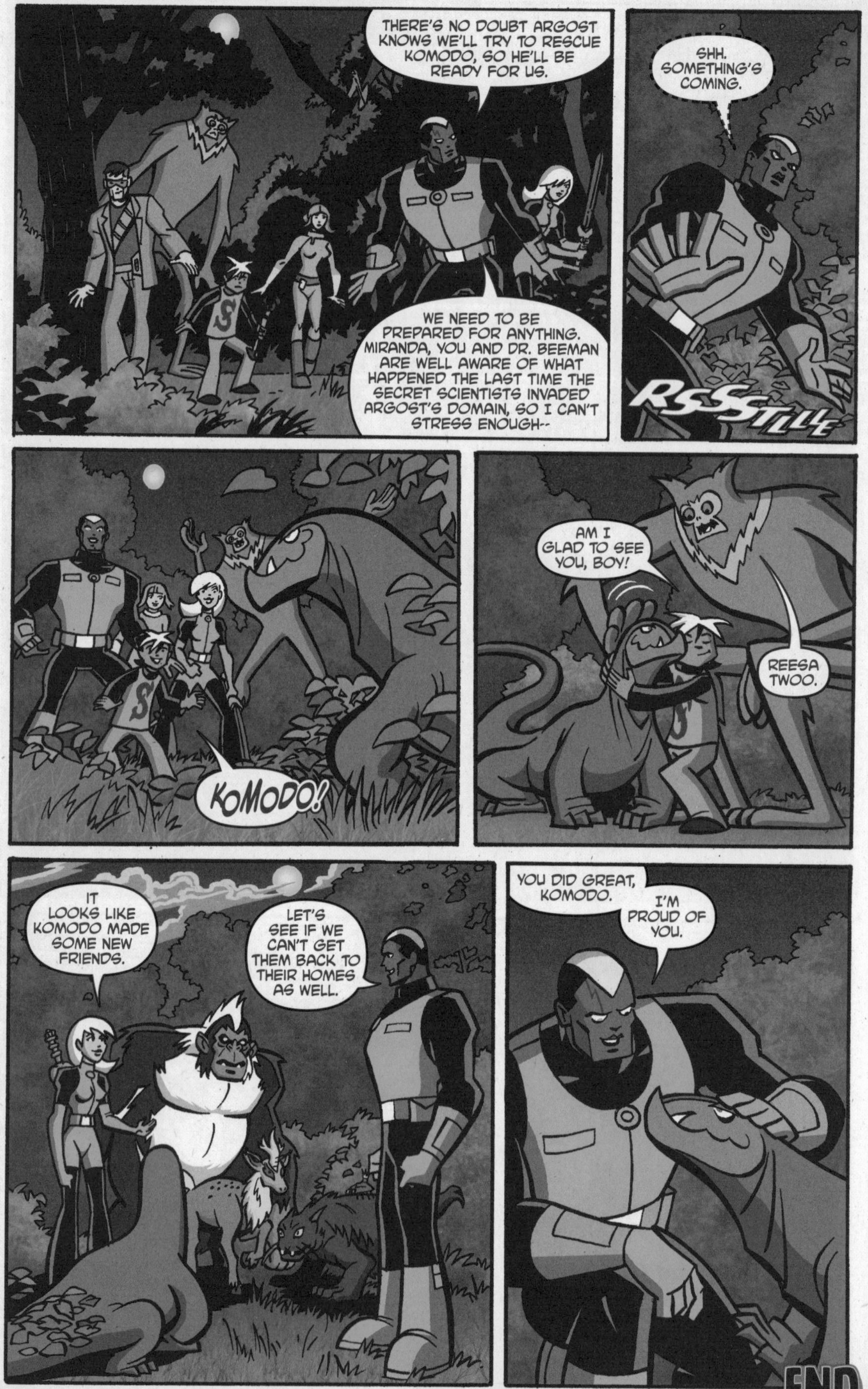
THERE'S NO DOUBT ARGOST KNOWS WE'LL TRY TO RESCUE KOMODO, SO HE'LL BE READY FOR US.
WE NEED TO BE PREPARED FOR ANYTHING. MIRANDA, YOU AND DR. BEEMAN ARE WELL AWARE OF WHAT HAPPENED THE LAST TIME THE SECRET SCIENTISTS INVADED ARGOST'S DOMAIN, SO I CAN'T STRESS ENOUGH--
SHH. SOMETHING'S COMING.
RSSSTLLE
KOMODO!
AM I GLAD TO SEE YOU, BOY!
REESA TWOO.
IT LOOKS LIKE KOMODO MADE SOME NEW FRIENDS.
LET'S SEE IF WE CAN'T GET THEM BACK TO THEIR HOMES AS WELL.
YOU DID GREAT, KOMODO.
I'M PROUD OF YOU.
END

THE CAVE of the CACUS

writer//JOHN ROZUM
penciller//WILL SWEENY
inker//MIKE MANLEY
colorist//HEROIC AGE
letterer//TRAVIS LANHAM
editor//SEAN RYAN
THE SECRET SATURDAYS
created by JAY STEPHENS

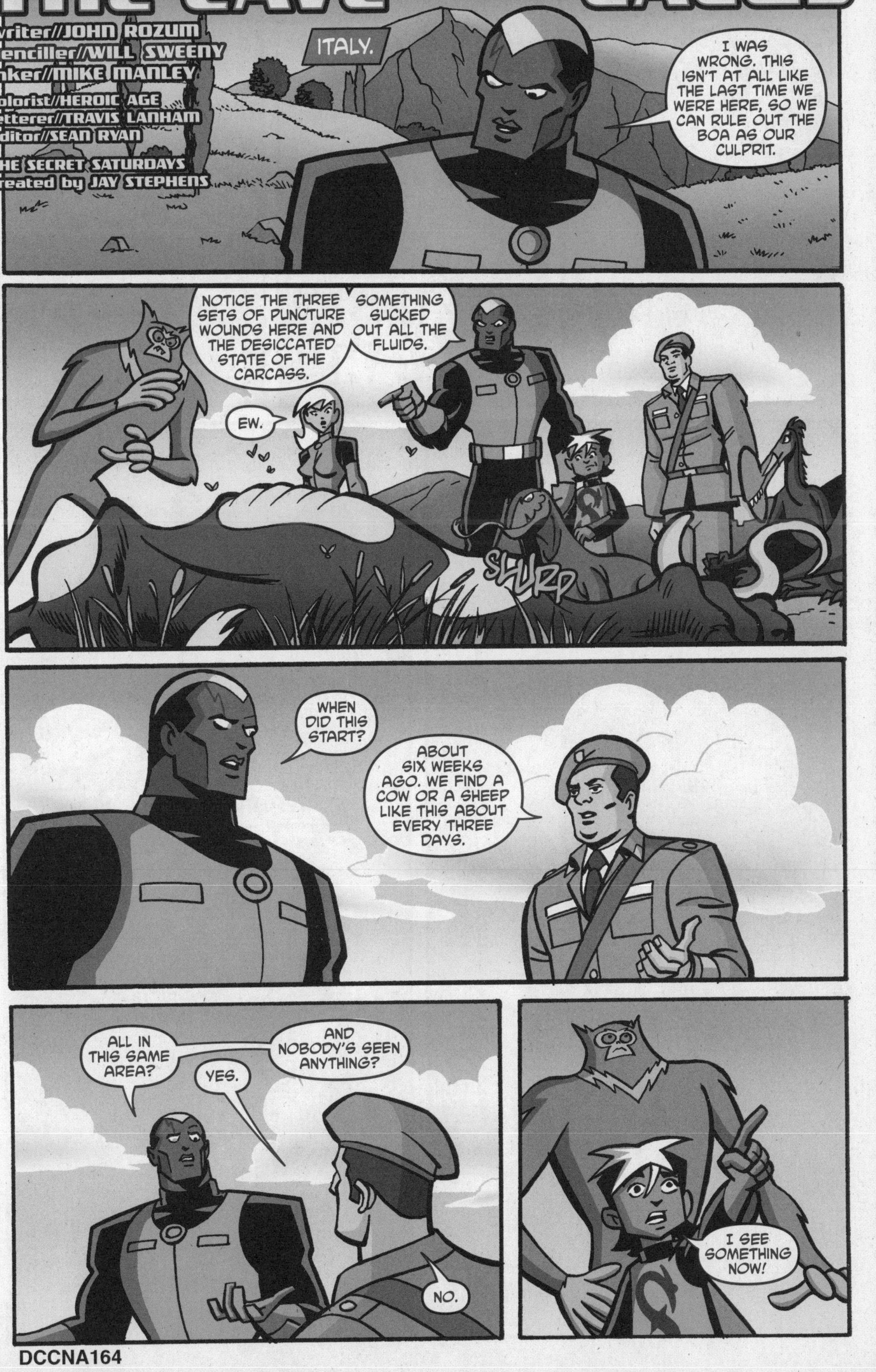
ITALY.
I WAS WRONG. THIS ISN'T AT ALL LIKE THE LAST TIME WE WERE HERE, SO WE CAN RULE OUT THE BOA AS OUR CULPRIT.
NOTICE THE THREE SETS OF PUNCTURE WOUNDS HERE AND THE DESICCATED STATE OF THE CARCASS.
SOMETHING SUCKED OUT ALL THE FLUIDS.
EW.
SHLURP
WHEN DID THIS START?
ABOUT SIX WEEKS AGO. WE FIND A COW OR A SHEEP LIKE THIS ABOUT EVERY THREE DAYS.
ALL IN THIS SAME AREA?
YES.
AND NOBODY'S SEEN ANYTHING?
NO.
I SEE SOMETHING NOW!

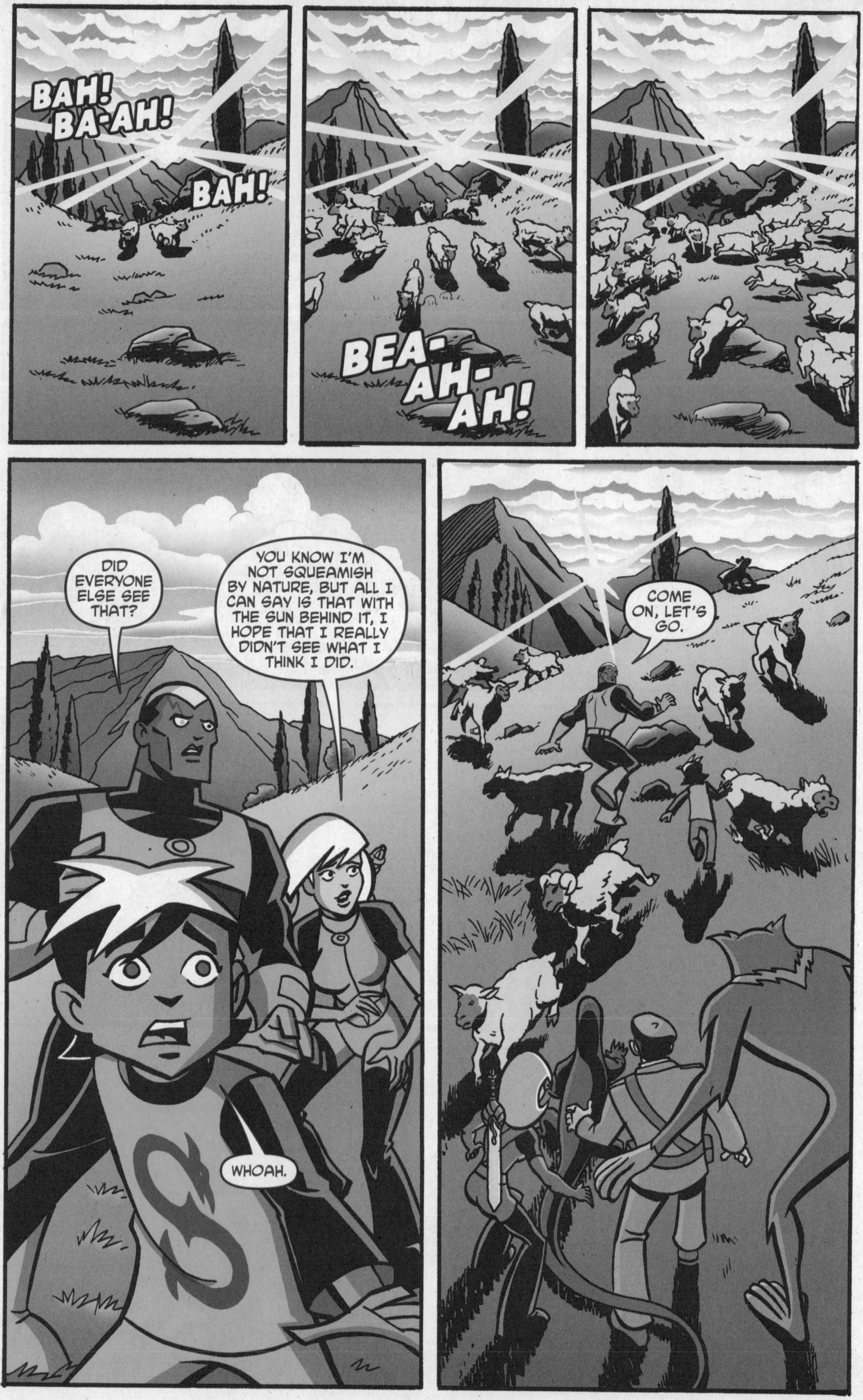
BAH! BA-AH!
BAH!
BEA-AH-AH!
DID EVERYONE ELSE SEE THAT?
YOU KNOW I'M NOT SQUEAMISH BY NATURE, BUT ALL I CAN SAY IS THAT WITH THE SUN BEHIND IT, I HOPE THAT I REALLY DIDN'T SEE WHAT I THINK I DID.
WHOAH.
COME ON, LET'S GO.

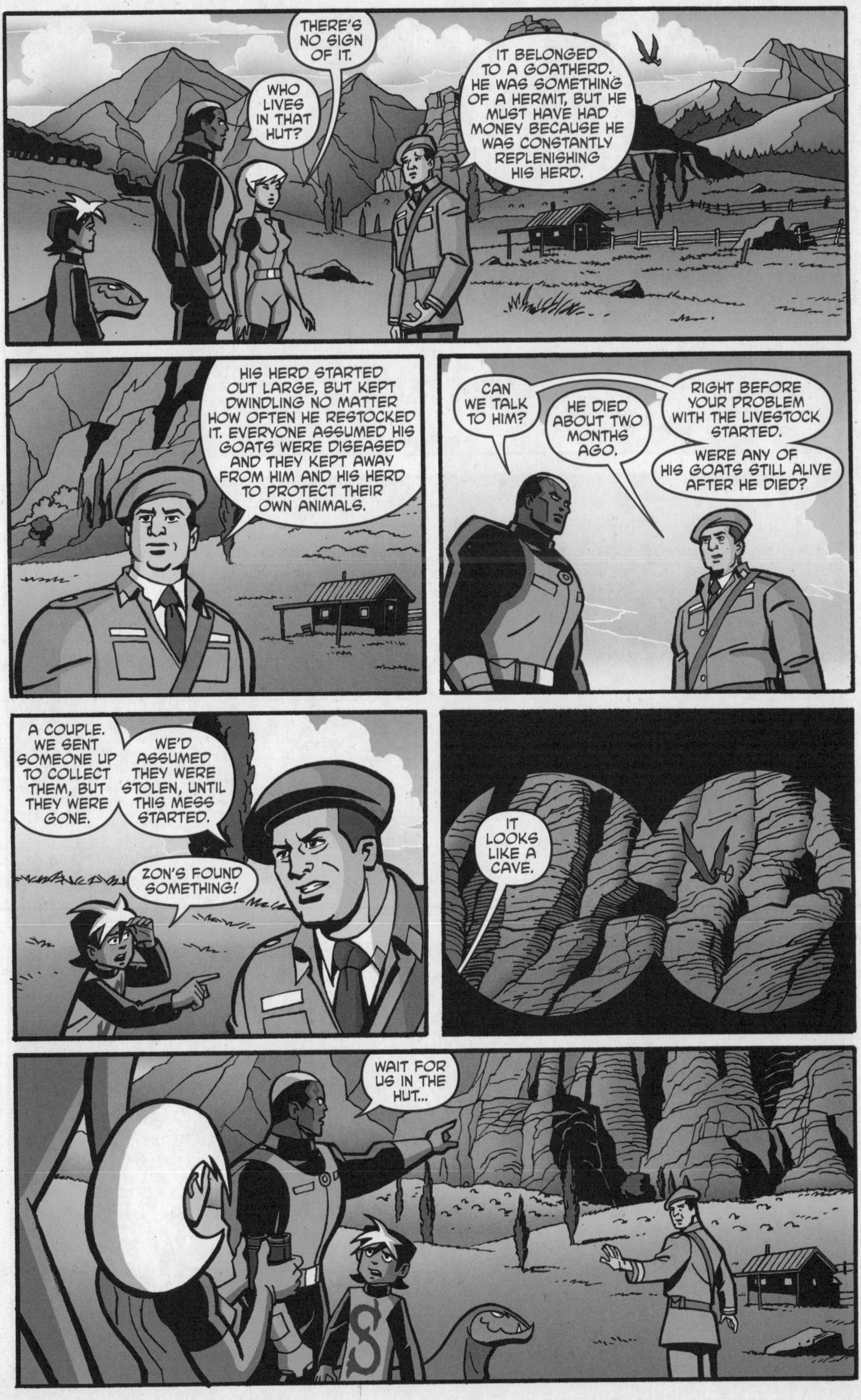
THERE'S NO SIGN OF IT.
WHO LIVES IN THAT HUT?
IT BELONGED TO A GOATHERD. HE WAS SOMETHING OF A HERMIT, BUT HE MUST HAVE HAD MONEY BECAUSE HE WAS CONSTANTLY REPLENISHING HIS HERD.
HIS HERD STARTED OUT LARGE, BUT KEPT DWINDLING NO MATTER HOW OFTEN HE RESTOCKED IT. EVERYONE ASSUMED HIS GOATS WERE DISEASED AND THEY KEPT AWAY FROM HIM AND HIS HERD TO PROTECT THEIR OWN ANIMALS.
CAN WE TALK TO HIM?
HE DIED ABOUT TWO MONTHS AGO.
RIGHT BEFORE YOUR PROBLEM WITH THE LIVESTOCK STARTED.
WERE ANY OF HIS GOATS STILL ALIVE AFTER HE DIED?
A COUPLE. WE SENT SOMEONE UP TO COLLECT THEM, BUT THEY WERE GONE.
WE'D ASSUMED THEY WERE STOLEN, UNTIL THIS MESS STARTED.
ZON'S FOUND SOMETHING!
IT LOOKS LIKE A CAVE.
WAIT FOR US IN THE HUT...

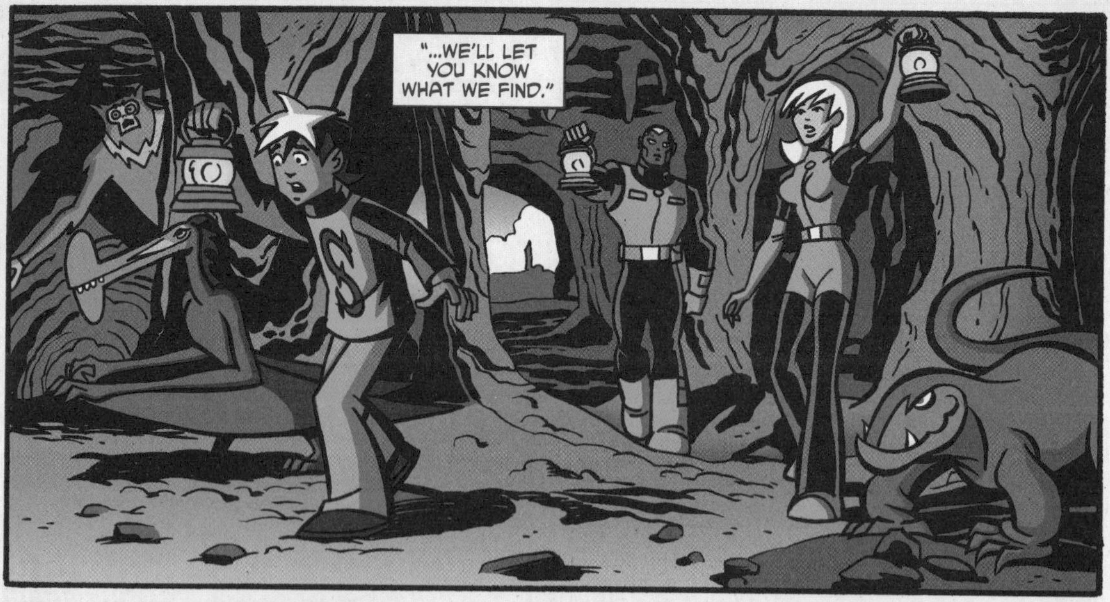
"...WE'LL LET YOU KNOW WHAT WE FIND."

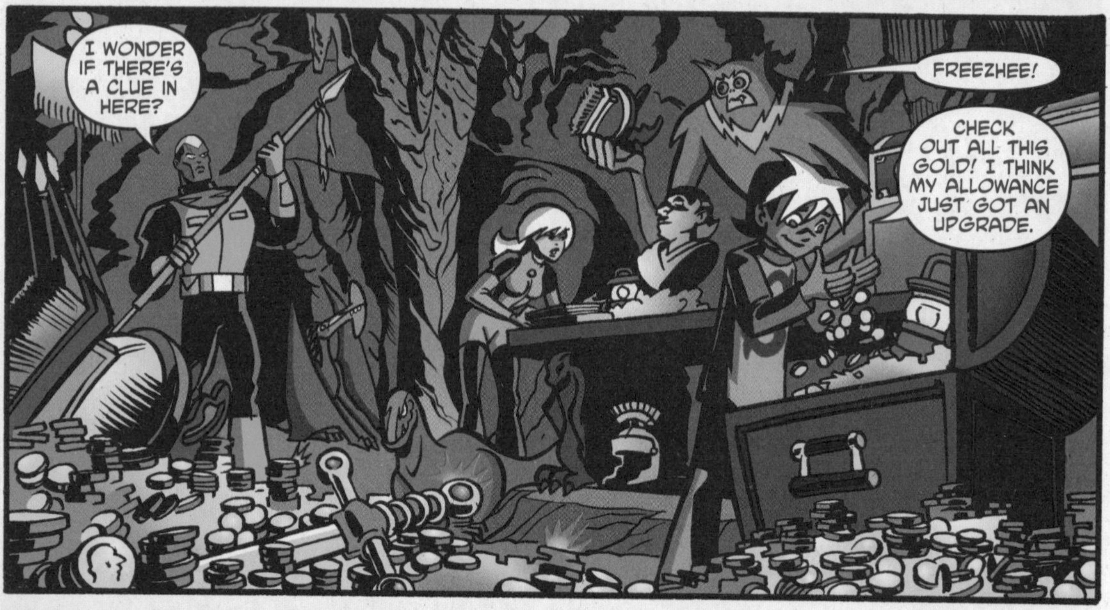
I WONDER IF THERE'S A CLUE IN HERE?
FREEZHEE!
CHECK OUT ALL THIS GOLD! I THINK MY ALLOWANCE JUST GOT AN UPGRADE.

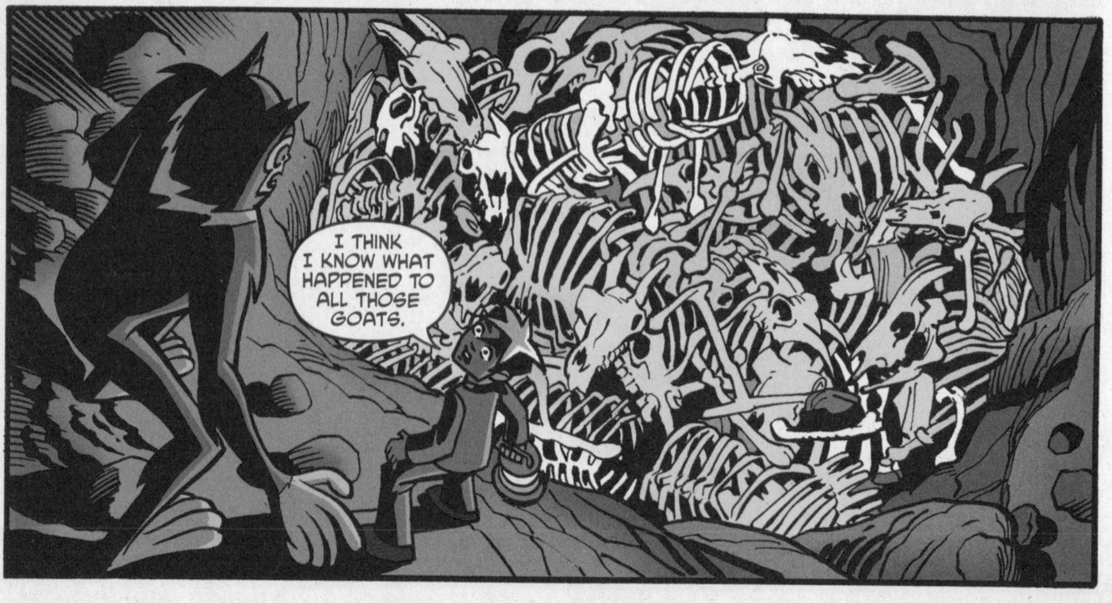
I THINK I KNOW WHAT HAPPENED TO ALL THOSE GOATS.

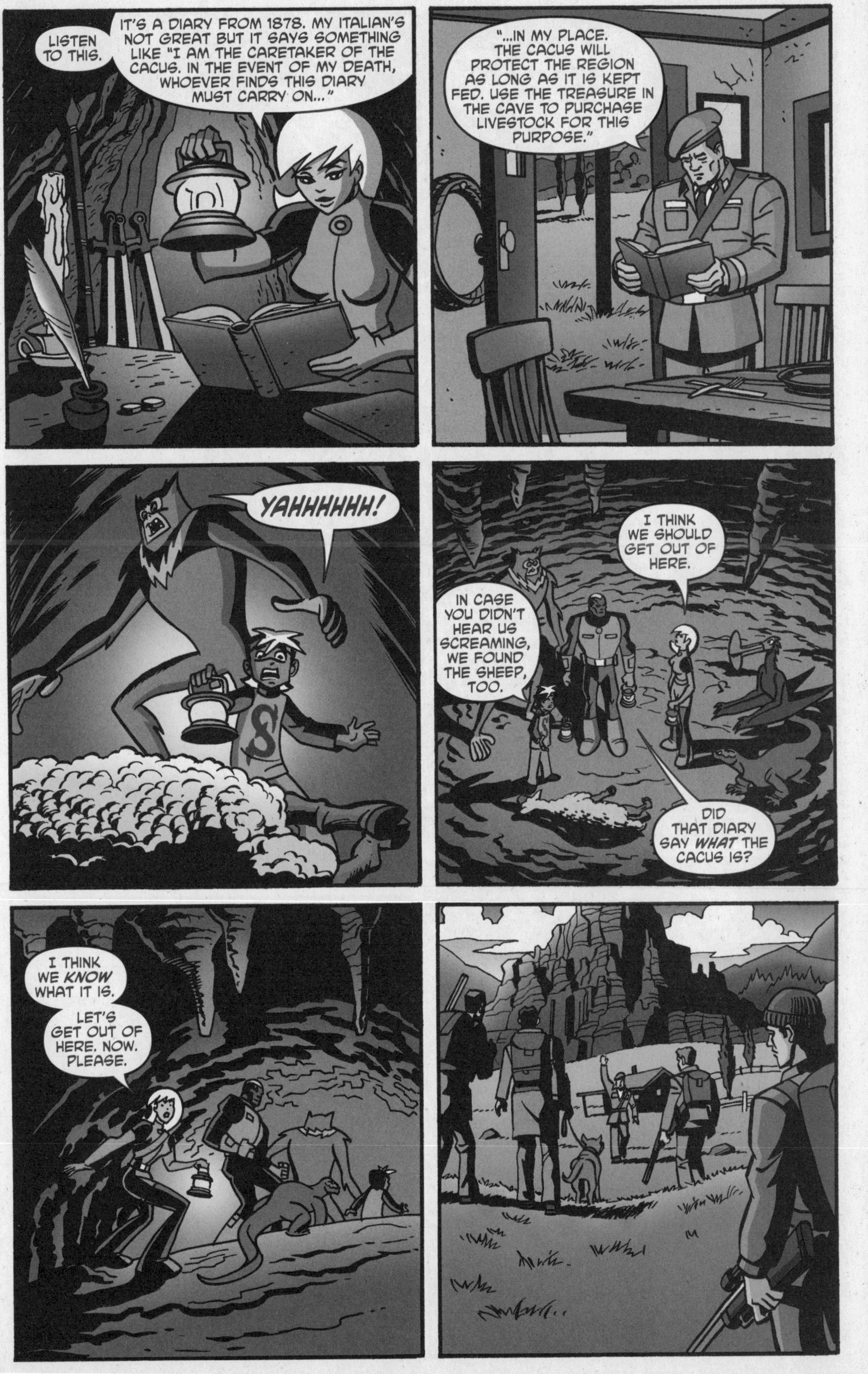
LISTEN TO THIS.
IT'S A DIARY FROM 1878. MY ITALIAN'S NOT GREAT BUT IT SAYS SOMETHING LIKE "I AM THE CARETAKER OF THE CACUS. IN THE EVENT OF MY DEATH, WHOEVER FINDS THIS DIARY MUST CARRY ON..."
"...IN MY PLACE. THE CACUS WILL PROTECT THE REGION AS LONG AS IT IS KEPT FED. USE THE TREASURE IN THE CAVE TO PURCHASE LIVESTOCK FOR THIS PURPOSE."
YAHHHHHH!
I THINK WE SHOULD GET OUT OF HERE.
IN CASE YOU DIDN'T HEAR US SCREAMING, WE FOUND THE SHEEP, TOO.
DID THAT DIARY SAY *WHAT* THE CACUS IS?
I THINK WE *KNOW* WHAT IT IS.
LET'S GET OUT OF HERE. NOW. PLEASE.

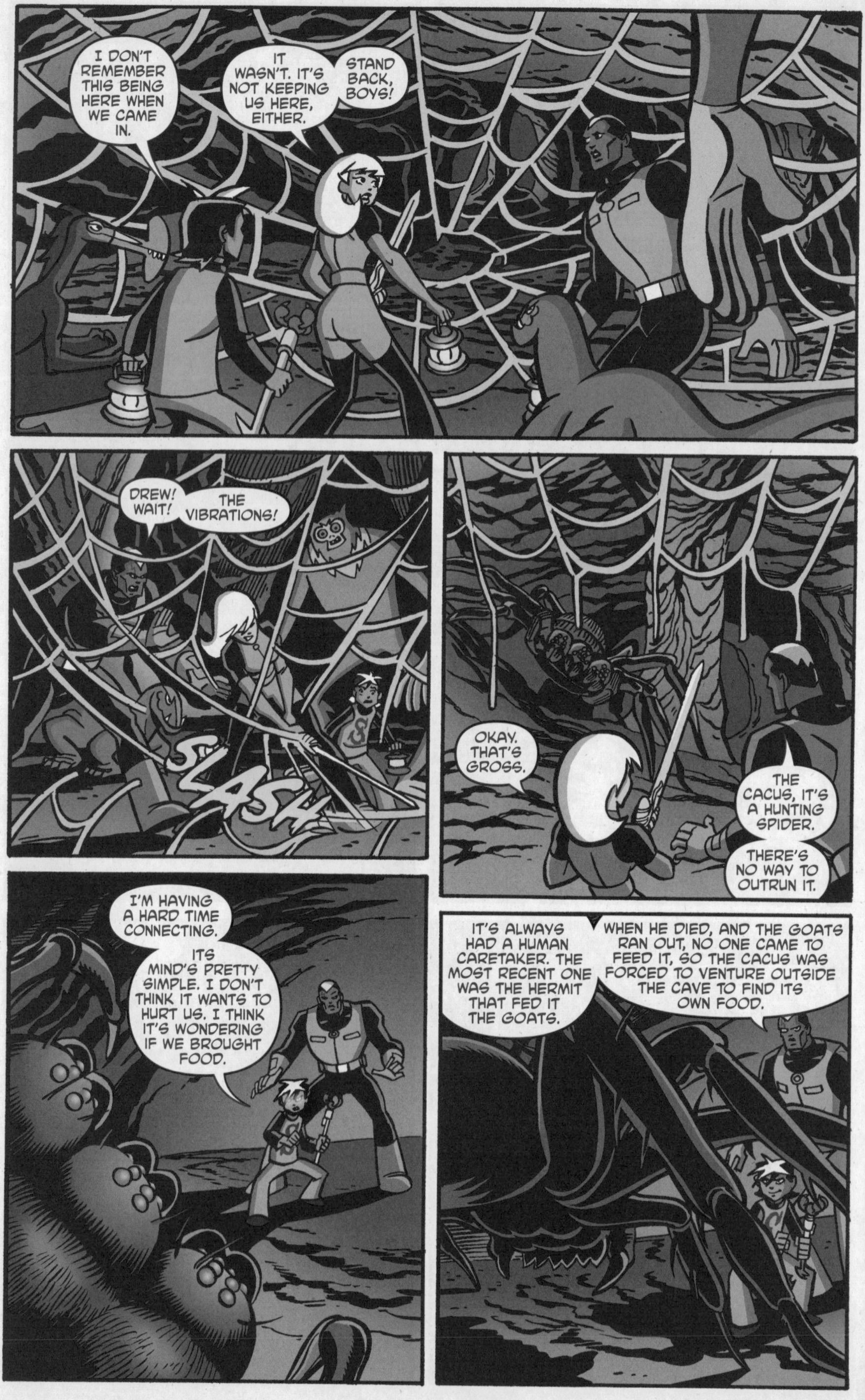
I DON'T REMEMBER THIS BEING HERE WHEN WE CAME IN.
IT WASN'T. IT'S NOT KEEPING US HERE, EITHER.
STAND BACK, BOYS!
DREW! WAIT!
THE VIBRATIONS!
SLASH
OKAY. THAT'S GROSS.
THE CACUS, IT'S A HUNTING SPIDER.
THERE'S NO WAY TO OUTRUN IT.
I'M HAVING A HARD TIME CONNECTING.
ITS MIND'S PRETTY SIMPLE. I DON'T THINK IT WANTS TO HURT US. I THINK IT'S WONDERING IF WE BROUGHT FOOD.
IT'S ALWAYS HAD A HUMAN CARETAKER. THE MOST RECENT ONE WAS THE HERMIT THAT FED IT THE GOATS.
WHEN HE DIED, AND THE GOATS RAN OUT, NO ONE CAME TO FEED IT, SO THE CACUS WAS FORCED TO VENTURE OUTSIDE THE CAVE TO FIND ITS OWN FOOD.

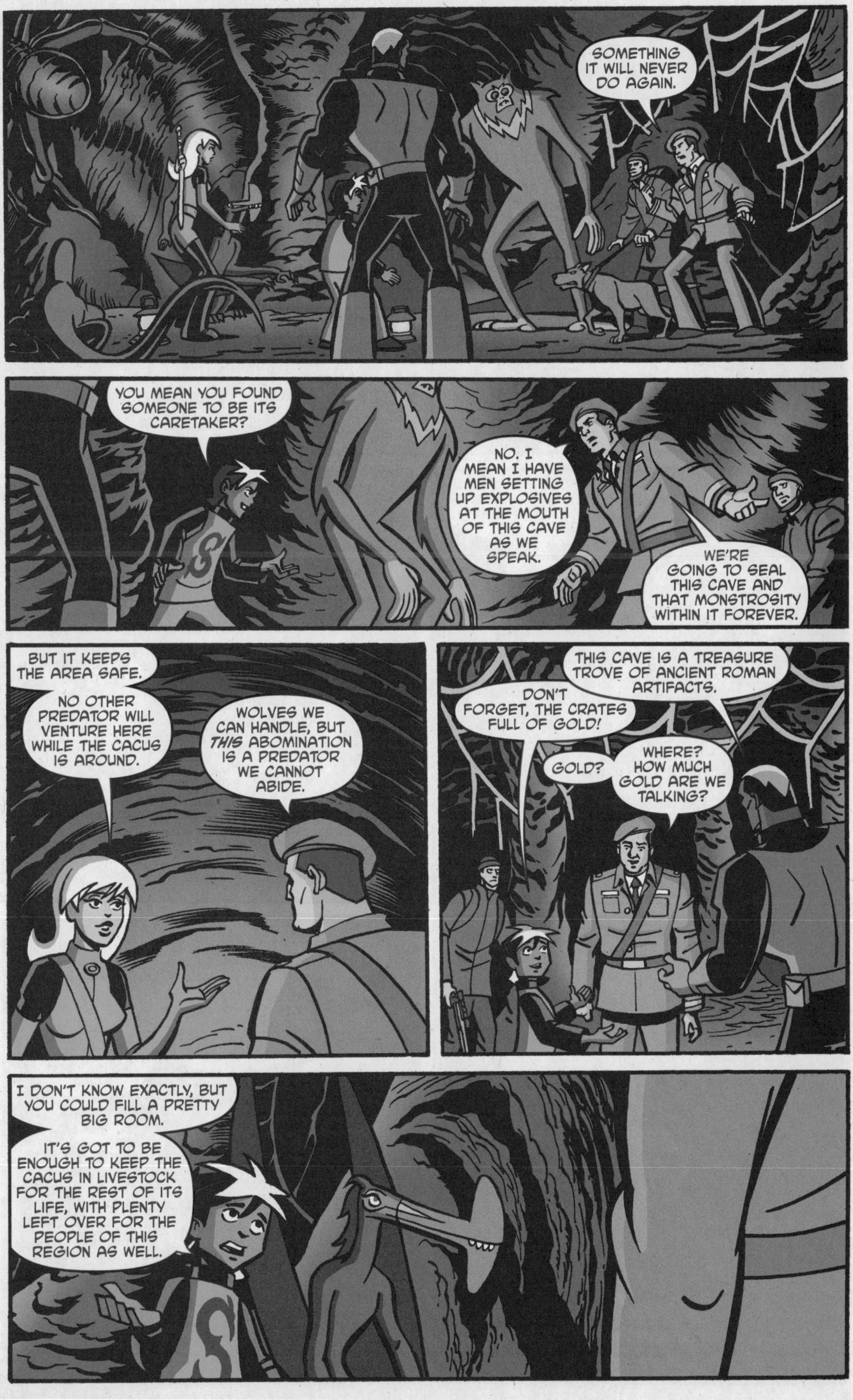
SOMETHING IT WILL NEVER DO AGAIN.
YOU MEAN YOU FOUND SOMEONE TO BE ITS CARETAKER?
NO. I MEAN I HAVE MEN SETTING UP EXPLOSIVES AT THE MOUTH OF THIS CAVE AS WE SPEAK.
WE'RE GOING TO SEAL THIS CAVE AND THAT MONSTROSITY WITHIN IT FOREVER.
BUT IT KEEPS THE AREA SAFE.
NO OTHER PREDATOR WILL VENTURE HERE WHILE THE CACUS IS AROUND.
WOLVES WE CAN HANDLE, BUT *THIS* ABOMINATION IS A PREDATOR WE CANNOT ABIDE.
THIS CAVE IS A TREASURE TROVE OF ANCIENT ROMAN ARTIFACTS.
DON'T FORGET, THE CRATES FULL OF GOLD!
GOLD?
WHERE? HOW MUCH GOLD ARE WE TALKING?
I DON'T KNOW EXACTLY, BUT YOU COULD FILL A PRETTY BIG ROOM.
IT'S GOT TO BE ENOUGH TO KEEP THE CACUS IN LIVESTOCK FOR THE REST OF ITS LIFE, WITH PLENTY LEFT OVER FOR THE PEOPLE OF THIS REGION AS WELL.

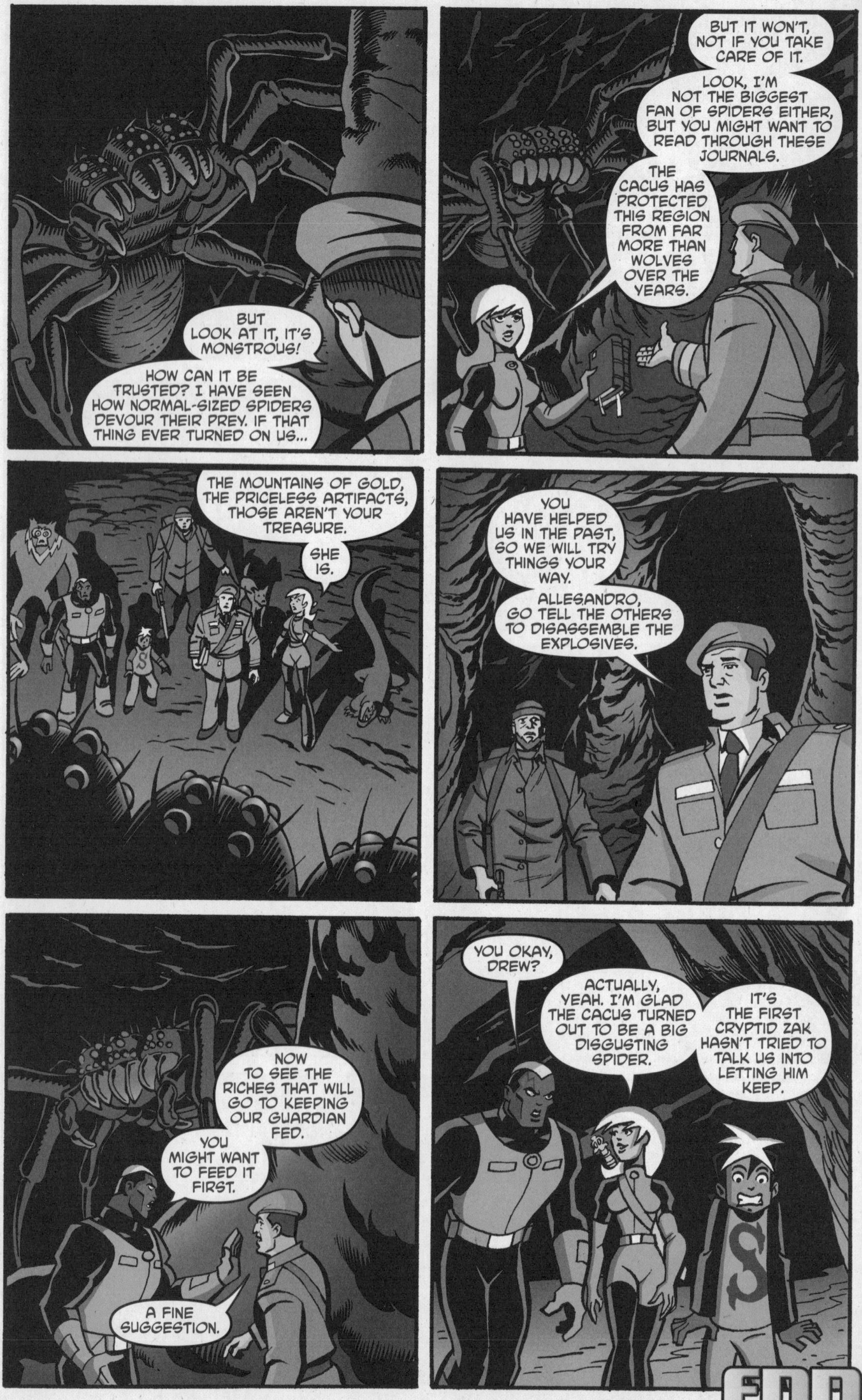
BUT LOOK AT IT, IT'S MONSTROUS!
HOW CAN IT BE TRUSTED? I HAVE SEEN HOW NORMAL-SIZED SPIDERS DEVOUR THEIR PREY. IF THAT THING EVER TURNED ON US...
BUT IT WON'T, NOT IF YOU TAKE CARE OF IT.
LOOK, I'M NOT THE BIGGEST FAN OF SPIDERS EITHER, BUT YOU MIGHT WANT TO READ THROUGH THESE JOURNALS.
THE CACUS HAS PROTECTED THIS REGION FROM FAR MORE THAN WOLVES OVER THE YEARS.
THE MOUNTAINS OF GOLD, THE PRICELESS ARTIFACTS, THOSE AREN'T YOUR TREASURE.
SHE IS.
YOU HAVE HELPED US IN THE PAST, SO WE WILL TRY THINGS YOUR WAY.
ALLESANDRO, GO TELL THE OTHERS TO DISASSEMBLE THE EXPLOSIVES.
NOW TO SEE THE RICHES THAT WILL GO TO KEEPING OUR GUARDIAN FED.
YOU MIGHT WANT TO FEED IT FIRST.
A FINE SUGGESTION.
YOU OKAY, DREW?
ACTUALLY, YEAH. I'M GLAD THE CACUS TURNED OUT TO BE A BIG DISGUSTING SPIDER.
IT'S THE FIRST CRYPTID ZAK HASN'T TRIED TO TALK US INTO LETTING HIM KEEP.
END

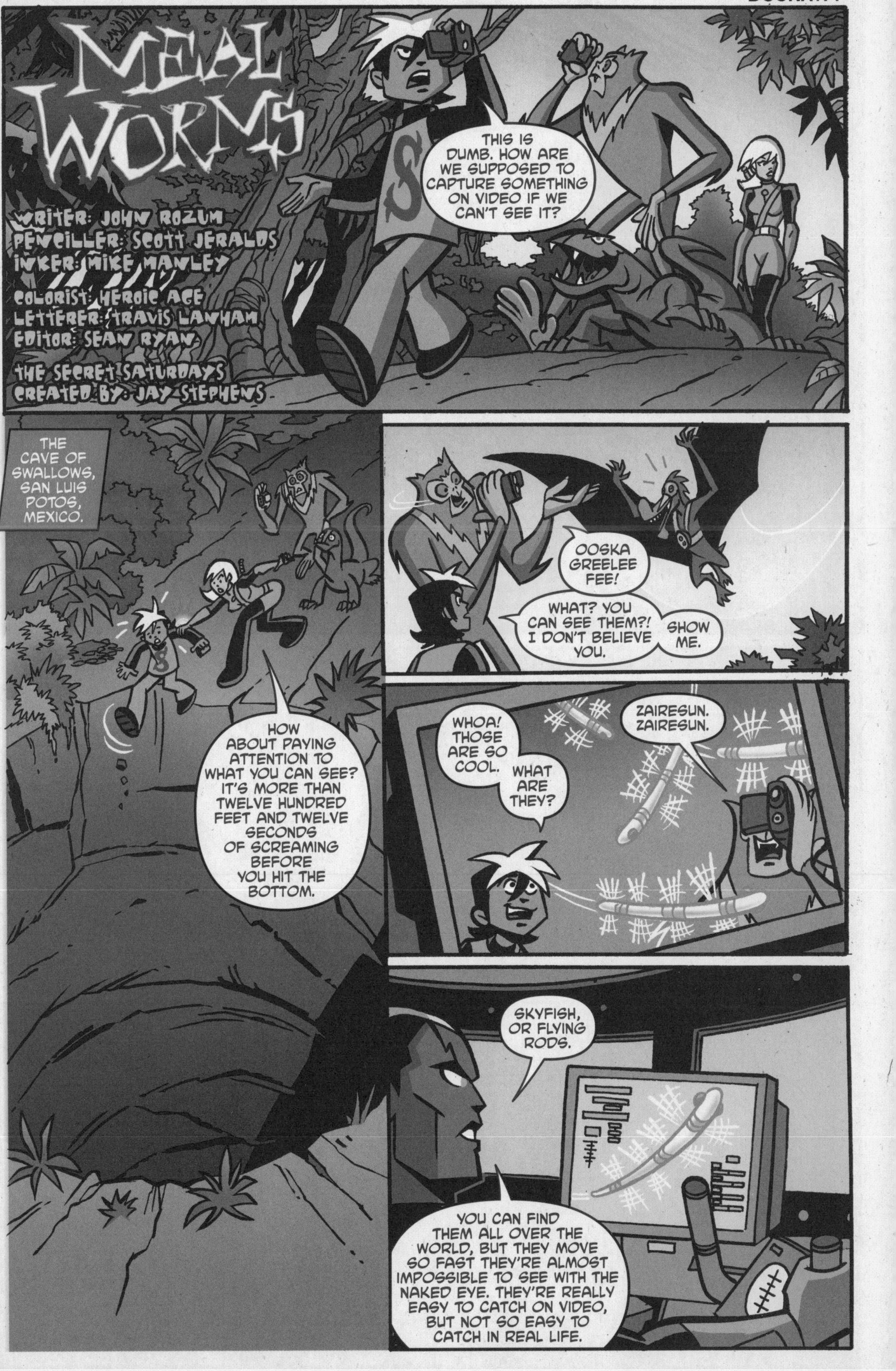
MEAL WORMS
WRITER: JOHN ROZUM
PENCILLER: SCOTT JERALDS
INKER: MIKE MANLEY
COLORIST: HEROIC AGE
LETTERER: TRAVIS LANHAM
EDITOR: SEAN RYAN
THE SECRET SATURDAYS CREATED BY: JAY STEPHENS
THIS IS DUMB. HOW ARE WE SUPPOSED TO CAPTURE SOMETHING ON VIDEO IF WE CAN'T SEE IT?
THE CAVE OF SWALLOWS, SAN LUIS POTOS, MEXICO.
HOW ABOUT PAYING ATTENTION TO WHAT YOU CAN SEE? IT'S MORE THAN TWELVE HUNDRED FEET AND TWELVE SECONDS OF SCREAMING BEFORE YOU HIT THE BOTTOM.
OOSKA GREELEE FEE!
WHAT? YOU CAN SEE THEM?! I DON'T BELIEVE YOU.
SHOW ME.
WHOA! THOSE ARE SO COOL.
WHAT ARE THEY?
ZAIRESUN. ZAIRESUN.
SKYFISH, OR FLYING RODS.
YOU CAN FIND THEM ALL OVER THE WORLD, BUT THEY MOVE SO FAST THEY'RE ALMOST IMPOSSIBLE TO SEE WITH THE NAKED EYE. THEY'RE REALLY EASY TO CATCH ON VIDEO, BUT NOT SO EASY TO CATCH IN REAL LIFE.

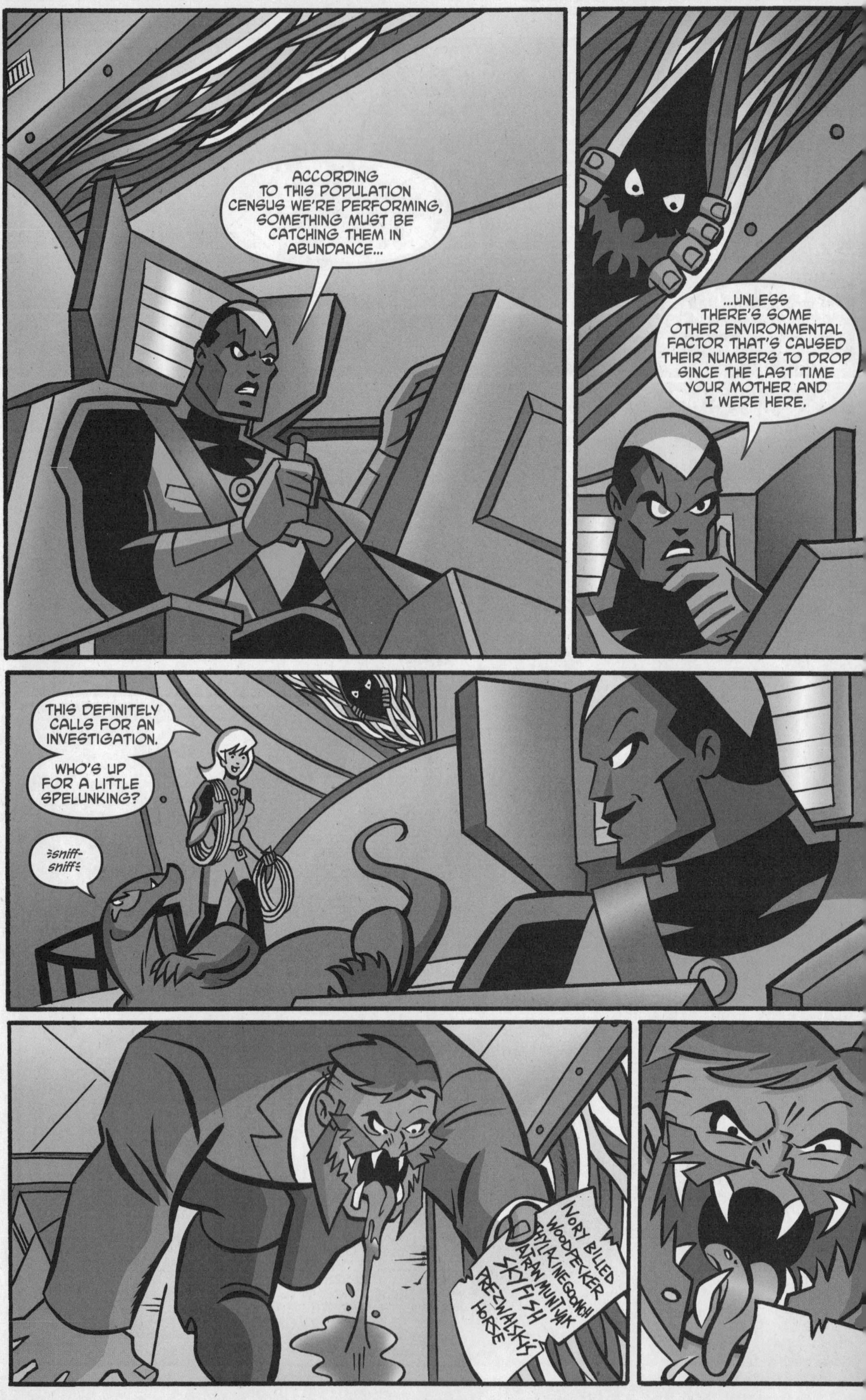
ACCORDING TO THIS POPULATION CENSUS WE'RE PERFORMING, SOMETHING MUST BE CATCHING THEM IN ABUNDANCE...
...UNLESS THERE'S SOME OTHER ENVIRONMENTAL FACTOR THAT'S CAUSED THEIR NUMBERS TO DROP SINCE THE LAST TIME YOUR MOTHER AND I WERE HERE.
THIS DEFINITELY CALLS FOR AN INVESTIGATION.
WHO'S UP FOR A LITTLE SPELUNKING?
sniff-sniff
IVORY BILLED
WOODPECKER
HYLACINE GOONCH
ATRAN MUNTJAK
SKYFISH
PREZWALSKI'S
HORSE

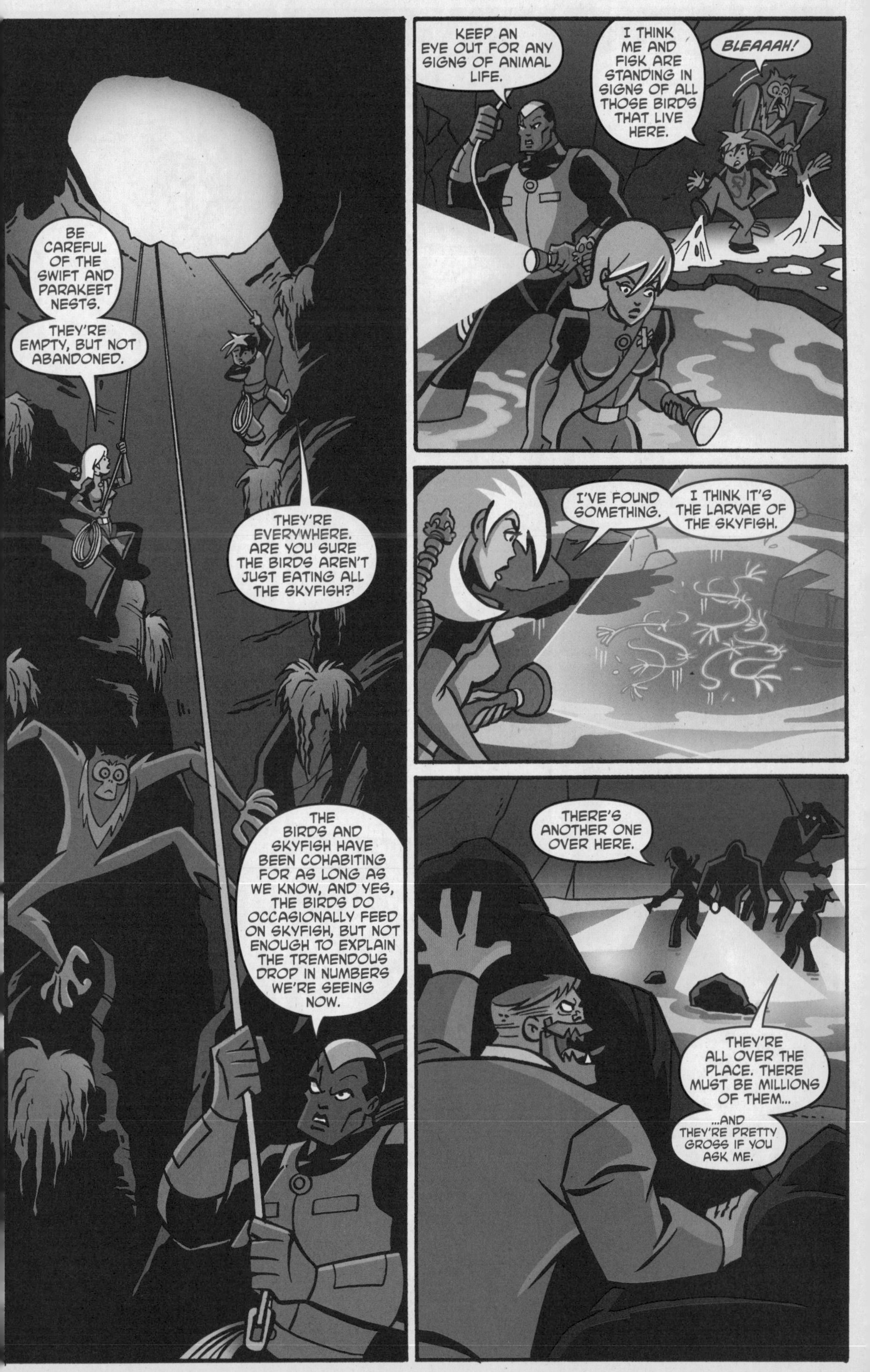
BE CAREFUL OF THE SWIFT AND PARAKEET NESTS.
THEY'RE EMPTY, BUT NOT ABANDONED.
THEY'RE EVERYWHERE. ARE YOU SURE THE BIRDS AREN'T JUST EATING ALL THE SKYFISH?
THE BIRDS AND SKYFISH HAVE BEEN COHABITING FOR AS LONG AS WE KNOW, AND YES, THE BIRDS DO OCCASIONALLY FEED ON SKYFISH, BUT NOT ENOUGH TO EXPLAIN THE TREMENDOUS DROP IN NUMBERS WE'RE SEEING NOW.
KEEP AN EYE OUT FOR ANY SIGNS OF ANIMAL LIFE.
I THINK ME AND FISK ARE STANDING IN SIGNS OF ALL THOSE BIRDS THAT LIVE HERE.
BLEAAAH!
I'VE FOUND SOMETHING.
I THINK IT'S THE LARVAE OF THE SKYFISH.
THERE'S ANOTHER ONE OVER HERE.
THEY'RE ALL OVER THE PLACE. THERE MUST BE MILLIONS OF THEM...
...AND THEY'RE PRETTY GROSS IF YOU ASK ME.

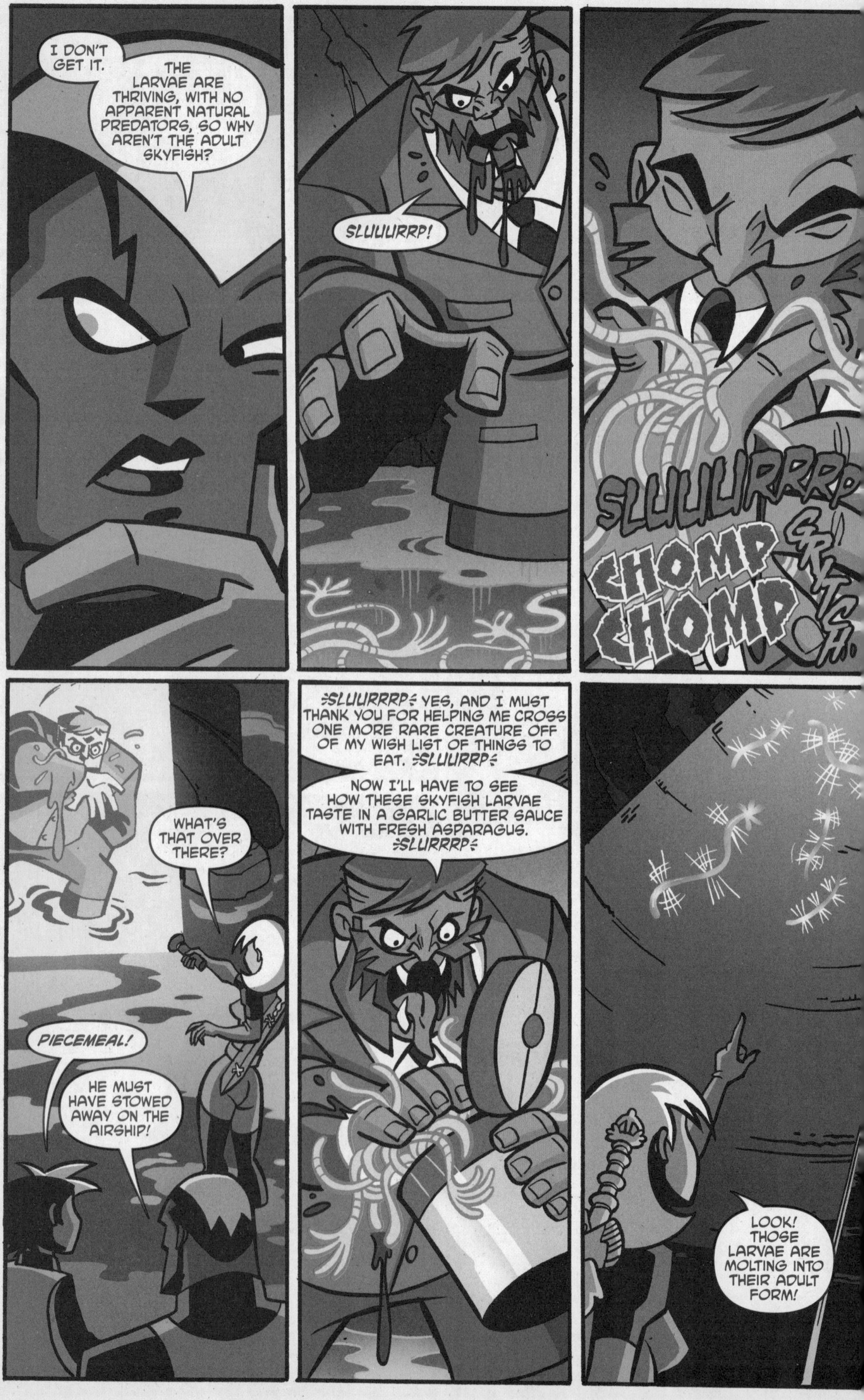
I DON'T GET IT.
THE LARVAE ARE THRIVING, WITH NO APPARENT NATURAL PREDATORS, SO WHY AREN'T THE ADULT SKYFISH?
SLUUURRP!
SLUUURRRP
CHOMP CHOMP
WHAT'S THAT OVER THERE?
PIECEMEAL!
HE MUST HAVE STOWED AWAY ON THE AIRSHIP!
SLUURRRP YES, AND I MUST THANK YOU FOR HELPING ME CROSS ONE MORE RARE CREATURE OFF OF MY WISH LIST OF THINGS TO EAT. SLUURRP
NOW I'LL HAVE TO SEE HOW THESE SKYFISH LARVAE TASTE IN A GARLIC BUTTER SAUCE WITH FRESH ASPARAGUS. SLURRRP
LOOK! THOSE LARVAE ARE MOLTING INTO THEIR ADULT FORM!

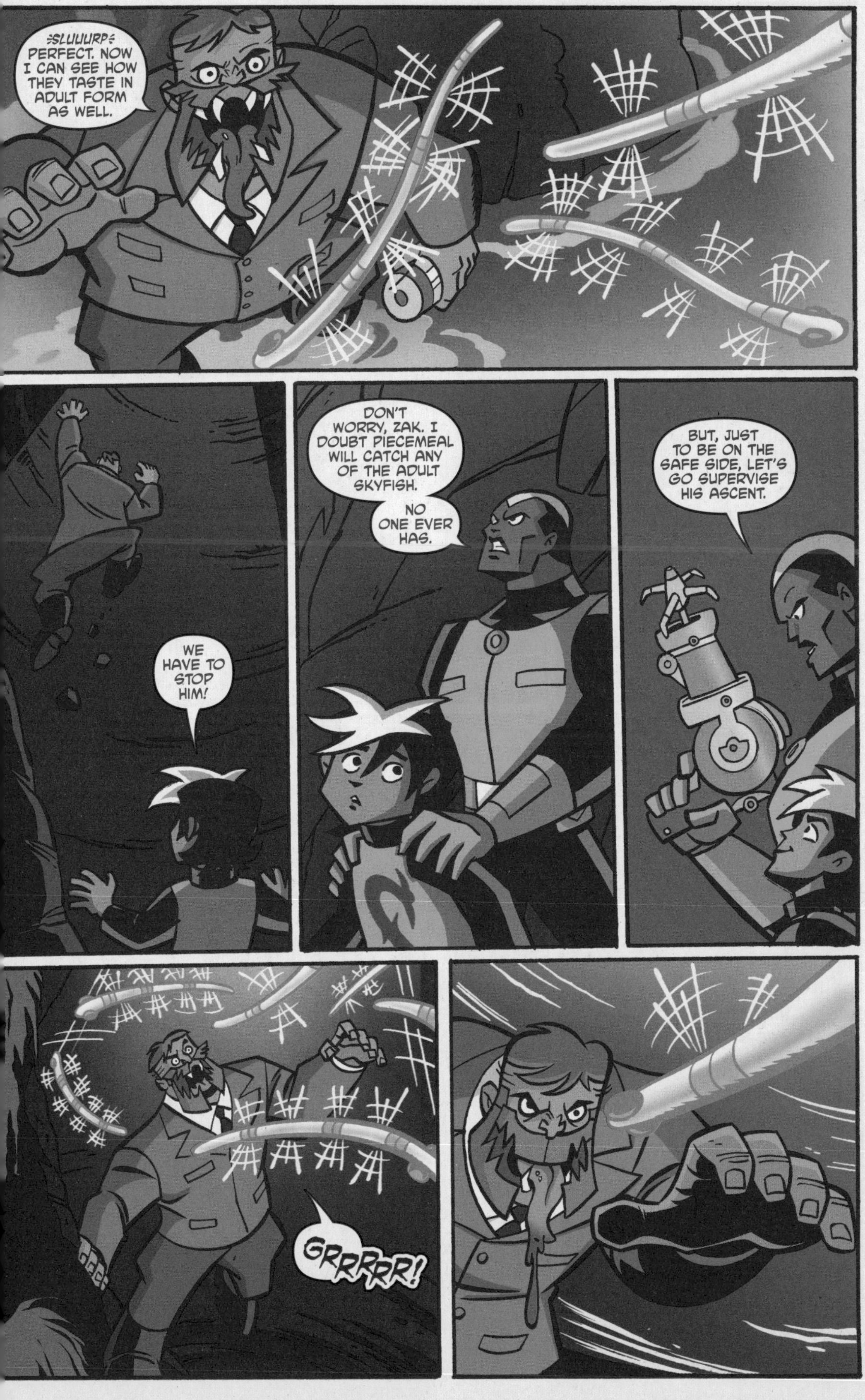

≈SLUUURP≈ PERFECT. NOW I CAN SEE HOW THEY TASTE IN ADULT FORM AS WELL.
WE HAVE TO STOP HIM!
DON'T WORRY, ZAK. I DOUBT PIECEMEAL WILL CATCH ANY OF THE ADULT SKYFISH.
NO ONE EVER HAS.
BUT, JUST TO BE ON THE SAFE SIDE, LET'S GO SUPERVISE HIS ASCENT.
GRRRRR!

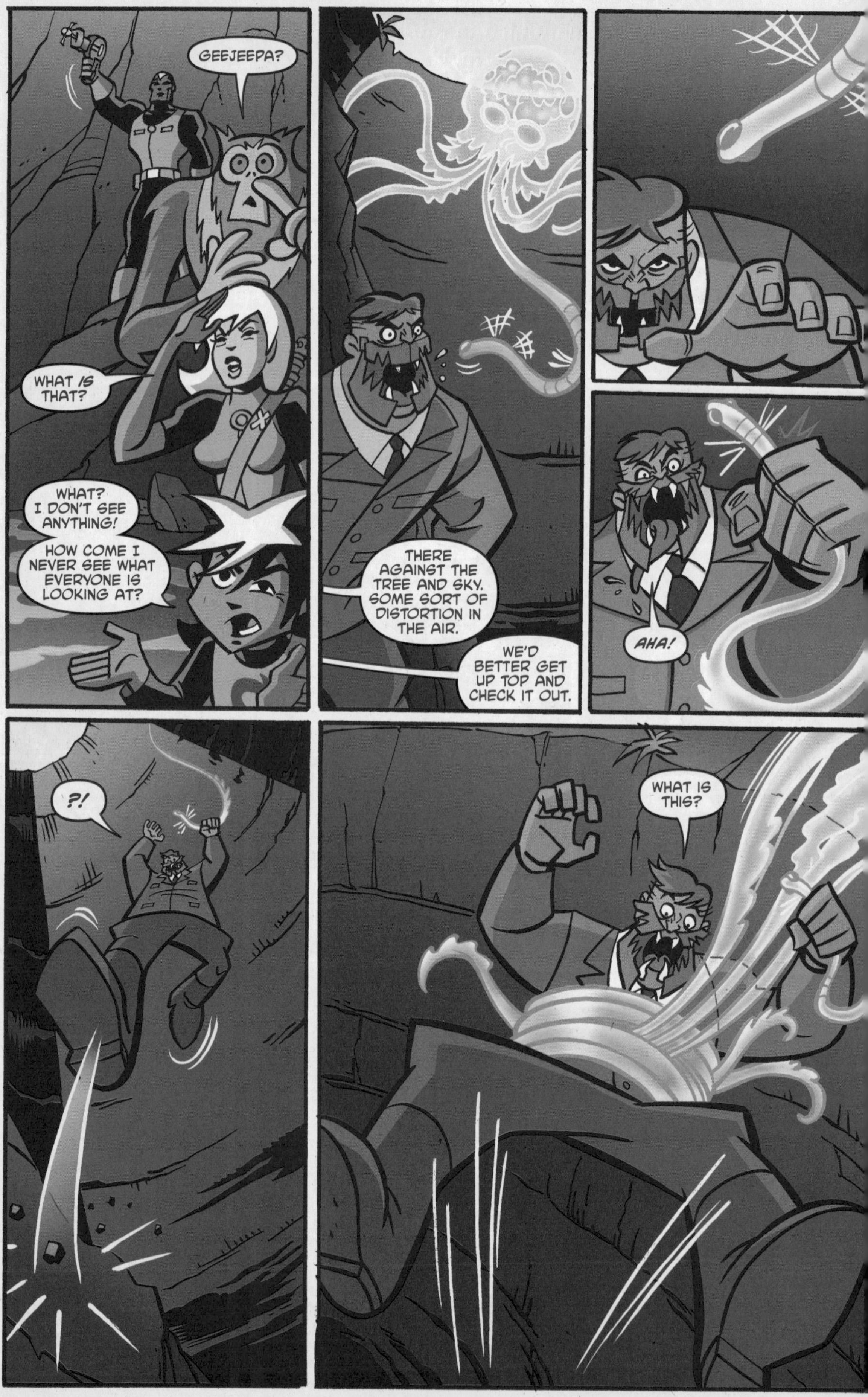
GEEJEEPA?
WHAT *IS* THAT?
WHAT? I DON'T SEE ANYTHING!
HOW COME I NEVER SEE WHAT EVERYONE IS LOOKING AT?
THERE AGAINST THE TREE AND SKY. SOME SORT OF DISTORTION IN THE AIR.
WE'D BETTER GET UP TOP AND CHECK IT OUT.
AHA!
?!
WHAT IS THIS?

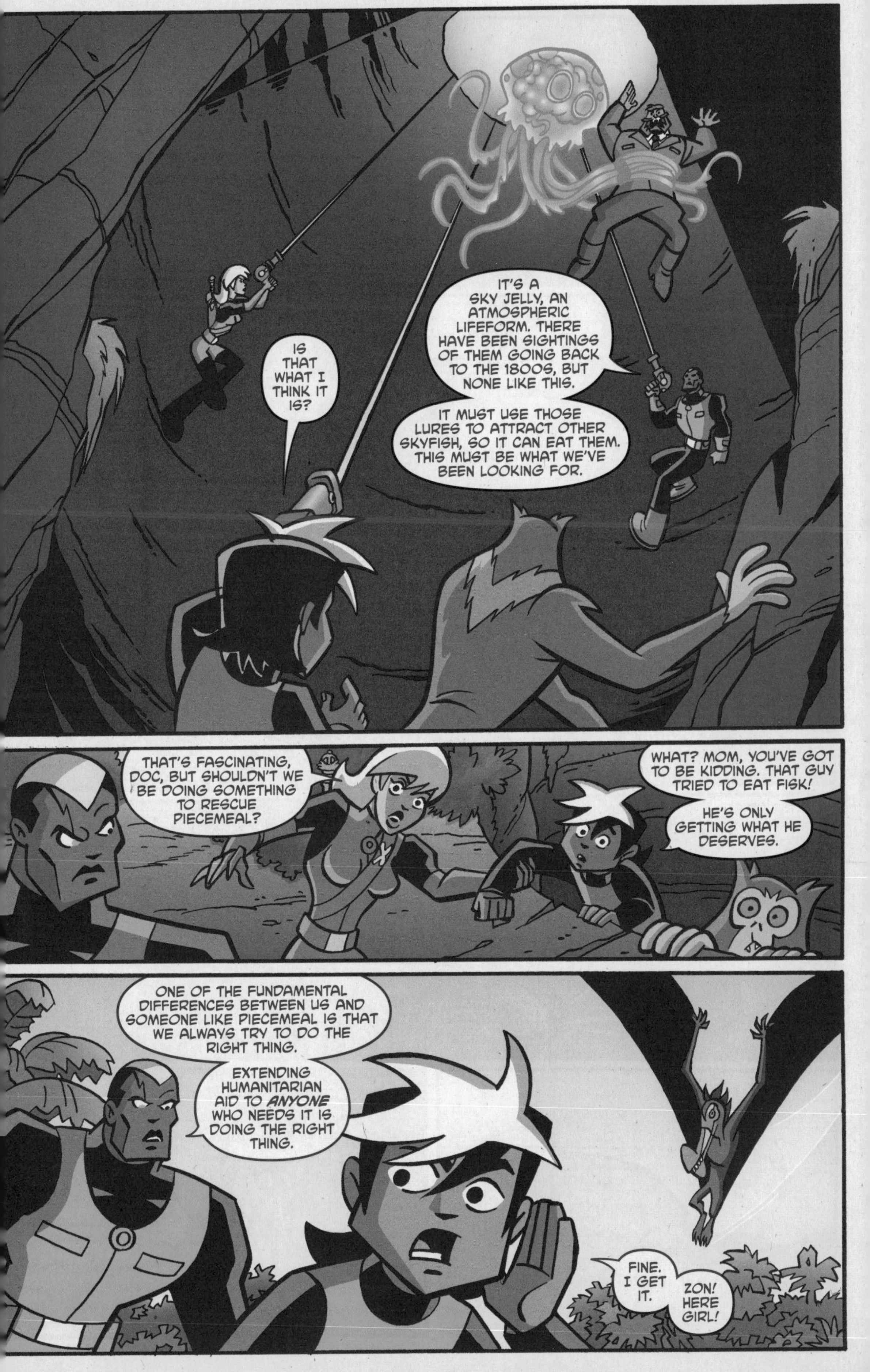
IS THAT WHAT I THINK IT IS?
IT'S A SKY JELLY, AN ATMOSPHERIC LIFEFORM. THERE HAVE BEEN SIGHTINGS OF THEM GOING BACK TO THE 1800S, BUT NONE LIKE THIS.
IT MUST USE THOSE LURES TO ATTRACT OTHER SKYFISH, SO IT CAN EAT THEM. THIS MUST BE WHAT WE'VE BEEN LOOKING FOR.
THAT'S FASCINATING, DOC, BUT SHOULDN'T WE BE DOING SOMETHING TO RESCUE PIECEMEAL?
WHAT? MOM, YOU'VE GOT TO BE KIDDING. THAT GUY TRIED TO EAT FISK!
HE'S ONLY GETTING WHAT HE DESERVES.
ONE OF THE FUNDAMENTAL DIFFERENCES BETWEEN US AND SOMEONE LIKE PIECEMEAL IS THAT WE ALWAYS TRY TO DO THE RIGHT THING.
EXTENDING HUMANITARIAN AID TO *ANYONE* WHO NEEDS IT IS DOING THE RIGHT THING.
FINE. I GET IT.
ZON! HERE GIRL!

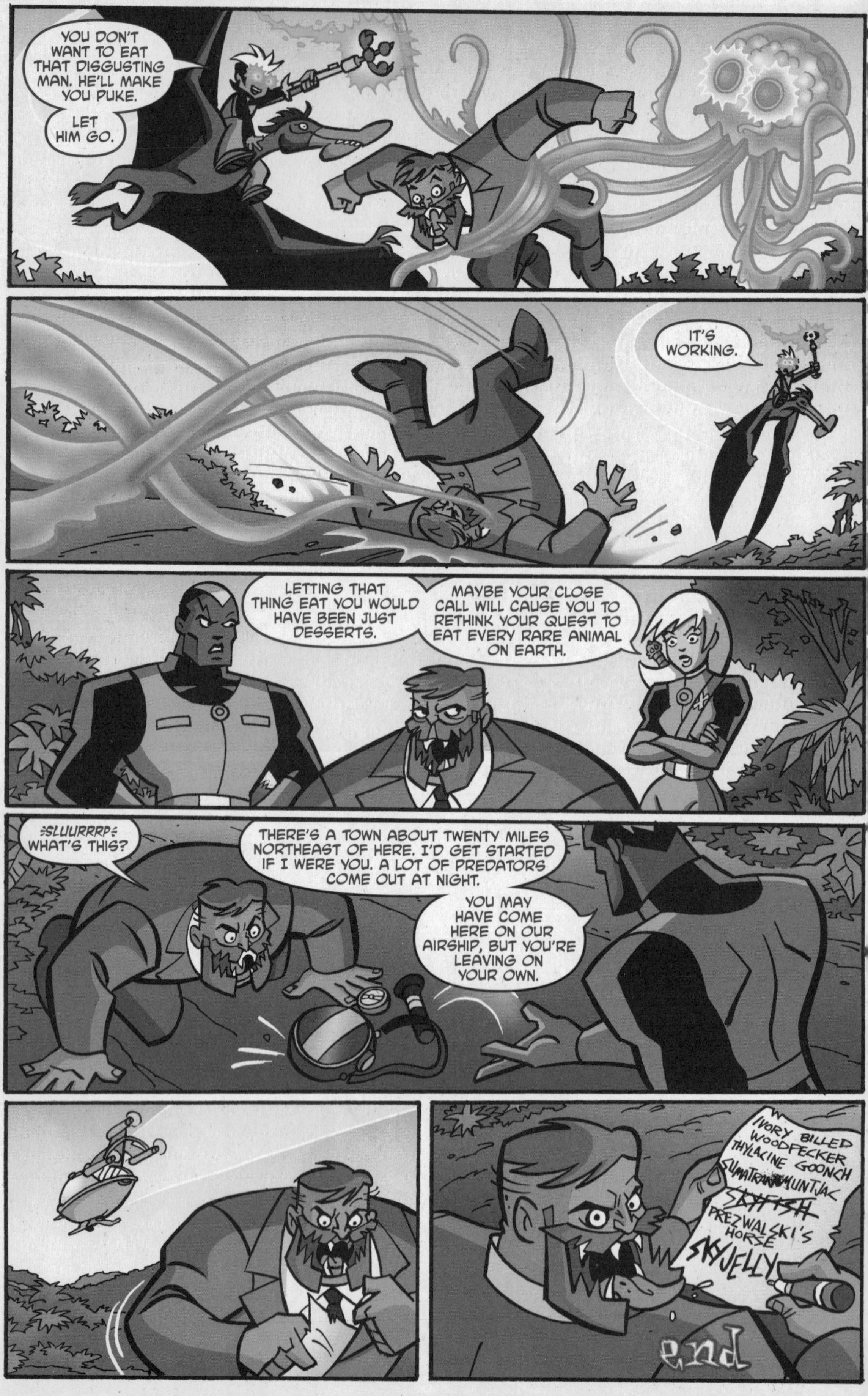
YOU DON'T WANT TO EAT THAT DISGUSTING MAN. HE'LL MAKE YOU PUKE.
LET HIM GO.
IT'S WORKING.
LETTING THAT THING EAT YOU WOULD HAVE BEEN JUST DESSERTS.
MAYBE YOUR CLOSE CALL WILL CAUSE YOU TO RETHINK YOUR QUEST TO EAT EVERY RARE ANIMAL ON EARTH.
SLUURRRP WHAT'S THIS?
THERE'S A TOWN ABOUT TWENTY MILES NORTHEAST OF HERE. I'D GET STARTED IF I WERE YOU. A LOT OF PREDATORS COME OUT AT NIGHT.
YOU MAY HAVE COME HERE ON OUR AIRSHIP, BUT YOU'RE LEAVING ON YOUR OWN.
IVORY BILLED WOODPECKER
THYLACINE GOONCH
SUMATRAN MUNTJAC
~~SKYFISH~~
PREZWALSKI'S HORSE
SKYJELLY
end